DIGITAL COMPOSABLE ENTERPRISES

An Evolutionary Approach to Innovate Organizations

from the Core of the Business

Ingo Paas

KDP Kindle Direct Publishing

Language: English

Book title: DIGITAL COMPOSABLE ENTERPRISES

Book subtitle: An Evolutionary Approach to Innovate Organizations from the Core of the Business

Edition Number: 1.2

Author: Ingo Paas

Published by: KDP Kindle Direct Publishing

First published: April 2023

ISBN 9798387639999

Disclaimer: The information presented in this book is based on the author's research and personal experiences. While every effort has been made to ensure the accuracy of the information, the author and publisher are not liable for any damages or consequences that may arise from the use or interpretation of this information. Readers should always consult a qualified professional before making decisions based on this book's information.

Two important things before getting started:

1. Thank you for reading this **BOOK**.

2. Thank you for reading the **FOREWORD** (page 9) and **PROLOGUE** (page 11).

AUTONOMOUS ACHIEVEMENTS

A free interpretation of philosophical discussions in practice,
inspired, supported, and encouraged by my family.

There is no greater opportunity in life than attempting the unknown and impossible.

The fact that something seems impossible should not be the reason not to pursue it.

But enduring this challenge is just what makes it worth trying with courage.

Where would learning and experience come from if success was certain and there was no risk?

Instead, the general risk in life is to shrink from its challenges and fail to learn and grow.

It requires autonomy in decision-making, accountability for the consequences, and deep trust.

Ultimately, it is not about the outcome but the courage to do and achieve it.

I dedicate this book to my family with passion and endless love

Ingo Paas

TABLE OF CONTENT

FOREWORD

Johan Magnusson, PhD
Professor of Information Systems at the University of Gothenburg
Director of the Swedish Center for Digital Innovation (SCDI), Gothenburg

"For the past 20 years, I have been a researcher and advisor about IT Governance. I have, throughout the years, met my share of creative, visionary, and profoundly intelligent Chief Information Officers. None, however, have blown me away like Ingo Paas.

When I first heard about what Ingo Paas was doing at Green Cargo, I thought it must be some ruse or blatant mistake. The approach that he was pursuing was a borderline heretic, going against the grain of what was currently seen as best practice in the industry. Ingo was upending the traditional perception of IT as the business's supporting infrastructure. To put it bluntly, he was utterly iconoclastic in his approach to IT.

After conducting a deep case study of Green Cargo, the other researchers involved and I were even more perplexed. What was this approach, and how would it pan out? Was it possible to approach IT from the perspective of Ingo Paas, dramatically turning the tables on previous core assumptions such as alignment, support, and reactivity? After following Green Cargo's transformation for over a year, the answer to the latter question is affirmative. As you will see in this book, true transformation of incumbent organizations is possible and reproducible.

When considering the Green Cargo and Ingo Paas case, I mind wandering to Giuseppe Tomasi de Lampedusa's iconic novel" The Leopard". A story of the crumbling aristocracy in Sicily in the late 19th century. De Lampedusa describes a society existing on the laurels of the past, completely separated from the general times, increasingly irrelevant, and disconnected from reality. The aristocracy continues its rites and ceremonies, sticking to protocol, but there is a profound insight into the obsoleteness of it all. In the words of de Lampedusa, they have understood that "If we wish for all to be as it was, everything must change".

This parallels many incumbent organizations we see struggling with digital transformation today. They have been relevant and even magnificent in the past. They have the regalia to show for it, the exquisitely decorated board rooms and offices, yet there is a brooding feeling of unrest. Everything must change if we wish for all to be as it was.

This is the core learning of digital transformation, but how can we lift ourselves from the bootstraps? Where do we start the transformation journey, and how do we ensure that it is conducted in a manner that does not involve exposure to unnecessary risk? The answer, as found in the case of Green Cargo and this book, is composability. It is one of dismantling old truths and antiquated best practices to get away from the myth and ceremonies related to technology deeply ingrained in CxOs through streamlined educational programs and consultancy firms re-packaging previous truths into new ones.

As such, the direction set out by the author of this book may be considered either trail-blazing or sacrilegious, in both interpretations deeply troubling to the established order. But this is a time for action, and there is ample support for the path proposed by Ingo Paas, both in emerging research and an increasing stream of practical examples from the industry.

For many of the firms we work with, transformation is no longer a question of optimization but rather an existential one. There is a rapidly increasing awareness among firms that the current operations' stalemate, deadlock, and sclerosis are no longer viable. There is increased uncertainty in the surrounding environment, increased fluctuation of demand, and an ever-increasing need for adaptivity and agility. Where early approaches to digital transformation involved decoupling it from the core business, ensuring that digital did not interfere with the core, we see increasing examples of digital transformation as more foundational change. Not limited to merely increased efficiency of existing operations through continuous improvements, but dramatically changing the whole identity of the firm.

In this setting, Ingo Paas's book profoundly and significantly contributes. If everything must change, how can we make this possible?"

Gothenburg, 2023-02-04

Johan Magnusson, PhD

Professor of Information Systems
Director Swedish Center for Digital Innovation
University of Gothenburg

PROLOGUE

Discovering and monetizing the next digital breakthrough technology is challenging for enterprises undergoing digital transformations. Many perform as if they would stand on a technology watchtower, trying to identify the next revolutionary technology-inspired innovation to deliver outstanding benefits by maximizing the promises of exponential technologies. Not surprisingly, innovative technology investments often lead to fragmentation and disappointment rather than valuable and scalable innovation.

Successful transformations have not dominated the latest wave of digital turmoil. Instead, many enterprises recognize the challenges of managing increasing operational and business model complexity and costs. At the same time, they are struggling to integrate their legacy IT systems seamlessly with their new and accelerating fragmented digital technologies.

The initial promise of rapid returns on digital investments has become a disappointing reality, as many organizations face increased running costs and difficulties in scaling and monetizing their investments effectively. Decision-makers have no choice but to rethink their strategies, leadership, and digital investments to tackle this dilemma as a key priority. Their lack of knowledge or unawareness of this challenge and appropriate responses might introduce unpredictable future risks as digital enterprise resilience deteriorates.

Leveraging enterprises is possible but does require a new approach to balancing competing objectives. "The Rise of the Ambidextrous Organization - The Secret Revolution Happening Right Under Your Nose" (Zabiegalski, 2019), discusses the importance of balancing revolutionary and evolutionary change. The resolution outlined in his book is the practice of organizational ambidexterity, the ability to be simultaneously exploitative and explorative, managing both dimensions in a balanced way that promotes both short- and long-term performance and success. According to the author's argument, ambidextrous organizations have underlying components such as culture, leadership, learning, and structure. He argues that the science of complexity, which incorporates balance, symmetry, systems, emergence, chaos, and governance, can more effectively tackle complex environments than traditional and isolated approaches.

Eric Zabiegalski discusses strategies to encourage an ambidextrous transformation by overcoming selected obstacles while being authentic in balanced ways to arrive at organizational ambidexterity over time.

In the case of digital transformations, organizational ambidexterity is the ability to explore new opportunities and exploit existing ones simultaneously. It is the ability to digitally innovate and develop new processes, business models, or services while maintaining and optimizing current operations. Organizational ambidexterity refers to an organization's capacity to simultaneously pursue and excel at two seemingly conflicting strategies or approaches. On the one hand, it focuses on exploitation and routine to secure legacy interoperability and enterprise-wide integration. On the other hand, the focus is on exploration and innovation by embracing digital composability. Organizational ambidexterity implies that enterprises must simultaneously balance seemingly contradictory strategies: to exploit (routine) and explore (innovate).

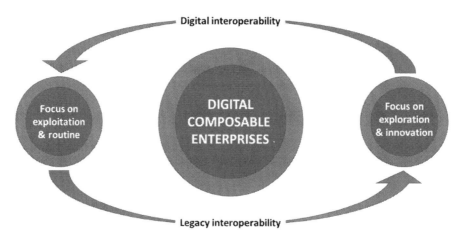

Figure 1 Demystifying the transformation into digital composable enterprises by utilizing the theory of ambidexterity to actively engage in exploitation and exploration

Traditionally, companies have often set distinct priorities, selecting one in preference of the other, while in today's rapidly changing business environment, this approach has been proven ineffective and risky. Instead, companies must adapt quickly to changing conditions, take advantage of new opportunities, and scale as they arise.

This is a core capability for digital composable transformations, while most enterprises are making decisions disregarding this robust and unrecognized approach, not combining and integrating those two varieties to transform traditional and digital enterprises into digital composable enterprises.

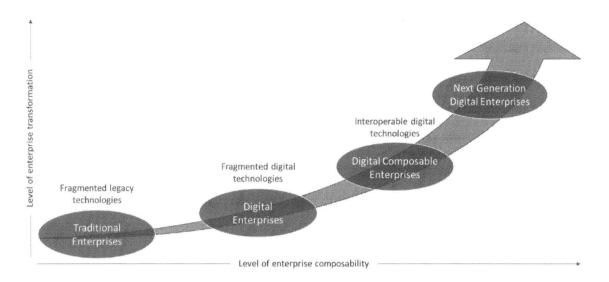

Figure 2 The transformational evolution of enterprises toward "DIGITAL COMPOSABLE ENTERPRISES"

To overcome this dilemma, enterprises may find a reasonable response and answer in the evolutionary transformation toward digital composable enterprises and greater digital resilience. Enterprises that understand the conceptual power of organizational ambidexterity may find that digital composable transformations are much less complicated to explore than anticipated. The time has come to demystify this complexity and open up new ways that enable enterprises to evolve from the existing status quo into "the nirvana of digital composability".

In comparison to digital transformations, digital composable transformations are necessary to achieve the following strategic objectives:

1.   To optimize and scale digital investments.
2.   To leverage digital and business resilience.
3.   To augment volatile (explosive) and future technologies.
4.   To evolve innovation from the core of the business.

Enterprises must recognize the need to significantly advance and change the direction of their transformations and investment strategies to position their organizations in this challenging context more distinctively. They must better understand why they have no choice but to take their organizations on this extended journey of digital transformations to evolve successfully to this next level.

As AI is one of the most fundamental game changers for digitally transforming enterprises, it brings additional but avoidable complexity, costs, and difficulties to monetize such investments, where the four strategic objectives of digital composable enterprises address those major concerns distinctively.

Digital enterprises must define, transform, and scale the opportunities of composability, leveraging their investments in more evolutionary but transformative ways. Therefore, transitioning enterprises toward digital composable enterprises comes with a request for new leadership to evolve digital collaborative cultures and innovation **from the core of the business**. Boards and senior executives must enhance their tech-savviness, knowledge, and conceptual thinking to make better-informed strategic decisions and understand potential consequences and risks.

Organizations can evolve into digital composable enterprises if they balance exploitative and explorative practices, while the starting point may be unrelated to their future accomplishments. Complexity does not mean complicated, and asymmetric patterns must be explored to create better conditions for success. Individual authenticity permits others to be authentic while evolving the organization's culture is eventually the most important capability of digital leaders. Balance is imperative for ambidextrous organizations, while leadership must combine all of it to help not to rely on learnings and what has been successful or unsuccessful in the past.

This book will demystify the process of digitally transforming enterprises, guiding readers to achieve maximum levels of composability. It will make the process more understandable by explaining how transparency, collaboration, communication, and cultural change help to achieve fundamentally better results. This book will discuss and suggest, in repeatable ways but with multiple perspectives, a new but viable approach to making transformations work. After reading it, you will have gained more profound foundational insights on making digital investments a permanent and scalable success.

"Implementing digital transformations in line with the elements of advice in this book will significantly increase the chances of achieving digital composability by maximizing return on those investments. Getting there requires talented teams, new strategic thinking, risk-tolerance leadership, personal courage, and discipline in evolutionary execution."

Enjoy reading!

Ingo Paas

INTRODUCTION

About the author

Ingo Paas is the Chief Information Officer (CIO) and Chief Digital Officer (CDO) at the Swedish railway transport company Green Cargo. He received the Award CIO of the Year in 2022 in Sweden from the International Data Corporation (IDC/IDG) and was recognized as one of Sweden's TOP50 tech influencers in 2023.

Throughout his career, Ingo has been at the forefront of innovation and digital composable transformations, demonstrating his leadership skills and ability to bring about positive change. He has over 28 years of international executive experience in multinational enterprises such as Ericsson, adidas Group, and ICA Group in Sweden. He is a visionary, innovative, technology-savvy, business-oriented executive and leader who worked on various digital, data, and technology-driven transformations, to generate new profitable technology-inspired business improvements and innovation. Ingo thrives in complex environments where he can inspire and lead change, foster a culture of innovation and learning, and drive digital composable transformations. He has worked on numerous digital, data, and technology-driven transformations, helping multinational enterprises generate new profitable business opportunities. His personal values and intuitive approach to leadership make him an outstanding and appreciated leader with a strong perspective, continually embracing change while establishing and developing high-performance teams.

Contact details

Author.ingo.paas@gmail.com   https://www.linkedin.com/in/ingo-paas-aa655a9/

Thought leader contributions

The following leaders have voluntarily contributed with their expertise or applied experience by writing individual short outlines, commenting on their contribution or perspective on how to evolve digital composable enterprises. They represent an exclusive group from different industries with outstanding in-depth experiences, skills, and leadership. I'm excited and deeply grateful for their contributions with their wisdom, experiences, knowledge, and thought leadership. THANK YOU!

Thought Leadership

The following thought leaders have contributed by writing a prologue to each chapter with their in-depth knowledge and leadership perspective from digital transformations from major enterprises, partners, and recognized research companies.

- Martin Althén, President, Securitas Digital
- Ted Söderholm, CEO, Green Cargo
- Hans van Grieken, Boardroom advisor on Digital Transformation
- Emmanuelle Hose, GVP & Regional General Manager, Rimini Street
- Daniel Akenine, National CTO, Microsoft
- Marc Dowd, Executive Partner, Executive Advisory - Research and Consulting, IDC Europe
- Tiago B. Azevedo, Chief Information Officer (CIO), OutSystems
- David Logg, Vice President Global Business Engineering, CGI
- Stefan Gustavsson, Managing Partner, Gartner

Applied Technology Leadership

The following technology leaders contributed by writing a complementary applied leadership section describing selected highlights from Green Cargos' digital composable transformation.

- Anna Skoog-Dabestani, Senior Application Specialist, Green Cargo, Consultant Dynamant
- Carl-Evert Dahlin, Senior Application Specialist, Green Cargo
- Helena Wetterwik, Head of Project Management Office, Green Cargo
- Johan Svensson, CTO/CIO, Sonat
- Oscar Wide, Chief Information Security Officer, Green Cargo

- Richard Tyregrim, Lead Solutions/Strategic Architect, R&D Lead, Consultant
- Emil Hellström, Product Manager Mainframe, Green Cargo
- Peter Marcusson, Business Enterprise Architect, Consultant IzeoTech, Green Cargo
- Christian Ericsson, Head of Architecture, Green Cargo
- Andreas Lindmark, Manager CCoE, Consultant IzeoTech, Green Cargo
- Thomas Wickman, Head of IT Development, Green Cargo, Consultant & Agile Coach
- Jörgen Lindholm, Consultant MaxiTech, Green Cargo
- Kasem Chahrour, Executive Digital Leader I Author I Advisor at Digital Vibrations AB & Lowcodi AB
- Filip Mood, Product Owner OutSystems, Green Cargo
- Per Jalmelid, Enterprise Architect, Green Cargo
- Steve Binning, Consult at Green Cargo, Business Intelligence Specialist, Atea AB
- Åsa Blom, Head of Applications, Green Cargo
- Dennis Eklöf-Lundin, Head of IT Operations, Green Cargo
- Pekka Rinne, Enterprise Architect and Digital Strategist
- Jonathan Hammander, Tech Lead, Green Cargo

Thanks for all your contributions and for sharing valuable leadership perspectives with your complementary individual writings in this book!

About Green Cargo

The Swedish State owns Green Cargo. The company transports 21 million tons of freight, has 1,900 employees, and has an annual sale of about SEK 4,2 billion (2021). Electric trains comprise over 97 percent of our ton kilometrage, meaning the climate impact is next to zero. We run more than 400 freight trains every weekday and thus replace around 9,000 trucks daily. This corresponds to 2,300,000 trucks – annually. We serve close to 300 locations in Sweden, Norway, and Denmark through our network, and with our partners, we reach all of Europe. Our efforts are not only about a comprehensive reduction of carbon dioxide emissions but also about space efficiency and safer roads. Together with partners, Green Cargo connects the Swedish market to nearly 2,000 destinations in continental Europe.

About Green Cargo IT

In September 2019, when Ingo joined Green Cargo as the CIO, IT was an immature organization with a complex, underdeveloped, and non-supported IT landscape, suffering over a decade of ineffective IT strategies and inadequate decisions. The financial situation was challenging, resources were restricted, the motivation was low, and there was no trust in the business to discuss or explore business development with IT, while the dimensions of leadership and engagement were dissatisfying.

Green Cargo faced an impossible challenge to overcome the trenches of nearly a decade of failed mainframe and ERP replacement strategies and insufficient strategic decisions. At the same time, Green Cargo realizes the need to consider a digital transformation to respond to growing customer needs and new digital challenges triggered by evolving digital ecosystem requirements and compliance demands in the European railway transportation sector.

The starting conditions were challenging, with a long list of significant difficulties, without any appropriate risk mitigation activities. The IT department struggled without a realistic IT strategy, two not-maintained mainframe systems, an outdated and incorrectly implemented SAP platform, and 10+ ERP-like disintegrated and incorrectly designed planning systems. Two unsupported AS/400 systems for our intermodal business worsened the situation. Based on a dysfunctional investment strategy and corporate governance, the IT department could not support the business, causing a backlog of critical IT development spanning over a decade. The IT landscape was fragmented, the infrastructure was outdated, and information security and cybersecurity conditions were ineffective. The IT organization was ineffective, while the absence of governance, compliance, and information security capabilities posed significant risks to the company. The poorly managed outsourcing environment was not governed and well implemented, and agile development methods or in-house development capabilities did not exist. In-house application, integration, and analytics development were also missing, and the company could not mitigate substantial business risks ingested by insufficient IT capabilities. With all these challenges, transforming Green Cargo into a digital composable enterprise was more than just daunting.

Initially, the preconditions for success were not in place, and the situation seemed like a "mission impossible" with no hope for Green Cargo to embark on a customer-centric digital composable transformation. At that time, Green Cargo was a deliberate mover in digital transformation with very constrained resources, zero willingness, and no ability to execute. However, significant changes have taken place since then.

The seemingly impossible journey for Green Cargo became the reference for developing this book and framework about "digital composable enterprises". The framework in this book relates to Green Cargos's journey of transforming from a truly traditional to an evolving digital composable enterprise. Throughout this book, experts from Green Cargo comment on the journey and success, with their applied technology leadership perspective providing practical insights and experiences. Enjoy reading!

Research on the Green Cargo case by the University of Gothenburg

The University of Gothenburg wrote a research paper about the Green Cargos transformation:

"BURIDAN'S ASS: ENCAPSULATION AS A POSSIBLE SOLUTION TO THE PRIORITIZATION DILEMMA OF DIGITAL TRANSFORMATION" by Magnusson, J. et al., 2022).

Abstract: "With organizations pursuing digital transformation with limited resources find themselves in a dilemma between prioritizing IT transformation or digital transformation. With the intricate dependencies between business and the digital infrastructure, lack of continuous IT transformation hinders digital transformation, and access to capital and other resources force organizations into a situation where they need to prioritize either IT transformation or digital transformation. We refer to this dilemma with a parallel to Buridan's Ass, i.e., the paradox of a donkey destined to die of simultaneous thirst and hunger since its needs are as equal as the distance to the haystack and water trough. This study addresses an IT transformation strategy where a combination of real-time data layers, enterprise hybrid integration and low-code cloud-only environments are utilized explicitly to avoid tradeoffs with digital transformation. The case is analyzed as an instantiation of Buridan's paradox, offering direct insight and a feasible solution to the dilemma of IT or digital transformation.

Conclusion: "This study answers the research question for how a strategy for IT transformation can avoid the tradeoffs with digital transformation. As found, the strategy of encapsulation offers a potential for avoiding said tradeoffs through amortizing the digital- and technology debt while leaving the technical debt unchanged. The strategy affords the organization to avoid decreasing the pace of digital transformation while at the same time decreasing the operational risks associated with the existing digital infrastructure through a combination of technologies such as real-time data layers, enterprise integration and cloud-only LowCode environments. The strategy entails a choice for outer rather than inner focus on renewal rather than established in a fashion of emergent rather than deliberate."

ONE – TRANSFORMATIONAL MISCONCEPTIONS

THOUGHT DIGITAL LEADERSHIP

Martin Althén, President, Securitas

"CIOs face a major challenge when driving business and IT transformation in a world with rapidly evolving technologies. They must manage complex IT legacy while at the same time leveraging new digital technologies. In response and to become true technology leaders, CIOs should strategically drive a value-driven transformation towards the interoperable and composable enterprise.

While organizations are occupied with extensive transformation programs, the world moves on. In my 25 years in the industry and 15 as a global CIO, I have been there several times. In many cases, hard and committed work by the teams led to program success. But often it was clear that more was needed to realize the full potential.

At Securitas, new customer needs and societal change challenged the industry and our competitiveness. We required new ways of working and new solutions driving innovation and efficiency. We embarked on a journey five years ago combining IT modernization, digitalization and building new digital businesses in parallel. We knew we needed a creative approach.

With digital capabilities and new agile working methods maturing, there is an opportunity to think and act differently. A more inclusive but also less risky way to make a sustainable difference. A way to allow you to adapt and evolve with fast-changing market needs that do not wait for your traditional change program to complete. However, there are traps along the way, and most notably, we, as IT professionals and business leaders, must challenge our comfort zones. We tend to apply pre-digital learnings of the past to the present and the future. Driving digitalization aligned with a complex IT legacy requires a change in leadership from CIOs, IT organizations, and CEOs.

Digital composable transformation can and should approach differently. In this book, Ingo Paas will tell you Why and How in a way that is easy to relate to, providing ample examples and hands-on advice. Let's challenge ourselves and embrace new ways of working for sustainable results, enjoy the reading!"

Written by Martin Althén, President, Securitas Digital

Reconsider the value of large programs

The dilemma of digital transformations refers to organizations' challenges and trade-offs when implementing digital technology and changing their business processes and operations. These challenges include the cost and effort required for digital transformations, the potential to disrupt existing systems and processes, and the need for organizational and cultural change to fully realize digital technology's benefits. Additionally, there can be concerns about data privacy and security and the potential for increased inequality and job loss as large-scale programs mainly address automation.

In the case of digital transformations, organizations have recognized the dilemma of making the right choices and finding the most valuable investment strategies. As the majority is still struggling, organizational ambidexterity is a new way and ability to explore new opportunities and exploit existing ones simultaneously.

As indicated in the introduction of this book, the concept of organizational ambidexterity refers to an organization's ability to balance two seemingly opposing strategies: exploitation (routine) and exploration (innovation) in digital transformation. It involves the capacity to pursue and excel at two strategies simultaneously, such as optimizing current operations while developing new processes, business models, or services. Organizational ambidexterity requires maintaining legacy interoperability and enterprise-wide integration while embracing digital composability to foster innovation and growth.

Traditionally, companies have often set distinct priorities, selecting large programs in preference of the other, while in today's rapidly changing business environment, this approach has been proven ineffective and risky. Instead, enterprises must adapt quickly to changing conditions, take advantage of new opportunities, and scale as they arise.

This is a core capability for digital composable transformations, while most enterprises are making decisions disregarding this robust and unrecognized approach. They are not combining and integrating those two significantly different varieties to transform traditional and digital enterprises into digital composable enterprises.

This dilemma of digital transformations for traditional enterprises refers to the challenges and trade-offs established organizations face when implementing digital technologies and changing their business processes and operations. Some of the key challenges include:

- **Legacy systems**

  Traditional organizations usually have complex legacy systems and infrastructure that are difficult to maintain. It is often costly to upgrade, develop, replace, or integrate with new digital technologies or external digital ecosystems. Digital readiness is the preference of risk-averse CIOs to motivate upfront investments in IT legacy systems to support digital transformations.

- **Risk aversion**

  Established companies may be more risk-averse and hesitant to invest in advancing state-of-the-art technologies and digitally enabled business models that may disrupt their operations. To become digitally ready, they invest in large-scale programs, such as modernizing IT legacy systems. Existing governance systems and leadership often do not appreciate and encourage risk tolerance.

- **Organizational culture**

  Organizations may have established cultures and working methods that can make adopting new technologies and change processes difficult to embed new digital technologies. Reluctance to change is ingested by large programs that do not engage with the line organization collaboratively. Organizational culture is usually the most difficult factor and is ignored in digital transformations. The not-invented-here syndrome is generally ignored, leading to acceptance and engagement problems.

- **Resistant to change**

  Organizations may resist change because their current business models have succeeded and may not see the need to adapt to new technologies. The willingness to change is often related to insufficient involvement and the ability to solve urgent business problems, while silo-thinking hinders collaboration.

- **Competition**

  Organizations may also face competition from digital-native companies with an inherent advantage in leveraging digital technologies. They may not see competitive advantages in utilizing digital technologies and agile development and struggle to develop successful investment and technology strategies.

- **Technologies**

  Organizations must implement new digital technologies and platforms while securing full interoperability with various inconsistent and outdated IT legacy systems and underlying infrastructures. They often select cutting-edge technologies that are difficult to integrate and utilize that were implemented in fragmented approaches. New business-driven technology leadership on the enterprise level is often missing. Without solid platform strategies, they risk continuing to invest in isolated technologies.

- **Investments**

  Major investments are required to modernize and adapt existing IT legacy systems to support digital transformations, where organizations struggle to understand complexity, why, how, and when to prioritize investments into large-scale programs and digital transformations. In the shadow of unbalanced investments into digital transformations, balanced digital investment strategies do not exist or are ignored.

These challenges can make it difficult for organizations to realize the benefits of digital technologies and can put them at a disadvantage compared to digital-native companies.

Enterprises may think they must make quantum leaps to catch up on digital leaders. With significant internal challenges and increased external competition, they prioritize cutting-edge technologies and large-scale investments to drive digital transformations. Unbalanced investments, overpromising business cases, and rapidly implementing fragmented technologies are often typical outcomes of actions without aligned strategies and comprehensive support of modern tech-savvy architectural teams.

Given this complexity, organizations cannot effectively judge and select the most appropriate strategies and investments to respond to those challenges. Judging and selecting the most appropriate strategies and investments is difficult, as traditional best practices may refer to different large-scale programs to drive change. Ignoring this challenge or jumping into action without aligning digital investments with the organization's purpose, vision, strategy, goals, and business priorities is not a good idea.

Non-tech-savvy executives and boards may negatively impact strategic decisions and the company's future. They may not understand digital transformations' potential opportunities and risks without a comprehensive understanding of digital technologies. This lack of knowledge may lead to poorly informed technology decisions and investments and unsuccessful digital transformations.

Insufficient prioritizations may cause other challenges, such as effective risk mitigation risks management with the introduction of digital technologies and the integration with IT legacy systems. It can be difficult for organizations to fully realize the potential benefits of digital technology if its boards, and executive teams are not tech-savvy.

Based on those learnings, digital transformations are a primary investment concern for most enterprises. As investments and programs fail to deliver on their promises, the challenges of large-scale programs only seem to increase. This situation is becoming increasingly complicated, as many organizations still prioritize strategies and road maps to replace their existing IT legacy systems before starting digital transformations. They often believe they must replace their technical debts and IT legacies before they start digital transformations on a broader scale.

Large-scale IT legacy replacement programs are often about risk mitigation, while many large-scale programs introduce new but more significant risks to organizations. It is also noticeable that organizations make such conclusions and investment decisions without embracing and considering alternative options. Uninformed or primarily risk-averse decisions on large-scale investments may therefore introduce significant consequences.

Understanding and exploring different alternatives requires a better understanding to avoid transformational misconceptions about enterprises going digital. The consequences of inappropriate interpretation and one-directional decision-making processes might mislead organizations in their ability to find the right choices, especially as leaders are inadequately and (in most cases) unintentionally misinformed about the potential choices and opportunities they have.

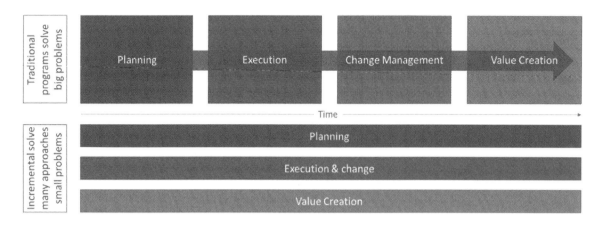

Figure 3 Large programs versus incremental change

Traditional organizations struggle to manage their technical debts effectively while introducing new digital technologies. Large programs often solve large and complex problems, while digital transformations require a more responsive approach to ever-changing business needs and priorities faster, with increased pressure to adapt greater resilience to enterprise-wide digital and IT capabilities.

Extensive IT system replacement strategies often prioritizes before digital transformations. They increase though certain risks with insufficient business cases, including poor Return of Investments (ROI), insufficient Time to Market (TTM), and a much too high Total Cost of Ownership (TCO).

Unforeseen problems usually harm large-scale programs with budget overspending, delays, reduced scope, and low investment returns. Beyond those undesirable outcomes, rapid and significant business improvements are rare, assign critical resources for a long time, and urgent business needs are constantly rejected or postponed by large-scale programs.

Trust within the organization is decreasing while unresolved business problems are postponed, delayed, or in worst cases, stalled entirely for a more extended period. This spiral of issues with large-scale programs is causing new complications and escalating, leading to significant concerns and risking the credibility of large-scale investments. Wrong assumptions, incomplete scope, or other planning-related challenges can significantly affect the realization of desired business goals and business cases regarding budget, time, quality, and scope.

Major programs usually cause damage to trust and confidence with growing criticism and disbelief across organizations. In many cases, organizations may recognize, far too late, that urgent business investment and a healthy approach disregard inflexibility or even wrong approaches to large-scale programs. With their inability to satisfy individual business problems, new risks and problems may arise, and organizations may experience significant disruptions, eventually encouraged and reinforced by inadequate strategies.

Large-scale programs often lead to general complications, such as:

1. Significant time and budget overrun,
2. Delayed or insufficient business case realization,
3. High-risk undertakings in comparison with alternative approaches,
4. Restrained innovation capacity,
5. Inadequate responsiveness and delivery in scope.

Organizations prioritize significant investments related to digital transformations around three major categories of large-scale programs/projects:

1. **Large-scale IT legacy programs**
2. **Large-scale data center/infrastructure shifting to the cloud**
3. **Large-scale digital transformation programs**

Those programs and investments have different purposes, objectives, motivations, rationales, and business benefits. They are preferred investments for CIOs, as they solve legacy problems, minimize legacy risks, and promise scalability and cost controls. Large-scale investments are preferred choices for CEOs, as they have greater control over well-organized investments and overall business cases.

Enterprises prioritizing large-scale IT legacy programs may make precarious decisions with severe consequences. Even if unconsciously initiated, they consequently postpone crucial investments in digital transformations.

Decision makers may misjudge the pervasive impact of their decisions on more urgent and business-driven digital transformations. Making the best possible investment choices is difficult, while traditional risk-averse leaders and organizations tend to promote large-scale investments, as they usually do not support seamless and evolutionary digital transformations.

Organizations should therefore rethink their major transformational programs and strategies to find more evolutionary alternatives, advocate, pursue digital evolutionary transformations, and make better and more realistic investment decisions.

Evaluate investment decisions

Major programs require detailed investment plans and business cases, even though those investments and complex undertakings are difficult to estimate, leading to major risks and problems during execution.

Many organizations still prefer to make large-scale transformative investments, even if they doubt their estimated value. Large-scale IT investments tend to go substantially over budget, deliver under the agreed scope, often land far below the estimated ROI (Return of Investment), and come with much higher TCO (Total Cost of Ownership) than initially promised even though those programs are still a preferred choice for many organizations.

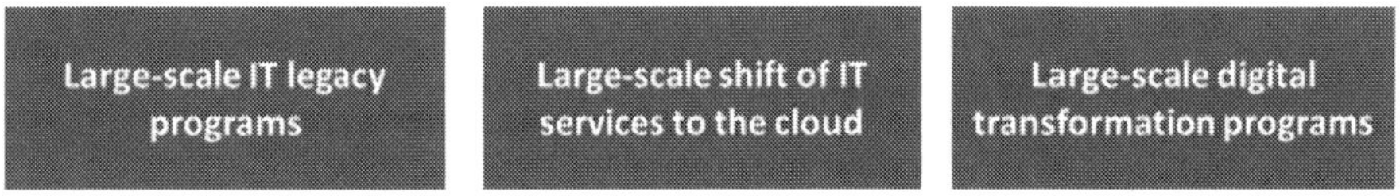

Large-scale IT legacy programs	Large-scale shift of IT services to the cloud	Large-scale digital transformation programs

Figure 4 Three large-scale investments scenarios

Those investments shall solve general problems, often prioritized by CIOs, as they are concerned about traditional IT risks caused by outdated technologies.

APPLIED TECHNOLOGY LEADERSHIP
Anna Skoog-Dabestani, Senior Application Specialist, Green Cargo, Consultant Dynamant
Carl-Evert Dahlin, Senior Application Specialist, Green Cargo

"Green Cargo started its mainframe development project as a proprietary local wagon identification in 1987 and was completed in 1992. Initially, this planning system was a true innovation for our industry for many decades. Bravo was introducing single wagon booking in trains, with two weeks of planning time ahead, an ability in which Green Cargo was alone for many decades within the European Railway sector.

With thousands of tables and a large amount of unknown code insufficiently used and inadequately documented, a strategic decision was made in early 2010 to replace this mainframe system. A new second solid integrated mainframe system for asset and service management, plus a not well-implemented SAP system, were implemented. However, developments in Bravo and SAP were uncoordinated and insufficiently implemented, with contracts hardcoded into SAP.

About a decade ago, a new IT strategy led to a total stop in system development, uncoordinated outsourcing of internal skills, and unreliable offshore development. The strategy and plans to eliminate those IT systems were unrealistic. Business development with IT went into mediocrity, and many projects started, only to never be completed.

It all changed with our new IT leadership when we regained confidence and started to turn things around in late 2019. New and realistic decisions were made, business development went off from one day to another, and we shut down offshore development. With Dynamant, a local Stockholm-based mainframe consulting company, we reinvested in the parts of existing mainframe systems that worked. The most significant change was establishing agile development within our Mainframe system and establishing our intensive partnership with a local Mainframe consulting company Dynamant.

Now we are progressing at unforeseeable speed, control, and quality. We went from four poor releases per year to more than 300 incremental high-quality releases yearly.

New digital platforms encouraged us to integrate the mainframe into our digital development, with real-time and event-driven digitalization of stone age business processes. Unexpectedly, IT took the lead in business development and has become a driving force in developing the future of Green Cargo.

We (Anna and Carl) were part of this journey and never anticipated such an impossible turnaround with incremental, systemic, and sustainable improvements. We stabilized the system, improved our system performance, increased stability, and minimized complexity. In various projects, subsystems have been phased out and replaced by other systems in more modern platforms. And more is yet to come.

We incrementally adapted the mainframe system to digital development in lowcode, regained control, and started planning future technology platform migration. With business innovation, more changes, and new requirements, a platform upgrade is a risk mitigation activity, as the system may reach the critical limit soon.

It has been crucial that Ingo Paas has come to Green Cargo with its innovative power and engaged everyone to contribute to our incremental transformative approach. He initiated collaborative teamwork across functions and listened to a specialist like us. Having a board and management that dared to trust our new strategy and leadership has also been important. In just three years, we took Green Cargo to the next level, from chaos back to structured innovation, applying modern composable leadership to reunite the legacy and our digital foundational platforms. This unforeseeable and impossible "Hollywood story" continues while we (Anna and Carl) prepare for retirement after 40 years of dedication!"

Written by Carl-Evert Dahlin, Senior Application Specialist, Green Cargo

Anna Skoog-Dabestani, Senior Application Specialist, Green Cargo, Consultant Dynamant

Understanding and positioning large-scale investment scenarios in the bigger context of digital transformations with their risks, opportunities, consequences, and dependencies is necessary. In addition, they are often presented to decision-makers as the only way forward, while alternative approaches are often ignored or excluded.

CIOs must inform decision-makers about alternative approaches while they may not be able to qualify such alternatives without appreciated leadership, risk-averse thinking, and available best practices. Risk adversity is a critical concern for boards and CEOs, as they must demand and compare risk-averse and risk-tolerance alternatives to make better-informed decisions. It is necessary to inform CEOs more rationally about the risks associated with large-scale programs, including the lessons learned from unsuccessful programs and transformations.

Large-scale IT legacy programs

Large-scale IT legacy programs are often motivated to prepare the underlying IT systems digitally. Such programs involve significant investments to replace large, outdated, complex IT systems. Digital leaders or CIOs often argue that digital transformations require a modern and updated IT landscape, where the only way to solve these problems is to make large investments to modernize or replace critical IT legacy systems.

Resource-intensive investments include significant changes, usually involving larger parts of the organization during long-term and complex implementations. Risk-averse organizations prioritize those programs and investments, as they most likely trust traditional and top-down approaches. Such programs usually deliver under their promises and scope. They often include high risks because they underestimate the complexity, experience scope creep, introduce technologies and interdependencies, and are often surprised by unpredictable implementation challenges. They underestimate the organizational ability to adapt to change, ignoring effective collaboration needs and the consideration of cultural aspects, as they often struggle with integrating changes into the line organization. Significant delays in deliveries may cause higher costs for prolonged system maintenance and increase operational risks and stability. Return on Investments (ROIs), Total cost of Ownership (TCO), and individual business cases are often unrealistic and impossible to realize. Costs usually increase, and the ability of effective programs to deliver on time, scope, budget, and quality is generally at risk and weakening over time.

Large-scale shift of IT services to the cloud

Another preferred standard approach is to secure organizational readiness to shift and lift the IT legacy and data center operations (IT applications and infrastructure) into the cloud. Those transformations are usually reasonably technical, solve several critical IT technology problems, are complex, resource intensive, and introduce parallel costs during transition phases. Proposed benefits are significant cost savings (mainly focused on cost avoidance), improved redundancy, unlimited scalability, embedded security and controls, and more robust and cost-efficient disaster recovery capabilities. Most of those programs deliver nearly up to completion level, while the promises of infrastructure cloud operations may significantly diverge from originally presented Return of Investments (ROIs), Total cost of Ownership (TCOs), and individual business cases. In the meantime, those programs may significantly delay or postpone other more critical investments.

Large-scale digital transformation programs

Organizations still consider running digital transformations as large-scale programs. Those traditional perceptions may be motivated by fundamental misunderstandings and interpretations of the scope, benefits, and level of change reinforced by digital transformations. Boards and executives often demand a more traditional approach to qualify digital transformations as a program rather than an evolutionary approach to change. The dynamics and complexity of digital transformations managed as large-scale programs are relatively volatile and unforeseeable. Digital programs may involve complex investments and variations over time, with unforeseen technologies and capabilities, data, skills, and problems to convince the line organization to assume responsibility. Due to their nature and dynamics, with complex interdependencies between new digital technologies and existing IT legacy systems, traditional planning and scope management will probably fail. The complexity of introducing new technologies, leveraging data-driven organizations, and reshaping enterprise information flow are additional challenges to overcome.

Few digital leaders can draw a reasonable conclusion from the beginning and estimate how to plan and execute such programs. Identifying and spotting the proper scope, dependencies, and order of priorities is a highly complex, if not impossible, undertaking.

APPLIED TECHNOLOGY LEADERSHIP
Helena Wetterwik, Head of Project Management Office, Green Cargo

"With over a decade at Green Cargo working in various business functions, I have seen several IT strategies and roadmaps. Until I joined IT at the end of 2019, they were all based on large-scale IT legacy programs or projects suggesting replacing legacy systems individually. Each of these replacements required advanced and time-consuming investigations and preparations. Only a few initiatives led to action due to a lack of stakeholders, resources, and/or money. The gap between the strategic objectives and the ability to execute grew bigger with every initiative we didn't start or finalize. Green Cargo's traditional large transformation programs failed in all aspects, creating major problems and risks we thought we would never recover from.

Less than two months after Ingo Paas joined Green Cargo, he presented a strategy to the board of directors based on evolution, not revolution.

The strategy suggested building on our legacy, successively adding or replacing critical modules and components while synchronizing and replacing the legacy bit by bit. The main purpose was to create value and mitigate major risks by keeping the balance. Things changed rapidly, and we reorganized around our new strategy and leadership. We are constantly evolving our plan while we realize that we went from unrealistic strategies to controlled and business-driven execution. We came further these three and a half last years than we did 15 years before.

The digitalization journey began based on a set of principles from our IT transformation. The digital transformation that grew out of the evolutionary IT transformation is unexpectedly successful, requiring focus, continuity, balanced investments, and distinct utilization of our foundational architectural principles. Instead of relying on traditional approaches and consultants that took the lead before, we decided to rely on the organization itself. This significant shift towards autonomy and accountability in strategy ownership and execution helped us establish and earn trust, including our executive team and supportive board of directors. I can see how this ongoing evaluation also requires more coaching, patience, decentralized leadership, and cooperation from the management.

The role of PMO has changed, inspired by our composable digital transformation. Green Cargo's PMO is now an accelerator of business-driven development. Our investment portfolio and strategy have taken a balanced approach between tactical business and strategic platform-related investments. Our digital foundational digital platforms (such as lowcode, integration, and analytics) were financed, including business pilots from the PMO budget. In addition, we utilized our PMO budget to establish our DevOps teams through business projects. The PMO is driven by business priorities and effective governance bodies, aligning technology-driven business development initiatives and engaging in collaborative ways to ensure proactive ownership and align our roadmap. We focus on competence development, secure ownership during and after project execution, and engage to secure the value of our investments.

Our PMO is embedded into our agile ways of working, utilizing SAFe5.0 as our first choice while running some initiatives as projects with smaller-sized sprints. One of the most important changes we achieved is the collaborative approach within IT, where Architecture, IT Development, Applications, IT Operations, and our Security team collaborate and improve together. Our PMO strives to cut down larger initiatives into smaller deliveries with pilots/POCs (proof of concepts) to visualize and monitor opportunities and challenges in integration and IT compatibility, organization, and processes while we constantly learn and improve."

The role of our PMO has changed significantly to accelerate value-driven investments, secure benefits, and contribute to systemic business development. We have encouraged and initiated tech-inspired business development, supporting the business from ideation to delivering value. We think systemic, incremental, modular, and constantly adjusting our roadmap securing interoperability, durability, and architectural principles when investing in tech and IT. ROI and TCO are at the core of every investment as we continually learn from our failures and successes".

Written by Helena Wetterwik, Head of Project Management Office, Green Cargo

Large-scale programs/investments introduce significant risks to organizations concerning their ability to deliver on their promises (ROI & TCO) and business cases. Unsuccessful programs may significantly slow down or postpone digital transformations and business development. To wait with digital transformations until major initiatives and programs are delivering on their promises is not an option.

Digital transformations must engage differently to optimize business models and digitalize enterprises from the core of the business in incremental and experimental ways. They must consider a rather evolutionary approach, involve the entire organization, collaboratively evolve new digital capabilities, and verify their applicability, focusing on short-term results and continual development.

They demand new approaches and ways to implement change and realize promised business benefits. Executives shall cautiously evaluate and reconsider the total impact of whether to prioritize large-scale programs or more evolutionary approaches to digital transformations. Major investment decisions must be better informed and compared with potential alternatives.

Make well-informed investments decisions

Making upfront investment decisions for large-scale IT legacy programs, large-scale cloud infrastructure programs, or large-scale digital transformation programs is difficult, if not impossible, to make.

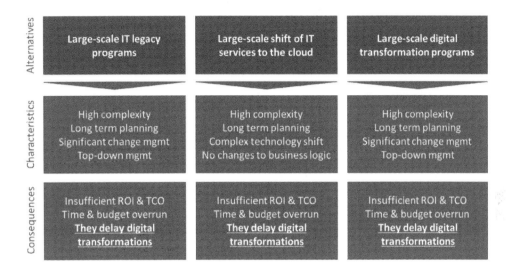

Figure 5 Three examples of large-scale implementation programs

Understanding and reviewing the outfalls and recommendations of those undertakings are inevitably critical for decision-makers to make better-informed decisions and investments. The following recommendations are indicative statements to review such investment decisions better. They may consider individual risks, business needs, compliance problems, issues with technical debts, and the existing IT legacy.

The following recommendations do not apply to every organization but should help senior executives make more balanced decisions, minimize risks, and optimize the ROI and TCO of their investments.

1. **Large-scale IT legacy programs**

   Recommendation: POSTPONE

   Large-scale IT legacy programs and replacements shall be postponed whenever feasible.

2. **Large-scale shift of IT services to the cloud**

   Recommendation: POSTPONE

Large-scale shift and lift programs of applications and infrastructure services from data centers to the cloud shall be postponed whenever feasible.

3. **Large-scale digital transformation programs**

   Recommendation: <u>AVOID</u>

   Organizations shall avoid running digital transformations as traditional large-scale digital programs whenever feasible.

Boards and CEOs must embrace and ask for and support alternative evolutionary strategies, to secure substantial and compelling, lasting digital composable transformations. Those recommendations go hand-in-hand with postponing and avoiding large-scale programs and investments.

Enterprises must consider different challenges associated with financing digital transformations as part of enterprise-wide investment strategies. They may consist of different issues, such as:

- **Lack of clarity on ROI**

  Measuring the return on investment (ROI) for digital transformation initiatives can be challenging, especially with strategic investments. Difficulties may arise in determining the financial benefits of investments, where innovation can hardly predict reliable business cases.

- **Limited Budgets**

  Digital transformations often require significant investments, while agile development, cloud operations and services, and security require large budget adjustments to finance agile development teams and organizations. Many enterprises may struggle to secure the necessary funds to support these budget-related challenges, especially if they have limited budgets or face other financial constraints.

- **Lack of Expertise**

  Many enterprises may not have the in-house expertise to budget, calculate, and estimate reliable investment plans and development budgets.

- **Uncertainty of change**

  The pace of technological change can be rapid and unpredictable, making it challenging to develop long-term investment plans for digital transformations.

- **Insufficient or missing investment strategies**

Investment strategies are more likely to be found for business assets, such as machines, trucks, and production units, but are often not appropriate for digital transformations.

The true reasons and pitfalls of digital transformations shall guide executives and boards to make better-informed decisions and to ask more comprehensive and challenging questions. With a more profound understanding, better and more balanced decisions are possible, while organizations can prevent traditional risks associated with large-scale programs.

Understand common pitfalls of digital transformations

To discuss and demystify the true reasons enterprises typically fail with their digital transformations, executives must apply a new and more holistic approach to identifying and addressing the underlying pitfalls and necessary mitigations and actions.

Traditional pitfalls have not been very helpful, as they offer standard responses to standard problems without realizing that they may be addressing the wrong issues while overlooking the root cause of problems.

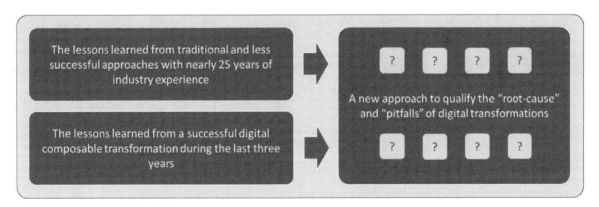

Figure 6 The true pitfalls of digital transformations are based on nearly 30 years of experience

Those experiences have led to the definition of new foundational pitfalls why many digital transformations fail or do not deliver on their promises. With an attempt at a more in-depth analysis of both successful and less successful digital transformations, those new pitfalls suggest a new comprehensive approach and guide for enterprises to increase their chances of success.

This book will provide in-depth expertise and insights on how to overcome those pitfalls. The suggested pitfalls are interconnected and describe a systemic and evolutionary approach to improve the chances of succeeding with digital transformations.

The proposed responses to digital composable transformations shall guide enterprises to find tailored and adaptive ways to establish greater awareness and engage in sustainable change to deliver on the potential of digital transformations.

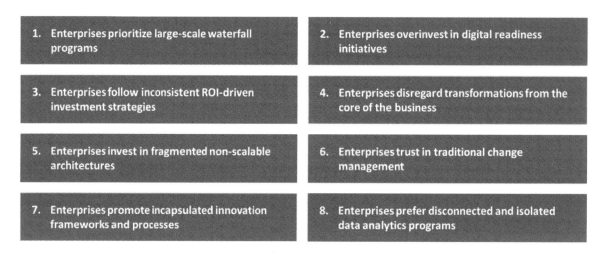

Figure 7 The eight pitfalls of traditional digital transformations

Pitfall 1   Enterprises prioritize large-scale waterfall programs

Problem: Enterprises prioritize large-scale and top-down waterfall programs, disregard learnings and failures from the last decades, and disbelieve in less risk-averse and more innovative evolutionary approaches. Decision makers easily relate to initiatives, as the majority of executives have experiences from large-scale programs from the last decades.

Reason: Risk-averse cultures encourage behaviors with risk-averse leaders and decision-makers. Traditional enterprises with risk-averse cultures are more likely to prioritize large-scale investments in the belief of control and structure. They prioritize significant investments such as moving data centers and infrastructure into the cloud or driving digital transformations as a program. Irrational attempts serve the need for control, command, and structure but reveal that digital composable transformations are often perceived as one-time investments.

Concern: Large-scale programs are not the appropriate answer to successful and sustainable implementations of support digital composable transformations. Prioritizing major programs and investments is rather counterproductive, possibly delaying digital transformations.

Without appropriate and distributed accountability, large-scale programs will not embrace and motivate incremental and scalable change with sustainable investments. Business cases with promising ROIs and TCO cases rarely deliver on their promises, leading to overdrawing budgets, scope creep, and overall failure.

Recommendation: Enterprises must postpone traditional large-scale and top-down programs whenever feasible.

Pitfall 2   Enterprises overinvest in digital readiness initiatives

Problem: CIOs often identify significant risks with their IT legacy, often perceived as not being digital-ready. The argument is that digital readiness is critical for enterprises to remain competitive and relevant by ensuring that their technologies, skills, and processes are adaptable and ready for digital interoperability with new digital technologies and processes.

Reason: Risk-averse cultures encourage risk-averse behaviors and risk-averse leaders. Traditional enterprises with high-risk awareness and risk-averse cultures are more likely to prioritize larger-scale programs to run their digital transformations.

In the absence of knowledge and choices, senior executives depend on the expertise of their CIOs or consulting companies. Fundamental misunderstanding and insufficient tech-savviness are other reasons for inadequate decisions to make large-scale investments in digital readiness initiatives.

Concern: Organizations are planning complex, time-consuming, and resource-intensive modernization investments into their IT legacy systems to prepare for future digital transformations. They may decide on up-front investments into IT legacy programs and projects. They prioritize avoidable large-scale investments without genuinely understanding the scope and benefits. It is unlikely that organizations can identify the necessary changes to make IT legacy systems digitally ready up-front, as they are difficult to define and to set clear goals and scope.

Recommendation: Enterprises must avoid traditional large-scale and top-down programs to ensure digital readiness before starting digital transformations.

Pitfall 3   Enterprises apply inconsistent ROI-driven investment strategies

Problem: Inconsistent investment strategies are often motivated by short-term ROI (Return on Investments) promises with rapid business impact investments.

Reason: As Boards and CEOS demand strong ROI-driven investments, enterprises are shifting their investment strategies toward tactical investments. Technology-inspired digital investments often motivate strategies to solve isolated business problems with fragmented technologies. Technology deployments risk being inconsistent and non-compatible with existing and future technologies, not supporting digital foundational and composable architectures.

Concern: Investments must secure strong short-term ROI, balanced TCO (Total Cost of Ownership), and strategic fit. Unbalanced investments can lead to ineffective deployment of fragmented technologies, limiting the enterprise to further scaling its capabilities and investments. Prioritizing interoperability over fragmentation will have long-term consequences with constrained and counterproductive investments with non-scalable ROIs and insufficient TCOs.

Recommendation: Enterprises must avoid inconsistent, fragmented, and non-scalable ROI-driven digital investments.

Pitfall 4 Enterprises disregard transformations from the core of the business

Problem: Enterprises disregard digital transformations from the core of the business as they most likely focus on digital investments and, at first hand, more popular customer-focused investments with less complexity.

Reason: The reasons vary, mainly because of various obstructions, barriers, and difficulties. Driving digital transformations from the core is often considered too complex, too little "digital," and too abstract to consider such changes as digital transformative activities and valuable investments. Existing IT legacy systems may dominate business models and processes at the core of the business, and digital investments often seem to add no or too little value. Enterprises may be concerned about high complexity, costs, and the absence of appropriate strategies. They most likely prioritize state-of-the-art technologies with significant improvements on dedicated business processes (such as e-commerce, digital customer portals, pricing optimization engines, digital marketing, and product enhancements). They lack strategies, technologies, and skills to make digital transformations work from the core of their business.

Concern: Digital transformations that exclude considerable digital investments at the core of their business cannot build digital composable enterprises. They disable enterprise interoperability and may cause ineffective processes, leading to sub-optimization of customer-facing processes with considerable problems, insufficient flexibility, and major inconsistencies. Enterprises investing in digital transformations without considering their core will not be able to build digitally resilient and composable enterprises. Digital ecosystems demand this agility with impossible internal and external ecosystem integrations. Business processes, such as e-commerce, order management, warehousing, and logistics, may be disconnected as non-collaborative transformations disregard the need for interoperability and transparency between several functions across multiple digital ecosystems and customer processes.

Conclusion: Enterprises must avoid digital transformations <u>not</u> driven from the core of the business.

Pitfall 5   Enterprises invest in fragmented non-scalable architectures

Problem: Enterprises invest in fragmented and non-scalable architectures!

Enterprises do not design their targeted architecture for composability. Their architecture is fragmented while disregarding the essential need for enterprise interoperability and composability.

Reason: Digital transformations often focus on solving specific business problems, using technologies without having a visionary approach. Individual investments into fragmented technologies usually support isolated problems.

Scalability is often not considered, as technologies are dysfunctional to support enterprise-wide interoperability and integration with the existing IT legacy systems. Unrecognized consequences of unbalanced prioritizations and fragmented investment decisions mainly cause architectures that are not scalable, as the primary focus on short-term ROI-driven investments does make platform investments unattractive.

Concern: Organizations disregarding critical foundational investments do not balance their investment decisions with short-term tactical ROI (finance the transformation) and long-term strategic digital foundational technologies and platforms (scale the transformation). They may introduce fragmented digital technologies, generating new future risks (new digital IT legacy) and costs (redundancies, ineffective buy versus build decisions). Fragmented and unbalanced non-foundational platform investments are not supported or reinforced through aligned visionary approaches to the vision, strategy, goals, and business priorities. Without appropriate architectures, enterprises will not mature and utilize their digital investments to become composable digital enterprises. Fragmented technologies and the absence of enterprise interoperability will instead dominate their future digital landscape. Those organizations suffer from incomplete or missing digital foundational and composable architectural design and principles and modern layered digital foundational platform strategies to design and build scalable and interoperable composable architectures.

Recommendation: Enterprises must avoid rigid investments in fragmented and non-scalable digital architectures.

Pitfall 6   Enterprises trust in traditional change management

Problem: Enterprises trust traditional change management initiatives embedded into traditional large programs. With little buy-in in the line organization and disengaged teams, there is insufficient ownership and a reluctance to change.

Reason: Objectives with change management are to share, inform, create awareness, find acceptance, and establish new knowledge and ownership about changes, usually emphasized by projects or programs. Change management is still necessary if separate projects or programs introduce changes, reaching out to a larger group of stakeholders and users. Another issue is that employees often lack clear understanding and involvement and have little influence on the changes.

Concern: Digital transformations are ineffective if they are not led as collaborative implementations and are not embedded with key business stakeholders and employees. Changes are not developed collaboratively, embraced, or owned by the line organization. Burning business problems are not recognized or solved, while new problems are becoming a serious challenge. Employees do not learn how to apply digital technologies and become disengaged. Change management does not motivate and inspire learning organizations and does not support agile development and implementations. In addition, product organizations will not rise, and digital transformations depending on change management are not transformative concerning culture. Adapting to cultural development necessitates collaboration and continuous learning to bring about change, which indicates that programs and traditional change management are no longer appropriate. Employees must collaborate in ongoing processes to adapt to cultural development while actively participating in change and working together to solve urgent problems. Without involving and inspiring employees in change, digital transformations will continue to experience acceptance problems.

Recommendation: Enterprises must avoid traditional change management initiatives whenever possible.

Pitfall 7   Enterprises promote incapsulated innovation frameworks and processes

Problem: Enterprises promote incapsulated innovation frameworks and processes, while senior executives and decision-makers disregard integrated innovation and digital development from the core of their business. They unintentionally promote encapsulated, ineffective, and incoherent innovation processes and frameworks. They are applying "best practices" that are inappropriate and ineffective, as they lack access to information about appropriate alternatives.

Reason: Organizations usually prefer traditional top-down approaches regarding innovation. They disengage their organizations in the absence of trust, missing abilities, and fear of inconsistencies that may arise with more democratized approaches to innovation.

They trust that traditional "waterfall innovation frameworks" function effectively as a discrete process. They do not embrace democratized agile and collaborative innovation opportunities. They recognize innovation investments as a separate funding process and have no incentives and tools to apply collaborative processes to foster a culture of innovation.

Concern: Innovation becomes a constrained and bureaucratic approach, disconnected from daily innovation opportunities and the involvement and utilization of creativity and skills. Those frameworks do not solve business problems with a sense of urgency and from the core of the business. Innovation is a separate and isolated concern, with distinct budgets, different decisions, and prioritization processes. Digital foundational platforms and technologies are not utilized. Innovation is not embedded into daily innovation prioritizations and is connected to collaborative, agile teams. The running innovation disregards a culture of innovation as a fragmented process, a static and traditional undertaking. Without leveraging innovation and engaging a broader group of employees, those organizations will never experience a collaborative and cultural transformation utilizing innovation embedded into everything. Separate funding processes and budgets (owned by senior management) for innovation will never encourage collaborative innovation and cultural adaptation. Those organizations eventually unintentionally choose not to empower their organizations in democratized and collaborative innovation.

Recommendation: Enterprises must avoid trusting and investing in encapsulated, rigid innovation frameworks and processes.

Pitfall 8   Enterprises prefer disconnected and isolated data analytics programs

Problem: Digital transformations prefer disconnected and isolated data analytics programs outside their digital transformations. The main reason is that data analytics is often disregarded as a core competence and critical undertaking of digital transformations. Instead, data analytics programs are often separated and disengaged.

Reason: This is due to their complexity and dignity, isolated data science teams, and the solitary focus on data-driven transformations. Risk-averse enterprises with conservative data protection principles and roles struggle to prevent disruptions in their transformations caused by an archaic exaggeration of data governance, compliance, and protection. Digital transformation does not recognize the need to establish platform capabilities and utilize data analytics to deliver such capabilities to the line organization.

Concern: Investments often focus on solitary or isolated programs, especially in analytics and data management. However, the return on investment depends heavily on integrated data and analytics capabilities, contrary to what decision-makers may think. Failing to strategically invest in data innovation and strategic analytics and data platforms will cause transformations to miss out on short- and long-term scalable benefits. Enterprises must rethink their approach to data integrity, ownership/stewardship, access, distribution, quality, security, privacy, and more, regardless of interpretability and dependencies. They must also realize and embed extensive data security and compliance activities. Including data analytics in digital transformations helps organizations identify new growth opportunities and efficiencies and solve fundamental business problems and inconsistencies with business logic. Data transformations cannot fulfill their promises and potential if analytics programs are separate from digital transformations.

Recommendation: Enterprises must avoid separating analytic data transformations outside their digital transformations.

In summary, traditional pitfalls usually come with standard arguments, such as the necessity of top-down CEO support, customer focus, and similar arguments. Consulting, research companies, and universities repeatedly highlight and communicate arguments explaining the confusion among senior executives about practical learning from failed transformations. It is not surprising that this confusion exists.

The immense complexity of digital transformation requires various strategic, tactical, and operational responses. They provide a foundational understanding of why to address digital transformations differently. Those eight pitfalls summarize the main reasons WHY digital transformations are failing, making this book a new and comprehensive guide to finding answers to such fundamental questions. Traditional pitfalls mainly address digital transformations requiring top management engagement, careful planning, clear communication, and a willingness to adapt to change.

Understanding comprehensive and systemic responses when developing digital strategies should at least include answers to the eight most common pitfalls of digital transformations. Implementing and realizing composable enterprises will be impossible without reconsidering the necessary depth and systemic approach to digital transformation. Instead of focusing on digital strategies, every digital transformation must identify the essential business drivers and be clear about the purpose and desired goals.

Deciding on strategic conceptions before the start or reviewing ongoing digital transformations is essential. If digital transformations facilitate the development of digital composable transformations, those eight pitfalls are mandatory to ensure successful efforts. Enterprises must embrace a cultural adoption, with innovation institutionalized at the business's core, and decide on their conceptions before starting.

Decide on conceptions before starting

When starting digital transformations, organizations should consider innovating their business from the core, ignoring the perceived degrees of complexity of their IT legacy systems and business processes. Organizations can make different choices for digital transformations categorized as investments that are or are not eligible for digital transformations.

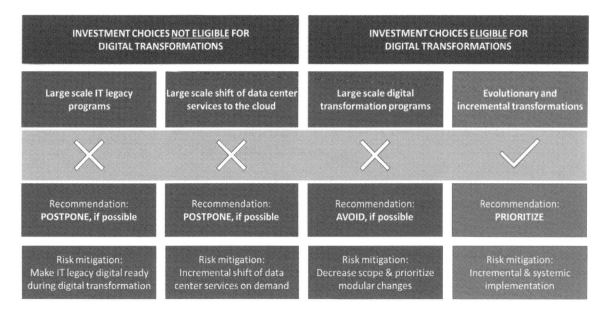

INVESTMENT CHOICES NOT ELIGIBLE FOR DIGITAL TRANSFORMATIONS		INVESTMENT CHOICES ELIGIBLE FOR DIGITAL TRANSFORMATIONS	
Large scale IT legacy programs	Large scale shift of data center services to the cloud	Large scale digital transformation programs	Evolutionary and incremental transformations
✕	✕	✕	✓
Recommendation: POSTPONE, if possible	Recommendation: POSTPONE, if possible	Recommendation: AVOID, if possible	Recommendation: PRIORITIZE
Risk mitigation: Make IT legacy digital ready during digital transformation	Risk mitigation: Incremental shift of data center services on demand	Risk mitigation: Decrease scope & prioritize modular changes	Risk mitigation: Incremental & systemic implementation

Figure 8 Upfront strategic investment choices for successful digital transformations

- **Large-scale IT legacy programs - postpone if possible.**

  Large-scale IT programs can delay digital transformations and require the long-term allocation of key resources for longer periods. Organizations should instead allocate their focus and resources to digital transformations.

- **Large-scale shifts of data center services to the cloud - postpone if possible.**

  Large-scale IT programs can delay digital transformations and require the long-term allocation of key resources for longer periods. Organizations should instead allocate their focus and resources to digital transformations. Enterprises replace larger parts of on-premise services and infrastructure incrementally rather than shift and lift those in major programs.

- **Large-scale digital transformational programs - avoid if possible**.

  Large-scale digital programs often have a higher risk of failure than digital evolutionary transformations due to their complexity, lack of flexibility, lack of buy-in and adoption, and longer timeframes with high levels of complexity. They are difficult to predict and take longer to complete, while original objectives, budgets, and effects may change.

- **Evolutionary digital transformations – prioritize, if possible.**

  This business-driven and evolutionary approach to driving digital transformations comes with various new approaches to why and how to establish digital composable enterprises successfully.

The remaining part of this book focuses on this new evolutionary and transformative approach, what seamless and continual implementation would require from enterprises, and what they could gain. Successful digital transformations do not require upfront digital-ready IT legacy systems, as the scope of "digital-ready IT legacy systems" is nearly impossible to define upfront. Instead, this book suggests different measures, such as making incremental choices while establishing valuable and digitally resilient enterprises.

Digital readiness must consider continual approaches to make IT systems digital-ready by making adjustments in more incremental ways, while DevOps teams shall engage in identifying and prioritizing required changes during digital development. This approach will help avoid large-scale upfront investments that have little or no impact on digital transformations.

APPLIED TECHNOLOGY LEADERSHIP
Johan Svensson, CTO/CIO Sonat

"Green Cargo had about 180 existing applications in a total defragmented IT landscape, including a significant lack of transformational capabilities to contribute with relevant business value. After a decade of unsuccessful major IT legacy programs to replace our two mainframes and insufficient SAP platform, the IT landscape was at high risk. Unsustainable decisions and unrealistic promises led to total stagnation and chaos of IT's ability to deliver valuable IT services and mitigate those significant IT and business risks. Competencies were abandoned and outsourced, only to be insourced again without the willingness to invest in skills and the enormous IT debt.

With new IT and executive leadership, things changed rapidly and significantly in late 2019. We made a 180-degree change in direction, from major IT legacy replacement revolutionary strategies and failures, towards a more realistic but non-proven evolutionary approach. Investments were made to stabilize our systems, insourcing off-shore mainframe development was initiated, and we turned mediocrity IT chaos into a controlled and managed approach.

Our new IT strategy was risk and business-driven, realistic, and value-focused. Our brand new, business-driven, cutting-edge platform technologies were implemented to mitigate the major business initially, and IT risks in coexistence with our existing legacy. The stepwise implementation of our new digital foundational platforms gave us the momentum to achieve strategic goals and drive hands-on business innovation.

Based on our evolving platform strategy, we started to renew and replace insignificant and misplaced legacy business capabilities with integrated and composable components.

With our new strategy in execution, IT significantly shifted from chaos to business leadership. It was like an inspirational nirvana, where great people and skills suddenly created the new and digital future of Green Cargo. It was a collaborative transformation of leadership where IT went from being recognized as a disintegrated and shunned department to take the lead in our accelerating business and IT transformation.

We invested energy in new ways of working and value creation, focused on solving business problems and shaping opportunities and innovation at an extraordinary scale. I still call it the impossible journey and trust in the foundational investments of a digital composable future for Green Cargo. A future that will help Green Cargo and its people evolve stronger than ever. In a broader abstract but hands-on approach, this book describes how others may find hope and inspiration from our transformation at Green Cargo."

Written by Johan Svensson, CTO/CIO Sonat

The main narrative outlined in this book is about finding realistic but evolutionary alternatives to large-scale digital transformations. Based on best practices, the suggestions go beyond the learnings from unsuccessful transformations. They also prepare enterprises to embed digital as the new normal of enterprise development, as digital will keep organizations engaged as long as technologies continue to evolve.

"Digital enterprise composability is not a separate strategy, undertaking, or project. Digital composability must instead be seeded and matured from the core of the business enabled by evolutionary change with revolutionary innovations and technologies, but gradually and incrementally."

Ingo Paas

Key conclusions and takeaways

The key conclusions and takeaways from the chapter "**TRANSFORMATIONAL MISCONCEPTIONS**" are:

1. Enterprises must postpone traditional large-scale and top-down programs whenever possible.

2. Enterprises must avoid traditional large-scale and top-down programs to invest in digital readiness before starting digital transformations.

3. Enterprises must avoid prioritizing inconsistent, fragmented, and non-scalable tactical digital investments.

4. Enterprises must avoid digital transformations that are not evolving from the core of the business.

5. Enterprises must avoid rigid investments in fragmented and non-scalable digital architectures.

6. Enterprises must avoid traditional change management initiatives whenever possible.

7. Enterprises must avoid trusting in encapsulated and rigid innovation frameworks and processes.

8. Enterprises must avoid separating analytic data transformations outside their digital transformations.

9. Enterprises must avoid running digital transformations as a program or project, as digitally inspired enterprise development is the new normal.

TWO – COMPOSABLE PROFICIENCIES

THOUGHT DIGITAL LEADERSHIP

Ted Söderholm, CEO Green Cargo

"When the transformation case of Green Cargo initially was presented to me as to-be CEO, it quickly became apparent that parallel work in multiple layers was needed to improve the company's performance and adapt the business model to the future. Sure, there are always opportunities to find low-hanging fruit in the starting phase of a major transition, and from the outside, it can seem very simple to get going. However, there are also significant risks and pitfalls when choosing the angle of attack. If you get it wrong early on, you might later find that you missed the plot and that you either are on the wrong path or have significantly slower or more costly progress than planned due to the need to continuously revisit and adjust your strategy.

I would claim that being an incumbent player in a mature traditional industry is a challenging starting position. Even if there is a sense of urgency and a clear understanding of the need for change in the organization, the legacy is always there to remind you and influence your thinking pattern. Worst case, it hampers your creativity and locks you in, while being a startup challenger player makes it easier to question the obvious and think outside the box. For me, it was evident that to successfully renew a traditional player in a traditional industry, a very solid platform is required – a foundation to build upon made up of good order and solid processes. The maturity and clear understanding of the importance of making it right the first time, in combination with a humble personal style, was the deciding factor when I hired Ingo as CIO to get started.

Ingo and I discussed the digital transformation at length early on, and quite soon, it became apparent that our discussion mostly circled around the word "risk". Rather than kicking off a major IT transformation which was my spontaneous approach, Ingo clearly advocated a rather surprising slow, steaming start. From an IT perspective, it meant that less sexy and more administrative pieces of the puzzle had to be laid first. The chosen approach was centered around stabilizing the legacy IT platform and ensuring uptime and stability whilst a long-term roadmap was formulated. All our focus in the initial year was put on establishing the critical reusable building blocks needed. Ingo's view was that this was the only way of modernizing the business model from the core with new leadership and a digital foundational platform strategy. With strategic clarity and the fundamentals in place, you can quickly pick up the pace. The ambition was set to become a "tech company on tracks".

The lengthy initial discussions on how to digitize and transform the IT landscape also had a great side effect in the sense that mutual trust between myself and Ingo was built. For me, knowing that my CIO was as keen as I was on minimizing risk, being cost-conscious, ensuring that the needs were driven by the business and customers rather than from technology itself, and that organizational readiness was an important pace-setter made it easy for me to let go and trust the process. By asking questions, at times challenging but mostly supporting Ingo and his organization, we have built a digital journey that works.

There is still much work left, but less than four years in, we have clearly avoided the statistical failure rate and are accelerating our composable transformation. In many aspects, IT is a binary thing, but when it comes to digital transformation, it is still up to the people involved to make change happen. Green Cargo's chosen approach and Ingo's stewardship might just become the exception from the rule."

Written by Ted Söderholm, CEO Green Cargo

Embrace the art of composability

In 2020, Gartner (Gartner, 2021) introduced the concept of digital composable enterprises, which presents a challenging new undertaking. These enterprises must develop enterprise-wide capabilities and respond effectively and rapidly to critical business challenges. Digital resilience is generally underdeveloped, while composable enterprises are fundamentally rethinking and changing their approach to composability.

Composable enterprises apply composable-inspired design principles and capabilities, design and implement digital foundational architectures, and invest in appropriate technologies that leverage enterprise-wide interoperability.

Many enterprises have IT legacy systems that restrict their ability to develop and adjust processes effectively for digitalization. The key challenge for these organizations is to design dynamic and resilient capabilities, ensure the integrity of data and application objects, and collaborate with APIs from different IT legacy systems, multiple digital platforms, various applications, and multiple internal and external data sources. The ability to rapidly adjust business core business processes is a key demand for resilient and responsive IT organizations.

Enterprises must adopt modern digital composable architectural designs to respond more effectively to future business disruptions, realize rapidly changing business needs, and scale digital investments.

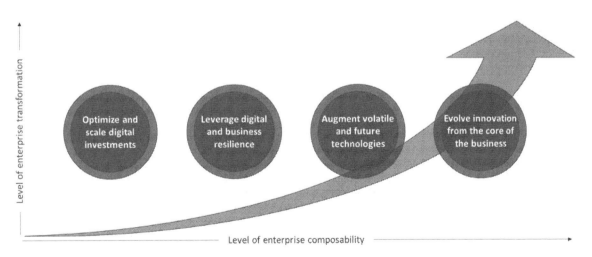

Figure 9 The four strategic objectives of digital composable transformations

The four strategic objectives of enterprise composability are indispensable from each other and may not be compromised. They act like a compass, supporting the overall direction of the enterprise and guiding strategic and daily decision-making.

"CEOs should only declare the digital transformation of traditional enterprises successful if their investments are scalable, leverage resilience, augment volatile technologies, and evolve innovation from the core of the business."

Ingo Paas

By utilizing principles of composable design, organizations can accelerate digital transformations in sustainable ways, essentially from the core of their business. Enterprises must rethink their approach to building a resilient business by looking at their most significant risks, opportunities, and business needs on all levels of the organization. By considering foundational principles of composable design, organizations can achieve rapid and responsive digital changes and facilitate digital transformations while fostering a digitally inspired culture from the core of the business.

In the context of digital transformations with complex technologies, volatility describes the degree of unpredictable variations in the performance or outcomes of digital transformations. Volatility is considering factors such as the complexity of implemented and future technologies, changes in market conditions, shifting customer preferences, or unexpected challenges in the implementation process. To navigate volatility in digital transformations with complex technologies, organizations should adopt agile and flexible approaches that allow them to respond quickly to changes and adapt their strategies accordingly. This may involve breaking down the transformation initiative into smaller, more manageable components. By embracing volatility and using it as an opportunity for scalability, flexibility, and scalability, organizations can more successfully navigate the challenges and complexities of digital transformation initiatives.

Through thoroughly re-evaluating the organization's IT legacy risks, digital transformations can foster a culture of digitally resilient business environments embedded in collaborative approaches, making adjustments at any time or process with fast responses. They do not need to rebuild their entire IT legacy to become a digital composable enterprise and must instead explore the impact of composability in their composable strategy.

Explore the implementation of composable enterprises

Digital transformations use digital technologies to drive substantial business models and process changes. Digital transformations do not just transform existing processes; they utilize new ways of working, inspire, and facilitate substantial changes everywhere. They have the power to transform entire organizations and impact and create digitally enabled ecosystems with customers, partners, vendors, and other relevant stakeholders.

Digital transformations, executed properly, will leverage, and scale the evolution of enterprise-wide composability. Great transformations will shape new digitally enabled packaged business capabilities (PBCs) as introduced by Gartner (Gartner, 2021). Packaged business capabilities are essential for realizing composable enterprises, introduced as a new layer on top of well-defined processes.

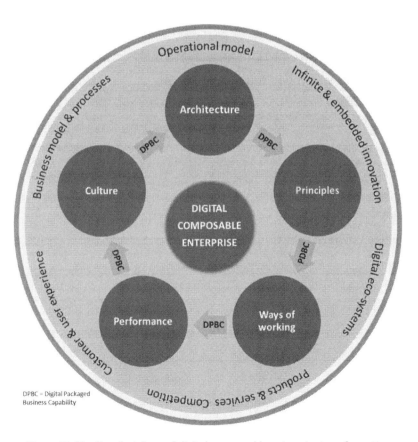

Figure 10 The five disciplines of digital composable enterprise transformations

The design of digital composable enterprises and the framework consider five critical core disciplines of digital composable enterprise transformations:

1. **ARCHITECTURE**

   To design, implement, and operate a composable architecture.

2. **PRINCIPLES**

   To develop and orchestrate digital foundational platforms based on guiding principles.

3. **WAYS OF WORKING**

   To utilize advanced collaboration and facilitate new ways of working.

4. **PERFORMANCE**

   To embrace and realize the core capabilities of high-performing organizations.

5. **CULTURE**

   To enable organizational adoption, advancement, and cultural development.

Digital transformations are complex undertakings to respond to opportunities, evolve existing business models, expand offerings (such as products and services), streamline cross-functional business processes, drive automation, leverage customer experiences, increase innovation capabilities, optimize costs, and encourage profitable growth opportunities. It is a broad and complex concept encompassing many aspects of enterprises. Consequently, the goals of digital transformations can vary greatly depending on the organization's specific needs and priorities. While developing digital composable enterprises may not always be an explicit goal of most digital transformations, it must be a desirable outcome for every traditional enterprise to stay competitive and relevant long term. This framework explains the purpose and potential of digital composable enterprises. It involves the entire organization and suggests making composability an explicit objective of transformational efforts and giving a detailed and consistent overview of the dependencies, correlations, and interconnected elements of digital transformations and composable enterprises.

"Enterprises must make composability an explicit objective of their digital transformation strategies, foundational and scalable and from the core of the business."

Ingo Paas

Enterprises that actively pursue digital transformations do shift away from traditional fragmented and silo-oriented ways of working. They leverage more collaborative, experimental, and systemic approaches to change. Organizations must reconsider their tactics and undertakings, why and how they drive change. Consequently, enterprises must reinforce and integrate composability at the core of their digital transformations with new approaches to digital packaged business application development (DPBCs). According to Gartner, the solution is to identify, and design packaged business capabilities, which is challenging for many organizations. Most enterprises struggle as they confuse processes and business capabilities or have issues identifying the right approach to effectively design their business capabilities and re-architect their business processes into digitally packaged business capabilities.

Digital transformations profoundly impact business models and processes, forcing enterprises to adopt new ways of working and automating processes and decisions while aligning and integrating fragmented business processes and systems. They take a much broader perspective, including customers and other external stakeholders, to leverage digital ecosystems and to promote digital changes from the core of the business rather than to concentrate on digital leadership transformation of the customer experience.

Advanced and intelligent analytics capabilities fundamentally change how organizations make decisions, follow up, apply predictive and preventive measures, and create end-to-end visibility and transparency throughout their core business processes.

Successful digital transformations build their digital capabilities exclusively in the cloud (even though there may be good reasons for exemptions). They utilize platform strategies, create digital foundational architectures, and guarantee scalability, reusability, transparency, stability, sustainability, autonomy, accessibility, and rapid and relentless innovation power. They do this to secure control and empowerment regarding privacy, security (detect & respond), compliance, and controls, embedded into the design principles and underlying architecture.

They adopt rapid changes and promote a shift from traditional software to product development, ingesting that applications are treated as products, enabling packaged composability of continual application development, facilitating infinite development, to establishing the capabilities of continually changing digitally developed applications.

Collaborative organizations mature out of initial agile development and optimize their technology investments systematically and holistically. They engage tech-savvy and enthusiastic business leaders to apply the fundamental principles of platform strategies rather than to promote fragmented ROI-driven technology investments and SaaS-centric (Software as a Service) fragmented approaches.

Organizations must embed innovation into daily prioritizations as a standard approach to innovate and develop the enterprise. They must learn how to utilize technology-enabled innovation utilizing cloud-based platforms from hyperscalers, such as Google Cloud Platform, Microsoft Azure, and Amazon Web Services.

Enterprises with platform strategies adapt and package technologies and digital capabilities and drive digital transformations by building networks and ecosystems for scalability, collaboration, and growth.

Augmentation and stability in digital transformations must be realized and accepted as a digital architectural design principle, while a more holistic architectural design secures systemic and sustainable development. Problem-solving will be more result-oriented, done in smaller incremental steps, and sustainable, allowing successfully implemented digital solutions to reuse. The future of work and digital user experience is changing, setting new demands on user-centric digital development. Another critical example is the workplace transformation during the global pandemic accelerated digital adaptation at never before seen speed and acceptance, radically and forever changing the digital user workplace experience.

Changes to people, culture, and leadership entrenched by digital transformations are tremendous and often underestimated and undervalued. New skills and competencies are required to rethink and reimagine the future of enterprise resilience in the digital age. Without unified enterprise-wide competence development strategies, organizations may struggle to leverage the new digital capabilities at scale within the business and IT functions. Those strategies must consider new roles and responsibilities for the entire organization. They must significantly involve analytics and data science skills, development skills, test skills, product owners, and roles within agile teams to utilize. They must likewise learn how to most effectively utilize new technologies inspired by ever-advancing technology-inspired opportunities and turn those from ideation into realistic and practical digital autonomous capabilities.

Evolving the organizational culture requires collaborative, agile, and adaptive organizations, where technologies, people, and values must grow together. Embedding digital thinking into cultural adoption and acceptance is critical for long-term success in evolving and engaging people, cultures, and skills.

Implementing incremental, experimental, and systemic changes will gain greater acceptance during implementation than large-scale programs and top-down implementations. Transformations require modern collaborative leadership to secure accountability at every level, as they empower and reinforce more distributed and autonomous (well-guided) decision-making processes. Collaborative development will set the scene for how organizations learn, engage, and realize digital transformations together. Organizations that successfully embrace agile cooperative development will make better decisions together and minimize the risks of fragmented technology investments while accelerating their digital transformations.

Adapting to digital leadership and considering effective risk management is critical for organizations planning and realizing digital transformations.

Understand organizational execution capabilities

Designing and developing a composable enterprise is complex, requiring designated and distinct execution capabilities and profound levels of digital maturity. Key differentiators can be financial strengths and funding capabilities, skills, IT complexity, infosec maturity, maturity of boards, executive teams, organizational limitations, and other factors.

Traditional enterprises must perform significant investments during their digital transformations. For organizations in low-margin industries, such as the transportation industry, those investments substantially hinder boards and CEOs from investing in complex digital transformations. Without securing funding, digital transformations are nearly impossible, hindering entire industries from leveraging technology innovation at scale. Complex business environments, overshadowed by outdated technologies and insufficient degrees of digital maturity, rarely make significant advancements while unable to leverage their IT legacy.

When considering the organizational willingness to combine action with the availability of critical resources, organizations must consider their starting point and perceived ambition level to understand their ability and requirements to master their digital transformations effectively. The two main dimensions are the organization's willingness (readiness, eagerness, and desire to change) and the required resources (funding, skills, people, legacy, and ability to change).

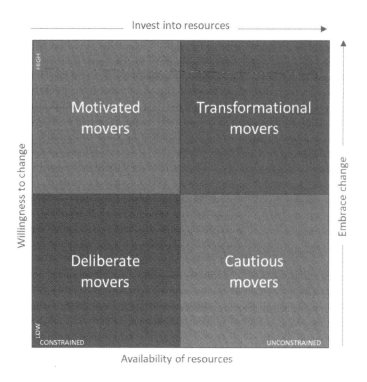

Figure 11 The four different categories of organizations undergoing digital transformations

The four categories differentiate organizations into four categories:

1. **Deliberate** organizations have constrained resources and a low willingness to change.
2. **Motivated** organizations have constrained resources and a high willingness to change.
3. **Cautious** organizations have unconstrained resources and a low willingness to change.
4. **Transformational** organizations have unconstrained resources and a high willingness to change.

Those four different categories of digital transformation are not remarkably static, as success, failure, mismanagement, or wrong strategic decisions may lead to variations between those four categories. As conditions shift and change because of external factors (such as a global pandemic), deliberate organizations may progress in their digital transformations, shaping better pre-conditions and leading to greater engagement and success in their digital composable transformations.

Deliberate movers - unconstrained resources and low willingness to change

Situation: Deliberate movers do not have the required resources or the willingness to change. Given those preconditions, they often fail to achieve digital composable transformations. Deliberate movers are insufficiently equipped with resources (skills and investment budgets), with insufficient capacities to realize digital transformations. In most cases, the chances of even starting a digital transformation are low, if not unrealistic. They may experience significant constraints while they expose their long-term relevance without the ability to explore or implement basic digital capabilities.

Risks: Deliberate movers do not find opportunities, deliberately agree with their "hopeless" situation, and give up.

Response: They may instead choose evolutionary and experimental activities to start digital transformations at a smaller scale while finding promising financing opportunities, such as digital platforms with business-driven pilots. They may prefer smaller investments and project funding with realistic ROIs, while they should utilize those projects to reprioritize and complement critical skills and resources. They shall focus on systemic incremental and experimental execution instead of engaging in intensive strategy work and planning. They should be able to find and solve burning problems, reuse and scale those initial capabilities effectively with a growing ROI focus, and finance future investments. Foundational investment decisions shall utilize project funding from prioritized digital business investments.

Motivated movers - constrained resources and high willingness to change

Situation: Motivated movers have higher chances to succeed, often caused by more vital visions, purposes, and business success. Motivated organizations have a high degree of willingness to change but are eventually not equipped with sufficient resources, which hinders them from delivering on their promises. They may jeopardize their credibility because they overpromise and fail to deliver on the promises and ROIs of digital investments. The chances to start a digital transformation are high, even though their ability to execute depends on allocating critical resources and the trust they can establish with executives and boards. They easily engage with others to support their approaches while struggling to find approvals on necessary investments and resources.

Risks: Motivated movers often face risks caused by their difficulties in making necessary investments, assigning required resources and skills, and eventually adjusting their investment priorities around approval and popularity. They are overpromising ROIs without engaging the organization in a cultural adaptation. They eventually make inadequate and imperfect strategic composable investments that require cross-functional commitment, ownership, and compliance with a strategic architectural design of digital composable enterprises. Investment decisions may be inadequate, not delivering on their promises and business cases.

Response: They may choose smaller investments with rapid ROI and should prioritize existing resources for those projects and shall avoid intensive strategy work and visionary planning. They should find and fix burning problems, establish cost-effective digital foundational platforms, and scale those initial capabilities if possible. They should also shift their focus from presenting and promising digital transformations toward execution and MVPs (Minimum Viable Products).

Cautious movers - unconstrained resources and low willingness to change

Situation: Cautious movers have appropriate access to sufficient resources, while the organization's willingness to change is relatively low. With those given preconditions, digital transformation initiatives deliver on their scope and agreed investments, even though their activities may not lead to more significant business benefits and strong ROIs. Cautious movers could engage in more moderate business cases, eventually under-promising and under deliver conceivable ROIs on their investments. They may find insufficient acceptance within the organization while creating disparity and distance between their programs/projects, the line organization, and other key stakeholders.

Risks: Risks for cautious movers come from collaborative engagement, insufficient cultural adaptation, and the ability to deliver solid ROIs, as they may fall short of cross-functional commitment and support. Interoperability and composability of the IT legacy and the investments from digital transformation (tech, data, platforms, capabilities, SaaS, ...) often disregards, as they instead invest in promotable digital capabilities to capture greater attention and increase the organization's support. They are like motivated movers, making inadequate, imperfect, non-strategic, non-composable investments requiring cross-functional commitment and ownership.

Response: Cautious movers must avoid making investment decisions and consider inappropriate technologies and skills. Their main risks of making ineffective investments are mainly related to their over trust in technologies without aligning those investments with the organization's vision, strategy, goals, and business priorities. If those risks materialize, they may invest in a solid architectural design, including digital foundational platforms. Their investment portfolio shall be more strategic, build foundational composable architectures, be ready to scale, and have business-driven investments with good ROI.

Transformational movers - constrained resources and high willingness to change

Situation: Transformational movers have all preconditions to effectively realize digital transformations and establish the required capabilities to evolve composable organizations. As most digital transformations will not deliver on their promises and potential, there is little evidence that most organizations will deliver on the maximum potential of their digital transformations. They do not effectively utilize their unconstrained resources to implement future composable enterprises. Transformational movers most likely overinvest in large-scale digital transformations, optimize, and organize their resources at maximum scale. Transformational movers are most likely to experience significant challenges in their transformations if confronted with rigorous risk-averse cultures and investment frameworks/governance.

Risks: They risk overinvesting into exhilarating ad-hoc and fragmented technologies, investment portfolios that can lead to friction and insufficient interoperable and conflicting technologies. They unintentionally reinforce future digital debts while eventually risking disconnections between real business needs and problem-to-solve capabilities with short-term benefits and more responsive approaches from the core of the business. They most likely promote more significant and complex changes with large-scale investments and programs. They may likewise end up implementing conflicting and redundant technologies, causing short-term issues (such as costs, complexity, integration, and business logic issues) and long-term issues (such as sustainability, digital development, interoperability, data integrity, maintenance, and resilience).

Response: Transformational movers should consider balanced investments into digital foundational capabilities rather than prioritizing isolated and fragmented investments into independent technologies. They should also avoid large-scale and complex technology implementations in the form of projects or programs.

They should design and implement a solid composable architecture and define an aggressive but business-driven realistic plan and road map. It is essential to oversee strategic investments with balanced priorities rather than intensifying the digital transformation unproportionally and disorganized. Investment committees and prioritization boards must secure more significant "strategic digital composable alignment" and "effective utilization of resources and individual investments." Governance bodies (such as investment committees) must also consider enterprise architecture perspectives and the significance embedded into governance and decision frameworks. They must prioritize necessary adjustments of their portfolio investments, evolve their enterprise governance frameworks, and simplify archaic processes and administrative excess to support their digital transformations to deliver. Architectural solid guidance and support are required to ensure that investments guarantee strategic fit and support the agreed digital architecture. Sustainable digital transformations require foundational investments, accelerating and shattering business-driven development with strong ROIs. The governance and decision frameworks must assume broader responsibilities and secure that the right preconditions are in place to simplify execution and minimize complexity.

All four scenarios must consider that investment decisions guarantee a coordinated and governed realization of well-balanced digital foundational investments to build the organization's future composable architecture.

Enterprises must emphasize appropriate measures to systematically build and secure full interoperability between their core IT legacy systems and their new digital foundational investments to build a solid composable architecture as a foundation for composable enterprises. Independent of their **access to resources** or **the organization's willingness**, enterprises must reconsider and respond to the inevitable necessity and importance of transforming traditional organizations into composable enterprises. They require a systemic approach to interoperability beyond packaged business capabilities.

Every digital transformation should carefully consider the organization's willingness to change and the availability of critical resources required to engage everyone concerned and contribute to digital transformations. The eight pitfalls of digital transformations (as discussed in Chapter 1) help key decision-makers better understand how to utilize those learnings to find the most appropriate responses to their organizational pre-conditions.

APPLIED TECHNOLOGY LEADERSHIP
Ingo Paas, CIO & CDO Green Cargo

"When I joined Green Cargo in September 2019, the organization was a deliberate mover, with no preconditions or abilities to consider a digital transformation. The situation was critical, and even reestablishing basic IT capabilities seemed impossible.

At Green Cargo, we assumed responsibility and started leveraging initial success stories, establishing accountability for our actions, even though we realized we had a long way to go. Our relentless approach of creating autonomy, accountability, and trust at every level helped us to engage with a high sense of urgency. Even though we experienced significant constraints in terms of resources, we started a risk-driven and risk-centric transformation to address the most urgent business risks. Those risks included the inability to

- *develop the business with IT,*
- *prevent business disruptions due to poorly maintained IT legacy systems,*
- *handle significant end-of-life problems IT problems,*
- *prevent business disruptions as a consequence of poor cybersecurity protection.*

The board approved our first IT strategy of directors within the first two months in office without any external consultancy support. The new IT strategy was a risk-driven and evolutionary approach to regain control and reinvest in business development with IT. In the absence of a realistic plan, the board agreed to implement the new strategy without having a clear roadmap proposed. Instead, the suggestion was to let IT make required decisions on leveraging technology, skills, partnerships, and processes to mitigate those risks. As the CIO, I proposed continually developing our plan and making incremental but realistic steps. The idea was to constantly evolve and establish a growing but robust foundation with distinct investments into IT legacy systems, interoperable technologies, and risk-mitigating activities concerning our IT legacy systems. The IT organization recovered from over a decade of frustration within a few weeks. Our employees started engaging, driving, and delivering various activities aligned with our new strategy. By this time, there were no expectations to include digital development into the IT strategy but rather gain control in the first two years in office.

With rapidly growing self-confidence, high energy levels, and a ten-year backlog of business development with IT, the race was on to realize the IMPOSSIBLE turn-around.

Green Cargos CEO played a crucial role in making this transformation possible. He supported this rare approach with outstanding trust and confidence in our risk-based and evolutionary strategy. With this exceptional CEO leadership in UNCERTAINTY, IT felt empowered to realize a substantial turnaround. By the end of 2020, the first sights of digital transformation became visible to everyone. With new leadership, unconventional methods, and unpredictable outcome, we made decent progress by revitalizing the organization to secure accountability at every level and started small but grew big at scale!"

Written by Ingo Paas, CIO & CDO, Green Cargo

Decision-makers shall support understanding organizational execution capabilities to leverage opportunities while intentionally creating the most suitable conditions for long-term success. This approach to deliberately making aligned and governed investment decisions shall guide enterprises to promote not just appropriate investment strategies, and they must understand and encourage risk-averse versus risk-tolerance decision cultures in their enterprises.

Promote a risk-tolerance decision culture

Risk-tolerance decision culture is essential for successful organizations that can transform their business from the core, while this is eventually a rare capability amongst CIOs and CTOs. Boards and CEOs have compelled CIOs and CTOs to meet expectations as risk-averse leaders for decades, which essentially goes against the core values and leadership characteristics of modern CIOs or CTOs. This is a major issue, as new demands on leadership require a radical change in the perception of boards and CEOs to support digital leaders changing their values and leadership perspective on risk-taking.

The paradox of risk management is that while it is necessary for avoiding major failures, excessive risk aversion can hinder innovation and prevent organizations from taking advantage of new opportunities.

This can lead to an excessive focus on stability, cost-consciousness, and compliance at the expense of innovation and business development. CEOs and boards have historically encouraged IT organizations and CIOs to make moderate, linear changes.

At the same time, exponential technologies are accelerating change and exposing organizations to new risks. This has created a tremendous dilemma for CIOs, who must identify and understand the core technologies required to build a sustainable digital composable enterprise while they might have to accept isolated business-driven investments in fragmented technologies.

Several challenges are associated with this, as technologies such as cloud, AI, and quantum computing rapidly change the digital agenda. With the rapid development of exponential technologies, most organizations are not sufficiently leveraging innovation at scale.

CIOs are facing enormous choices in finding the right technologies, especially with the rise of the cloud. They must deal with new business development opportunities with overlapping and competing technologies and increased complexity with new overlying multi-dimensional technology domains. All decisions require full interoperability and may eventually introduce new threats and vulnerabilities caused by data protection problems, cybersecurity, and business continuity challenges.

At the same time, processes, skills, roles, and methodologies change, while traditionally built versus buy decisions introduce new dimensions of complexity. CIOs play a critical role in helping their organizations take advantage of the opportunities presented by exponential technologies while effectively and proactively managing associated risks and challenges. However, expectations and traditional ways of utilizing IT may hinder CIOs from solving and effectively leading enterprises through this dilemma of complexity and uncertainty.

With PaaS, SaaS, and IaaS services, complexity has increased significantly with new options, including their underlying variations. Those new options enable the consumption of ready-to-use services in the cloud, with innovative alternatives but important strategic architectural choices.

The cloud has significantly impacted the strategic response and required leadership of CIOs, providing increased flexibility and scalability in IT infrastructure while reducing costs. This has led to a greater focus on using the cloud for strategic initiatives such as data analytics, machine learning, and digital transformation.

CIOs can easily provide organizations with access to new technologies and services through the cloud, responding more quickly to the evolving needs of their organizations. Unlimited access to cloud technologies allows CIOs to drive innovation and business value across the enterprise through applied technology leadership in sustainable ways.

Sustainable economic development is a well-understood responsibility, supported by an economic theory based on the work of Nobel laureate Harry Markowitz from the middle of the last century, explaining the logic of portfolio optimization. In modern organizations, decision-makers are overly reluctant to take risks, prioritizing solid business cases and safe investments. Seventy years later, executives are still reluctant to propose and advocate risky investments.

The theory of Nobel laureate (Harry Markowitz, 1990), could be utilized in digital transformations to help organizations optimize their portfolios of digital investments. Modern Portfolio Theory suggests that investors can optimize their investment portfolios by balancing risk and return. This involves selecting a diverse mix of investments that collectively provide the desired level of return while minimizing risk. In the context of digital transformations, this theory can help organizations optimize their digital investment portfolios and take more and better-informed risks. The theory involves assessing each investment's potential impact on the organization's strategic goals and the risk associated with each investment. By managing portfolios of digital investments that collectively provide the desired level of return while minimizing risk, organizations can maximize the value of their digital investments. It helps organizations manage risk by diversifying their digital investments across various technologies, platforms, and initiatives. Applying Markowitz' theory can reduce the impact of investment failures, help ensure that the organization is not overly reliant on single technologies or solutions, and help organizations make more informed and strategic decisions regarding their digital investments. Considering those conceptual capabilities could enable enterprises to achieve their digital transformation objectives while minimizing risks.

Managing risks is a well-established profession among most enterprises, with risk management defined in policies and quarterly processes. Enterprises do not address risk management as a cultural concern and critical aspect of enterprise innovation and digital transformation. The organizational approach to normalized risk aversion and avoidance is a major concern regarding risk-taking and the ability of enterprises to make the right choices in transformative undertakings.

Corporate governance frameworks mainly encourage low-risk investments, promoting a risk-averse culture. From a career development perspective, risk-averse leaders may increase their chances of promotion by conforming to the overall risk culture and behaviors. However, these incentives only reinforce risk-averse behaviors and may be one reason for less successful innovation programs. In risk-averse enterprises, corporate governance systems, individual incentives, and control of processes discourage decision-makers from promoting and taking risks. If risk-averse organizations hold leaders individually accountable, they will eventually not prosper and grow. This can hinder digital composable transformations from proceeding and accelerating due to cultural implications. Promoting risk-averse behaviors in organizations can create significant barriers to fostering innovation and enabling digital transformation.

Creating a culture that encourages calculated risk-taking and supports decision-makers in taking risks that align with the organization's strategic objectives is usually never discussed on the board or executive level. But by doing so, organizations can increase their chances of successful digital transformations and achieve their long-term goals.

If risk-averse behavior is predominantly, it can ultimately lead to a business culture where:

1. Investment decisions are limited, as risky investments are never or only sporadically promoted and supported,
2. Organizations do not optimize their potential, as they are not overseeing and balancing the risks of valuable investments of their entire investment portfolio,
3. Managers must navigate cautiously with less or non-transformative investments/projects,
4. Organizations do not evolve their culture toward greater risk tolerance,
5. Organizations do not promote and encourage accountability to increase performance,
6. Governance frameworks disengage collaborative processes, decision-making, and prioritization, especially in agile environments,
7. Information security and cybersecurity risks are overrated, while the cloud is a narrative for senior leaders to <u>not</u> store and share critical data outside the organization's traditional firewall.

Risk-averse cultures will eventually hinder digital composable transformations because they discourage new attempts at experimentation and innovation. In a risk-averse culture, decision-makers act reluctant to take on new projects or try new technologies for fear of failure or negative consequences.

Such personal considerations can make it difficult for organizations to seize new opportunities and stay competitive in a rapidly changing digital landscape. In the context of digital composable transformations, a risk-averse culture can make it difficult for organizations to experiment with new technologies and approaches and to quickly adapt to changing business needs. Digital composable transformations require organizations to be more agile, responsive, and iterative, changing how they work and delivering value to their customers.

On the other hand, more risk-tolerance decisions can tremendously influence the success of transformations while accelerating the organizational ability to adhere to changes while mitigating risks, illustrated in the following figure, describing the impact of risk-tolerance cultures on digital transformations.

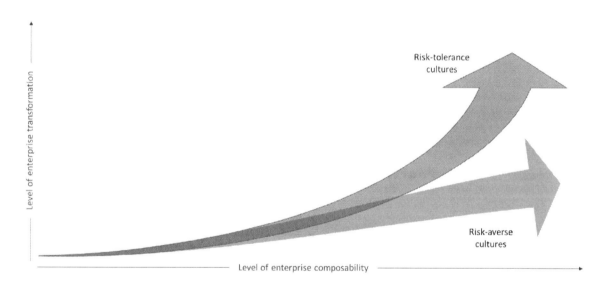

Figure 12 Digital composable transformations outcome in comparison between risk-averse and risk-tolerance cultures

To overcome these obstacles, organizations must create environments encouraging experimentation and innovation, where failure is an opportunity to learn and improve. Managers can influence their cultures by creating and promoting a culture of experimentation and learning. They may encourage cross-functional collaboration and experimentation and provide the resources and support their teams need to undertake new projects and try new technologies.

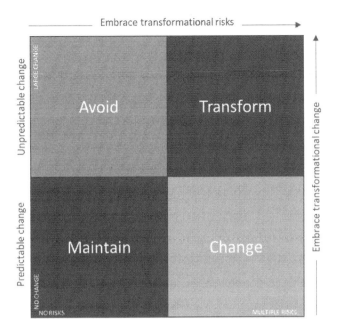

Figure 13 The impact of risk-tolerance cultures on digital transformations

Risk-tolerance organizations realize predictable and unpredictable change levels to embrace, empower, and realize transformational change, while risk-averse organizations will avoid unpredictable change, preventing digital composable transformations from rising.

If culture and governance promote and support risk-averse investments and decisions, digital transformations will be less transformative, ineffective, scalable, and innovative. If the culture and governance allow and support risk-tolerance investments/decisions, digital transformations will adopt more transformative, scalable, adaptive, agile, collaborative, and innovative ways of working.

Digital transformations require more than technologies, digital platforms, and other digital capabilities. They also demand new tactics and acceptance when selecting appropriate risk levels to initiate and deliver digital transformative change.

Select appropriate risk tactics

In most organizations, IT complexity is emerging rapidly as new digital technologies are introduced on a broader scale and at an accelerated speed. Organizations shall use new risk tactics and slowly adapt to more extensive cloud services. Those new technologies must coexist with complex business models supported by complicated and unyielding IT legacy systems and infrastructures. As organizations have no choice but to accelerate the pace of digital transformations, they must find new ways to respond rapidly and adapt to changing customer and market needs. Organizations face challenges and risks as CIOs experience difficulties managing and balancing risk-averse architectural requirements with new digital business demands.

IT decision-makers have learned to deal with and respond to business and technology challenges over decades. Many best practices are effectively leveraging IT legacy systems with robust risk mitigations or with major transformations of ERP systems into the cloud. During the last decades, IT organizations constantly adapted their skills, processes, and ways of working, while most organizations have not made significant advancements in digital technologies, especially in business environments with highly complex IT legacy systems and diverse technology landscapes.

Traditional skills and experiences worked perfectly until the pace of technology development forced IT organizations to turn their responses into a defensive mode to protect and secure their IT legacy environments. With new technologies, cloud-based applications, and new risks introduced, IT organizations are usually unprepared to respond effectively to those risks, and new skills are essential.

Managing risks is a critical discipline that has developed and matured across most organizations, especially within industries that are typically highly regulated, governed, and overseen. But it is not enough to professionally manage enterprise risks, as risk cultures may play a vital role in how organizations effectively utilize or adjust their approaches to risk management. A more conservative approach to risk management might significantly impact the enterprise's ability to understand and apply risk management effectively in the context of digital transformations.

The key challenge with transformations is an issue for those organizations that manage their risks entirely focused on risk-averse approaches. Risk mitigations can lead to delays, obstruction, and poor effectiveness of digital transformations with long-term consequences on enterprises' competitiveness and innovation ability.

RISK-AVERSE APPROACH – TRADITIONAL LINEAR	RISK-TOLERANCE APPROACH – FORWARD THINKING
▪ Known markets, limited external networking	▪ Unknown big picture, digital ecosystems
▪ Low technology exposure	▪ High technology exposure
▪ Little innovation and focus on business as usual	▪ Industrialized innovation at scale
▪ Small and predictable change	▪ Continual and scalable but unpredictable change
▪ Focus on solving big, isolated problems	▪ Focus on solving small problems but continually
▪ Repeat best and common practices	▪ Explore new tactics, act experimental, learn
▪ Focus on risk elimination and avoidance	▪ Focus on shifting risk perspective
▪ Isolated and defined risks	▪ Interdisciplinary, complex, and dynamic risks
▪ Tendency of over-compliance	▪ Focus on risk appetite with appropriate levels of compliance

Figure 14 Differences between risk-averse and risk-tolerance organizations are significant

As many organizations are overwhelmed by the complexity of legal requirements, rules and regulations, policies, and other concerns (such as cybersecurity risks), organizations rather promote risk-averse than risk-tolerance cultures. This is especially problematic, as every risk culture comprises several layers. Those layers include the personal predisposition to risks, personal ethics, behaviors, organizational culture (governance, policies, roles, rules, and regulations), and, finally, embedded into the organization's risk culture.

The Institute of Risk Management (see next figure) has identified and described those layers. Further developing this model adds the perspectives of risk-averse and risk-tolerance cultures to this hierarchical and centric model.

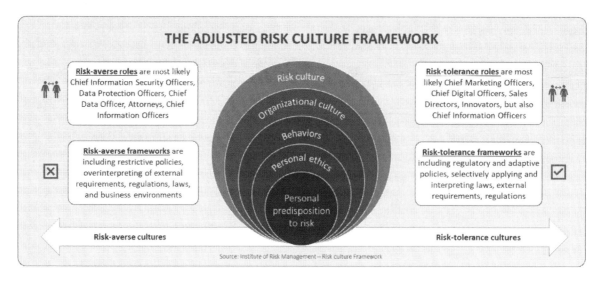

Figure 15 Implications on risk cultures through risk-adaptive leadership (adjusted framework Risk culture Framework) (Institute of Risk Management)

The dominating risk culture is usually more influenced by high-profile roles, influencing organizations' risk appetite through their predisposition to risks. They are most likely professionals with a well-established knowledge of how to evaluate and interpret external requirements. Their attempts to establish risk-averse frameworks have a huge impact and are often anchored deep within the organization's governance frameworks and policies, strongly emphasizing their need to secure compliance and conformity.

Risk-averse roles, such as DPO (Data Protection Officer), CISO (Chief Information Security Officer), and Compliance Managers, can be critical in protecting sensitive information and ensuring compliance with regulations. However, if these roles become too risk-averse, they can be obstructive and counterproductive to an organization's digital transformation efforts. By focusing too heavily on risk management, these roles can create a culture of fear and caution that stifles experimentation and innovation. Organizations may experience difficulties taking advantage of new technologies and approaches and staying competitive in a rapidly changing digital landscape. They may slow development, as risk-averse roles may be overly cautious about new technologies, which can slow the development and deployment of new applications and services. Those approaches to risk assessments of new technologies can make it difficult for organizations to respond quickly to changing business needs and take advantage of new opportunities.

They may likewise cause a lack of flexibility. Too strongly governed risk-averse approaches can make it difficult for organizations to adapt to changing business needs and new technologies because of inflexible systems and processes, which may limit the realization of new requirements and technological innovation.

Organizations must balance effective risk management with the need to drive innovation and increase enterprise agility. This is achievable by creating a culture that values experimentation and learning, encourages cross-functional collaboration, and does provide the resources and support needed for teams to take on new projects and try new technologies. Additionally, early on, involving risk-averse roles in the digital transformation process and aligning their goals with the overall business objectives can help mitigate these risks.

CIOs must deal with huge technology debts and risks concerning their critical IT legacy systems. Such complex undertakings could include the demand for risk-mitigation investments, such as the replacement/modernization of IT systems or essential infrastructures of IT, mitigation of compliance issues, information security and cybersecurity measures, implementation of disaster recovery, and more. It is noticeable that IT decision-makers usually argue in line with traditional risk management approaches, motivated by their incentives to secure business performance, stability of operations, and stable customer services.

Organizations encouraging senior leaders to discuss more balanced and risk-tolerance strategies, cultures, and leadership will increase their chances of successful digital composable transformations. It is noticeable that digital composable transformations are not just tech or risk driven; they must consider additional important organizational factors to succeed. Not considering those factors in digital transformations can significantly slow down or hinder successful change.

Avoid effects that slow you down

Digital transformations severely depend on IT organizations' ability to adjust their systems effectively, utilize data from legacy IT systems, and make urgent changes across various processes and systems seamlessly and rapidly. The introduction of agile development methods has caused additional challenges to engaging entire organizations in those new working methods.

Traditional outsourcing partners are not always ready to support agile and evolutionary digital composable transformations. The main reasons are their organizational structures, governance systems, existing contracts, or the inability to respond agilely. IT organizations may have been surprised how traditional outsourcing partners may, in the worst cases, endanger agile and evolutionary digital composable transformations. CIOs will likely find internal conditions (in addition to archaic risk-averse cultures) potentially slowing down digital transformations.

The most significant issues and obstacles are organizational complexity, over-administration, oversized traditional outsourcing, administrative complexity, and corporate governance.

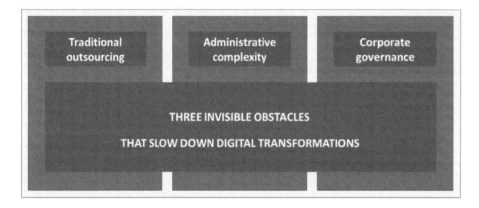

Figure 16 The three invisible obstacles that slow down digital transformations

To be effective, the following areas could potentially slow down digital transformations:

Situation: Traditional outsourcing may expose risks for digital transformations, as this can hinder digital transformations, restricted by vendors with archaic structures, complex governance, design of their services, and revenue models. Given those conditions, their lead times, processes, and ability to respond might restrict their ability to fit and engage in digital composable transformations effectively.

Problem: The demand from customers to provide agile services and structures, and to engage in value-driven initiatives, strongly contrasts their ordinary business models and structures. Major traditional outsourcing vendors seem to make adjustments to support digital transformations.

Leveraging existing traditional outsourcing relationships is difficult, as their organizations are not designed, skilled, or ready to adjust their working methods, relationship management, and operating models. Considering the role of traditional outsourcing vendors in digital transformations is important, digital leaders and CxOs must find new ways, to secure more sustainable and responsive processes effectively. Digital leaders should carefully consider why, how, and when they engage (intensify or reduce) their scope with outsourcing vendors aligned with changing demands from their digital transformations. Implementing agile ways of working with traditional vendors can be challenging. To effectively shift perspectives and mindsets and to establish agile, integrated working routines is simply a time-consuming effort. With an agile mindset and processes in place, this is a liability for outsourcing-intensive IT organizations. The outsourcing industry is trying to adjust but eventually may need to undergo significant changes to respond to those changing demands effectively. This applies to other external partners and licensing models with contractual constraints, which may negatively affect the development of digital composable enterprises.

Recommendation: Outsourcing partners must adopt an agile and collaborative approach to their services to succeed in the current business environment. This means repackaging their skills to provide modular services that meet customer needs, supporting incremental innovation. The focus must shift towards continuous improvement, where the delivery organization identifies and solves problems. To achieve this, outsourcing partners should integrate themselves to provide the best solutions to their customers. This transformation requires a shift from a contract-governed operating model toward a customer-centric approach. Outsourcing partners must understand their customers' needs, goals, and work closely with partners to co-create solutions. Enterprises must evolve their traditional relations with outsourcing partners to build new collaborative relationships, renew or update contractual frameworks, apply selective sourcing, adjust outsourced services, and insource critical services. It is essential to address any hindrances with outsourced services promptly and effectively. Changes take time and require support from internal stakeholders and external vendors.

Evaluating and investigating alternative options, such as finding specialized partners for critical services like mainframe development, is crucial. Outsourcing partners must embrace agility, collaboration, and flexibility to provide modular and customer-centric services that meet the evolving needs of businesses.

Administrative complexity

Situation: Administrative complexity can have a significant impact on digital transformations. They can slow decision-making, as traditional structures make it difficult for organizations to make decisions quickly and efficiently. This can impact the effective development and deployment of new applications and services, making it difficult for organizations to respond to changing business needs and take advantage of new opportunities.

Problem: Such complexity can create silos, where complex organizational structures and processes can make it difficult or impossible for different departments and business units to work together effectively. This can lead to inefficiencies and may delay the transformation process. Complex administrative processes and systems can cause a lack of coordination, making coordinating efforts across different departments and business units difficult. This can lead to duplication of efforts, wasted resources, and a lack of alignment between different teams. Especially complex changes across multiple departments and systems may become a major issue during transformations.

Another problem is the lack of responsibilities in complex organizational structures and processes, making it difficult to hold individuals and teams accountable for their actions and decisions to improve dysfunctional processes. This lack of ownership can cause ineffective decision-making, delay the execution of critical tasks, slowing down the digital transformation process. Especially complex processes with concerns of enterprise-wide interoperability may become major showstoppers. Measuring and tracking progress and resolving complicated issues is difficult. This can make it hard to identify the status of critical improvements and make timely adjustments by identifying and resolving root cause problems. Unnecessary bureaucracy can easily distract digital leaders and their agile teams, leading to frustration and loss of talent.

Recommendation: Recommended actions may include overseeing processes, defining new roles and responsibilities, reducing silos, and simplifying complex corporate structures.
Organizations must improve coordination between different parts of the organization, simplify complex administrative processes and systems, define clear ownership, empower agile teams' decision-making, measure, and track progress by identifying and resolving root cause problems, and reduce unnecessary bureaucracy.

Corporate governance

Situation: Corporate governance can significantly impact digital transformations with ineffective processes concerning decision-making processes and allocation of resources. Agile ways of working and agile budgeting require changes in traditional governance systems to allow for more effective prioritization and utilization of resources. Traditional governance can be a major hinder to digital transformations, impacting the speed and ability to execute the organization's digital transformation efforts. This can include making priorities, identifying key initiatives, and allocating resources. It does prevent organizations from effectively applying collaborative, agile principles from ideation to monetization and scaling of investments. It does not help if all IT folks are certified and skilled if the organizational governance is not counter-productive.

Problem: Adjustments of risk-managing governance can play a critical role in managing risks and ensuring that the organization's digital transformation efforts are aligned with the organization's overall risk management strategy and culture. Governance bodies and frameworks tend to overprotect when interpreting relevant laws, regulations, standards, data protection, privacy, and security policies. Other fields of governance are investments and financial processes. Due to indifferent budgets and approval processes, the most significant challenge lies in empowering decentralized and cross-functional teams to make decisions and gradual investments. If budget decisions are entirely centralized, teams may experience delays and challenges in utilizing resources effectively. Governance structures are hindering digital transformations making fast and rapid adjustments in line with their agile methods. Traditional governance understands late requests for approval as insufficient planning, while agile development considers late as timely rather than bad planning.

Those conflicts are difficult to overcome, and digital leaders who do not understand why the system blocks them and how to overcome this challenge may be unable to address those root-cause problems.

Recommendation: Governance systems must facilitate digital transformations by enabling and supporting them rather than imposing restrictive regulations and policies. To support digital transformations effectively, organizations must adjust restrictive policies and compliance requirements, introduce agile budgeting, simplify resource allocation, and empower decentralized decision-making. This requires new roles and responsibilities with more decentralized mandates.

Organizations must oversee and align digital transformation with overall business objectives to mitigate risks, and top management may need to adjust governance frameworks to enable empowered decentralized decision-making and agile prioritization processes. Establishing greater awareness, risk-tolerance structures, processes, and governing bodies can also ensure effective governance of digital transformation efforts. Decision-making processes must be clearly defined and transparent. A balanced approach is crucial to avoid impeding digital transformations due to overworked compliance and risk requirements. Digital leaders should collaborate effectively with key stakeholders and encourage faster, more incremental, experimental approaches within the adapted governance framework. Speed is sometimes more important than quality, particularly at the beginning of agile transformations, given that there is a solid foundation. Continual learning helps organizations oversee and adjust restrictive governance hindering digital transformations and cultural evolution.

Considering those three obstacles, the key to success is to find out why, how, and what must be changed, ideally before problems occur. The number of potential obstacles is enormous, and digital leaders must actively assume responsibility to identify hinds that potentially cause productivity issues of agile transformations, introducing new ways of working to the organization.

Applied Technology Leadership
Oscar Wide, Chief Information Security Officer (CISO), Green Cargo

"When joining Green Cargo in early 2021, I realized a lot of challenges within IT relating to governance and IT legacy, as well as a somewhat basic and fragmented IT security architecture and a precarious cyber security posture. In my first 30 days, I put everything aside and focused on learning the risk culture, organization, people, and IT environment to fast-track a foundational understanding of the overall risks and hurdles. It was obvious early on that several of these issues boil down to the root cause of having insufficient knowledge and control over the IT environment, lacking security baseline, and a lot of legacy IT.

In a digital composable strategy, security is critical from the beginning and throughout the whole lifecycle. As the strategy relies on combining various components to create a larger system, ensuring each component is secure and not introducing any vulnerabilities to the overall system is important.

At Green Cargo, we applied four security and risk-related principles:

1. *Fixing the basics and paving the way for proactive security*

   We addressed risks and pains with a practical approach by shifting focus to address low-hanging fruits and critical gaps from a technical, process, and organizational governance perspective, which enabled the prerequisites for change. We eliminated old policy exceptions and took a hard stance on enforcing strong authentication over the whole board, using offensive security testing, and ensuring an efficient detection and response capability to weigh up for the lack of protective capabilities. We accept that things will fail, but we make sure we are resilient enough to handle it.

2. *Applying a business-driven risk mindset to enable change momentum*

   We addressed the fast-paced digitalization with a business-driven and risk-tolerance mindset. We applied lean principles for security risk management, addressing operational security vulnerabilities and hardening our cloud platforms. We avoided getting stuck in the best practices framework but focused on what enables transformational change velocity and momentum while remaining resilient towards tomorrow's threats. We avoided overreliance on traditional information security standards. Instead, we focused on practical security capabilities so as not to become bogged down by philosophical compliance discussions.

3. *Stop policing and start empowering others to take responsibility*

   We addressed the chaos by establishing functional governance for proactive security. We stopped trying to catch up with the fast-paced change.

   We implemented the necessary gates to align with already existing processes. We re-oriented and became a lean virtual security team focused on supporting, raising awareness, and identifying key cross-functional security champions to act as gatekeepers.

> 4. *Applying a holistic security mindset as the superglue in the digital composable strategy*
>
> *We addressed the lack of control by using a strategic security platform that seamlessly consolidated our security vendors and solutions within the multi-sourcing environment. We enforced a lean security baseline with an agile mindset to adapt and apply situational requirements. We also partnered with an independent third security provider to ensure logging and monitoring throughout our multi-sourcing environment, which enabled us to take ownership and actively manage our security.*
>
> *We did not want to apply a security-by-lock-down approach by enforcing rigid governance and overprotective security measures. Instead, we took a distinct approach to prevent greater risks and vulnerabilities that could hinder enterprise-wide innovation and digital business resilience."*
>
> *Written by Oscar Wide, Chief Information Security Officer, Green Cargo*

Enterprises must consider all critical elements, including those three dimensions, to avoid effects that may slow them down. Organizations must collaborate internally and externally for effective digital transformations, simplify processes, and minimize complexity. They should strive to avoid unnecessary administrative conflicts, risks, and delays that can slow down the pace of their digital initiatives. Those and other changes and complications usually demand senior and strong leaders capable of embracing and mastering indispensable leadership principles.

Apply indispensable leadership principles

To lead digital composable transformations aligned with the enterprise's long-term vision and business priorities requires compelling leadership qualities and a huge personal commitment to relentless discipline during execution. Fundamental leadership principles are essential to engage organizations, teams, and individuals in large-scale transformations.

Figure 17 Three universal leadership principles for transforming digital organizations

They are unique and must adjust to the situation and the organization's culture, values, individual preferences, and leadership. The right principles shall facilitate the creation of high-performance teams, empower decision-makers, and foster collaboration on every level. They ingest the basics for greater independence, reinforce liabilities, and secure confidence in execution into uncertainty.

The three proposed universal principles of digital leadership are:

- **Autonomy**

  Encouraging autonomy is essential to leverage, eliminate, or reduce dependencies on every level. Autonomy is a core leadership principle that enables and sustains change in indispensable ways. Autonomy secures sovereignty, independence, liberty, self-direction, self-reliance, and self-determination, making it a universal formula for success.

- **Accountability**

  To facilitate the unconstrained transfer of responsibilities while promoting risk-tolerance decision make, including options of failing and learning, overdelivering, and constantly stretching own ambition levels & targets, to take full responsibility for their actions. Accountability does leverage maximum performance through constantly evolving comfort zones, relentless learning, and self-determination of evolving and scaling high-performance individuals and teams.

- **Trust**

  To increase confidence with everyone concerned, encourage learning and collaboration, generate better and sustainable outcomes, encourage to fail fast and to learn and grow, inspire, support, and collaborate, and create belief in everyone engaged. Trust is another foundational principle, as without trust, there is no growth, and accountability will not evolve.

Autonomy, **Accountability**, and **Trust** are the most critical universal leadership principles or values that could help transform organizations, especially in tackling digital transformations' real pitfalls and issues.

> **"The most authentic way to leverage leadership in evolutionary transformations is to lead by example, help others grow, and empower individuals and teams to create high-performance organizations. Autonomy, accountability, and trust are my principles for creating and maintaining high-performance organizations."**

Ingo Paas

Leaders with robust leadership principles to support their digital transformations might significantly increase their chances of success. They can make a difference by fostering a powerful culture of engagement and confidence. Once they are applied, sustainable results will be achievable, and employees and teams will embrace and adopt greater autonomy, enabling high-performance teams to prosper and grow.

Those three universal leadership principles require authenticity and a relentless determination to those principles in daily execution. They shall be understood as complementary leadership principles and not replace the agreed enterprise leadership principles.

Autonomy is a prerequisite for successful digital composable transformations, not only from a leadership perspective. With greater levels of **Accountability,** organizations transform into high-performance teams with high-performing individuals. The willingness to assume responsibility, expand comfort zones, and accept failure to create a learning culture is only possible if **Trust** earns from actions and outcomes, not words!

Key conclusions and takeaways

The key conclusions and takeaways from the chapter "**COMPOSABLE PROFICIENCIES**" are:

1. Enterprises must utilize digitally packaged business capabilities from the core of their digital transformations.

2. Enterprises must reinforce collaborative development embedded into their agile ways of working.

3. Enterprises must shift from risk-averse cultures towards risk-tolerance cultures to pave the way for future innovation and digital composable transformations.

4. Enterprises must identify and address risks with outsourced services timely and actively supported by committed internal stakeholders and external vendors.

5. Enterprises must reduce administrative complexity and corporate governance to support and encourage agile digital transformations.

6. Enterprises must identify or attract leaders who promote and evolve a digital culture based on relevant principles.

7. Enterprises must avoid overprotecting the business with rigid governance and overprotective security measures, instead taking distinct approaches to prevent greater risks and vulnerabilities that could hinder enterprise-wide innovation and digital business resilience.

THREE – VISIONARY EVOLUTION

THOUGHT DIGITAL LEADERSHIP

Hans van Grieken, Boardroom advisor on Digital Transformation
Digital DNA: People-Centric, Process Focused and Value Driven (Research)

"When my good friend Ingo Paas asked me to write the prologue to the third chapter on the Visionary Evolution of his new book Digital Composable Enterprises, I could not help but think of the research piece above. It appears that in his approach, Ingo has managed to solidly "marry" the more "foundational and Talent Driven approach" of Talent and Strategy Leaders to the far more "agile, speedy and risk-tolerant" approach of Fast Moving Experimenters.

To digitally transform traditional enterprises is a difficult undertaking. Making "digital" work by applying technologies and data is not enough. Visionary Evolution is just as much about technology as it is about incrementally organizational and cultural change." And part of that change - most of the time - is a fundamental recalibration of the organization's Technology partner network and its sourcing strategies, which makes this chapter relevant, as well as Ingo's analysis of four different relationships with Technology Partners - ranging from traditional Outsourcing to full fletched dynamic collaboration - and how they play out in practice.

One thing is for sure: Visionary Evolution will not only change your technology stack, your ways of working, and your company culture, it will forever and fundamentally change your Make or Buy strategies."

Written by Hans van Grieken, Boardroom advisor on Digital Transformation

References:

Research Publication (Hans van Grieken, 2017) & Conference presentation on the research

Balance digital investments

Successful digital transformations shall be guided and driven by the organization's purpose, vision, strategy, goals, and business priorities. Digital composable transformations shall be predominantly business driven, while organizations experience difficulties aligning business demands and technology-driven architectures and strategies.

There are two types of vision-driven digital investment strategies:

1. **Tactical digital investments are ROI-driven**

   They are usually ROI-driven (Return of Investments) and have a short-term and problem-solving focus, often driven at the business unit or department level.

2. **Strategic digital investments**

   They are usually not ROI-driven, having a long-term and systemic focus, but driven on a business unit or enterprise level.

The key challenge with tactical digital ROI-driven and strategic digital investments is to find and execute the right balance of both investment strategies, ideally combining them into one. Tactical investments often focus on instant financial returns, while strategic investments have longer-term goals and a wider range of potential, often with scalable benefits. The success of digital tactical investments is measured by metrics such as conversion rates and revenue, while the success of strategic investments is more difficult to quantify. ROI-driven tactical investments have lower financial risks but promise immediate rewards. The ROI of strategic investments is often long-term, difficult to qualify, and challenging to make business leaders commit to such business cases. They reinforce, strengthen, and enable higher ROIs over time, while they cannot promise immediate returns. Examples are long-term investments into scalable platform technologies with indirect returns. Tactical investments into fragmented projects and technologies focus instead on specific, measurable outcomes. Those investments can restrict interoperability, increase complexity, or jeopardize strategic goals with digital transformations. They solve specific business problems, often within certain business processes, eventually leading to process suboptimization. Tactical investments neglect a reasonable balance between tactical and strategic digital investments.

Organizations need transformational architectural governance to mitigate those risks, make better-informed decisions, and not overprioritize tactical investments. Those decisions must keep a certain balance to accelerate strong financial development and business performance. Compared to more tactical investments, they must also secure alignment with the business vision and strategy. Initially, those investments seem to make organizations more responsive and agile, while considering their long-term implications, the opposite might be the case. Organizations must take appropriate measures to analyze, evaluate, and decide on actively chosen investment strategies.

Executives, including CEOs and CFOs, must ensure that investment strategies consider

- Balance tactical and strategic investments,
- Consider architectural advice on interoperability,
- Make investment decisions in systemic ways,
- Align investments with enterprises' business and IT strategies.

The implications of digital ROI-driven investments in digital transformations have different and important but sometimes conflicting purposes. Those conflicts are often unrecognized or ignored in favor of tactical options, especially as those investments can make stronger impressions on less technology-savvy decision-makers.

The overweight of tactical ROI-driven investments may not be aligned with overall business strategies and may cause a lack of strategic alignment leading to undesirable implications on short- and long-term digital transformations. They may delay or risk strategic investments into foundational digital technologies essential for successful digital transformations.

Overinvesting in tactical technologies can increase an organization's long-term risk exposure by limiting interoperability and leading to fragmented digital technologies. Unbalanced investment decisions require better-informed decision-making, supported by a strong architectural vision and greater awareness of potential risks associated with unbalanced tactical investments.

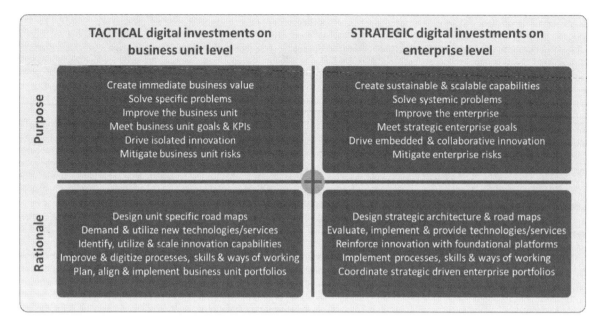

Figure 18 Balance competing for purpose and rationales of digital investment strategies

In contrast to business-driven tactical investments, IT often drives strategic investments. The main goals should be to secure enterprise-wide critical capabilities, such as interoperability, sustainability, reusability, flexibility, scalability, and security.

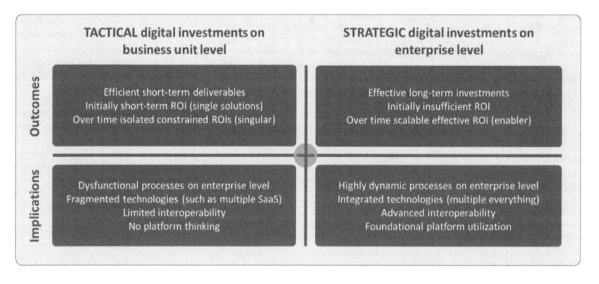

Figure 19 Both strategies lead to different outcomes and require a more balanced approach

The success or failure of digital transformation depends on an enterprise's ability to leverage the best possible and affordable digital investments with a clear understanding of their investment purposes and long-term effects. CxOs and IT play crucial roles in identifying and motivating decision-makers to consider these investment strategies in a balanced way to prevent unbalanced digital systems and overcome internal power games. Investment decisions must balance tactical ROIs with strategic, reusable, and scalable ROIs and TCOs. Enterprises must avoid silo thinking and partitioning to ensure scalability and reusability wherever feasible. Digital composable transformations require utilizing foundational technologies to the largest extent possible.

In retail, prioritizing the digital customer journey and personalization of offerings and services is crucial and should be given priority over individual business unit priorities. The digital customer journey is a prime example of this.

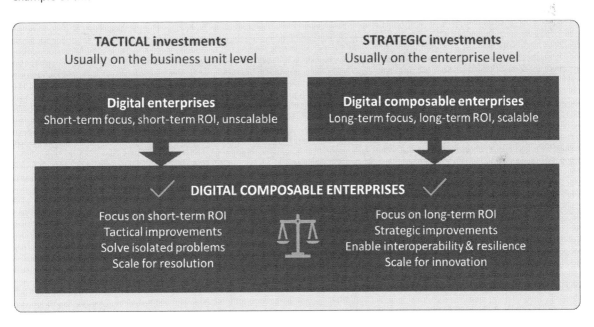

Figure 20 Business value-driven investments must be in balance with technology-driven investments to build the composable enterprise

Digital composable enterprises are only achievable if tactical investments are balanced with the enterprise's strategic investments.

"To evolve digital composable enterprises, organizations need to balance tactical and strategic digital investment to secure interoperability, composability, and long-term digital superiority."

Ingo Paas

Enterprises must increase their digital resilience to respond better, withstand, and recover from disruptive events such as natural disasters, economic downturns, and cyber-attacks. Their ability to quickly adapt and recover from these events is becoming increasingly important in today's rapidly changing business environments. Digital resilient enterprises must prepare themselves to identify and mitigate potential risks and threats, which helps to ensure business continuity and maintain customer trust and loyalty. They are better positioned to adapt and capitalize on new opportunities, such as digital disruption, and to navigate with effective investment strategies to constantly explore and utilize opportunities in the rapidly changing business environment. Digital resilience is critical to secure maximum responsiveness to changing business needs and effectively introduce innovative and disruptive technologies. To become a digital composable enterprise and increase its digital resilience, organizations must safeguard their tactical and strategic technology investment strategies and evolve digital composable enterprises from the core of the business.

Transform the business from the core

For several reasons, enterprises may avoid driving digital transformations from the core of their business. Most enterprises avoid this challenging undertaking because of the complexity combined with their fear of disrupting business operations. Inflexible IT legacy systems increase this complexity and usually make changes impossible, especially as they often come with high costs and low returns. As skills are critical and enterprises often face a lack of expertise, ideas to pursue such cross-functional changes often find a hard stop because of organizational silos and the mentality of independent operating business units or departments. Combined with short-term focus and highly operative business, business stakeholders intend to focus on daily problems and short-term gains instead.

Most enterprises shift their focus toward their customers instead of realizing digital transformation from the core of their business. Ignoring the necessity to transform enterprises from the core can cause major problems in delivering on the customer's expectations.

Disconnected business processes may cause difficulties, workarounds, and manual efforts to align operations and customer-faced processes, especially in the shadow of digital transformations.

After three decades of major ERP implementations, enterprises face unprecedented choices and complexities with major investments in digital technologies. Enterprises must find new ways to resolve this dilemma to balance costs, complexity, and change, manage diversity, and avoid fragmentation, complexity, and the first wave of digital legacy.

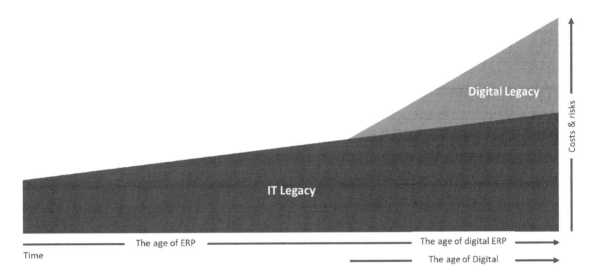

Figure 21 The age of ERP is not over, and substantial IT legacy costs & risks will only increase during the digital age with the introduction of new Digital legacy costs & risks

The era of ERP will not just vanish because of the digital age, and the digital age will only add new digital technologies and legacies with new costs & risks. ERP is transforming from on-premise into the cloud, while digital transformations will increase the costs of IT as new technologies drive long-term total cost of ownership (TCO). Boards and executive teams must distinguish and understand "good" costs from costs for replacing existing IT capabilities with new digital capabilities. The expectations may be complicated and irrational, but they are comparable to the industrial revolution. Substitute handcraft with machines and electricity was impossible to overcome by simply shifting existing costs for labor to new industrial costs. The same goes for digital investments and their existential role in the future of digital composable enterprises.

"The age of ERP is not over, will demand further investments, and will convert on-premise ERP into the cloud. CIOs must eliminate redundant IT costs when introducing new digital costs, wherever and whenever possible. However, boards and executive teams must help to finance additional digital investments and costs that are profoundly necessary to transform and not only to replace."

Ingo Paas

The value proposition of IT has changed significantly, and new digital foundational capabilities emerged just recently. Cloud offerings have sustained their abilities, and enterprises mainly utilize cloud services to run their current IT legacy in infrastructure and applications.

Google and Microsoft demonstrate technology leadership and continual cloud platform technologies development (see Chapter 7). The ongoing transformation of Google's and Microsoft's digital foundational platforms reflects the shift of new deployment capabilities of massive technology innovations exclusively in the cloud.

- **Microsoft**

  Microsoft will embed OpenAI to innovate further its digital platforms, such as in the Microsoft Dynamics or Power platform. OpenAI's natural language processing (NLP) and generative AI capabilities will enhance their PaaS services significantly, increasing the ability to understand better and respond to customer inquiries, making it more efficient and effective in delivering customer support. Using OpenAI's machine learning and AI capabilities will further improve Dynamics's intelligence and automation capabilities, making it easier for customers to use and helping reduce the time and effort required to complete tasks. OpenAI's GPT-3 language model will be embedded into Dynamics to improve its ability to generate natural language text across multiple platforms, such as emails, chatbot responses, and document summaries. This integration can enhance Dynamics' predictive analytics and forecasting capabilities, helping organizations make better data-driven decisions and optimize operations. Enhanced data visualization capabilities will make it easier for users to understand and interpret large amounts of data. In the future, low-code development will experience further acceleration with automated AI-enabled development of applications, APIs, and other capabilities.

Microsoft's plans to use OpenAI further to develop its digital platforms aim to make them more powerful, user-friendly, and capable of providing valuable insights and predictions to help organizations make better data-driven decisions and optimize their operations.

- **Google**

   Google develops its Cloud Platform (GCP) through ongoing research and development to build, test, and improve cloud-based infrastructure, services, and tools. GCP includes digital innovations such as Artificial Intelligence and Machine Learning, with as TensorFlow, Google Cloud AutoML, and Google Cloud AI Platform. It includes Big Data and Analytics, including Google BigQuery and Google Cloud Dataproc. Compute Engine, Google Kubernetes Engine, and Google Cloud Storage are other examples, while the platform also includes the Internet of Things (IoT), with offerings such as Google Cloud IoT Core and Google IoT Edge. With embedded database and security services, such as Google Cloud SQL and Google Cloud Key Management Service, GCP is rich in completeness. Besides those fundamental capabilities, it includes developer tools and platforms like Google App Engine, Google Cloud Functions, and Google Cloud Build. These services help businesses scale, store, analyze data, develop and run applications, and secure digital assets.

As investments into monolithic systems have considerably different purposes and goals than today's investment portfolios and IT investments, IT organizations experience difficulties balancing and constantly realigning their skills, strategies, architectures, and processes. The role of IT is changing significantly, with increasing responsibilities to keep track of those developments and assume greater responsibility to influence and reshape business strategies.

The future has never been predictable, but recent technological developments will continue to challenge the fundamentals of IT organizations and the role of CxOs (such as CIOs - Chief Information Officers, CDOs - Chief Digital Officers, and CTOs - Chief Technology Officers). They will have to see and understand the bigger picture to leverage future opportunities supported by strategic investments that will strengthen the scalability and reusability of digital investments. Making frequent changes to the core of the business models and processes requires distinct architectures, investment strategies, and new leadership to utilize new technologies with new designs of digital composable architectures.

They are necessary and critical to enable transformations from the core of the business. Designing responsive technology landscapes and service-oriented architectures is essential to enable more adaptive and responsive approaches to digital composable transformations. Without a solid design of digital foundational architecture, organizations might face significant complications and risks due to inconsistent choices and implementations of non-coherent digital capabilities.

Utilizing the right technologies (see Chapter 7) and allowing rapid adaptations and developments from the core of business models and processes is critical for digital composable transformations.

> **"Enterprise digital transformations that do not generate increased levels of digital autonomy, interoperability, and significantly higher levels of digital sustainability (maintainability) shall NOT be considered successful."**
>
> *Ingo Paas*

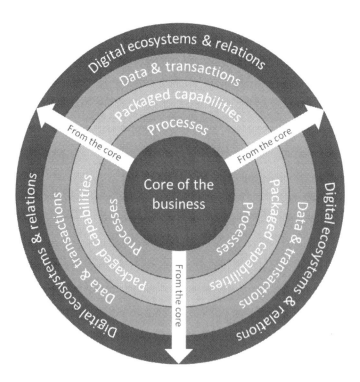

Figure 22 Evolutionary digital composable transformation from the core of the business

Driving digital transformation from the core of the business can be a significant challenge for many organizations, requiring significant investments, cultural changes, and complicated transformations. However, the benefits of embracing digital transformation can be significant, including increased agility, efficiency, and competitiveness in a rapidly changing digital landscape.

Digital transformations must evolve from the core of the business because it allows for technology integration throughout all aspects of the organization rather than just in isolated departments or functions. This centric focus allows for a more holistic and strategic approach to digital transformations, ensuring alignment with the strategies and goals of organizations. This new approach is critical for digitally enabled customer centricity because it enables organizations to understand better and respond to their needs and preferences.

Seamless technology integration and interoperability ensure that the entire organization can take advantage of technology's benefits, such as increased efficiency, cost savings, and improved customer experiences. By integrating technologies throughout all aspects of the business, organizations gain a more comprehensive view of their enterprises with a shift toward real-time and event-driven processes and decision-making. By providing more personalized, data-driven products, services, and experiences, this information can guarantee significant business value and improve the customer experience.

"It is necessary to digitally transform enterprises from the core of their business, which is essential for securing evolutionary, incremental, and experimental changes."

Ingo Paas

Enterprises that understand and utilize the power of visionary evolution and apply critical principles are considerably better prepared to lead their enterprises into a composable, sustainable, and digitally resilient future based on strong foundational principles.

Identify and apply foundational principles

Digital transformation is about utilizing technologies to change how organizations fundamentally operate, deliver value to their customers, and interact with stakeholders.

To ensure a successful transformation, organizations must establish guiding principles to help them navigate the complex and rapidly changing digital landscape.

In this context, foundational principles are crucial, as they support the organization's approach to technology and digital initiatives and provide a framework for decision-making and prioritization. Such principles are fundamental guidelines that help to secure the execution of the organization's IT strategy and inform how to use technology. These principles ensure that the IT function operates consistently and efficiently and aligns with the organization's broader objectives. They must likewise guide and help organizations make the most of digital technologies and transform their operations. They provide a framework for innovation and experimentation, encourage collaboration, and foster a culture of continuous improvement.

Distinct principles are critical in digital transformations as they provide a common framework for decision-making and prioritizations that enables teams to collaborate effectively. They help to align technology investments and business objectives, and digital initiatives are prioritized based on their impact on the organization. They foster a culture of innovation and collaboration by allowing them to continually reflect, learn, adjust, and improve their principles. By applying distinct principles, organizations can successfully navigate the challenges of digital transformation and stay competitive in the digital age.

If IT organizations do not start to implement in line with their core principles or have no such principles in place, they risk losing sight of their objectives and priorities and may make ineffective or wrong decisions, not aligned with the needs of the business and overall investment strategies. Insufficient clarity can result in wasted resources, failed projects, and, ultimately, a failure to achieve the desired outcomes of digital transformations.

Core principles provide a solid foundation for executing a successful digital transformation, guiding decision-making, and ensuring alignment with business objectives, investment strategies, and interoperability of technologies.

Principles play a crucial role in the implementation of collaborative digital transformations, as they:

- **Provide guidance**

  Principles provide clear guidelines for decision-making and implementation, ensuring that the transformation aligns with the organization's values and goals.

- **Encourage collaboration**

  Principles promote open communication, collaboration, and stakeholder engagement, critical for successful digital transformations.

- **Protect and scale investments**

  Principles ensure that the investments into digital transformations secure effective ROI and TCO, as they reuse, and scale already made investments.

- **Promote transparency**

  Principles ensure stakeholders understand how their information is used by promoting data collection and transparency.

- **Drive continuous improvement**

  Principles engage organizations to establish a culture of continuous improvement, encouraging teams to continuously evaluate and refine digital developments to meet evolving business needs. Scalability and reusability significantly contribute to continued improvements at scale, fostering incremental innovation from the core of the business.

- **Ensure standards and compliance**

  Principles guarantee that the changes are guided by relevant factors, such as privacy, security, and data protection, and foster fairness and inclusivity.

Enterprises that adhere to relevant principles minimize their risk exposure to digital transformations and foster effective development aligned and guided by the organization's vision, strategy, and more to secure sustainable development in the long term.

Digital principles are important to design digital foundational architectures because they provide guidelines and best practices on utilizing technology to implement and integrate within organizations. These principles ensure that the design of digital foundational architectures aligns with the organization's overall goals and objectives. Those principles will further evolve culture and values in collaborative implementations.

The right principles will secure that even new or complementary investments utilize existing investments or avoid conflicting investments, monitored by decision-makers and inspired by the architectural framework. They align decisions with the overall design of the digital foundational architecture, ensuring security. Those foundational principles provide that the targeted architecture is flexible, scalable, and adaptable to changing business needs and technological advancements. They play an important role in designing and developing new digital products and assets. They define how digital products shall be built, orchestrated, maintained, and managed during their life cycle. They can also help ensure that the architecture is designed with a focus on user experience to make it easy and intuitive for users (employees, customers, and other stakeholders) to interact with digital technologies in action. In addition, they guarantee that the architectural principles are understood, applied, and driving value while ensuring overall compliance with regulations, laws, and standards.

PRINCIPLES	PRINCIPLES EXPLAINED
Strategic principles	▪ Implement digital resilient enterprise with digital transformation from the core of the business ▪ Make architectural governed tactical and strategic digital investments ▪ Transform and innovate from the core and safeguard digital business resilience ▪ Identify and implement critical/core Packaged Business Capabilities (PBCs
Business transformation principles	▪ Digital transformations must be business and technology driven ▪ Prioritizations shall be guided by vision, strategy, goals, and business priorities ▪ Secure rapid and sustainable monetization by solving many small problems, not big ones ▪ Foster a data driven business culture
Architectural principles	▪ Secure a composable and interoperable business and IT architecture ▪ Maximize utilization of loosely coupled services ▪ Secure composability, reusability, flexibility, scalability, agility, and relentless orchestration ▪ Protect stability, performance, with real-time, and event-driven orchestration
Technology principles	▪ Never compromise on standardized foundational digital platforms ▪ Utilize digital foundational capabilities based on service-oriented architectures ▪ Leverage and scale loosely coupled services when building digital capabilities ▪ Disregard investments into non-API and non-cloud services and solutions
Execution principles	▪ Foster autonomous decision making and collaborative decentralized prioritizations ▪ Implement incremental, experimental and collaborative business collaboration ▪ Promote risk-tolerance behavior but safeguard security and privacy by design

Figure 23 Selected principles of digital transformations

Principles shall safeguard the quality and foster a climate of undisputed, uncompromising, reflective focus during execution. They are not just applicable to making better technology and development decisions but are critical to secure the expected effects of strategic investments.

Those principles are examples of securing practical guidance for everyone concerned at any time and every level of the organization.

- Make more sustainable decisions (such as buy versus build),
- Secure strategic alignment of digital transformation,
- Simplify collaborative ways of working,
- Support more federated decision-making,
- Secure simplicity,
- Support composability,
- Avoid digital legacy,
- Make better-balanced investment decisions,
- Secure collaborative ownership,
- Secure improved ROI and acceptable TCO.

The right principles build the foundation for success and are critical to the overall success of digital composable transformations. It does require highly skilled architects to understand and describe those principles at the early stages of digital transformations. Effective principles are critical to avoid technology risks and issues, such as interoperability, scalability, stability, and performance of systems, platforms, and applications.

> ### *Applied Technology Leadership*
> *Richard Tyregrim, Lead Solutions/Strategic Architect, R&D Lead, Consultant Manager*
>
> *"I remember discussing the possible future of fully integrated enterprise systems, distributed solutions, and how to tackle digitalization challenges with this book's author.*

There were many long sessions, with many very clever people also involved. From domain experts to business leaders to some of the best software developers I've ever met.

What resulted from this was one of the most dynamic and open-ended technology platforms I've had the great pleasure of putting my name to. Successful digitalization's core is the ability to remain agile and open-ended. Too many efforts fail because the Problem is approached like an all-in effort. Such an approach will fail because not all systems can be expected to be at the same maturity level, nor can all lines of business be expected to cope with a radical change similarly. Thus, the principle of evolution, not revolution, is key to success.

This starts with the platforms and tooling. Invest in good, open-ended tooling that follows standard means of communication to be easily extended or replaced in an ever-changing world where things move rapidly. It's very easy to get sidetracked looking at all the shiny features in product x, forgetting the base that is supposed to make all systems interoperable and open up information exchange. At Green Cargo, in particular, we faced challenges with a landscape of old systems still critical to the business and a fragmented IT landscape of silos, where interoperability was limited, cumbersome, and complex.

The way we solved this is by opting for a base cloud native and event-driven integration platform and consolidation towards a unified domain model and master data representation, so we could achieve a standard understanding of the core business events and processes and their relationships and build bridges across the silos using a standardized and centrally managed communication model.

We also adopted an approach where, instead of replacing them, we added new components to the existing mainframe and ERP systems to enrich them with modern communication and messaging capabilities. Because parts of those systems were core to the business and well-built, replacing them in an all-in effort would have been detrimental and highly disruptive. Merely by opening up messaging, allowing for tool assist workflow design, and using low code tooling to build applications on top of common data models, we managed to modernize in steps and evolve digitalization organically instead of it becoming too complex and expensive to stand a chance of success outside of the business vision documents."

Written by Richard Tyregrim, Lead Solutions/Strategic Architect, R&D Lead, Consultant Manager

Organizations that successfully design, apply, comply with, and adapt distinct principles will transform their organizations more rapidly, collaboratively, and self-controlled. Strong principles will ensure more successful utilization of their investments and deliver greater ROIs with controlled and lower TCOs.

Successfully utilized digital foundational principles will motivate everyone to engage in embedded innovation in a sustainable and vision-driven execution. The right principles will support effective collaboration and more autonomous decision-making, aligned with the execution of agile planning and prioritization processes. They will further support the evolution of the organization's culture with greater autonomy in several domains. Effectively utilizing those principles will secure sustainable benefits and leverage organizational independence and levels of sovereignty in unforeseeable ways.

Foster a culture of autonomy

Autonomy is not just a concern of leadership and creating high-performance teams. Autonomy is essential in digital transformation and a prerequisite for establishing digital composable enterprises. The following four domains of autonomy are examples of how enterprises can leverage autonomy to make digital transformations work.

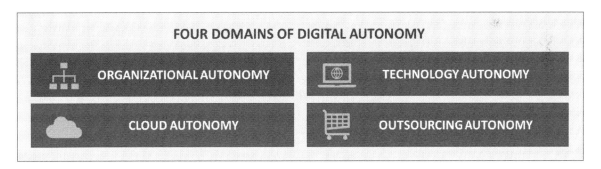

Figure 24 A culture of autonomy consists of different components, of which those four are selected representative examples critical for digital transformations

This chapter further explains four representative and important domains of critical capabilities to develop and evolve a culture of autonomy beyond the aspects of leadership.

ORGANIZATIONAL AUTONOMY

Organizational autonomy refers to the degree of independence and self-governance an organization has in making decisions and pursuing its goals, less dependent on external control or influence. It encompasses the authority, freedom, and discretion that an organization has to determine its policies, procedures, and activities, as well as the power to make decisions that affect its operations and direction. Organizations must encourage greater autonomy to realize the promises of agile working methods.

They can achieve greater autonomy if they take actions such as:

- Communicate clearly on the organization's strategy, goals, and priorities to allow more autonomous decision-making,
- Promote consistency by ensuring that all employees follow common guidelines, assuming greater accountability in decision-making and execution,
- Encourage ownership, provide employees with clear expectations, and inspire them to feel more accountable for their decisions and actions,
- Empower employees to make better-informed decisions by giving the organizations the data and information they need,
- Remove administrative burdens and complexity (such as sourcing and contract management),
- Democratize digital services in governed and controlled ways by reassuring broader utilization of tech and data outside traditional IT or tech organizations,
- Redistribute budget responsibilities by allowing collaborative consumption,
- Empower decentralized decision-making and agile, collaborative teams to make more autonomous decisions and prioritizations.

Principles support an environment of creativity and innovation by encouraging employees to take risks and experiment with new ideas. Those can facilitate a culture of autonomy where they become empowered to assume ownership and make responsible decisions, which leads to greater innovation, productivity, and engagement. From an organizational perspective, autonomy paves the way to increase self-sufficiency in evolutionary transformations and foster a culture of accountability and high performance.

Digital transformations can increase the autonomy of traditional organizations by automating repetitive tasks, allowing employees to focus on higher-value work. Every enterprise can establish organizational autonomy, which is critical for enabling agile collaboration across enterprises and their ecosystems.

 CLOUD AUTONOMY

Cloud autonomy is an ever-increasing field of responsibility for traditional IT organizations, significantly changing the role and level of autonomy. With the rise of digital foundational platforms, the purpose and meaning of the cloud have changed operational responsibilities, resulting in an increased shift and lift of IT applications and infrastructure into the cloud. Organizations undergoing this change may reconsider their approaches to cloud services and embrace new ways of utilizing the cloud to increase their independence and levels of autonomy significantly.

As digital transformations often neglect the significance of utilizing the entire range of cloud services at the core of their digital transformations, they most likely dismiss the opportunities for rapid adoption of new cloud-based platform services from hyper-scalers. They provide a wider range of standards of innovative technologies for experimentation, utilization, implementation, and orchestration at scale. Enterprises transforming their IT operations must reconsider their cloud strategies to utilize such platforms' innovation and interoperable new levels of autonomy. This means that digital transformations must consider a cloud-centric approach. They must leverage the cloud differently and embrace unreleased opportunities by redefining their level of autonomy concerning in-house cloud service management. They must take action and assume full-scale accountabilities, responsibilities, and ownership of their digital cloud portfolio. They selectively assume responsibility and accountability for operating and managing their cloud services, implementing more advanced cloud service management teams, and establishing CCoEs (Cloud Centers of Excellence).

Organizations implement Centers of Excellence (CCoEs) as the ultimate level of cloud autonomy to:

- Standardize processes and technologies across the organizations,
- Increase autonomy and assume ownership of their cloud transformations,

- Foster collaboration and knowledge sharing among teams,

- Improve business support and increase responsiveness,

- Drive innovation and continuous improvements,

- Secure strategic ownership of the organization's core cloud services,

- Reduce costs and improve efficiencies,

- Enhance the organization's ability to adopt new technologies and methodologies,

- Improve the quality of services and products,

- Enhance the organization's reputation and competitiveness.

A well-functioning CCoE does provide organizations with a competitive advantage by facilitating the development of best practices, promoting the adoption of new technologies, and enabling the organization to continuously improve and adapt to changing market and business conditions. This example of organizational autonomy is viable across various domains, where autonomy enables enterprises to select partners, contribute with special skills and 24/7 delivery models, and assume clearly defined responsibilities. As CCoEs owns administrative access rights about their cloud tenants, they can change their vendors with relatively short notice and without major transformative projects.

Organizations increase their autonomy significantly through the implementation of cloud operations to manage and change vendors' access rights in their cloud environments to:

- Monitor and log cloud activity to detect and respond to potential security incidents,

- Use cloud services that offer centralized user management and access control,

- Regularly review and revoke access rights for inactive or terminated user/vendor accounts,

- Establish a clear process for requesting, granting, and revoking vendor access,

- Regularly audit vendor access to ensure it aligns with current business needs and security requirements.

By implementing these capabilities and a CCoE, organizations can maintain control over their cloud environments and easily adjust vendor access rights, increasing their agility and ability to respond autonomously and independently to vendor relationships or security requirements.

🌐 TECHNOLOGY AUTONOMY

Technology autonomy does include more than just the ability to implement new technologies. Organizations can substantially take over control of their core IT services that are mission-critical to support critical digital business capabilities.

Autonomy in technology utilization, development, and deployment is crucial as digitally transforming organizations may reconsider the effectiveness of outsourcing their digital capabilities. Rather than finding partners assuming full-stack responsibility, digitally transforming enterprises must assume full responsibility. This includes autonomous digital architectures with full interoperability and the ability to constantly add, replace, or change digital technologies without always depending on third-party vendors.

- Foster innovation by allowing businesses to experiment with new technologies and ideas,
- Enable businesses to scale their digital infrastructure and development processes as needed,
- Allows for rapid growth and expansion without the need for major capital investments or significant changes to the existing architectures,
- Secure greater flexibility and innovation in developing state-of-the-art compelling, unique digital products without having dependencies on other vendors,
- Develop, scale, and deploy own digital development and future maintenance,
- Secure maximum responsiveness and digital resilience,
- Enable time and cost savings through significant changes in the enterprise sourcing strategies and future vendor selections,
- Integrate enterprise digital security in every aspect of digital capabilities.

By leveraging autonomy, enterprises will significantly increase their ability to innovate the enterprise and secure digital resilience. They must reinvent and reorganize their sourcing strategies, finding partners that can fill the gaps and help to scale where limitations of autonomy create risks. Examples are 24/7 services for cloud or security services, where new partners could offer dynamic utilization of skills and services on demand.

OUTSOURCING AUTONOMY

Organizations can transform traditional outsourcing to remove restrictions and increase autonomy in agile development and digital transformations. Examples include activities such as:

- Adopt a collaborative and co-creation approach with vendors,
- Incorporate flexible contract terms that allow for adjustments to project scope and timelines,
- Encourage vendors to adopt agile methodologies and digital tools,
- Emphasize clear communication and increase collaboration in agile development,
- Replace dependencies of external coding and development with new capabilities,
- Test and evolve hybrid models to combine outsourcing with in-house development,
- Engage vendors in business prioritizations and create engagement,
- Foster a continuous learning and improvement culture.

By implementing prioritized activities, organizations can increase their control over the development process, improve collaboration, and foster a more agile and adaptable collaboration with their traditional IT outsourcing vendors. Organizations traditionally did not make radical changes concerning their ways of working with outsourcing partners. Increasing autonomy is a key challenge, usually impacted by traditional outsourcing contracts and relationships, limiting the autonomy of organizations in agile development and digital transformations.

Ineffective outsourcing relations can cause a variety of issues, such as the following:

- Inability to align outsourcing with strategies, business goals, and priorities,
- Lack of control over processes and decision-making,
- Communication and coordination difficulties,
- Dependence on a single vendor or service provider,
- Inflexibility in the ability to respond to changing market conditions or business requirements.

These four domains of autonomy suggest critical changes and new thinking, how digitally transforming organizations must reinvent their roles, and the ability to become agile, innovative, adaptable, and responsive to secure digital resilience.

Enterprises must reconsider their strategic approach to outsourced IT services to adjust their vendor management strategies to their desired and necessary level of autonomy. The vendor's ability to contribute to digital development must define digital vendor dependency and autonomy levels. To strive towards agile sourcing is a selective and incremental process, as enterprises should focus on those core services which are critical to work. Implementing agile sourcing does not necessarily require completely redesigning entire sourcing relationships.

It is most likely that core business capabilities define the scope and intensity of necessary transformative changes to achieve agile sourcing or dynamic sourcing capabilities. However, enterprises shall consider strategic changes to make strategic adoptions, establish co-creation capabilities collaboration, engage vendors in agile development, and incorporate flexible contract terms to allow for continual adjustments to costs, scope, and timelines. By doing so, enterprises may evolve their sourcing relationships to secure digital composability without disruptive problems caused by ineffective sourcing relationships.

"Enterprises must reinforce digital autonomy by overcoming traditional behaviors and cultural aspects. Establishing digital autonomy across the enterprise is foundational for evolving digital composable enterprises."

Ingo Paas

Only enterprises that may evolve their sourcing relationships to dynamic or agile sourcing levels may achieve composability without interruptions. Inflexible and stagnant outsourcing may cause ineffective relationships and lead to incoherent or non-functioning composable business capabilities. They may lead to major struggles and risks, as insufficient outsourcing will restrict enterprises' ability to pursue digital transformations successfully. Bottlenecks caused by traditional outsourcing relationships must be considered a major risk to digital transformations.

Transform traditional outsourcing

The impact, importance, and complexity of traditional outsourcing relations in digital transformations are worth further discussing in this field of expertise. While technologies are revolutionizing nearly every aspect of traditional business models and utilization of technologies, outsourcing remains a major concern, heavily impacting the execution of digital transformations. As outsourcing is a major obstacle for many digital transformations and establishing digital composability on an enterprise level, outsourcing deserves a separate break-out. Companies that undergo a digital transformation may seek partners with expertise in areas such as cloud computing, data analytics, or artificial intelligence, which is rare in traditional outsourcing arrangements.

There is a variety of domains that can become hindrances to using traditional outsourcing partners in digital transformations for varying reasons:

- **Lack of business model flexibility**

  Traditional outsourcing partners often have business models based on delivering fixed services/products packed for larger clients with limited flexibility. This can hinder digital transformations that require experimentation, iteration, and adaptation to find services matching their tailored needs. Instead, digital transformations require outsourcing partners with business models based on flexibility, modularity, agility, and scalability (costs and scope), which may not be compatible with traditional outsourcing models.

- **Lack of innovation**

  Traditional outsourcing partners may not have a culture of innovation or only think of innovation in the context of large-scale projects. Their approach to large-scale projects and complex solutions may help solve larger problems but will not foster a culture of innovation which can hinder incremental development. Instead, evolutionary transformations require a culture of risk-taking, experimentation, and innovation, which may not be present in traditional outsourcing partners.

- **Lack of business alignment**

  Traditional outsourcing partners may not align with their client's strategic goals and visions, as they may have disconnected approaches to support their clients with what they can offer rather than what their clients eventually need. This can lead to complicated negotiations and insufficient business proposals that may be way off compared to the client's expectations and needs.

- **Lack of vendor governance**

  Traditional outsourcing partners often operate within rigid governance structures, including fixed processes, policies, and decision-making hierarchies. As a result, they may confront clients with complicated negotiation processes and struggle to provide agile responses when business needs or scope changes. Their rigid structures may hinder them from responding to client needs and acting on a scale. This can hinder digital transformations that require agile decision-making, experimentation, and iterative processes that can constantly adapt to changing business needs. Similarly, implemented services may be difficult to adjust rapidly for enterprises.

- **Lack of expertise**

  Traditional outsourcing partners may not have the deep expertise and knowledge required to support digital transformations, particularly in emerging technologies such as artificial intelligence, blockchain, or the Internet of Things (IoT). This may limit their ability to provide the support and guidance required for successful digital transformations with dedicated expertise in solving small but critical tech problems or customizations. They may have perfect expertise in delivering larger projects but cannot support clients with edge skills when required.

- **Size and hierarchical structures**

  Traditional outsourcing partners often have global organizations and hierarchical structures, making it difficult to work collaboratively and agilely. Digital transformations require cross-functional teams, continuous learning, and experimentation, which may not be compatible with the hierarchical structures of traditional outsourcing partners, often causing difficulties. At the same time, such hierarchies may be excellent for international enterprises utilizing their outsourcing partners' global or regional presence.

- **Lack of contract flexibility**

  Traditional outsourcing contracts with fixed pricing, scope, and service levels can be inflexible and hinder clients from engaging in responsive relationships and service provisioning. Outsourcing vendors may also be constrained by their contracts and inflexible service level agreements, making it difficult to adapt to changing requirements in digital transformations. These contracts can even cause problems in realizing business cases and securing cost reductions when outsourcing services have been replaced with new digital solutions. Eliminating these costs can take a long time and risk business cases with ROI calculations and TCO due to double the costs of parallel services.

- **Inflexible services/products**

    Traditional outsourcing partners may offer inflexible and oversized services/products that do not support the evolving needs of digital transformation enterprises. If contracts allow changes in demand, the products may not be that flexible, hindering clients from realizing their business cases with committed ROI and TCO calculations.

Overall, governance, contracts, lack of expertise, inflexible contracts, size, hierarchical structures, business models, and rigid services/products are new demands that outsourcing vendors must adapt to be based on the need of their customers. Enterprises should define clear strategies, seek alignment, openly discuss with their outsourcing vendors, and align their future demand with a governance model. By doing so, enterprises will eliminate major difficulties and better articulate their needs. This will reduce problems in ineffective negotiations and endless trials of solving unsolvable problems.

Categorizing vendors and projects will help to simplify and improve communication with new prospects and projects. This may involve adopting new contract models, building cross-functional teams, and collaborating with partners with deep expertise in emerging technologies.

As traditional outsourcing vendors are scaling up technologies and exciting industry-specific large-scale innovation, their underlying business models may distract them from offering and delivering outsourced IT services will appropriate levels of agility.

DXC Technology is a global information technology (IT) services company that provides various digital solutions and services to businesses and organizations across various industries. DXC is s focused on helping its clients leverage digital technologies to transform their operations, improve efficiency, and drive growth. The company is strongly committed to sustainability and social responsibility and aims to create long-term value for its stakeholders by delivering innovative digital solutions and services. DXC offers large-scale innovation and digital capabilities and adjusts traditional outsourcing services to offer and provide more scalable and agile services on demand. Offering and embedding agile capabilities on demand to support digital transformations is a transformative undertaking and challenge, even for those global vendors providing enterprises with disruptive digital services.

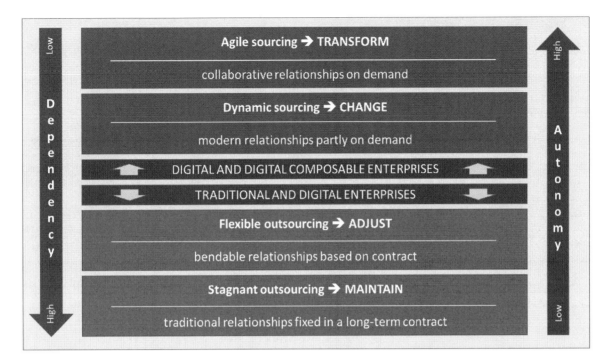

Figure 25 To leverage digital autonomy to utilize external relations differently

Organizations that choose a more diverse and dynamic collaboration with their digital vendors configure and manage their portfolio of services based on their individual needs and capabilities.

While vendors struggle to identify more agile service offerings, some evolve digital service offerings to address changing enterprise partnerships and consumption behaviors. Tietoevry, a leading Nordic digital services and software company, has introduced unique approaches that address the new agile sourcing demands of enterprises undergoing digital composable transformations. This shift in perspective and leadership is the future of agile sourcing, replacing traditional outsourcing over time.

Traditionally organizations must apply all four scenarios in parallel, as they will most likely navigate between those four approaches, depending on the scale of the desired level of elasticity required. IT organizations with multiple sourcing approaches shall select their vendors based on their ability to support individual needs distinctively. They may consider the following distinctions while applying their strategies and differentiating their efforts in line with a realistic evaluation of their efforts and chances of success, by understanding given limitations.

AGILE sourcing = TRANSFORM

An agile sourcing strategy characterizes transformational relationships that engage in transformational partnerships. They prefer fully agile development and agile responses from their partners. They want to share business goals, understand business priorities, and focus on value creation. They only select partners that proactively and quickly adapt to changing business needs and requirements. IT organizations with an agile sourcing approach typically have a collaborative, flexible, and adaptable workforce. Transformational sourcing generally leverages new elasticity and innovation opportunities to support and encourage incremental, experimental, and evolutionary development. Agile sourcing is the ideal level of sourcing and guarantees the most significant possible levels of elasticity!

Agile IT sourcing is essential for digital transformations and agile organizations, where flexibility, speed, adaptability, and elasticity are crucial considerations. Agile sourcing is necessary to enable digital foundational transformations and digital composable enterprises.

Agile sourcing does

- Enable enterprise-wide composability,
- Enable digital autonomy and independency from external partners,
- Enable agile development and service adaption,
- Reduce lead times and time-to-market,
- Accelerate digital transformations from the core of the business,
- Engage selected partners in goal-driven partnerships.

DYNAMIC sourcing = CHANGE

Dynamic sourcing strategies emphasize the ability to constantly change the sourcing of external services and skills. Dynamic sourcing approaches include continuous improvement and innovation in sourcing processes, with high degrees of flexibility. Dynamic sourcing approaches focus on enabling agile development and finding partners to scale and adapt their services. They continually evolve their technology stack and prefer dynamic sourcing partners to support them in different phases of technology adaptation.

Dynamic IT sourcing is an approach to procuring and managing IT and digital services responsively and flexibly. It emphasizes collaboration, adaptability, and rapid iteration in procurement and delivery, as opposed to traditional, more rigid approaches. Dynamic IT sourcing is important for digital transformations and development, where flexibility and speed are important but not the only considerations. It does support digital foundational transformations and digital composable enterprises.

Dynamic IT sourcing does

- Support enterprise-wide composability,
- Support digital autonomy and independency from external partners,
- Support agile development and service adaption,
- Reduce lead times and time-to-market,
- Accelerate digital transformations from the core of the business,
- Engage selected partners in goal-driven partnerships.

FLEXIBLE outsourcing = ADJUST

A flexible outsourcing approach emphasizes the ability to adjust long-term and often complex outsourced IT services for enterprises. Their changes are more focused and at lower frequencies, with the ability of short-term adjustments to make short-term adjustments to changes in demand and supply. Their need to buy high-volume services, such as data center operations, makes them less volatile to unpredictable changes. Flexible outsourcing is an approach to procuring and managing IT and digital services traditionally but still in a somewhat flexible manner. Flexible outsourcing emphasizes standard processes, governance models, and contractual agreements. It does not directly support digital transformations and development but might help digital development with industry best practices or dedicated knowledge and experiences from outsourcing vendors.

It does focus on standardized IT services in traditional delivery models. Modern and more flexible outsourcing contracts with greater flexibility make the basis for flexible outsourcing relationships as they enable greater responsiveness and continual changes to standard outsourcing services.

Flexible outsourcing does the following:

- Only partly support enterprise-wide composability,
- Not support digital autonomy and independency from external partners,
- Only partly support agile development and service adaption,
- Not reduce lead times and time-to-market,
- Not accelerate digital transformations from the core of the business,
- Not engage selected partners in goal-driven partnerships.

TRADITIONAL outsourcing = MAINTAIN

A traditional sourcing strategy is characterized by a lack of innovation and a tendency to stick with conventional sourcing models. IT organizations that remain focused on traditional sourcing strategies may resist change, focus on cost efficiencies, and assume lower autonomy and less accountability. The most traditional way of IT outsourcing is stagnant outsourcing, which emphasizes rigid processes, governance models, and contractual agreements. Stagnant outsourcing supports normal IT deliveries of standardized services within traditional scope and delivery models based on traditional outsourcing agreements. They are strategic, with contract periods spanning multiple years.

Traditional outsourcing does the following:

- Not support enterprise-wide composability,
- Not support digital autonomy and independency from external partners,
- Not support agile development and service adaption,
- Not reduce lead times and time-to-market,
- Not accelerate digital transformations from the core of the business,
- Not engage selected partners in goal-driven partnerships.

IT organizations that manage multiple sourcing approaches tend to be more adaptable and responsive to changing business needs while creating ultimate levels of elasticity in their sourcing strategies. They foster collaborative relationships with vendors capable of supporting agile or dynamic approaches. Their choices are demand-driven, and they select their partner depending on their ability to adapt.

Modern IT organizations will have to navigate across all four levels until modern digital capabilities replace their IT legacy domains. Most sourcing strategies might require significant adjustments to add the layer of agile and dynamic sourcing to traditional sourcing approaches with flexible and standard sourcing relationships. The more IT organizations shift their sourcing volumes toward dynamic and agile sourcing, the more their level of autonomy will increase. The more they will see the significant benefits of dynamic and agile sourcing relationships, the more they contribute to their digital transformations. Depending on the chosen level of sourcing strategy adoption, those changes may take a considerably long time. Intensive collaboration with prioritized outsourcing vendors is essential to align on necessary changes and create a common foundation for change. Simply demanding a change will not result in acceptance. Instead, collaborating purposefully and making changes in partnership can facilitate successful implementation. It is beneficial to learn from initial mistakes and failures to improve and enable the transition from outsourced services to more agile or dynamic sourcing services by isolating and eliminating those. Examples are file server or storage management, application servers, firewalls, and on-premise services. This includes the shift from traditional outsourcing services to cloud-based services. Awareness and early action will help to identify critical gaps and risks addressed and mitigated as proactively and early as possible.

Organizations can become digital composable enterprises if their outsourcing strategies allow migrating digital packaged business capabilities towards DYNAMIC or AGILE sourcing models. Such transformations are necessary for those critical business processes from the core of the business that enterprises must transform. Enterprises must recognize that those undertakings must happen within a relatively short time frame, as digital initiatives have little tolerance for delay. Taking action is critical to seek alternatives to mitigate risks from the beginning proactively. Searching for new options after failure is not appropriate or recommended. Issues will most likely increase the urgency for traditional outsourcing partners to respond more effectively to those new demands, significantly changing the direction of future service provisioning. Only enterprises with a strong focus on agile and dynamic sourcing, concerning their most critical services to secure enterprise-wide transformations or changes, can support their digital transformations with collaborative and modern sourcing vendor relationships. The absence of this strategic ability may have severe implications on digital composable transformations and the establishment of digital composable enterprises. Transforming and evolving enterprises must effectively operate on and across all four categories but may experience difficulties delivering services at levels one and two in collaborative or cooperative ways.

Insourcing of application development

IT organizations that strive for greater application development autonomy on an enterprise level must push the boundaries of traditional IT sourcing towards agile or dynamic outsourcing relationships and strategies. IT organizations often rely on external development for their outsourced IT applications, but when those relationships become inflexible, they might need to act distinctively and implement significant changes.

Digital autonomous organizations must adhere to their architectural design at the core of their business models and assume full-stack responsibility and accountability for their digital development. Outsourced applications or systems with complex external application development require significant changes to better integrate the application development of monolithic or complex systems into agile development processes. With greater digital autonomy, organizations make more and better independent decisions and move faster while eliminating complexity in decision-making processes. IT organizations must insource application development to accelerate their digital transformations. From a business perspective, enterprises must engage with their vendors to transform outsourced development.

Insourcing of application development in general:

- Allow IT organizations to increase agility and respond more quickly to changing business needs and take advantage of new opportunities as they arise,
- Improve and foster agile collaboration between different development teams and lets business directly engage with application developers,
- Encourage increased innovation and experimentation, as IT organizations are free to build and test new applications and digital solutions that may not have been possible with traditional development methods,
- Enable faster enterprise integration development to secure enterprise composability,
- Allow IT organizations to control better and improve the quality of their applications and ensure that they meet today's and tomorrow's standards and requirements.

Insourcing application development increases agility and speed to optimize internal skills and leverage those skills to find more effective solutions to business problems. It gives IT organizations more control over their digital transformation, allowing them to decide what applications to build, when, and how to build them.

It enables IT organizations to integrate their applications more easily with existing systems and data, ensuring their digital transformations are aligned with strategies, goals, and business priorities. This can result in cost savings over the long term, as IT organizations can build applications that meet their specific needs rather than having to purchase or license pre-built applications that may not fit their needs exactly.

By insourcing application development, IT organizations can achieve a faster, more efficient, and more effective digital transformation while maintaining control over their technology landscape and ensuring that their applications align with their goals and standards.

Individuals and teams that navigate in such autonomous frameworks will

- Foster a culture of communication and learning,
- Increase confidence in decision-making,
- Challenge the average ambition level when setting goals,
- Promote more risk-tolerance decision-making,
- Gain independence from external partners,
- Give better feedback (to everyone concerned),
- Assume accountability for failures and correct those instantly,
- Increase levels of accountability in ownership of IT and digital services,
- Improve the trust between each other,
- Learn from their mistakes,
- Solve problems in sustainable ways,
- Accelerate time to market and time to value, and
- Promote a culture of high-performing teams and individuals.

Insourcing may help to mitigate business and IT risks and, in small steps, reorganize and transfer decision power, control, and supervision downwards into the organization. This can accelerate autonomous decision-making, more autonomous and rapid development, and create enterprise-wide digital composable architecture and capabilities. Without making this move and establishing autonomy in critical application development, ownership, and the ability to execute, organizations will continue to struggle to act independently, coherently, and distinctly, especially during complex digital transformations. Insourcing application development will help organizations to transfer power and autonomy back to their teams.

This power transfer is important for IT organizations in traditional outsourcing environments, where the lengthiest part of the development process (often in outsourced development activities) will determine the overall speed within the agile development framework of different DevOps teams. Complexity grows as application development requires integrations and development within core legacy systems. It usually forces developers to rebuild critical business processes or data structures to make them fit in digital development projects.

To eliminate and find new solutions to such substantial problems, organizations must cautiously shift critical application development back to their organizations or harmonize their vendor's development processes with their agile processes. They must be aligned with other DevOps (Development Operations) teams to secure ERP system integration and the ability to develop integrations, especially of complicated applications, such as SAP, mainframe systems, AS/400, and other critical systems. Especially the development of enterprise applications will force organizations to effectively leverage agile development processes involving their monolithic systems.

Real-time integrations with IT legacy systems require changes in those systems, a prerequisite for enterprises to build interoperability across systems at the core of their business. This is another critical prerequisite for digital composable enterprises to leverage interoperability through agile, collaborative development teams.

Without the ability to develop and implement digital composability across their core business processes, their enterprises may never achieve enterprise-wide composability and interoperability. They will be unable to foster and embed the ability to build and evolve enterprise-wide digital resilience.

APPLIED TECHNOLOGY LEADERSHIP
Emil Hellström, Product Manager Mainframe, Green Cargo

"Green Cargo traditionally outsourced most IT services, including all IT development. Green Cargo outsourced our mainframe development to India without having the proper skills and resources within Green Cargo. With more than ten years of trials to replace the mainframe system, investments were cut, and mainframe skills were outsourced and unavailable.

This approach was changed significantly with the new IT strategy, approved by the board of directors. A new team was established to take care of our mainframe. This was done in a new partnership with a local Stockholm-based mainframe consulting company Dynamant. After onboarding new consultants from Dynamant, we started implementing the basics. Green Cargo reconfirmed initial success and initiated the insourcing of mainframe development from India back to Stockholm. As a consequence of this decision, we had to invest and accept increased costs but could achieve major improvements, such as:

- *Improved system performance, stability, and quality,*
- *Enhanced agile demand management with business and our DevOps teams,*
- *Reinforced business development and increased collaboration with the business,*
- *Introduction of agile development with an increase from four up to three hundred releases/year,*
- *Reduced system complexity by reducing unused code and programs with a complexity of thousands of tables in the system.*

At the same time, we were stabilizing our mainframe by shutting down several old systems to make them more stable and manageable. To integrate our mainframe into our growing efforts of composable development, we added new technologies and built real-time integration capabilities with a general API to our mainframe system Bravo. This was another essential milestone to enable agile enterprise development in a more than forty-year-old system. We migrated the old and unsupported relational database management system running on mainframes to reduce risks further. This also allowed us to download data to our enterprise lowcode OutSystems platform as we had to rewrite almost five hundred programs. Development in our mainframe is considered best practice agile development, where we constantly leverage the strengths and skills of every individual. Our teams have a high sense of focus to ensure we constantly deliver smaller, high-quality packages. Agile development methods are embedded into all agile planning and development. Even though our mainframe development team is located within the Applications department, we apply the same principles and utilize the same Microsoft DevOps tools as all other DevOps teams within the IT Development department.

We perform smaller, simpler tests and correct potential problems or incidents responsively and rapidly after new releases. A rollback is created on the deployed application to the previous application package in the event of major incidents. Instead, we have ended up in the position that the customers do not have time to accept as we deliver solutions.

We have prolonged the life cycle of our mainframe and initiated investigations to verify future opportunities for leveraging our mainframe with modern technology platforms. We went from chaos to mastering our mainframe."

Written by Emil Hellström, Product Manager Mainframe, Green Cargo

Dynamic organizations with strong reasoning to utilize and implement higher grades of digital autonomy inside their organizations collaboratively must leverage digital transformations in new and unprecedented ways. Those organizations must not only focus on becoming more autonomous while they increase their level of dependencies, but they must also embrace and promote the evolution of business processes and systems that can be several decades old.

Independent of the given complexity, they should consider radical changes concerning outsourced application development to enable evolutionary and collaborative development approaches across various necessary processes and systems, guided and driven by clear business priorities. Truly agile partners, such as Dynamant, a Stockholm-based mainframe development consulting firm, represent value-driven sourcing partnerships, outperforming other vendors due to their focus on creating sustainable business value. They assume responsibility and always prioritize their clients in open and constructive discussions, often focused on learning more to better engage in realizing new opportunities or solving real business problems.

Organizations can make those significant shifts as they must embrace autonomy at a larger scale from the core of their business. They must find new ways to build and sustain interoperability even if conditions are difficult and impose new technology and investment risks initially. If they want to proceed and establish composability at the core of their business, they have no choice but to promote evolution rather than revolution. By engaging the organization in distributed execution, they can ideally encourage more decentral and unconstrained demand-driven digital development by allowing employees and consultants to engage. They can do this by introducing stimulating and well-supported citizen developer capabilities.

Embrace citizen developer opportunities

Citizen developers emphasize a more distributed and democratized digital development in business functions – where applicable, ideally without losing control of their digital development. Organizations can empower employees to utilize distributed but well-governed development tools or platforms to eliminate traditional obstacles of resource constraints in IT organizations to rapidly and spontaneously allocate their resources to solve individual development needs.

Citizen development empowers non-technical employees to create software applications or digital solutions (such as reports, queries, and APIs) to realize specific business needs rapidly and instantly. Greater business involvement, ownership, and ability to execute are important for organizations because they can lead to increased efficiency, better alignment of IT and business goals, faster innovation, and greater employee satisfaction and engagement. If users assume ownership, they can help develop applications that better fit their unique needs, leading to increased productivity and improved business outcomes. Citizen development can help organizations save time and resources, increase efficiencies, better align IT and business goals, and improve employee satisfaction and engagement through relevant and supportive user experiences.

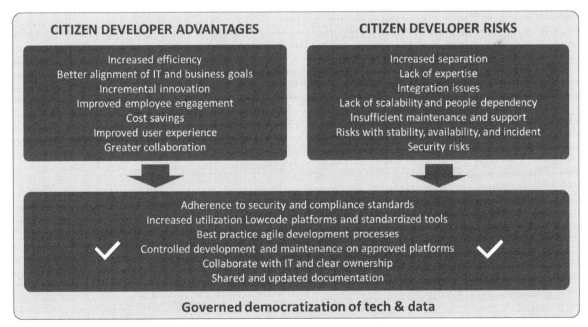

Figure 26 The advantages, pitfalls, and appropriate governing principles to utilize effective digital development by applying citizen development in sustainable ways

While citizen development approaches can bring many benefits, they can also have some pitfalls that organizations must be aware of. Mitigating those risks is important and should support distributed development rather than making it impossible. Those risks could include the lack of expertise and understanding of general IT development practices, Inconsistent quality, safeguarding appropriate support, maintenance, release management, and security and compliance requirements. Other issues can be related to insufficient documentation, dependencies on individuals, and problems with performance, access rights, and scalability.

Organizations must have clear guidelines and governance around citizen development to mitigate these risks. They must provide training and support to citizen developers and have a clear process for ensuring the quality and security of the applications created.

Citizen developers can develop more sustainable applications and digital solutions with appropriate governance or self-governance if they adhere to security and compliance standards, use low-code platforms, follow a defined development process, seek feedback, document their work, test their applications, and collaborate with the IT organization. By doing so, they can build maintainable and reliable solutions to meet business needs aligned with the organization's governance and standards.

Standardized tools, such as lowcode platforms, provide a visual, drag-and-drop interface to build high-quality applications without extensive technical skills. A defined development process ensures that applications are tested and validated before deployment. The IT organization ensures proper integration of applications and digital tools with existing systems through collaboration and provides support and guidance to citizen developers when needed. Through collaborative user groups, citizen developers can support and align their development processes. By doing so, they can create a more autonomous approach to creative, compliant, and controlled development. Appropriate governance and self-governance can help maintain the applications' quality and security over time.

As citizen developers can make great contributions, they cannot replace enterprise application development as usually performed by DevOps teams, with greater organizational complexity, funding need, effective compliance with architectural frameworks and complex technologies, and external relationships. Collaborative and more autonomous approaches to utilizing citizen-developers concepts include a wider development scope, including APIs, analytics, and algorithms. Even though citizen developers develop within a limited but agreed scope, they contribute to an evolutionary approach to digital transformations.

Promote evolution rather than revolution

The theory of technology-enabled digital evolution refers to the idea that the advancement and adoption of technology drive changes and evolution in how businesses operate, adapt, and compete. This theory suggests that technology acts as a catalyst for innovation and change and that enterprises must adopt and leverage technologies to enable incremental development. The concept of technology-enabled business evolution recognizes that organizations use and leverage technology as a crucial catalyst or enabler for driving evolutionary changes. Technology and data-driven business strategies find support with this approach, ultimately aligning with the company's digital investment strategies.

The evolutionary principle in digital transformations also implies that smaller changes enable new incremental digital advancements inspired in evolutionary ways. According to Gartner (Gartner, Combine, Cluster, Complement: 3 Fundamentals of Combinatorial Digital Innovation, 2021). "Combinatorial digital innovation is the practice of using components of different digital technologies and trends together to uncover new or better value". By applying this theory, enterprises can increase their chances of securing strategic and tactical rewards for their technology investments as they explore and capitalize on the advantages of combinatorial approaches.

Combinatory technologies are reusable and can interoperate and be combined in countless ways to drive even more incremental digital evolutions. This results in new digital-inspired opportunities constantly pushing the boundaries of what is possible in the digital age. In practical terms, the theory of technology-enabled business evolution suggests that businesses must be more proactive in their approach to technology and data, continuously leveraging new and innovative technologies that can help them to improve business operations and increase effectiveness. Utilizing technologies, data, and new skills will allow enterprises to continually advance their business models and processes, inspired, and encouraged by a systemic and adaptive combination of technologies.

Organizations that want to evolve towards composable enterprises using evolutionary approaches must integrate the underlying technologies systemically. They must focus on disciplined utilization of technologies, preferably digital foundational platforms on an enterprise level. Applying evolutionary thinking is a methodic and more reliable approach supporting the theory of ambidextrous organizations.

In the broader sense, evolution means change over time, propelling continual adjustments to constantly evolving systems. In technology and business-related innovations, random events and patterns create changes that lead to dynamic developments and relentless adoptions with infinite opportunities. As technologies evolve and advance continuously (often unrecognized at an exponential scale), they undergo rapid but evolutionary developments, principally applying the uncompromisable logic and mechanisms from evolutionary biology. Evolutionary change is continual and must not necessarily reach an end-state and might not even have this goal. It has various implications, such as the <u>speed</u>, <u>degree</u>, <u>risks</u>, <u>impact</u>, and <u>effects</u> that evolutionary changes may cause.

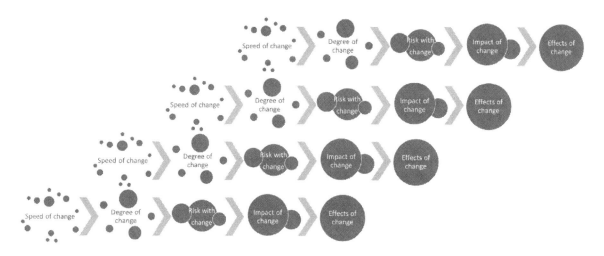

Figure 27 Evolutionary change leads to major change, but in incremental steps

Many factors determine the evolutionary success of organizations when enterprises adopt new digital technologies while accelerating their digital transformations. The speed of technological change can pressure organizations to keep up with the latest advancements, while incremental enhancements and development can compensate for risks by introducing continual changes. The evolution of complex systems consequently inhibits the logic of natural selection, as proven by evolutionary theories. Natural selection is not necessarily negative, as it is part of the process to evolve complex systems which constantly improve on optimizing their ability to fulfill and evolve their purpose. Those systems will continue to develop until even the most advanced systems may be discarded by the process, by unforeseeable events, or because of more successful, stronger, adaptive, or competitive systems. If those systems behave adaptive and resilient, they have a greater chance to contribute to evolutionary and systemic development.

Evolutionary design and development logic will lead to systemic enhancements based on distinct principles or rules. While those principles and rules remain stable, conditions and technologies might change more frequently. This approach will guarantee more successful evolutionary digital transformations while facilitating collaborative development and utilization of incremental enhancements. New methodologies, more systemic thinking, and incremental and experimental design are most likely increasing the success of digital transformations. This leads to the conclusion that organizations might review and eventually abandon the traditional concept of revolutionary digital transformations, large-scale unpredictable development, and major transformational changes.

"Instead of implementing large-scale revolutionary change, organizations should adopt evolutionary strategies to digital transformations, focusing on systemic incremental and experimental change. This approach allows for more flexibility and adaptability in responding to changes, rather than overhauling the entire system at once."

Ingo Paas

Collective commitment from the organization is essential for securing sustainable and evolutionary technology development. This challenging undertaking involves jointly transforming and leveraging complex systems through technology investments' incremental but visionary value propositions. Adopting an evolutionary approach to digital transformation is advantageous compared to large-scale transformations and a necessity. Some advantages of evolutionary transformations are:

- Minimized risk during execution (such as scope creep, costs, time plans, ROIs),
- Minimized complexity of digital development,
- Continual and rapid deliveries with shorter ROIs,
- Reduced TCO and more timely investments (not too early and not too late),
- Continual learning and teaching of the organization's employees (tech, data, processes),
- Embedded innovation processes and advanced problem-solving capabilities,
- Cultural advancements and development in collaborative engagements,
- Less complexity by segregating big problems into many small ones,
- Continual prioritization with improved business responses to change priorities,
- Collaborative learning informs decision-making processes of larger investments,
- Technology investments are possible timely with lower initial costs and scaled when needed.

Digital evolutionary transformations require dedication, leadership, and vision-driven inspiration, to overcome numerous challenges, difficulties, and unprecedented problems. They require focused execution, significant learning and risk-taking, and the ability and willingness to deal with constant conflicts and utilize them to evolve behaviors and cultural changes without reinforcing them.

The leadership perspective and the necessity to relentlessly accept and implement evolutionary development requires systemic thinking, a positive mindset, and relentless discipline from everyone involved.

APPLIED TECHNOLOGY LEADERSHIP
Ingo Paas, CIO & CDO, Green Cargo

"Our IT strategy implemented in October 2019 intended to realize systemic evolutionary changes and to establish the fundamental capabilities required, to transform our business model from the core. We utilized systemic methods to make progress everywhere at the same time. We focused on solving small problems (rather than big ones) with a relentless focus on execution. We made gradual improvements everywhere, engaged the entire IT organization and the business (stepwise) in our agile processes, initiated collaborative product ownership, and worked with our leadership.

We designed and implemented our digital composable architecture while we were setting the baseline for a professional IT delivery organization. Financed by various projects, we implemented our state-of-the-art digital foundational platform architecture, built composability and interoperability into our IT legacy (as much as affordable), and started integrating Green Cargo into multiple digital ecosystems. We embedded innovation into our agile processes and started making prioritizations with the business, always from the core of our business. Innovation suddenly started to evolve gradually. Our collaborative initiatives engaged over time to identify new improvements by reusing digitally developed packaged business capabilities. Our new architecture aligns with our principles, fully interoperable, reusable, adaptable, and scalable, enabling incremental digital transformation from the core of our business.

We continue to evolve and develop our business capabilities to strengthen Green Cargos' evolving data-driven culture collaboratively. We constantly learn, fail, solve, reuse, and scale our innovation capabilities embedded into our digital development, originating from the core of our business. We accelerate digitally inspired business development wherever feasible and reuse already-built digital assets to solve business problems. We engage key business stakeholders in our new ways of working and utilizing technologies and data seamlessly and evolutionarily. Innovation can also come from vertical industry solutions with business optimization capabilities and algorithmic technologies.

Looking to optimize locomotive planning and reduce costs, Green Cargo turned to DXC Technology's rail cargo management solution (RCMS), customized to provide a locomotive optimization system called LOOP. Green Cargo has increased productivity by 5-10% in terms of kilometers per locomotive and saved over 100,000 km in travel, all while reducing greenhouse gas emissions. DXC is shifting away from managing our infrastructure to becoming a strategic partner in supporting new innovative projects with leading industry-specific solutions while enabling our transformative business strategy by 2030 and replacing IT legacy systems.

The business has assumed a leading role in developing the core capabilities required to radically change our business model, supporting Green Cargos' strategy towards 2030. We have a strong road map and aligned plans to innovate the business model, seamlessly secure enterprise-wide interoperability, and mitigate business risks."

Written by Ingo Paas, CIO & CDO Green Cargo

Promoting evolution rather than revolution is a core success factor for digital transformations. Even in terms of organizational development and transformations, it is necessary to drive digital transformations collaboratively, engage, and align the entire organization over time. Evolutionary digital transformations enable organizations to overcome concerns with traditional management approaches, where most time is consumed by planning, explaining, and approving instead of proving experimental steps and letting the business verify what works best. Even though digital transformations are complex, organizations must prepare to manage and normalize those undertakings like "business as usual".

As technologies will continue to evolve exponentially, digital transformations are the new normal. Enterprises must secure their ability to deliver continual evolutionary changes by incrementally ingesting investments and organizational adjustments. Getting there does require enormous discipline, focus, and appreciation of risk-tolerance cultures and leadership. By identifying the most appropriate foundational principles, such as autonomy, accountability, and trust, evolutionary change will improve the ability to execute. Organizations should prefer digital evolutionary transformations to utilize and promote experimental and incremental development and change. Those insights are fundamental to creating, fostering, and encouraging the primary conditions for evolutionary digital composable transformations and cultural adaptation.

Key conclusions and takeaways

The key conclusions and takeaways from the chapter "**VISIONARY EVOLUTION**" are:

1. Enterprises must balance business tactical (short-term ROI) with strategic (long-term scalable ROI) digital investments.

2. Enterprises must drive digital transformations from the core of the business, converging those processes towards excellence in the customer experience.

3. Enterprises must secure that digital transformations shall be guided and driven by the organization's purpose, vision, strategy, goals, and business priorities.

4. Enterprises must apply distinct digital principles across various domains (such as strategic, transformational, execution, architectural, and technologies).

5. Enterprises must encourage and sustain a culture of organizational, operational, and sourcing autonomy.

6. Enterprises must promote evolution rather than revolution to foster a culture of incremental and experimental change.

7. Enterprises with their boards and executive teams must plan for the unavoidable budget increase caused by NEW additional and essential digital investments and costs that are profoundly necessary to transform and not only to replace.

8. Enterprises must principally reinforce digital autonomy at the core, which is foundational for evolving digital composable enterprises.

9. Enterprises must assume full accountability to define and implement strategic technologies and platform strategies to drive business innovation, even without business demands. Waiting is not an option!

FOUR – VALUABLE IT LEGACY

THOUGHT DIGITAL LEADERSHIP

Emmanuelle Hose, GVP & Regional General Manager, Rimini Street

"In today's climate of fierce competition and a relentless focus on growth, organizations must be cognizant of future economic, technological, and political uncertainty. Increasingly, change is coming from unprecedented directions, and organizations must be prepared for and expect change without knowing when and where it is coming from. When the unexpected happens, a composable strategy can engrain an agile culture that adopts the most appropriate, cost-effective, and timely technology.

Digital transformation is a priority for organizations focused on better interaction with customers, partners, and stakeholders in a more dynamic fashion. With these goals in mind, depending on - and innovating at the speed of -one monolithic software vendor is no longer viable.

ERP suites will remain the backbone of many organizations' everyday operations. According to Grandview Research, the on-premise segment held over 70% of the market share in 2022. We must acknowledge that these critical proprietary systems have years or decades of data on customers, employees, finances, and partners and are surrounded by unique, refined, customized business logic.

But where ERPs were built to last today, they need to be built for change - and we now have access to a seemingly endless number of solutions that provide the almost instant capability to make that happen.

Embracing the value of legacy IT in combination with digital solutions in a harmonized, composable model allows organizations to extend or replace parts of the enterprise landscape where better business outcomes can be achieved with a favorable ROI. However, transitioning to a composable model can be an arduous journey. Fortunately, strategies, guiding principles, building blocks, packaged business capabilities, frameworks, architectures, and third-party support tools can aid the evolution with spend vs. value top of mind."

Written by Emmanuelle Hose, GVP & Regional General Manager, Rimini Street

Embrace a composable strategy

Packaged business capabilities refer to pre-built, reusable components that encapsulate a documented and defined specific business capability as a component of a business process. These components are critical to identifying the business capabilities that support a range of business needs, of which the most critical ones describe the core of the business. They function as the building blocks/components of business processes, such as supply chain management, pricing, order management, financial management, and human resources, while one or more business capabilities combine to illustrate a process.

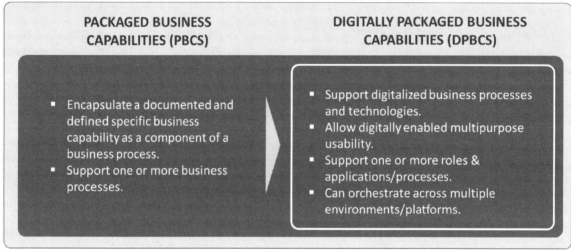

Figure 28 Packaged business capabilities (PBCs) and digital packaged business capabilities (DPBCs)

Digital packaged business capabilities (DPBCs) digitally designs as reusable components to support digital business processes and technologies. DPBCs support digitalized business processes and technologies and are digitally enabled components allowing multipurpose usability for multi-purpose utilization supporting various applications and business processes. This means that one DPBC supports one or more applications/processes orchestrated across multiple applications and platforms. Developers create packaged applications using independent, loosely coupled microservices utilized in multiple DPBCs orchestrated into the cloud. PBCs trigger actions/events in real-time, while public and REST APIs will trigger actions/events in other DPBCs or systems. They are composed of microservices, small-scale, independent, autonomous services combined in various ways. They are a combination of microservices that form or pack individual business capabilities.

The role of DPBCs in evolving composable enterprises is to provide organizations with a flexible and modular way to digitally build and manage their business processes from the core of the business. They enable organizations to assemble, modify and evolve their processes in response to changing market conditions and business requirements. This approach helps those organizations increase agility and responsiveness to changes and reduce the time and cost associated with process development and maintenance. Transforming composable organizations use pre-built and pre-tested business capabilities that rapidly assemble and form new or updated processes. They play a key role in developing composable enterprises by providing organizations with the most flexible and efficient way to build, manage, and evolve their processes in response to changing business needs. Composable enterprises consider the entire spectrum of their core business model & processes, their operational models, their ability to industrialize infinite & embedded innovation, and how to utilize capabilities to embrace and establish digital ecosystems, digitalize, or digitally enable their products & services. They must do this to understand and approach the most critical disciplines essential to transformation.

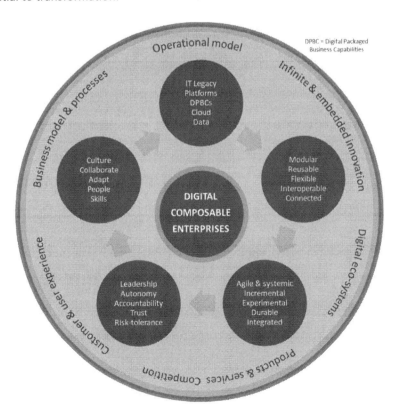

Figure 29 The framework of digital composable enterprises

The five critical core disciplines of enterprise composability explained:

ARCHITECTURE: Design, implement, and operate a composable architecture

IT Legacy
Platforms
DPBCs
Cloud
Data

Composable architectures consist of an organization's IT legacy and new digital capabilities, fully integrated and composed, where needed and when applicable. Composable architectures contain modern foundational platform technologies with superior architectural design. Designing digital foundational platforms does require effective utilization of the distinct and general principles for the entire enterprise.

The three most essential and foundational platforms include enterprise-wide Enterprise hybrid integration platforms (such as Microsoft Azure), enterprise lowcode development platforms (such as OutSystems), and enterprise analytics (such as Google Cloud Platform and Microsoft Power Platform) are must-have platform capabilities of digital composable transformations. Those cloud platforms usually come with accessible and ready-to-use technology innovation leveraged and provided by the world's leading CSPs (Cloud Service Providers). They offer on-demand options with unlimited innovation capabilities, constantly being upgraded and enriched as technologies develop radically. They empower traditional organizations to utilize innovation capabilities at unparalleled levels. Additional platforms are more specialized, such as Automation, Workplace, security, and IoT.

Composable enterprises and digital transformations rely on packaged applications as their core. Enterprise lowcode development platforms have made composable development more feasible and less complicated. Digital packaged business capabilities (DPBCs developed on these platforms offer new opportunities for development and deployment. Well-designed and implemented composable architectures can even overhaul parts or entire IT legacy systems. The selected platforms with systemic capabilities facilitate collaborative thinking, execution, and adaptation in new and sustainable ways. Integrating hybrid enterprise applications with existing IT legacy systems enables revolutionary business processes and application development with real-time and event-driven enterprise applications. Development teams can use highly modular approaches to integrate, adjust, and migrate existing IT legacy systems.

The ever-increasing investments and advancements of intelligent analytics capabilities are mandatory technology innovations for digital composable enterprises. Data-driven capabilities, such as skills, access, tools, data quality, data governance, and security, must be aligned with the increased pace of changes in the IT landscape, with its IT legacy systems and new digital capabilities.

Digital composable organizations must be capable of constantly orchestrating business processes and their digital objects across their digital foundational platforms, embedded into and controlled to operate effectively with their IT legacy systems at maximum scale.

PRINCIPLES: Develop and orchestrate digital platforms based on guiding principles

Guiding principles are fundamental and, at the core of any future digital composable architecture, supporting the transformation and realization of composable enterprises. Those guiding and fundamental principles are to secure a distinct, effective, and controlled transformation into digital composable enterprises.

Modularity is a critical design principle to secure the optimized and unconstrained design and development of new applications and digital assets, supremely to utilize loosely coupled services architectures. Reusability is one of the most profound scalable capabilities digital transforming organizations must ensure. Building flexibility is at the core of composability and digital resilience and must be embedded deep into the architecture (from loosely coupled services to DPBCs and applications/digital assets). Flexibility is essential for composability at scale, as flexibility will enable a shift from traditional application development towards elasticity and responsiveness to change constant business demand, with rapid response abilities from development teams. Connectivity is essential for enabling high-performance operations across multiple environments and orchestrating digital services across multi-connected environments. Interoperability will relentlessly support variations of integrated technologies and technology platforms to ensure controlled protocols and information exchange between different products and technology stacks.

Adaptivity, simplicity, stability, sustainability, and other relevant principles may accompany those foundational ones. They all supplement each other and create the foundation for the success of every composable design. Those principles support and enable the development and orchestration of composable applications in highly effective ways, mainly enabled by enterprise Lowcode development (such as OutSystems). They usually guide the design of digital foundational platforms, adjustments, and investments into the IT legacy, digital ecosystems, and more, while they are essential for the endless utilization of those architectural design patterns.

WAYS OF WORKING: Utilize advanced collaboration, and facilitate new ways of working

Agile & systemic
Incremental
Experimental
Durable
Integrated

Agile development is a well-established practice with many organizations and a well-recognized modern practice. Challenges concerning agile development are often visible when agile investments or decisions conflict with rather conventional and non-agile governance structures, processes, and business planning. Ideally, organizations should implement agile development, not just IT development and fusion teams. Organizations that apply agile development may also appreciate more systemic thinking and acting. They will impose incremental changes not just in their development processes but may shift their entire transformation into a systemic approach, eliminating complexity through continual decision-making and prioritizations driven by a common sense of urgency. Incremental development is critical for agile development practices and introducing foundational product-driven organizations (shift from application to product development). It will allow organizations to make smaller improvements faster, reduce risks, and rapidly learn from failure and success. It will foster a culture of continual problem-solving at the core of the business and with continual development. Such organizations will collaboratively prioritize their development resources and effectively manage maintenance and backlog management.

The experimental approach to digital product development will foster new and innovative thinking. Experimental thinking in digital transformations can help enterprises to test and verify ideas with a more controlled and low-risk approach. It helps to make better-informed decisions about which initiatives to pursue and how to implement them most effectively. It will increase flexibility, focus on critical and high-business-value activities, and foster a culture of innovation and learning within the organization, increasing collaboration and cultural adoption. Organizations must still distinguish and secure long-term planning, where necessary, and not blindly trust experimental approaches to avoid chaos and risk-full misconceptions.

Durable development in digital composable enterprises describes the shift from traditional application development to lasting, resilient, dynamic digital development. Learning organizations and teams guide and encourage the elimination of risks through more sustainable patterns based on those principles. During development, the modular design of digital assets/services increases reusability and secures stability in deployment and orchestration.

The risks of traditional fragmentation are eliminated by seamlessly integrating enterprises and utilizing enterprise-wide platforms. By adopting composable architectures, businesses can evolve advanced hybrid enterprise integration capabilities at the core of their technology and business transformations.

PERFORMANCE: Embrace and realize the core capabilities of high-performing organizations

Leadership
Autonomy
Accountability
Trust
Risk-tolerance

Leadership in digital transformations is shifting radically, requiring a more comprehensive and systemic approach to leadership. With the wrong leadership and more traditional thinking and acting, realizing digital composable enterprises might be unachievable. Digital autonomy enables digital transformations by allowing organizations to assume full responsibility, own their digital core, establish digitally savvy leaders everywhere, make data-driven decisions, scale initiatives quickly, drive innovation, and become digitally independent. Leaders must leverage autonomy wherever possible and make teams and individuals more independent (utilizing important things such as speed, time, control, and quality). Organizations that increase their level of autonomy create more qualified and effective preconditions for success. This requires leveraging accountability to empower individuals and teams in more federated and distributed decision-making activities. With greater levels of accountability, organizations foster a culture of high-performing teams. Teams and individuals increase their confidence, relentlessly increase their comfort zones, and start setting ambitious but realistic goals, utilizing the trust they experienced.

Another key criterion is the organization's risk-tolerance ability to effectively understand and manage its definite risk portfolio organizations purposely identify and leverage more relevant risks, make better-balanced risk-based decisions, and leverage complex technologies more sustainably.

CULTURE: Enable organizational adaption, advancement, and cultural development

Tradition
Collaborate
Adapt
People
Skills

Adapting and influencing the tradition of conventional organizations in digital transformations is a long-term process and not a one-time happening. Digital transformations must find incremental ways to engage and involve the organization, mainly through intense cross-functional collaboration and cooperation. They should focus on incremental changes to help the organization understand the benefits and improvements with continual adaptation rather than big-bang change management initiatives. With an increasing focus on people, digital transformations must transform competencies and behaviors with new ownership and levels of engagement. Digital transformations must focus on people as much as they focus on new technologies. With such fundamental changes, organizations must identify when, why, and how to develop, hire, or buy necessary skills. They must redefine those business and IT implications on their workforces across the enterprise.

Digital transformations are not a different approach to composability, as they are instead inevitable and highly dependent on each other. Therefore, the outcome of digital transformations must result in the development of digital composable enterprises! Establishing composable enterprises does require setting a modern architecture based on guiding principles, utilizing new ways of working, establishing high-performing teams, and fostering collaborative cultural change.

Set a composable architecture.

Even digitally mature organizations must consider composability, as their investments into digital technologies might have grown into a new modern and digital but non-composable and non-resilient architecture. Many digital leaders might not be ready and prepared to effectively implement composable capabilities at the core of their digitalization efforts. Those organizations have not been considering Packaged Business Capabilities (PBCs) when designing and implementing their digital architectures. They have not built modular digital capabilities and cannot rapidly respond to changing business requirements. They use APIs but have not considered strong API strategies, ensuring that business functions and processes are encapsulated and designed in interchangeable components.

With well-architected core digital foundational platforms, development teams become product organizations, while they cannot orchestrate those components across their enterprises and secure full interoperability. Very few organizations have reached that level of digital composable maturity, where composability is at the core of everything they do. With enormous efforts and finding invested in agile but traditionally encapsulated software development, organizations may claim that they have built composable applications. They may also claim they leverage composability to support their critical business capabilities, but this is not always true.

Traditional coding does not inherently prevent composable architectures and applications, but there are still difficulties in leveraging coding to meet the requirements of large-scale composability and interoperability. Traditional coding is not as automated and scalable as high-performance enterprise lowcode platforms because design choices and architecture patterns used in coding practices may not prioritize modularity, separation of concerns, and scalability. They are essential for creating composable systems and may never be compromised.

The lack of appropriate abstraction and encapsulation mechanisms in traditional coding concepts can make it difficult to isolate and reuse components in composable architectures compared to digital foundational platforms and enterprise Lowcode development.

Modern software development practices must emphasize modular, reusable components and employ design patterns that promote the separation of concerns and scalability to overcome these limitations. This paradigm shift is possible for future application development but may turn completed development work and code into a new digital legacy. Efforts to rebuild and redesign developed applications to fit with composable design patterns and development frameworks may be enormous. Composable thinking is taking a very different perspective on the same question, but rather trying to encapsulate services into components, which in the case of retail companies, could be encapsulated services such as on-stock, customer orders, embedded into business processes and enabled by applications, integrations, and data.

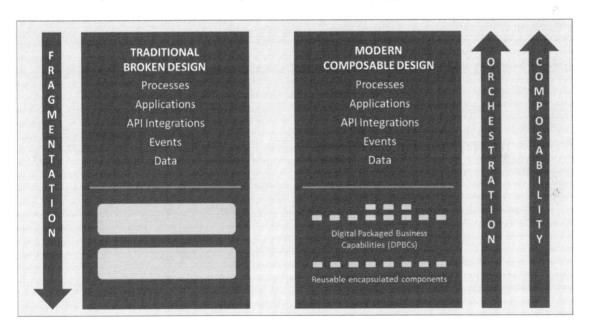

Figure 30 Composability is a bottom-up approach compared to fragmented application-centric design

Reusable encapsulated components designed as loosely coupled services will be necessary to materialize the composable architecture. Packaged business capabilities (PBCs) are created by combining reusable encapsulated capabilities as autonomous components in multiple PBCs.

They interoperate in event-driven and real-time environments and orchestrate into cloud-native digital foundational platforms. They function as loosely coupled services in various products, such as applications and integrations, composed of microservices. On the macro level of composable business processes, relentless integrations will ensure a highly collaborative landscape where IT legacy systems and digital capabilities coexist and overcome the separation between the distinctly different micro and macro levels, operating like interchangeable components. This distinction will not change processes significantly at the surface in the composable world. At the same time, we build the logic bottom-up, not top-down, focusing on achieving interoperability of components and leveraging autonomous operations and applications at an unprecedented scale. Microservices is an architectural style for building scalable, resilient, and maintainable software applications composed of loosely coupled and independently deployable services. This approach allows organizations to package their business capabilities as small, autonomous, self-contained, developed, deployed, and independently managed services.

Microservices deployed in the cloud give enterprises major advantages of the cloud's scalability, reliability, and cost-effectiveness. Cloud providers such as Microsoft Azure, Amazon Web Services (AWS), and Google Cloud Platform and leading enterprise lowcode platforms offer a wide range of services and tools to build, deploy, and manage microservices-based applications in the cloud.

One of the main benefits of deploying microservices in the cloud is that it enables organizations to package their business capabilities quickly and easily as services that can be reused and recombined in different ways. This concept is key to rapidly developing and deploying new applications and services that meet changing business requirements.

By deploying microservices in the cloud, organizations can improve their agility and ability to respond to changing business needs faster and more autonomously. They can scale their services up or down as needed, rebuild applications and processes, and use the cloud's automatic failover and disaster recovery capabilities to ensure their services remain available even during failures or outages.

Microservices and the cloud are a powerful combination that can help enterprises package their business capabilities in unprecedented flexible, scalable ways. This architecture enables them to respond quickly and easily to changing business requirements and deliver new applications and services.

Applied Technology Leadership
Ingo Paas, CIO & CDO Green Cargo

"At Green Cargo, we had no choice but to find new ways of establishing a very different and unproven concept of new digital development starting in late 2020. The overall ambition was to integrate our archaic and complex IT legacy with a new digital platform-enabled digital foundation exclusively in the cloud. Our strategy was to evolve gradually but deliberately. We built a highly integrated architecture with digital foundational platforms in the cloud, realizing full interoperability between our IT legacy and digital platforms. Thinking composable was a natural response, focusing on developing our digital future and IT legacy simultaneously from the core of our business. We designed an architecture around modular, reusable encapsulated components as packaged business capabilities, which we fully applied in Green Cargos digital composable architectural design. By implementing reusable encapsulated components (loosely coupled services) in our digital foundational platform architecture, we implemented composability as a concept for everything. We did this based on the realization of loosely coupled and autonomous services for applications development embedded and instituted in Green Cargos:

- lowcode enterprise application development platform from OutSystems,
- hybrid enterprise API-centric integration platform from Microsoft, and
- analytics platforms from Microsoft and Google.

At Green Cargo, we have realized composability by simplifying our digital design of digitally packaged business capabilities and logic to utilize our digital foundational platform strategy. Our utilization of the world's leading enterprise lowcode platform from OutSystems and our Microsoft Azure Hybrid Integration platform represents the core of our distinctive and effective composable architecture in production."

Written by Ingo Paas, CIO & CDO Green Cargo

A composable implementation refers to the ability to architecting all concerned IT stacks within the organization into seamlessly integrated and interoperable components, including at least applications, data, and API integrations. Composable implementations must address the ability of organizations to operate their digital composable core exclusively in the cloud (see also chapter five). Those digital foundational platforms can utilize advanced API integration services by securing enterprise-wide interoperability between the existing IT legacy and the enterprise's new digital core.

Enterprises successfully implementing composable architectures can apply distinct enterprise-wide principles across different systems, platforms, and technologies, securing full interoperability of new and existing components. Their composable efforts all support transforming the business long-term by organizing business capabilities in a more composable and autonomous way.

Composable enterprises must establish processes and teams that embrace the highest possible degrees of flexibility through relentless utilization of thinking small and practicing modular. They will evolve around composable thinking, while their digital and IT legacy capabilities will, over time, be organized around autonomous business teams, owning digital enterprise products (applications) developed in lowcode, analytics core models designed and managed in the analytics platform in the cloud.

Examples of ownership are cloud-native applications, core data models, algorithms, or the ownership of a set of customer-facing digital capabilities, including e-commerce platforms or customer portals with embedded REST APIs. It is a valuable option to transform major ERP and IT legacy systems over time, applying the core principles of digital composable transformations.

They are utilizing existing assets and are relentlessly developing new capabilities, seamlessly integrating, and orchestrating their modular digital capabilities, without reinventing and rebuilding their existing IT systems, services, and processes. With the ever-increasing complexity and the introduction of new platforms, technologies, and applications, adopters of composable businesses realize full-scale interoperability between their IT legacy, new digital technologies, and connected digital ecosystems (including their customers).

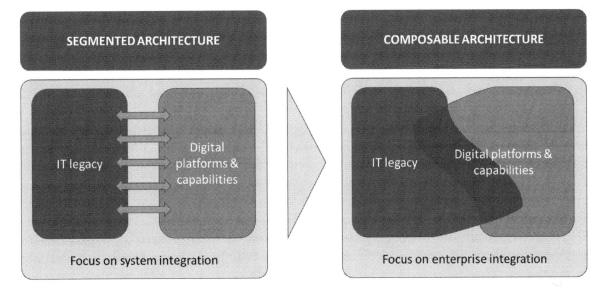

Figure 31 Segmented versus composable architecture

The terminology composable means modularity and expresses the ability of modular components (such as loosely coupled services) that effectively and unconstrainedly interact. They are fully autonomous and orchestrated in the digital foundational platforms at the core of digital composable enterprises. This composable architecture in traditional organizations will enable IT legacy systems to integrate with digital composable architecture fully. By utilizing enterprise-wide API integrations, the digital composable architecture will be securing unlimited collaboration and orchestration capabilities, connecting the individual components of:

- **IT legacy systems**
  Those systems tend to have a low degree of composability. Major investments are required to rebuild the systems architecture from monolithic to microservice design.
- **Digital assets (apps, data models, data objects, APIs, algorithms)**
  If developed and managed on digital foundational platforms, those digital assets secure the highest possible levels of enterprise composability if critical principles are defined and utilized in distinct and stringent ways.

- **PaaS (Platform as a Service) platforms**

  PaaS plays a key role in enabling digital composability. Those platforms allow modular, scalable, and reusable development, enabling businesses supported by those modular building blocks (loosely coupled services) to assemble and deploy enterprise applications and other digital assets.

- **SaaS (Software as a service) applications**

  SaaS applications cause problems with enterprise composability because they have proprietary data formats and APIs, making integrating them with other systems and applications difficult. This cloud service can limit digital interoperability with inflexible data and functional silos. They may lead to decreased flexibility and secure compatibility (vendor updates) typically maintained and updated independently by vendors, leading to compatibility issues with other systems.

Composable strategies utilizing those digital foundational capabilities to foster a collaborative culture involving all disciplines, skills, and parts of the organization, embracing and implementing composable thinking. Successful organizations engage and enable business and tech teams to collaborate effectively, diminishing the boundaries while clarifying new roles and responsibilities. Those collaborative teams focus on constant improvements, constantly learning from each other while incrementally, experimentally, and continually solving business problems that potentially were unresolvable before.

This approach to collaborative development is possible as organizations prioritize composable design, perfectly integrating their technologies across the enterprise, utilizing data, and rewriting business logic more effectively and sustainably. They embrace composable business building blocks and principles, leverage their digital investments more effectively, and consistently improve their daily business and operations.

Applying a distinct conceptual composability framework, especially within complex traditional enterprises, significantly affects business value, relevance, and responsiveness in digital transformations. Experts recommend that organizations adopt a composable architecture and embrace evolutionary approaches to execute their strategies effectively.

Implement composable processes

Organizations must establish composable digital processes to respond quickly and efficiently to changing business needs. Composable processes involve breaking down complex processes into smaller, modular components or services. Composable processes allow organizations to quickly adapt to new market opportunities, changing customer demands, and emerging technologies.

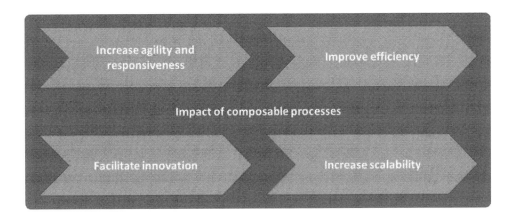

Figure 32 Implications of composable business processes

By having composable digital processes, organizations can:

- **Increase agility and responsiveness**

  Modular and reusable components create new processes and services, allowing the organization to respond more rapidly to changing business needs.

- **Improve efficiency**

  Composable processes can help organizations streamline and automate their operations, reducing manual intervention and improving efficiency.

- **Facilitate innovation**

  Composable processes can make it easier for organizations to experiment with new technologies and ideas, to help drive innovation and competitiveness.

- **Increase scalability**

  Modular and reusable components can be scaled up or down as needed, allowing organizations to manage their resources agile and dynamically and respond to change business needs more effectively.

Composable processes can be supported by digital foundational technologies, such as cloud computing and lowcode development, to enable organizations to take full advantage of these technology's benefits. This will allow organizations to become more agile and efficient, respond to market changes, improve customer engagement, and drive innovation.

Processes and business capabilities are related but distinct different concepts. Processes are tasks or activities carried out in a specific and repeatable way to achieve defined goals. Business capabilities are the skills, knowledge, technologies, and resources a company possesses or can access. Business capabilities often consider "what" a business can do, whereas processes are "how" a business performs activities. One business capability may encompass multiple processes and involve cross-functional teams, technologies, and other resources. Packaged business capabilities (PBCs) enable composable processes by providing a set of pre-built, modular, and reusable logical business objects. In digital composable enterprises, those logically packaged business capabilities are built as modular digitally enabled elements on the enterprise's digital foundational platforms. Digital packaged business capabilities (DPBCs) are digital modular building blocks for dynamic reconfiguration to create new processes or services quickly and efficiently without starting from scratch.

By using packaged business capabilities, organizations can:

- **Increase resilience**

  Packaged business capabilities can easily be changed and reconfigured, allowing faster adaption to change business needs as they significantly increase digital business agility and resilience. Their role is essential in digital composable transformations and is critical in building digital resilience in composable enterprises.

- **Rapid development**

  Packaged capabilities provide a starting point to build new processes, reducing the time and effort required to develop new processes from scratch. New digital development will ideally lead to new packaged business capabilities for reusing and scaling.

- **Improve quality**

  Packaged capabilities are typical autonomous entities or objects that repeatedly guarantee the same outputs with the same quality to ensure that processes perform effectively and meet the business requirements.

- **Increase consistency**

  Packaged capabilities can be used across different business units and functions and help to ensure consistency and alignment across the organization. By applying foundational principles, developers can satisfy new demands faster, more consistently, and rapidly.

- **Reduced costs and speed**

  Packaged capabilities can help reduce the costs of developing new processes by reusing existing components and services. The efficiency gains of shifting development towards packaged business capabilities bring major advantages to any developer teams, especially if they utilize enterprise lowcode platforms.

They allow organizations to create new processes quickly, efficiently, and consistently, making it easier to adapt to change business needs, improve customer engagement, and accelerate innovation from the core of their business. Organizations can quickly and easily assemble new business capabilities, processes, and products to leverage pre-built, reusable components. Reassembling business capabilities makes it easier for organizations to respond to changing business needs and adapt to new market opportunities.

Additionally, it allows for faster time to market, improved scalability, and better management of digital assets. Such abilities can enable organizations to be more competitive in the digital economy.

Packaged business capabilities enable composable processes with important capabilities, such as:

- **Reusability**

  Packaged business capabilities can be reused across different business scenarios, reducing the need to build new processes from scratch each time a new need arises.

- **Standardization**

  Developers can create packaged business capabilities that comply with industry standards and best practices, promote consistency, and reduce the need for customization.

- **Ease of integration**

  Packaged business capabilities can easily integrate with other technologies and systems, reducing the time and effort required to implement new processes.

- **Scalability**

  Packaged business capabilities can be easily scaled up or down to meet changing business needs, improving the organization's ability to respond to changes or rapidly test new features.

By using digitally packaged business capabilities, organizations can create new business processes and services more easily and efficiently, allowing them to respond more quickly to changing business needs, improve efficiency, and drive innovation.

The objective of achieving composability can guide digital evolutionary transformations by applying a flexible and adaptable approach to implementing and managing digitally inspired change. Organizations can more easily adapt to new opportunities by breaking down complex processes into smaller, modular components or services that they can assemble easily and configure to create new business capabilities, processes, and products. They can adapt to changing customer demands and emerging technologies, utilizing their architectural foundation with a modular design and the ability to augment and embed new technologies. They allow incremental changes to existing processes and systems rather than requiring a complete overhaul, making it easier for organizations to embrace digital transformation without disrupting their operations. Organizations can easily reconfigure composable processes and services to adapt to changing business needs, making them more agile and responsive to market changes.

As cloud-native-designed digital packaged business capabilities originate from digital foundational platforms, process composability can simplify and accelerate experimentation with new technologies and ideas to drive innovation and competitiveness. Organizations that apply composable thinking can fully take advantage of the benefits of digital foundational platforms and technologies.

Overall, composability can help organizations evolve their digital capabilities, allowing them to continuously adapt and improve their digital initiatives rather than undertaking a large-scale, disruptive transformation.

Realize an evolutionary strategy

A revolutionary strategy is fundamentally different from an evolutionary one, which instead is securing a more consistent, controlled, incremental, experimental, and systemic approach to strategy execution. In the case of IT legacy systems, an evolutionary strategy would impose a gradual and modular approach to managing the risks caused by old technologies, operating systems, and risk-full IT legacies.

The main difference between the evolutionary and revolutionary development of complex systems is the pace and degree of change, while evolutionary development is a gradual and incremental change process. In evolutionary development, small improvements are made over time to existing systems while new systems can be added and integrated. Evolutionary approaches optimize and refine current systems for continual improvements and are adaptable to changing circumstances. In contrast, revolutionary development is a more rapid and disruptive process, where change might impact entire systems or create major new ones to create radical innovations. These changes are typically driven by breakthrough technologies, new business models, or societal shifts. As both have advantages and disadvantages, evolutionary change comes with lower risks and continual improvements, while revolutionary change can offer significant benefits with higher risks and greater challenges to achieve results.

"By applying the principles and theory of ambidexterity approaches, a combination of evolutionary and revolutionary change should be the favored choice for most enterprises."

Ingo Paas

An evolutionary strategy would imply applying enhancements to existing systems, making those more agile and ready for interoperability in line with business priorities, needs, resources, and funding. The biggest concern for most CIOs is balancing increasing risks, costs, and overall complexity. In addition, IT legacy systems may have considerable implications on the ability to change business processes, a typical dilemma that most CIOs must deal with. Another specific consequence of evolutionary strategies is a much lower dependency on detailed long-term planning, as incremental planning still requires planning but on a much higher level.

At the same time, complex IT legacy systems require more strategic responses and planning. Those systems often come with major inconsistencies, problems with interoperability, and multifaceted dependencies (such as new digital technologies, complex integrations, distributed and inconsistent business logic, related projects, traditional vendors, and non-tech-savvy boards and owners). Those challenges cause additional and often significant risks, while digital transformations are ranked high on most CEOs' lists of priorities.

Business and IT executives consider their IT legacies costly, complex, hindering, and inflexible while underestimating the immense value and investments they have made over the years. Those investments are especially relevant, as IT legacy systems effectively operate and facilitate core business processes in reliable and controlled daily operations while they contain huge amounts of historical data. Although the IT legacy is the backbone of massive transactions and complex "often hard coded" business logic, organizations are most likely not utilizing and leveraging data to the extent they essentially could be doing. Effectively adapting, integrating, and embedding their IT legacy in the context of digital transformations is becoming exceptionally critical for organizations promoting digital transformations.

Encouraging long-term life-cycle-management strategies, rather than replacing IT legacy systems, keeps CIOs awake at night. In their desperate attempts to find new ways to utilize and leverage the value of their IT legacy systems, they are either replacing or reinvesting into their IT legacy systems. Supporting digital transformations requires smart investments to modernize the IT legacy systems, increase responsiveness to urgent business demand, including the organizations' ability to mitigate risks, advance existing business processes, and smoothly bridge the gap between traditional IT legacy and new digital technologies.

Embracing the value of the IT legacy in combination with digital composable transformations requires superior composability in the architectural design aligned with the organization's business priorities, which all stakeholders can support and consent with.

The alignment of processes, planning of prolonged maintenance periods, cost reductions, maintaining critical skills, optimizing vendor support, and lifting processes, such as increasing development, test, and release management frequencies, are critical in supporting and enabling rapid digital developments and deployments.

Effective digital composable transformations demand essential alignment on agile development capabilities in the most critical IT legacy systems, enabling the design and development of embedded and integrated digital enterprise applications. Developing composable architecture, including its integrations, is essential in complex and traditional business environments. Development teams in agile transformations must increase their collaboration with DevOps teams to leverage the number of releases per year significantly. Without such changes, enterprise application development might become a major constraint.

Evolutionary strategies could demand prioritization of focused activities in legacy systems (such as mainframes), including important considerations to:

- Revitalize expert level and skills,

- Regain control over data, processes, databases, and tables,

- Modernize and secure integrations for real-time and event-driven digital interactions,

- Decrease unused and poor code, applications, and processes,

- Build dedicated business processes outside their core systems (enterprise Low-code),

- Simplify the maintenance, development, and decommissioning of IT legacy systems,

- Implement agile methods in legacy systems (based on demand and viabilities),

- Modernize the end-user interface and experience,

- Improve performance, stability, incident management, and disaster recovery capabilities,

- Re-invest in underlying infrastructure or modernizing operating platforms in the cloud,

- Improve integrations and batch processing,

- Improve and scale release and change management processes to increase flexibility.

- Secure compliance, and controls, with necessary authorizations plus access rights,

- Support agile system development, testing, and deployment capabilities in critical IT legacy environments,

- Establish full governance and system controls, monitoring, and maintenance.

Those activities prolong systems life-cycle management and minimize risks while making the IT legacy more digitally ready for more responsive digital development. They should include more agile development processes, frequent releases, and smaller incremental changes while reducing business risks and incidents.

"Enterprises shall <u>AVOID</u> investing in a complete or major overhaul of the existing IT legacy but identify which systems are essential for agile development and digital modernization efforts."

Ingo Paas

Organizations choosing an evolutionary approach to their transformations will recognize new opportunities in mitigating existing and future risks while modernizing their IT legacy environments and processes. They rapidly respond to business needs and digital application development while delivering incremental value.

Highly complex IT legacy environments are not necessarily requiring complex transformational and revolutionary investments and programs. They rather require a clear and renewed understanding of how the IT legacy systems can support the complex attempts to realize digitalization and composability of the enterprises. CxOs need to discuss and agree on the limitations of evolutionary strategies with key business stakeholders, making them aware of potential future restrictions and limitations.

Hidden and insufficiently designed business processes with ungoverned business logic built into existing IT legacy integrations are typical examples of organizations gaining significant benefits from new digital foundational platforms in modernizing and risk-mitigating their IT legacy systems.

Enterprise Low-Code platforms and modern API enterprise hybrid integration platforms can reduce business and technology complexity by rebuilding functionality and simplifying IT legacy systems (such as mainframes or ERP systems) while incrementally shifting critical functionality into the cloud. Digital foundational platforms empower and change traditional IT organizations' responsiveness and development abilities, developing digital and modular business applications at an unprecedented scale. By utilizing those new capabilities, enterprises will minimize dependencies, streamline processes, and simplify a more incremental consolidation and modernization of their existing IT legacy systems.

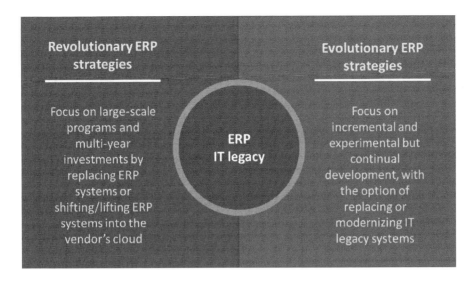

Figure 33 Evolutionary versus evolutionary ERP strategies

By applying this approach, organizations may embrace new ways of solving complex business problems by simplifying their IT legacy. They may become inspired by developing data-driven capabilities and finding modern solutions that integrate and orchestrate their data while developing event-driven and real-time modular digital applications to integrate with their IT legacy systems.

Successful CxOs and IT organizations are shifting their momentum towards evolutionary improvements rather than investing in large, ineffective, costly, and risk-full legacy multi-year programs or projects.

Developing composable architectures while seamlessly integrating the IT legacy and new digital capabilities will be critical for traditional organizations moving forward in their digital transformations. However, IT must be capable of effectively mitigating and responding to IT legacy risks by leveraging unmatched ERP services during their multi-year transitions.

Leverage unmatched ERP services

Leveraging digital transformations requires reconsidering large-scale ERP systems' purpose, value, strategic fit, and maintenance costs. Those costs are challenging CIOs and their IT budgets; they likewise need greater attention, as IT legacy systems usually include one, if not more complex, and outdated ERP systems.

Integrating and maintaining those systems during digital transformations requires special competencies and skills. As operating costs with significant maintenance fees also are considerably high, and major investments are needed, CIOs must leverage and upgrade older ERP systems. Nearly all organizations are about to make complex and very strategic decisions about their ERP installations' mid- and long-term future.

Most ERP systems and releases support business requirements in relatively stable, robust, and customized environments. Software vendors set those important assets and major investments under pressure, actively promoting the shift from traditional on-premises (data center) installations into their new and modern cloud environments. Those cloud transformations of existing ERP systems escalated and emphasized by most ERP vendors require new strategies involving long-term commitment to ERP vendors (such as SAP and Oracle), as much as they are demanding major investments from their clients. Initial investments concerning necessary modernizations are the first step and are usually followed by difficult transformations into the vendors' cloud environments, even though many vendors are promoting and offering comprehensive and state-of-the-art cloud environments.

CIOs increasingly establish alliances with third-party support partners to run and maintain their ERP platforms in searching for new options. Third-party vendors are extending the ERP life cycle and maximizing the value of current ERP and database software releases, allowing for further utilization of those investments. They are helping protect the stability, reliability, and security of ERP investments while they reduce ERP maintenance costs. Business cases are promising and realistic, offering great savings compared to maintenance costs from traditional software vendors.

As many organizations are reconsidering their dependencies on major ERP vendors, they are becoming uncertain about their long-term strategic ERP investments and unavoidable vendor commitments. In times when ERP costs are still a major part of most IT budgets, CIOs struggle to rapidly adapt to new and business development demands in their ERP systems. Keeping those systems up to date and maintaining appropriate Service Level Agreements while constantly keeping track of security upgrades, patches, and other critical maintenance activities is a major and costly undertaking. Consequently, CIOs are searching for alternatives to reduce costs associated with maintaining their ERP systems while keeping the same service levels and constantly leveraging innovation.

They offer those services by maintaining current systems for 15 years or more at significant annual support savings. With support from leading third-party maintenance vendors, CIOs may maintain their systems at lower costs, while such contracts significantly extend the lifespan of ERP systems. They are minimizing the criticality of ERP cloud transformations, offering CIOs alternative ways of financing their digital transformations through ERP cost reductions while driving revenue and growth initiatives. At the same time, they are avoiding major investments into major replacement or cloud transition programs.

Third-party vendors, such as Rimini Street, are helping keep ERP systems flexible and maintainable by constantly monitoring and acting upon critical components, such as obsolescence, operating-system compatibility, vendor certifications, hardware upgrades, and more, solving ERP-related technology challenges, including compatibility, migration, security, and integration, across operating systems, databases, middleware, browsers, integrations, even including cloud-based applications.

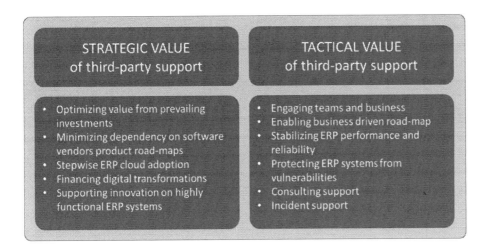

Figure 34 Value of third-party ERP support

Overall predictions indicate significant growth of ERP investments in the years to come. Oracle Netsuite predicts that most organizations are planning to transform their business processes, moving their ERP systems into the cloud, even though they may be struggling with funding and the approval of running such complicated, as well as time and resource-intensive multi-year programs. Research by Statista.com indicates that ERP in the cloud will grow by 13.6% annually and reach $40.5 billion by 2025.

Moving ERP systems into the cloud and retiring older generations of ERP suites while enterprises increasingly prioritize delivering business capabilities over replacing their entire ERP platforms is a complex undertaking, usually managed as large-scale programs.

DOMAINS	BENEFITS OF THIRD-PARTY VENDORS (such as Rimini Street)
Incremental ERP transformation	• They enable customers to continue running their ERP platforms for several years on-premise, prolonging the life-cycle of ERP systems to allow ERP system migration into new modular digital ERP cloud platforms-
Cost savings	• Offer their services at a lower cost than the original ERP vendor, enabling large cost savings for businesses.
Customization and flexibility	• Provide more flexibility and customization options than the original ERP vendor, allowing businesses to tailor their ERP systems to their specific needs and processes.
Support and maintenance	• Provide high-quality support and maintenance services, helping businesses ensure their ERP systems run smoothly and efficiently, reducing downtime and improving system performance.
Access to expertise	• Have specialized expertise in certain areas, such as software development or database management, providing access to expertise and skills, leading to better system performance and outcomes.
Risk mitigation	• Help to reduce reliance on a single vendor to mitigate the risk of vendor lock-in or other issues, providing businesses with greater flexibility and control over their ERP system.

Figure 35 Benefits of third-party ERP vendors

New choices are opening up for incremental ERP transformations, where enterprises only need support to maintain their ERP legacy to transform into the cloud. If time is not a constraint, enterprises may replace ERP systems incrementally. Instead of large-scale programs, they can deconstruct their ERP systems with selected cloud-based services in line with business priorities, risks, and road maps.

By selecting multi-cloud and multi-vendor ERP solutions (if feasible), enterprises are making significant progress in replacing parts rather than pursuing big-band implementations.

Applied Technology Leadership
Ingo Paas, CIO & CDO Green Cargo

"At Green Cargo, we are using third-vendor support for our SAP System maintenance and critical to secure operating-system compatibility, vendor certifications, and hardware upgrades. Rimini Street helps Green Cargo to solve ERP-related technology challenges, including compatibility, migration, security, and integration across operating systems, databases, middleware, and browser compatibility. We have significantly reduced ERP maintenance costs while guaranteeing extended life-cycle management support to secure operations, Performance, and security reliability. This strategy is also helping us to migrate ERP functionality towards our future Microsoft Dynamics platform, avoiding complex and major ERP programs and transitioning to SAP S/4HANA. Our migration will follow similar principles, with incremental replacement of SAP modules and stepwise migration towards Dynamics and complementary best-of-breed SaaS solution, when required.

Our cost savings are vital for financing our digital transformation, while Rimini Street is helping us reduce major risks and compliance problems. By trusting Rimini Street to maintain agreed service levels, we can shift our focus away from ERP towards rapid digital transformation and implementation of our composable architecture. We are also seeing greater transparency in costs and future cost savings, driven by the modular replacement of current SAP modules, where our costs with Rimini Street are scalable and will be adjusted when applicable, and the number of users starts to diminish.

We trust SAP as a software suite but cannot afford to rebuild, transform, and migrate into the vendor's cloud.

With our confidence in having the right partner with Rimini Street to secure the SAP ERP life-cycle management, we plan to migrate away from our SAP ERP system in the coming years. We trust Rimini Street to help us during this migration, eliminating technical risks and reducing costs in line with the initial business case."

Written by Ingo Paas, CIO & CDO Green Cargo

As the variety of services of third-party support vendors is considerable, this market has great potential. They include various services, from SAP to Oracle, to allow their clients to continue to optimize, evolve and transform their enterprise applications while keeping them highly secure. By effectively utilizing costs and constrained resources, CIOs should embrace the future differently, prioritize composable architectures opportunities, and seek comprehensive strategies to invest in digital foundational platforms.

Consider digital ERP platform strategies

Replacing enterprise IT legacy systems is complicated and expensive. It frequently leads to unfortunate investments, resource-intensive programs with long-term implications for the business, and complex changes driven by extensive change programs. As the competition of cloud-based ERP platforms is accelerating, organizations are making strategic vendor decisions that significantly influence their long-term business and IT strategies. The future of ERP is in the cloud, as organizations are applying cloud-based platform strategies to replace or migrate their legacy IT systems. Modern cloud-based ERP platforms offer new strategic choices significantly varying from traditional on-premise ERP systems.

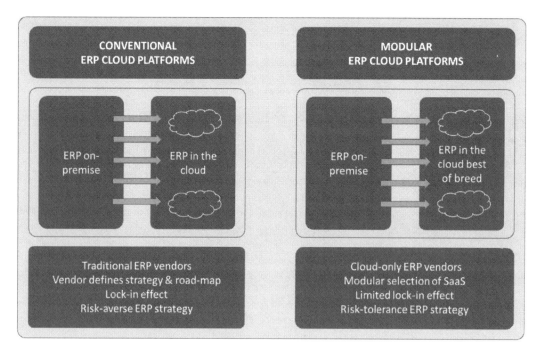

Figure 36 Comparison of two distinct different cloud ERP strategies

CIOs understand that selecting a cloud ERP vendor is a crucial strategic decision directly affecting an organization's operations and bottom line. Moreover, it significantly impacts the organization's capability to balance long-term strategic goals with the pressing need to establish enterprise-wide digital resilience. Vendor choices include substantial investments and costs for organizations, typically involving long-term commitments and substantial total ownership costs.

Comparing ERP vendors is a highly individual and complex case-by-case enterprise-specific process. But making such strategic choices requires fully understanding and considering both opportunities and risks to secure strategic and maximum scalable digital composability on the enterprise level. Enterprises may unintentionally make uninformed and ineffective strategic choices if they do not consider important requirements and strategic demands on future ERP platforms (see Chapter 7, Evolve composable ERP in the Cloud).

SaaS services for noncompetitive business processes will bring integrated digital capabilities like CRM, HR, Finance, Controlling, and more. Other differentiating and more competitive processes might benefit from selective best-of-breed SaaS services, supporting industry-specific capabilities and demands. While standardized API integration features almost disqualify criteria, even if SaaS services promise industry-specific advantages and have richer functionality.

Future ERP strategies are flexible collections of individual SaaS services, accelerating and utilizing extended collaborative opportunities. In addition, more intelligent and AI-enabled capabilities will support decision-making, predefined analytics/reports, integrations, and cross-functional connectivity. SaaS applications can easily be integrated and connected compared to traditionally siloed systems. With CRM as an example (exemplifying on Microsoft Dynamics Sales), sales teams are receiving a fully integrated system, with inbuild analytics, reporting available and changeable on demand, communication, and collaboration (emails, meetings, chats, conferencing, file sharing, ...) will all be embedded. Intelligent AI capabilities help organize contacts, collaboration, negotiations, sales activities, and decision-making processes.

Vertical attempts from specialized vendors (logistics, e-commerce, order industry-specific management are simplifying the introduction of new SaaS-based applications, applying templates, and utilizing standards rather than reinventing the wheel. Users embrace digital transformations in their daily work by utilizing platform-based SaaS applications on platforms complemented with best-of-breed solutions.

Applied Technology Leadership

Peter Marcusson, Business Enterprise Architect, Green Cargo; Consultant IzeoTech

"Green Cargo, as many companies today, is struggling with an aging monolithic ERP system and a wide cluster of complex applications. In addition, two very old mainframe systems are approaching their end of life for different reasons. The monolithic business system environment has created dependencies and interconnectivity within the system and processes, where significant changes are not appropriate anymore to scale business innovation without constraints.

Our strategy has taken enterprise interoperability to the next level with our digital foundational platform architecture, including seamless enterprise data integration. In this, we have already started building the composable enterprise of the future. Green Cargo is already leveraging and scaling its digital foundational platforms with its IT legacy systems to enable digitally packaged business capabilities.

To further advance our foundational composable architecture and address end-of-life IT legacy risks, we leverage cloud ERP systems (SaaS applications) in a Microsoft-centric strategy. Our business roadmap for migrating towards ERP in the cloud enables the replacement of existing non-satisfying business capabilities from Legacy systems. We started to add new capabilities that the business needs to scale up and to further innovate from the core of our business model. The combination of Microsoft platform services (PaaS) and their cloud software applications (SaaS) creates scalability on the standard business ERP system functions and is the foundation for our already-started digital ERP transformation. In this strategy, we are adding specialized business applications that will enable the drive to propel the company into the future. To achieve this, we continue to leverage and accelerate our digital foundational transformation by further evolving our sophisticated digital platform architecture. Green Cargos' digital cloud ERP transformation will be done in many small steps while securing full interoperability with our digital foundational architecture and in-house build digital applications.

We will selectively add competitive spearhead tools for the business to excel above our competitors with our developed applications and functions and specialized off-the-shelf SaaS systems.

> *We will continue leveraging Green Cargo's digital composable transformation to advance our composable enterprise transformation further. The future IT landscape, including our ERP, will give the business an additional edge to make changes quickly and agile in our future ERP and core IT systems in the cloud."*
>
> *Written by Peter Marcusson, Business Enterprise Architect, Green Cargo (Consultant)*

Establishing digital composable enterprises is complex, while the choices of future cloud ERP platforms are truly significant and of greater strategic importance than decision-makers may consider. The right decision can elevate digital composability and resilience, while an inappropriate decision can significantly limit the enterprise's ability to achieve digital composability for decades.

By understanding and considering those implications, strategic choices are affecting traditional outsourcing strategies and models, including the organization's governance, processes, skills, and levels of accountability.

Key conclusions and takeaways

The key conclusions and takeaways from the chapter "**VALUABLE IT LEGACY**" are:

1. Enterprises must understand the purpose and value of composability in digital composability's four critical building blocks: composable thinking, design, architecture, and technologies.
2. Enterprises must embrace digital composable strategies to address the five essential disciplines to implement digital composable enterprises.
3. Enterprises must embrace new and evolutionary strategies even for their IT legacy, ERP systems, most likely in the cloud.
4. Enterprises must consider whether they believe in lifting/shifting their ERP system into the vendor's cloud or want to increase their autonomy and future composability.
5. Enterprises must embrace evolutionary strategies for their IT legacy while accelerating digital readiness in line with development priorities.
6. Enterprises must reconsider their architectural readiness with ERP transformations to identify alternatives in their choices.
7. Enterprises shall AVOID investing in a complete overhaul of the existing IT legacy but to identify which systems are essential for agile development and digital modernization efforts.
8. Enterprises must find third-party support partners to help maintain expensive and complex ERP systems to reduce costs and refinance their future composable ERP transformations.

FIVE – TRANSFORMATIONAL CLOUD

THOUGHT DIGITAL LEADERSHIP

Daniel Akenine, National CTO, Microsoft

"How old is the cloud? We have learned that big technological shifts take time until they reach a tipping point and become ubiquitous – often they take a decade. One of the reasons is that tech transformation is not only about tech but also about people and organizations transforming and adapting to technology. And people and organizations tend to transform slowly, in smaller steps.

The cloud was born a little more than a decade ago, the result of decades of innovations in hardware, networks, and software platforms. It started as a baby with a couple of simple services, curious and eager to understand the world. It went on to become a child – observing, learning, and adapting to its environment. Cloud then become a teenager, challenging the world with new ideas and perspectives, and today it is in its early twenties. Professional and ready to work.

This is an evolutionary process with incremental and sustainable accomplishments. The cloud is further evolving and growing beyond the conception of traditional thinking. Its transformational capacity is rapidly entering the next phase enabling digital foundational platform strategies at scale. The cloud has proven to be the future engine for innovating enterprises from the core of their business, and its potential is adaptive, scalable, and innovative.

For the next ten years, we will see the cloud growing up, taking on more and more responsibilities and hopefully creating new technological transformations as its children."

Daniel Akenine, National CTO, Microsoft

Embrace a cloud-native future

Cloud services continue growing, which is a common finding when studying market forecasts and reading technology reviews. While the current market dominates by SaaS spending, infrastructure, and platform services are continually rising while other cloud services, such as information and cybersecurity, are still growing fast with lower sales volumes but still high growth rates. With continued significant growth rates, the cloud demonstrates its future potential and impact on enterprises' digital transformations.

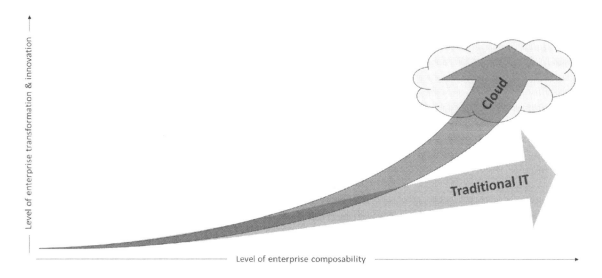

Figure 37 The future f enterprise transformation & innovation is in the cloud

Even though numbers are impressive and show the enormous potential of the cloud, most enterprises do not leverage its maximum potential. Even though an increasing number of organizations see measurable benefits from their cloud investments, the essential value of the cloud to leverage innovation and scale business improvements is not realized to a larger extent by most organizations.

Most cloud investments ignore or disengage the organization from leveraging innovation with cloud services to motivate and enable digitally enabled transformations. They are astonishing, as the cloud offers immense opportunities to encourage innovation based on foundational PaaS (Platform as a Service) technologies and to support digital transformations at an unprecedented scale.

Even though digital development is a key priority within many organizations, there seems to be a great level of uncertainty, ambiguity, and reluctance to build the digital future of organizations entirely in the cloud. Instead, more traditional development and coding dominate most digital development within enterprises.

As global CSPs (Cloud Service Providers) continuously develop, advance, and leverage PaaS services, organizations still observe those developments rather than align their digital initiatives based on those extensive cloud-native offerings. In comparison, cloud-native platforms' immense and rapid expansion enables fundamentally new digital development, even though most organizations only use small-scale elements of those capabilities.

Enterprises unintentionally restrict their innovation potential, disregarding new opportunities with infinite digital cloud-native innovation capacities at the core of their digital transformations. Beyond great features, tools, and technologies, they miss out on a near-limitless scale and elasticity and embrace, cultivate, and industrialize innovation in sustainable and monetizable ways.

Early movers will aggressively pursue and adapt outstanding cloud opportunities to enable state-of-the-art digital transformation innovations by utilizing PaaS capabilities from global CSPs. While most enterprises focus on more traditional cloud services, visionary cloud adapters apply and utilize those new digital capabilities, identifying new opportunities to innovate from the core of their business.

The potential is huge even though most enterprises do not utilize cloud opportunities to enable digital transformations and realize composable enterprises. Those ignored or missed potentials come at a time of increasing competitive pressure on companies and ongoing challenges to find new opportunities and realize their digital transformation while establishing composable enterprises.

PaaS platforms offer substantial foundational innovative capabilities and significantly support organizations in increasing their business resilience to utilize cloud-native platforms. A more aggressive approach to cloud-native adoption and transformation is potential revenue growth and efficiency engines. They might become the future's most solid and infinite basis for digital composable transformations to effectively realize more business value from digital investments. To utilize the cloud and PaaS at the core of digital transformations, innovative enterprises will prioritize those strategies to build their future digital architectures, eventually exclusively in the cloud.

Cloud-only strategies are possible and unavoidable and have proven effective, even in immature enterprises and IT organizations. Open-minded and experimental organizations experience better chances of competing with established and emerging digital players across ecosystems and industries.

Similar to other technology disruptions, the cloud has the potential to reduce barriers to entry into new markets and enable new competitors to scale their business development without large-scale investments and risks. Traditional organizations can embrace cloud platform investments without taking major financial risks and utilize consumption-based subscription models to utilize those services gradually and effectively. With this adaptive approach to financing, the cloud significantly reduces barriers to entry and allows for rapid digital transformation when necessary.

Among all those significant advantages, the cloud is still mainly utilized for moving traditional on-premise infrastructure and software for managing applications and infrastructure into the cloud, driven by the need to increase IT operations efficiencies, with expectations of decreasing operational costs.

Cloud-native superiority is achievable for most organizations to design future digital foundational architectures exclusively in the cloud. Becoming cloud-centric does not come free of charge and will require continued investments and costs.

This chapter about cloud-native supremacy provides additional insights into how organizations can leverage cloud services to drive innovation from the core of their business truly. It does also elaborate on how organizations can realize sustainable and effective benefits.

Applying such design patterns for digital foundational architectures is possible without significant upfront investments. Embracing those opportunities will be possible at low costs and risks but with great enhancements of ongoing or "completed" digital transformations. The capabilities of the cloud are there to enhance utilization and digital development further and better understand opportunities for future growth with infinite cloud capabilities.

Understand cloud capabilities

Deployment models of cloud services vary, considering organizations' individual needs, preconditions, and opportunities. Key selection criteria vary but must consider key concerns, such as compliance, security, risk, legal, internal controls, and accessibility.

Other alternative deployment models include stability, reliability, scalability, security, privacy, data storage, data ownership, and different important abilities. Undergoing significant shifts of services into the cloud may reduce complexity firsthand, while management of services in the cloud does require organizational capabilities and readiness, with new skills, dedicated resources, and appropriate tools and processes.

Enterprises must be capable of effectively managing their cloud services and new processes, such as onboarding, offboarding, maintenance, and effective governance of such services, including cost management, monitoring, decision support for lift-and-shift initiatives (such as software and infrastructure), configuring, and lifecycle-management of cloud services.

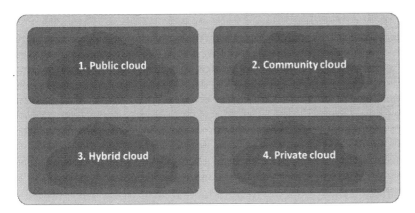

Figure 38 The four most recognized cloud deployment models

The four most recognized deployment models are:

1. **Public cloud**

   The cloud infrastructure is designed, dimensioned, and managed on the provider's premises. The cloud infrastructure provisions for exclusive use by a single provider comprising multiple enterprises. Public cloud has a multi-tenancy concept, where public cloud providers serve numerous customers who share the same infrastructure resources (such as servers, storage, and network devices). Those services are designed for scalability and elasticity, are quickly adjustable to changes in demand, and handle large amounts of data and traffic.

Their pay-per-use pricing models charge customers based on consumption of services (such as computing power, storage, and data transfer), allowing customers to pay only for the resources they use rather than investing in hardware and software upfront.

2. **Community cloud**

The cloud infrastructure provisions for exclusive use by groups of consumers from enterprises with shared concerns (such as mission, security requirements, policy, and compliance considerations). Shared infrastructure: A community cloud is a cloud computing environment where multiple organizations share resources with similar interests and requirements. It provides a collaborative platform for community members to share infrastructure, applications, and data. They include services with advantages such as controlled access for a community that can securely access and shares resources and greater control over data and applications compared to the public cloud while still offering the benefits of cloud computing. It also enables cost-sharing models, which can result in significant cost savings for all members involved.

3. **Hybrid cloud**

The infrastructure is based on individual entities tied together by standardized or proprietary technologies that enable data and application portability (such as load balance between clouds). A hybrid cloud is a concept describing integrating multiple cloud environments, such as public cloud, private cloud, and community cloud, to create a single, seamless environment. This concept provides greater flexibility but requires intense knowledge about multiple cloud environments, which might be more appropriate for large enterprises or enterprises with special compliance or security requirements. This concept provides greater flexibility and agility to respond to changing business requirements.

4. **Private cloud**

Private cloud refers to cloud computing environments dedicated to a single organization and not shared. A private cloud includes the computing resources (such as processing power, storage, and memory) belonging to a single organization. This ensures that the organization has complete control over its dedicated resources as they secure higher security and data privacy. Private clouds are customizable to meet their specific needs by configuring the infrastructure, applications, and security settings, making meeting compliance and regulatory requirements easier. They provide self-service capabilities to allow on-demand access without manual intervention from IT staff.

Different models are available that are constantly undergoing the process of refinement and change. New models are constantly under development, and the following three service models describe the most relevant and prominent models:

- **Software as a Service (SaaS)**

  Applications are highly standardized and ready to use, usually running on the provider's cloud infrastructure or an infrastructure provider to the application provider. The cloud provider manages applications, runtime, middleware, operating systems, virtualization, servers, storage, and networking. The customer (enterprises) does not manage or control the underlying data, processes, or cloud infrastructure, including network, servers, operating systems, storage, or individual application capabilities, except for limited user-specific application configuration settings. SaaS is a highly pre-configured application service usually offered in public cloud solutions.

- **Platform as a Service (PaaS)**

  Paas is a platform-based computing model with a third-party provider that delivers hardware and software tools. With PaaS, users can develop, run, and manage applications without the complexity of building and maintaining the infrastructure typically required for the development. This ability allows for faster development and deployment of applications, as well as scalability and ease of management. Customers usually only manage data and applications. The cloud provider manages runtime, middleware, operating systems, virtualization, servers, storage, and networking. The customer does not manage or control the underlying cloud infrastructure but has control over applications and configuration settings for the application-hosting environment.

- **Infrastructure as a Service (IaaS)**

  Infrastructure as a Service is a cloud model in which a third-party provider delivers virtualized computing resources over the Internet. This service model includes physical and virtual servers, storage, and networking. It allows customers to rent computing resources on-demand without needing upfront hardware investments. Examples of IaaS providers include Amazon Web Services (AWS), Microsoft Azure, and Google Cloud Platform (GCP). The cloud provider manages the systems, virtualization, servers, storage, and networking. The customer has no rights to address the underlying cloud infrastructure but may control operating systems, storage, applications, and possibly limited control of selected networking components (such as hosting firewalls).

Figure 39 Global cloud market according to Markets and Markets (CAGR compound annual growth rate) (Markets and Markets, 2021)

Making better-informed decisions about cloud technologies requires a fundamental understanding of why, how, and when to apply those different models. As CIOs, IT, and business professionals utilize those services, strategies and business-driven digital transformations are rare outcomes of global investments in cloud services.

The cloud does make it possible to provide easy access to applications, processes, transactions, data, and information. With cloud-enabled technologies, enterprises leverage their ability to deliver business services faster, better, and cheaper. They will support critical business processes and may potentially eliminate performance and scalability problems by leveraging cloud services.

The cloud is a new digitalized data center and the future for most enterprises and their digital composable transformations. They will continue and accelerate to establish enterprise digital foundational capabilities, predominantly through stronger utilization of PaaS services as their core provisioning capability to secure infinite innovation and digital composable transformations.

The cloud introduces new business and IT opportunities with technical and operational challenges. The cloud does not come free of charge; it will bring unknown risks and problems and will not only simplify IT operations.

It will, though, increase the level of autonomy of IT organizations and eliminate traditional dependencies in processes, technologies, and vendor relationships. However, enterprises continue to expand their cloud utilization and shape the necessary organization and operational conditions. Enterprises managing increased volumes of cloud services might often reconsider their organizational readiness. They consequently implement new capabilities to address those challenges effectively. The rise of cloud centers of excellence (CCoE) interconnects with access to such capabilities.

Organizations have successfully onboarded and run SaaS (Software as a Service) applications to replace on-premise software appliances with more standardized and pre-packaged solutions. SaaS applications have the full capacity to replace traditional on-premise provisioning of applications that organizations have managed for decades. On-premise systems dominated the software industry for decades, and ERP customers have already invested billions in moving their ERP and other portfolios to the cloud. Software giants such as Oracle, SAP, and Workforce have successfully driven their massive cloud technology-enabled transformations. They have all moved their platforms into the cloud and utilized new ways of providing SaaS ERP services over the Internet. Most of their new applications function as SaaS services without having governed or evaluated the long-term implications, limitations, or restrictions.

As SaaS (Software as a Service) applications are the most utilized cloud services, they provide substantial benefits, such as:

- Shorter ROIs (Return on Investments) with simplified service provisioning,
- Reduced costs for implementation and application maintenance with no upfront investments,
- Controlled costs as organizations only pay for usage and can easily influence costs,
- Simplified technologies with ready-to-use and scalable capabilities without the need to buy licenses and software,
- Modern and simplified integrations (reducing costs and easing enterprise integrations),
- Simplified operations, life-cycle management, and automated system release management,
- Easy to use and perform conceptual verifications with business needs,
- Secured compliance with appropriate policies, rules, and governance (such as data privacy and information security).

Most organizations have a pile of enterprise integrations, data privacy concerns, security issues, and challenges to managing access rights across their IT environments effectively. Key topics such as data ownership, compliance, effective digitalized on- and offboarding processes, and effective controls caused unexpected and new complications. Managing cloud services from different vendors in multi-cloud environments became more difficult than anticipated. Organizations find it difficult to define, evaluate, and decide which applications are most viable to fit the business requirements that SaaS services must support. Exploiting digital superiority in the cloud is a complicated and strategic shift of business capabilities, but undeniably necessary for most, if not all, digital transformations.

Exploit digital superiority in the cloud

Organizations must evaluate their specific needs and goals before investing in cloud services and developing strategies to support their short and long-term needs. Enterprises invest in transformational initiatives to shift and lift their IT applications and infrastructure from data centers into the cloud. Those complex and costly initiatives provide better scalability and elasticity at lower costs, eliminating the need for up-front and long-term infrastructure investments. Shifting large physical data center infrastructure and operations into the cloud is complicated and mainly considered a priority by IT executives to promote and elevate proposed transformations.

After years of intensive investments into those projects, enterprises must consider whether they shall continue prioritizing those major investments, potentially delaying more critical business investments into digital transformations. Organizations consistently underdeliver on their initial promises and business cases, overseeing new investments into skills, processes, and other capabilities (such as Cloud Center of Excellence) and reconsidering a new and eventually thought-provoking different TCO (Total Cost of Ownership). They increase costs for cloud services directly related to the increase of energy costs and more advanced requirements on environmental considerations of cloud service provisioning. Here are risks and opportunities, while IT executives must consider a more holistic perspective on the enterprise's prioritizations, why and when to make those strategic decisions.

From an IT operations perspective, there are clear benefits, such as scalability, manageability, elasticity, security, flexibility, Disaster Recovery, reduced upfront investments, lower costs, and more. Those benefits are usually understood and framed as the organization's cloud strategy to lift and shift the IT systems into the cloud. Although cloud services have developed significantly during the last few years, many IT organizations see the cloud primarily as their new "data center as a service."

There is no simple evaluation and answer to whether those infrastructure projects are right, wrong, effective, or contra-productive. Considering the complexity of digital transformations, the success of these transformations and the future of business will most likely not depend on whether IT applications run in the cloud or a data center. Other considerations are determining how the cloud can initiate and sustain digital transformation based on profound new thinking and acting.

Transformational opportunities to utilize advanced cloud services are potentially coming from digital cloud-native platforms provided by CSPs (Cloud Service Providers, such as Amazon, Microsoft, and Google), promising greater digital transformation potential than traditional strategies. Those digital foundational cloud-native platforms are at the core of digital transformations. The right utilization shall enable digital transformations that further enable transformative outcomes, such as composability and full-scale interoperability.

They combine unlimited innovation power and ready-to-use digital capabilities, are multi-purpose configurable, and adjustable to individual business needs and requirements. They challenge and enlarge business innovation with innovative technologies provided by digital cloud-native platforms. Global platform providers, such as Amazon, Microsoft, and Google, constantly invest in their digital platforms and advance existing ones while constantly adding and evolving new innovative capabilities, such as Microsoft, with the integration of OpenAI into their multiple platforms.

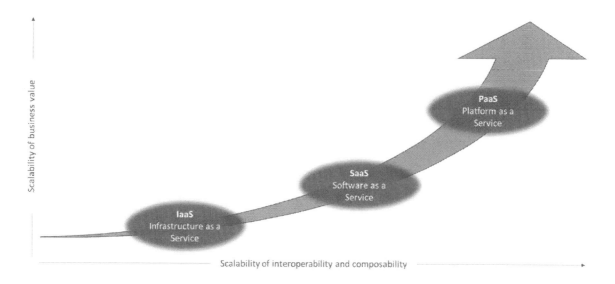

Figure 40 Cloud layers that enable digital transformations

Both scalability of business value and the scalability of interoperability and composability are significantly different when comparing those three different cloud delivery layers shall help to understand better that cloud strategies are highly complex and must be business capability driven. Decision makers shall review their decisions and prioritizations, reflecting on their strategic outcomes and relevance concerning their current strategies and investments in cloud services.

Reinforcing innovation and leveraging interoperability and composability across the enterprise differentiates platform-based cloud strategies from traditional ones. The efforts from standard transformation are widely addressing the shift and lift of data center operations into the cloud. The reality is different, as most enterprises do not utilize cloud platform strategies for their digital transformation.

Utilizing cloud services is a complicated and multi-dimensional undertaking, and cloud-native capabilities offer new ways to outline and implement digital transformations. Enterprises' choices of strategically managing individual cloud services (such as onboarding on their own PaaS in a private cloud versus relying on a vendor-managed private cloud) can significantly optimize cloud-first strategies.

The cloud has never before demonstrated this amount of freedom, choices, and relentless innovation capabilities that only needs to be better balanced and utilized in more cloud-agnostic and cloud-first strategies.

Decision makers can align their cloud decisions with a clear choice of what extent their investments and strategies will support composable transformations (see figure above).

Applied Technology Leadership
Christian Ericsson, Head of Architecture, Green Cargo

"Green Cargo was in a situation where a large-scale investment program to replace the most business-critical legacy systems had failed to get approval. The need for business development was great to try to come to terms with long-term profitability problems in the company.

From a technical standpoint, the need for new technologies and the capabilities to quickly adapt to new business needs was crucial; however, it severely hampers many old legacy systems and technology. We started building a very constraint-based architecture. Instead of driving large-scale investment programs, we built a composable architecture to add new technologies and functionalities to the older legacy systems. To get access to new technologies and new, consumption-based models, we realized a cloud-only strategy, which is the key cornerstone for our composable architecture. We built an integration platform and added a Low Code Platform, a process automation platform, and an analytics platform, all in the cloud. This approach allowed us to add new functionalities and augment the more rigid legacy systems.

Our Cloud Only strategy is crucial in realizing a composable architecture for digitalization and innovation at Green Cargo, and this has enabled us to add functionalities incrementally instead of driving large-scale transformation programs to replace our legacy systems. This approach has also enabled Green Cargo to build organizational capabilities incrementally. We have managed to transform the IT department fully and started delivering new functionalities and digitalization to meet the new business needs of the company.

We have not adapted a traditional lift and shift approach but instead used the cloud to get access to new and improved technologies, innovation, new, more agile ways of working, scalability, as well as creating flexibility in the possibilities of choosing partners to help the company with the cloud journey."

Written by Christian Ericsson, Head of Architecture, Green Cargo

Depending on the choices and preferred cloud adoption, cloud strategies significantly impact the ability to leverage digital composable transformations.

The opportunities how to utilize those platforms will eventually separate digital enterprises from digital composable enterprises, which truly embrace cloud-native platform strategies as the key differentiator for their business-driven digital composable transformations.

Embrace cloud excellence

Organizations that embrace more profound and innovative cloud strategies and architectures must establish new skills, processes, and tools to secure stability, control, and effective deployment of all relevant and self-managed cloud services. They experience more governed and sustainable benefits of cloud implementations than organizations that have not invested in more autonomous approaches to self-govern and self-operate even complex cloud services.

Increased complexity may only arise from insufficient knowledge, the absence of critical operations capabilities, and the inability to take control. The most effective solution to this problem is realizing a Cloud Center of Excellence (CCoE). The CCoE will lead and govern cloud adoption, provide IT and business with dedicated ownership, and realize the enterprise's cloud strategy. The CCoE supports the business in selecting the most valuable cloud services while it provides operational governance and highly effective monitoring and control capabilities.

CCoEs will accelerate the insourcing of traditionally outsourced services for several reasons. They provide better control and governance over outsourced services by centralizing expertise and resources. They ensure that outsourced services meet the organization's requirements. Enterprises will gain increased control and can make insourcing a more attractive option because it allows organizations to have greater oversight and control over service deliveries. Establishing a CCoE will save costs long-term by centralizing expertise and resources and applying economies of scale. They can also help scale up new services effectively and reduce costs, while they might identify areas where services can be optimized, terminated, or consolidated.

Another advantage of CCoEs is the ability to retain knowledge and expertise in-house. A well-functioning CCoE will also give organizations greater agility and flexibility in responding to changing business needs. By centralizing knowledge and resources, CCoEs can more quickly and effectively respond to evolving requirements, making it easier to deliver services in-house. This increased agility and flexibility can make insourcing more attractive because it allows organizations to respond more quickly, increasing autonomy and digital resilience.

The CCoE is a dedicated team or organization, often within IT Operations or architecture, responsible for driving cloud technology adoption and management. The main benefits of having a CCoE include the following:

- **Cloud strategy**

  The cloud strategy defines the enterprise's approach to the cloud and guides strategic decisions about cloud adoption and usage, which the CCoE will support during development, execution, and operations.

- **Adoption of new technologies**

  Adopting new technologies is essential to identify new cloud-based technologies that can help the company achieve its goals and facilitate the adoption of those technologies across the organization. The CCoE will be central in leveraging digital foundational platforms and services on those platforms and onboarding new technologies (such as SaaS).

- **Alignment of business and IT**

  Business and IT can easily align, agree, and execute relevant business goals and priorities to ensure that cloud initiatives align with the company's overall strategy.

- **Enterprise Interoperability**

  Enterprise interoperability assumes responsibility to secure service integration considering the entire cloud service portfolio. The CCoE plays a crucial role in accelerating and ensuring enterprise-wide interoperability by providing a centralized hub of expertise, establishing standards and best practices, providing governance and compliance mechanisms, facilitating collaboration, and providing a scalable framework for implementation.

- **Managed governance**

  Managed governance establishes and secures support, guidelines, policies, and processes for using cloud services, ensuring that the organization uses cloud services securely and promptly. The CCoE is critical in securing cloud governance through policies and procedures, providing expertise and best practices, governance oversight, and collaboration between different teams and departments. By providing a centralized hub of expertise and resources for cloud governance, a CCoE can help organizations use cloud services securely and competently.

- **Cloud operations**

  Cloud operations will guide decision-makers, collaborate with the business, architecture, or Operations teams, and secure knowledge sharing across the enterprise. The CCoE does play a critical role in securing cloud operations by providing expertise and best practices, establishing and enforcing policies and procedures, providing governance oversight, and facilitating collaboration between different teams and departments. As the centralized hub of expertise and resources for managing cloud services, a CCoE can help organizations operate their cloud services securely and effectively.

- **Compliance and security**

  Ensure that the enterprises comply with relevant regulations and industry standards, such as GDPR, and other frameworks, to establish security policies, frameworks, and protocols while continuously monitoring and ensuring compliance.

A well-established CCoE allows enterprises to centralize expertise, knowledge, and collaboration with other critical functions, such as IT Architecture teams. It makes it easier for the enterprise to make strategic decisions about cloud adoption and usage. It does operate at the center of the organization's digital transformation and is a critical capability at the core of digital capabilities.

> ### *Applied Technology Leadership*
> *Andreas Lindmark, Manager CCoE, Green Cargo; Consultant IzeoTech*
>
> *"Green Cargo has been adopting the public cloud to implement our cloud-centric digital transformation with new technical capabilities to support and enable the changed business requirements.*

Our technology landscape combines traditional monolithic systems hosted in a private on-premises data center and modern public cloud Azure Services. The IT organization is also a mix of a traditional IT, DevOps, and CloudOps mindset. Our agile teams are successors for our digital transformation to meet business requirements and scale transformation in the overall cloud-first platform strategy.

This strategy has created the need to establish a Cloud Center of Excellence (CCoE) using standardized frameworks and working methods. Our CloudOps functions as a proactive team, establishing cloud services using Microsoft Cloud Adoption Framework (CAF) that provides a structured path for developing and deploying our composable architecture. The CCoE also performs operations on systems and services with a different life cycle management than our traditional applications.

This is a major leap in Green Cargos' strategy to implement the CCoE because of our desire to increase our level of autonomy, taking full responsibility for owning and managing our critical cloud transformation. With this shift, we are preparing to transition our ERP system into a cloud-only ERP with multiple SaaS (Software as a Service) applications from Microsoft Dynamics. This is a major leap and strategic investment into our digital future.

This requires a mix of roles and functions from the business side and IT to deliver high-quality service with continuous secure system development. Everything is built and deployed as code to automate and optimize the Azure infrastructure, using build and release pipelines with approval flows in Azure DevOps.

The CCoE has been established to govern, support, and leverage our cloud adoption to accelerate and optimize services required to realize Green Cargos' digital foundational platform strategy and centralize key competencies and practices to build secure and re-usable services that are monitored and optimized. In addition, the DevOps culture evolved and implemented cloud technologies to automate business processes, drive innovation, and become cost-effective. The CCoE is a core enabler to advance our journey toward the future composable enterprise."

Written by Andreas Lindmark, Head of Architecture, Green Cargo; Consultant IzeoTech

Cloud operations create, manage, and maintain cloud-specific tasks, such as:

- Manage, plan, operate, and monitor workloads and performance,
- Stabilize functionality of core platforms,
- Improve resiliency and reduce latency,
- Control workload criticality, the effect of interruptions or performance issues,
- Establish cost and performance plans,
- Maintain asset and workload inventory,
- Maintain operational compliance,
- Protect workloads and associated assets,
- Analyze and improve cloud service deliveries,
- Improve costs/performance ratios of workloads aligned with the business.

Implementing a CCoE is an essential step for cloud-centric organizations to achieve substantial agility concerning business and technology. It has the role of coordinating, collaborating, and organizing cloud service management. It does this through intensive collaboration between various domains and roles with dedicated competence, such as cloud adoption (solution architects), cloud strategy (developers, product owners), cloud governance, cloud platforms (owners and developers), as well as cloud automation (cloud engineers and security engineers).

It will also improve quality and KPIs (Key performance indicators), enhancing stability, agility, speed, reliability, performance efficiency, security, maintainability, and user satisfaction. These gains are critical if the enterprise implements large-scale cloud-enabled innovations and digital composable transformations.

Gartner (Gartner, Execute Your Cloud Strategy With a Cloud Center of Excellence, u.d.) has defined the three pillars of a CCoE as governance, brokerage, and community, which are the minimum framework and responsibilities of CCoEs governance.

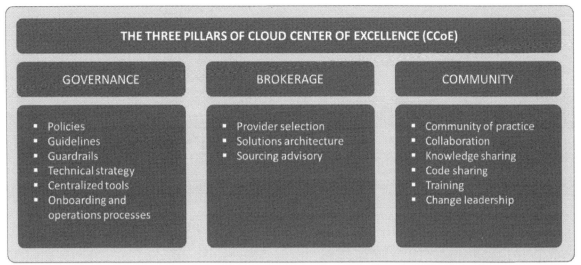

Source: Gartner, How to Deploy a Cloud Center of Excellence (gartner.com)

Figure 41 The three pillars of the Cloud Center of Excellence (CCoE) (Source Gartner)

The CCoE will be a major milestone for IT organizations to accelerate and elevate their cloud strategies, secure strategic alignment, and become trusted partners to the business. When successfully implemented, this function creates a significant shift in the long history of IT. The CCoE is a paradigm shift away from the traditional role of IT concerning standard deliveries of traditional IT and cloud services to assume full accountability for all cloud operations instead. It will accelerate innovation while increasing business agility based on autonomy, accountability, and trust principles.

The CCoE team will accelerate and secure controlled cloud adoption across the enterprise with the right set-up. It is likewise critical to digital transformations to support agile development and ways of working and automate/simplify the deployment of new cloud capabilities. It will define and align cloud services with operational procedures, review and approve changes with cloud-native tools/services and standardize and automate commonly needed digital foundational platform components concerning enterprise cloud service deliveries.

Define effective cloud governance.

Cloud governance can be very helpful in managing digital transformations in the cloud by providing a framework for the planning, deployment & utilization, and ongoing management of cloud-based resources.

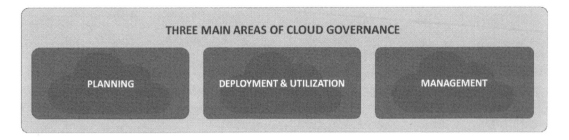

Figure 42 The three main purposes of effective cloud governance

Cloud governance can support digital transformations by ensuring security and compliance through supportive and guiding frameworks to ensure conformity with security and compliance requirements, securing procedures for data protection, access control, and risk management while reducing the risk of security breaches and regulatory violations. It will help to optimize costs by creating visibility into cloud resource usage and enabling cost optimization strategies to avoid overspending through effective utilization. Cloud governance frameworks can help streamline the deployment of cloud services through guidance, standards, skills, and best practices. Collaboration and cooperation across different parts of the organization will improve by establishing clear roles and responsibilities.

Skilled cloud engineers and teams will enhance performance and availability by establishing policies and procedures for monitoring and managing cloud resources while they can help improve user experience and avoid downtime. They will provide procedures and tools for data management, life-cycle management, and other critical capabilities required for large-scale successful cloud adoption. Cloud governance plays a critical role in supporting digital transformations by providing frameworks for managing cloud-based resources and ensuring they are aligned with organizational goals and objectives. Implementing automated governance is part of transforming its central role from fulfilling users' requests to empowering self-service for specialized teams, which demand greater agility to use cloud services with cloud-native tools.

New SaaS applications require distinct support governance for business and IT, with strong tech leadership reinforcing optimized and well-informed decision-making processes and finding the most appropriate ways to govern and utilize cloud computing applications.

Comprehensive cloud governance shall not hinder cloud utilization, as the role of cloud governance is to prevent problems, support decision-makers and projects, improve the utilization of services, and secure required levels of security and compliance.

Cloud governance shall:

- Secure preventative controls to avoid risky actions at their source, while retrospective controls enforce when an audit highlights a compliance issue to remediate in a multi-cloud environment,
- Identify the need to establish own tooling, as well as adopt third-party solutions such as cloud management platforms,
- Create effective and deployable policies to embrace the power of cloud services but to execute this transition with full control and effective risk management,
- Balance agility and autonomy for cloud users with the need to protect the organization,
- Implement cloud governance as a cross-functional approach by including teams from legal, sourcing, compliance, security, HR, operations, business, finance, and control to provide effective support throughout the entire lifecycle,
- Support business autonomy, but enforce policies and appropriate control processes that business owners must perform and comply with, not only in case of violations,
- Determine the best combination of tools that respond to the organization's enforcement strategy, including the cloud platform's native tools, third-party cloud management tools, and custom-developed extensions.

Relentless work and support of all decision-makers and cloud users will secure a more genuine and adaptive approach to the cloud, prevent insufficient decisions, and the introduction of uncontrolled risk levels (such as data ownership and compliance). Therefore, cloud governance aims to enhance data security, manage risk, and enable the smooth selection, introduction, operation, and life-cycle-management of SaaS applications and PaaS platforms. Besides those important goals, cloud governance has another distinct goal supporting decision-makers to make well-informed and superior buy versus build decisions.

Cloud governance shall inform decision-makers on how to make the most optimized decisions when considering new SaaS applications. Governance shall encourage, support, and empower decision-makers rather than drive complexity in solving well-identified business problems. Effective cloud governance avoids issues and informs stakeholders while prioritizing the most important issues to address.

Governance topics may include key domains, such as:

- Information security,
- Data privacy,
- Access rights,
- Data ownership,
- Physical data storage,
- Integration capabilities (APIs),
- Life cycle management,
- Single-sign-on,
- Vendor compliance and company assessment,
- Legal requirements,
- Licensing models,
- Performance and stability,
- Release management,
- Service provisioning.

Successfully utilizing public cloud governance must consider the right balance between self-service enablement and governance. Too much enablement will lead to turmoil, while too much control may lead to obstructive behavior and could become an obstacle to effective utilization, innovation, and integration of cloud adoption. Business-oriented and collaborative governance shall guarantee a more common approach to safer, controlled, robust, and effective usage and consumption of cloud services.

"The future of enterprises is in the cloud, and without digital transformations in the cloud, future technologies or innovations such as AI will not be deployable and scalable."

Ingo Paas

Digital composable enterprises must invest in cloud excellence at the core of their digital composable transformations. Cloud excellence is a critical and foundational capability at the core of every digital composable transformation, and decision-makers better understand, reinforce, and utilize cloud services wherever possible.

Transform any business in the cloud

Leveraging cloud technology is essential for success in today's fast-changing business environment. Companies must move beyond considering the cloud as an optional tool and adopt a cloud-first mindset encompassing all the components necessary for innovation: data, personnel, technology, processes, and partnerships. Enterprises must reconsider the power of the cloud when it comes to business and technology-inspired innovation.

The cloud has enormous, unlocked potential, as most enterprises are not using the cloud for transformative and evolutionary change. They ignore or misunderstand the capacity of the cloud to bring to most businesses across various industries. By utilizing cloud potential, enterprises could unlock enormous value by accelerating innovation to rapidly transform and create responsible and resilient strategies for the future.

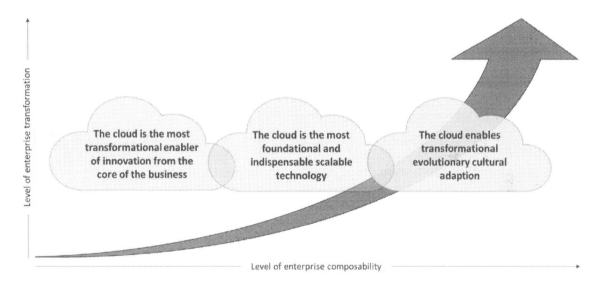

Figure 43 The cloud is the most transformational technology to enable digital composable enterprises

The three most significant value drivers of the cloud are:

1. **The cloud is the most transformational enabler of innovation from the core of the business**
   The cloud is the most profound and underrated foundational technology layer now and in the years to come. The cloud is not an isolated IT technology to be discussed within the IT organization as it must instead position in enterprises' business strategies and the core of the business. Enterprises must rethink their approaches, shape up, and prioritize their strategic goals for cloud adoption.

By leveraging the cloud as a foundational critical business capability, modern business strategies utilize the cloud to foster and encourage a culture of collaborative innovation. With cloud platform services, traditional IT deployment models have changed how IT organizations utilize Software as a Service and Infrastructure as a Service exclusively in the cloud. To utilize the maximum effect of future sustainable business innovation, IT is truly on the brink of challenges. With the cloud at the core of the business model, business innovation does not only come through infinite access to the latest state-of-the-art technologies, such as generative AI and ML. But even more important is the infinite utilization of innovation at the core of the business with unrestricted incremental and experimental development of enterprises, enabled and strengthened by digital foundational platforms from the world's most innovative organizations, such as Microsoft, Google, and Amazon. Boards play a vital role and must reconsider the integration of cloud strategies into business strategies. The full benefits of the cloud are possible when enterprises transform their digital capabilities to be faster, more agile, and more collaborative. This involves fundamental and new evolutionary approaches to support and enable cultural adoption and acceptance of the cloud as a key driver of business strategies.

2. The cloud is the most foundational and indispensable scalable technology

The terminology trusted hyper-scale cloud partners refers to a group of global cloud service providers with the unique ability to offer reliable, secure, and scalable cloud computing services. Hyper-scale cloud providers own a global network of data centers, allowing their customers to access computing resources independent of their location. They have earned their customers' trust by providing high-quality services that can be configured and scaled in line with their customer's needs.

They offer a wider range of cloud-based capabilities, such as infrastructure as a service (IaaS), platform as a service (PaaS), and software as a service (SaaS). Their security, data protection, and strict compliance with regulatory requirements are often far better than what enterprises can guarantee for their digital and IT services deliveries. Again, examples of trusted hyper-scale cloud partners include Amazon Web Services (AWS), Microsoft Azure, Google Cloud, IBM Cloud, and Oracle Cloud.

Their services are foundational and recognized as the most centric technologies at the core of digital transformations, while most enterprises have selected those services individually but not as a critical element of their scalable digital foundational platform strategies.

The traditional argument with scalability mainly addresses enterprises' need to immediately respond and scale up their infrastructure capacity if certain planned or unplanned peaks of service utilization occur. This definition is much too narrowly defined, as the true value of scalability comes from enterprise-wide and integrated platform strategies and well-designed architectures. The misconception of the scalability of cloud services to enhance business strategies, and outperform competitors, is a common issue globally, as hyper-scalers are still delivering the majority of their services on infrastructure and application services.

Enterprises may continue limiting scalability to infrastructure performance while overlooking opportunities with scalable platform technologies.

They lack awareness, as most enterprises may not be fully aware of the capabilities of scalable platform technologies in the cloud. In other cases, they might not fully realize how to leverage these technologies in their digital transformation efforts. Regarding the wider appreciation of risk-averse strategies, enterprises may be hesitant to adopt such technologies and implications, particularly if they have successfully leveraged their infrastructure services in the cloud. This goes hand in hand with skill gaps on all levels of enterprises, from architects to boards. The design and adoption of scalable embedded platform technologies in multi-cloud environments require specific skills and proficiencies, which seem to be restricted in many enterprises.

Consequently, enterprises may not select and try to adopt that comprehensive platform-enabled set of technologies and encourage their organizations to realize the benefits of these platforms collaboratively. CxOs must redefine their perception of those digital foundational platforms, as they ultimately contribute to scale value, not only computing power and transactions. As many CxOs push to deliver rapid ROIs, such investments may be down-prioritized, further ingesting collaborative misunderstanding and poor prioritizations of such strategic investments.

In the world of digital foundational platforms, scalability is about everything, from leveraging existing technologies, integrating new ones, and orchestrating digitally developed assets and products to scaling innovation.

CxOs do this by utilizing infinite opportunities of scalable architectures, enabling, and accelerating a sustainable digital transformation of traditional and digital enterprises into digital composable enterprises. Overall, while there are many benefits to leveraging scalable platform technologies in the cloud, enterprises may still face barriers to adoption.

Enterprises must evaluate these technologies' potential benefits and risks and develop a roadmap for adoption that addresses any challenges they may face. Thanks to cloud democratization, AI/ML knowledge is no longer confined to a select group of data scientists and specialists but is available to a wider audience. Boards should also ask themselves and their CEOs to evaluate whether the right leadership is in place to utilize the power of those technologies in scalable ways and utilize the cloud's potential impact. They must prioritize the cloud and evaluate their long-term enterprise performance on the potential level of the organization's readiness and ability to scale utilization of foundational cloud platform adoption strategies.

3. **The cloud enables transformational evolutionary cultural adaption**

The cloud is more than just a place to manage IT and utilize advanced services to run IT applications, utilize scalable technology environments to effectively scale for high workloads, or shift and lift applications and infrastructure from any data center into the cloud.

With its encouraging digital foundational platforms, the cloud enables unparalleled internal and external collaboration opportunities and incremental and experimental evolutionary change. The cloud includes organizations in collaborative ways of working with highly integrated tools and processes, encouraging, and fostering data and technology-driven organizations.

Digital foundational platforms in the cloud transform enterprise cultures to be more agile in collaborative agile prioritizations, development, and continual innovation. Those platforms provide effective tools and processes to encourage and embed agility to innovate and iterate faster, as cloud opportunities encourage a culture of experimentation and risk tolerance. Those platforms can foster and facilitate collaboration across enterprises, resulting in increased knowledge sharing, improved decision-making, adopting data and technology-enabled continual improvements, and a more cohesive culture.

Those capabilities provide better and more reliable insights into all important business dimensions, from customer to profitability and real-time performance.

These initiatives can help organizations to streamline their processes, reduce costs, improve efficiencies, and continually solve their business problems to scale on those improvements and realize continual but sustainable scalable improvements from the core of the business. They experience digital transformations in action and realize the immediate value of their engagement.

By doing so, organizations continually grow their commitment and trust in those new technologies. They learn and grow as they inspire others and become role models of change.

Enterprises must adopt those technologies without major change management programs as they experience the direct value and impact of those new opportunities for their daily business. Such organizations will encourage innovation by default, as they will realize the power of those platforms, exploring new ways of solving problems and why they are accelerating innovation as an evolutionary element at the core of everything they do. They will develop a more adaptable culture, utilizing the power of flexibility and scalability, coming with those new ways of working and technologies. They will use digital foundational platforms in the cloud, transforming enterprise cultures by fostering agility, collaboration, customer centricity, and digital transformation.

Enterprises must adopt DevOps and everything-as-code upfront as natural ways of thinking to establish foundational blocks for experimentation at scale, making data and insights from data-driven intelligence easily accessible for those who need it so that they can benefit from these resources to compete further and innovate. Enterprises need more data scientists, while the cloud will further democratize artificial capabilities and AI/ML knowledge not exclusively restricted to a siloed group of data scientists and analytics specialists. Businesses must have access to the data and tools they need, turning data into action, decisions, and better insights, finally realizing the data-driven enterprise.

The potential of the cloud is infinite, and the majority of enterprises must refine their perspective to reconsider their strategies and the future potential of the cloud for their enterprises and industries.

Consider the future potential of the cloud

The cloud will continue growing in popularity and importance in the future. Enterprises and individuals will increasingly turn to cloud-based services for innovation, collaboration, computing power, innovation, storage, and other needs. As a result, the demand for cloud-related products and services continues to rise. Artificial Intelligence and Machine Learning will also increase significantly as cloud-first capabilities.

Some predictions include adopting multi-cloud and hybrid-cloud strategies, integrating IoT and edge devices with the cloud, using containers and serverless computing more, and increasing focus on security and compliance. New technologies such as 5G and edge computing drive even more innovation in the cloud. The future of the cloud is promising, and it will increase its fundamental role in innovating modern business and technology.

The cloud is also a core technology for enterprises to reduce their carbon footprint. Cloud service providers invest significantly in energy-efficient data centers, consuming less power and generating fewer emissions than on-premises data centers. Cloud services enable server consolidation and virtualize multiple virtual servers to run on a single physical server. Cloud service providers often use the latest energy-efficient equipment and technologies, such as energy-effective cooling systems. Numerous enterprises can share computing resources and infrastructure. As CSPs promote their efforts, they will further scale and accelerate innovative energy consumption and utilization of green and renewable energy to secure enormous scaling effects across entire industries.

Utilizing the cloud will lead to more responsible and efficient use of resources, improving carbon footprint by reducing energy consumption and carbon dioxide emissions. Selecting a cloud service provider that prioritizes sustainability and has a strong environmental policy is important. Enterprises should also monitor their usage of cloud services to optimize their energy usage and minimize their carbon footprint. The cloud is a key accelerator for enterprises to make a significant impact.

Selected examples of predicted future development further drive utilization of cloud services:

1. **Artificial Intelligence and Machine Learning** will increase in the cloud as organizations look to gain insights from their data and automate processes.
2. **Multi-cloud and hybrid cloud strategies** leverage the strengths of different cloud providers to optimize cost, performance, and security.
3. **Edge computing** will grow in relevance as the volume of data generated by IoT devices grows.
4. **Serverless computing** will become more popular as organizations seek ways to reduce costs and increase agility.
5. **Containers** will become more widely adopted to deploy and manage cloud-native applications.
6. **Security and compliance** will become even more important as organizations move their sensitive data and workloads to the cloud.

7. **The Internet of Things (IoT)** does play a vital role in the future of the cloud, with increasing numbers of devices connected to the internet generating data in the cloud.

8. **Blockchain** integrates into the cloud for various use cases like security and supply chain management.

9. **Quantum computing** integrates with the cloud to solve complex problems and simulations.

10. **5G networks** will be more widely adopted, allowing faster, more reliable connectivity to cloud-based services and enabling new use cases such as VR (Virtual Reality) & AR (Augmented Reality).

The cloud is essential for enterprises in achieving digital enterprise composability as they must fully adopt the cloud as the predominant delivery model for digital technologies. Enterprises must secure their ability to constantly evolve and rapidly reconfigure and assemble digital assets (such as applications, services, and data). The cloud is critical to successful digital transformations because it gives organizations the flexibility, scalability, and agility to deploy and manage their digital assets in unprecedented ways. Cloud-centric strategies allow organizations to strengthen their transformation by advancing their critical resources into the cloud. But without significant investments and cloud adoption at scale, enterprises will limit their abilities to transform and innovate. The cloud is the future platform for integrating and orchestrating digital assets across the enterprise. Cloud platforms, such as public cloud providers or hybrid cloud environments, offer a range of tools and services for building, deploying, and managing digital assets. This includes tools for application development, data management, and integration, which can help organizations build and maintain a cohesive digital ecosystem.

> **"The cloud is not only the future of doing business. It is one of the most critical capabilities and preventive responsibilities enterprises must take to reduce carbon dioxide emission sustainably significantly."**
>
> *Ingo Paas*

Without the cloud, enterprises will not adopt a composable business model and not stay competitive in the rapidly evolving digital landscape. Different industries can have different levels of cloud maturity, depending on various factors such as their digital maturity, financial performance, regulatory requirements, and customer relationships. Some industries have been early adopters of cloud computing, such as software development, fin-techs, e-commerce, and media and entertainment.

These industries tend to have a high level of cloud maturity, with many industries relying heavily on cloud-based services while other sectors are unconvinced and act risk-averse. Other industries, such as healthcare and financial services, have been slower to adopt cloud computing due to data security and regulatory compliance concerns. Even though cloud providers have improved their security measures and compliance capabilities, these industries are steadily adopting the cloud. They are confronted with the fear of competition by fin-tech companies aggressively utilizing the cloud in their operations and customer experience. Cloud adoption also varies significantly within industries, with varying cloud maturity levels.

Financial services companies continue to adopt cloud technology to improve efficiency, reduce costs, and enable new services such as online banking and mobile payments. The media and entertainment industry increasingly adopt cloud-based solutions for storing and distributing content and powering streaming services and virtual reality experiences. Retail companies increasingly adopt cloud-based solutions for managing inventory, tracking customer behavior, and powering online stores.

The healthcare industry increasingly adopts cloud-based solutions for storing and sharing patient data and powering remote monitoring and telemedicine services. Manufacturers adopt cloud-based solutions for managing supply chains, tracking production, and analyzing data from sensors and IoT devices. And the transportation and logistics industry is expected to increasingly adopt cloud-based solutions for tracking vehicles and shipments, as well as for optimizing routes and managing inventory.

In contrast, the energy and utilities industry increasingly adopt cloud-based solutions for managing smart grids and analyzing data from sensors and other IoT devices. The education industry increasingly adopts cloud-based solutions for storing and sharing educational materials and powering online learning and distance education. At the same time, the public sector, including government and military organizations, is expected to increasingly adopt cloud-based solutions for storing and sharing data and powering online services and remote work. These are just a few examples, while many other industries will adopt cloud-based solutions in the coming years.

Evolve cloud-centric businesses

Enterprises must prepare for further cloud adoption and increased cloud-centric business modeling and digital collaboration. In the coming 3 to 5 years, some megatrends may force immature enterprises to rapidly change their approaches to respond to the continued growth of multi-cloud and hybrid-cloud strategies.

As organizations look to optimize cost, performance, and security, they should increasingly adopt a multi-cloud strategy to leverage the strengths of individual cloud providers. This multi-cloud approach will drive the development of new technologies and services to support increased deployments, such as cloud management platforms and cloud-agnostic services.

Integrating artificial intelligence and machine learning will drive the development of new AI and ML-powered services and tools and new cloud data management and governance approaches. The rise and continued growth of edge computing are also likely to be a key trend as more devices and sensors generate data that needs analytic capabilities in real-time, triggering automated, event-driven, and transaction-intensive processes.

The cloud will play a central role in modern business and technology, driving innovation across various industries and use cases in the coming years. Executives must rethink their approach to significantly investing in the cloud and reevaluate their strategic considerations of exclusively transforming the core of their digital capabilities into the cloud.

In the digital age, the cloud has become a fundamental technology for many businesses, providing significant competitive advantages. Industries experiencing rapid disruption, such as retail, healthcare, and finance, must adopt cloud-centric strategies and prepare their organizations. As cloud adoption increases, cloud utilization becomes less of a competitive advantage and more of a baseline requirement for survival in many industries. Enterprises that fail to adopt cloud technology at the center of their strategies risk being left behind and losing market share to more agile and technologically advanced competitors.

The competitive advantage of mastering cloud-centric operations for early adopters and innovative organizations is becoming increasingly essential for survival in a rapidly evolving digital landscape.

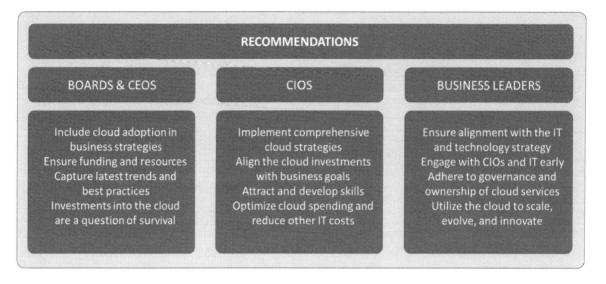

Figure 44 Three pieces of advice to secure transformational opportunities with the cloud

Enterprises not making significant investments into the cloud are increasing their risks, eventually without recognizing them. Investments into the cloud are not a question of competitive advantage; they are increasingly becoming a question of survival.

"Digital composable enterprises must assume full accountability and ownership of their cloud strategies from design to execution. Without establishing autonomy in cloud operations by implementing a Cloud Center of Excellence, risks will increase while benefits will deteriorate significantly."

Ingo Paas

Three pieces of advice to three important groups of decision-makers may help to explore further and leverage the transformational capacity of the cloud:

1. **Boards and CEOs**

   Boards and CEOs should include a strategic approach to cloud adoption in their business strategies. Ensuring their organizations have the resources and expertise to manage and secure their cloud deployments effectively is also important. Funding is critical to secure necessary investments and prepare the enterprise cloud. Most importantly, boards and CEOs must be aware of the revolutionary development of the cloud industry and stay up to date with the latest trends and best practices to ensure their organization stays ahead of the curve. Investments into the cloud are not a question of competitive advantage; they are increasingly becoming a question of survival.

2. **CIOs, CTOs and CDOs, and tech leaders**

   CIOs must develop comprehensive cloud strategies to align the goals and objectives of the organizations with their digital transformations. They should clearly understand the different cloud services and deployment models available, such as public, private, and hybrid clouds, and select the one that best aligns with the organization's needs. Another piece of advice is ensuring that their organization has the resources and skills to manage and secure their cloud deployments across their enterprises effectively. Secure a clear understanding of the ongoing costs of cloud adoption and regularly review, forecast, and optimize their cloud spending. CIOs should stay updated with the latest trends and best practices in the cloud industry and ensure their organization is well-positioned to take advantage of new opportunities and technologies.

3. **Business executives**

   Business leaders must ensure their cloud adoption approach aligns with the organization's IT and technology strategy and goals. Collaboratively engage and seek early support and guidance from the CIOs and IT teams responsible for the organization's overall technology strategy and infrastructure. Adhere to governance and ownership over cloud services, including data management, access rights, processes, compliance, costs, and more. Enterprises shall only have one IT and cloud strategy, which is not owned by the business but informed by the enterprise's purpose, vision, strategy, and goals. Business leaders must utilize cloud opportunities to further scale, evolve, and innovate the enterprise – but aligned with the IT and technology strategy.

Key conclusions and takeaways

The key conclusions and takeaways from the chapter "**TRANSFORMATIONAL CLOUD**" are:

1. Enterprises must prepare for highly scalable cloud operations with the continued exponential growth of AI-enabled services, such as OpenAI and Bard.

2. Enterprises must position the cloud at the core of their business strategies and digital transformations.

3. Enterprises must position the cloud as foundational to achieve digital composability.

4. Enterprises must invest in the cloud as a critical capability to secure digital resilience.

5. Enterprises must implement cloud-agnostic digital foundational platforms and architectures.

6. Enterprises must invest in strategic cloud capabilities (such as Cloud Center of Excellence, skills, processes, technologies, partnerships, and governance).

7. Enterprises must invest in cloud strategies to leverage scalable business innovation from the core of their business and empower disruptive business innovation initiatives.

8. Enterprises must secure investments into the cloud not only as a question of competitive advantage; but increasingly becoming a question of survival.

9. Enterprises must invest in cloud services to significantly reduce carbon dioxide emissions sustainably.

SIX – INDISPENSABLE CAPABILITIES

THOUGHT DIGITAL LEADERSHIP

Marc Dowd, Executive Partner, Executive Advisory - Research and Consulting, IDC Europe

"Moving to a composable architecture should be the goal of any organization that wants to thrive. IT departments and digital leadership must get the message that the future is a composable business. Often the difficulty is how to get there.

Legacy mindsets and understanding hold beak and subvert digital transformation efforts. So often, I hear the cry that if only I had a "green field" with no legacy, I could move as fast as a startup. Ingo is living proof that with the right leadership, legacy is not the issue. Leadership is essential, as it is an understanding of the holistic nature of Digital Transformation.

As you will see in this chapter, the key is to find or create the right attitudes and mix that with good technical knowledge. Also, you will need a good plan, and in this chapter, Ingo lays out all the elements you will need.

Plan for success. Adopting tools and technologies, you may already have without a coordinated plan will only fragment your digitization efforts. A composable architecture works. It relies on abstraction to save effort and complexity. But, to be successful, a willingness to change everything about IT has to be acceptable.

All elements outlined in this chapter must be carefully composed for your organization. Too many fall into the trap of tactical solutions creating a patchwork of competing priorities and investments.

Investment governance often becomes a resource competition, and Ingo rightly suggests a 4-layer model. This gets away from the issues of tactical ROI and ill-defined innovation. Moving from a point solution that promises to ease the pain in the short term at the cost of long-term legacy is a trap. The new shiny object is easier to resist once the tools, techniques, and architecture integrates to accelerate time-to-deployment.

Getting to exponential business agility relies on a change in mindset regarding IT. Trust must exist that the value of the investment in all the elements that make it possible. The framework and elements proposed by Ingo are understandable to businesspeople, and you must evangelize to build trust and understanding on moving to a fully composable environment.

Properly integrating APIs, microservices, distributed data, AIDevOps, Cloud, and low-code is key. In this chapter, Ingo explores how the benefits of each grow as they are integrated.

Getting to a composable enterprise is a business problem that IT cannot solve alone. Getting to a composable IT is something you cannot get to without understanding or trust. That is an IT leadership problem. I recommend you think deeply about integrating all the elements in this chapter.

Digital transformation will fail to be a business differentiator if these lessons in this chapter are not understood and implemented with great leadership and skill."

Written by Marc Dowd, Executive Partner, Executive Advisory - Research and Consulting, IDC Europe

Apply composable technology layers

Applying composable layers of distinct and different technologies is essential to secure successful and enduring digital composable enterprise transformations.

Enterprises are cautious in positioning digital foundational technologies at the center of their business and technology strategies. They are most likely not utilizing interoperable platform strategies in the cloud, designing and implementing such architectures at the core of their digital transformations.

One signal and piece of evidence for this assessment is the low adoption rate of PaaS digital foundational platforms, according to IDC. Those platforms are entirely cloud-enabled PaaS platforms and are critical to transforming traditional and even digital enterprises into digital composable enterprises. The low adoption rate of these platforms is another strong signal that most digital transformations do not leverage their enterprises toward digital composability.

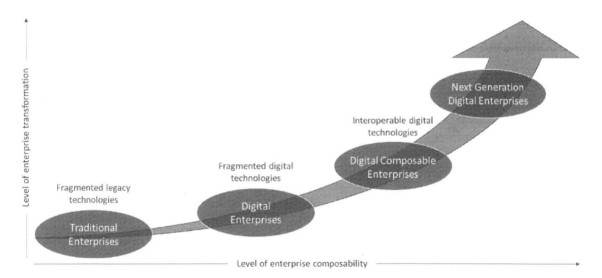

Figure 45 The rise of the digital composable enterprise

To apply discrete technologies is a masterpiece of work that requires tech-inspired brilliant minds (architects) and strong tech-savvy leaders, combined with the commitment to transform their organizations into digital composable enterprises.

To find tech-agnostic and visionary leaders and architects with a holistic and systemic perspective, able to identify the most appropriate technologies and how they shall be applied consistently, is a prerequisite to success. Those visionary leaders must understand the macro perspective of composable enterprise transformation as much as they must understand the micro perspective to design modular architectures. They must navigate the entire spectrum from the macro to the micro view to understand various technology layers and identify the patterns and principles to make them work collaboratively and coherently.

If organizations lack the critical skills for designing and leveraging digital composable transformations, it is unlikely that they will be able to do so. In addition, organizations that do not differentiate and utilize interoperable technology layers increase their risks of fragmented and inconsistent digital technology investments. This can even result in a new "digital IT legacy" in the worst cases. Therefore, decision-makers must understand and relate their technology investments in more comprehensive and enduring ways, as complex transformations require a fundamental and holistic architectural design. It is critical to ensure effective investments supporting digital composable architectures and prioritize them over primarily prioritizing ROI investments.

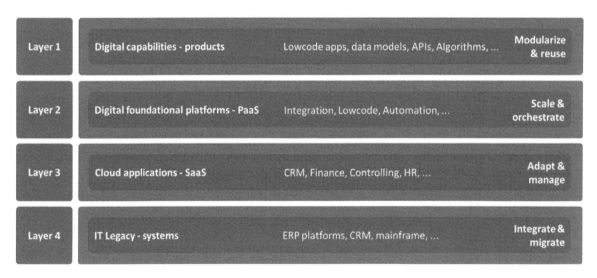

Figure 46 Overview of core technology layers of digital composable transformations

Those four layers of technologies are crucial for successful transformations playing significantly different roles in building future composable enterprises.

Layer 1	Digital capabilities - products	Lowcode apps, data models, APIs, Algorithms, ...	Modularize & reuse

Digital products such as applications, data objects, APIs, integrations, and algorithms are developed on PaaS platforms or similar tools. They are available as cloud-native products and for orchestration in the cloud. These products are digital versions of packaged business capabilities, business logic, or integrations. They are designed based on the core digital foundational principles, where they are designed and developed as **modular** components with high grades of **reusability**. Modularity and reusability are characterizing digital products critical to achieving digital composability.

Layer 2	Digital foundational platforms - PaaS	Integration, Lowcode, Automation, ...	Scale & orchestrate

Digital foundational platforms (PaaS) offer highly interoperable and **scalable** digital and IT business innovation and features. They are at the core of enabling enterprise-wide interoperability, integrations, and **orchestrations** of digitally developed products to secure enterprise-wide composability. By leveraging and enabling digital development and orchestration of digital objects in unprecedented ways, those platforms provide standardized and ready-to-use infinite business and technology innovation capabilities at the core of digital composable transformations. They ensure a stable and sustainable digital composable transformation, enabling seamless future integration of new innovative technologies. They help scale business development and minimize legacy complexity with maximum reusability, leading to faster development cycles, lower investments on IT legacy investments, and reduced risks, development, and maintenance costs. They can also develop code and functionality from IT legacy systems to diminish their role or complement missing functionality on standard applications. They allow organizations to solve unsolvable future business problems instantaneously, rapidly, and effectively to innovate at scale. They are transformative at scale and provide unprecedented new opportunities to transform enterprises with unparalleled scalable and sustainable technology innovation.

| Layer 3 | Cloud applications - SaaS | CRM, Finance, Controlling, HR, ... | Adapt & manage |

Cloud (SaaS) applications deliver standardized applications operated and provided by external vendors. The effective and standardized ability to **adapt** and onboard SaaS services are critical to effectively managing those services in the cloud. They require distinct and strategic **management** and governance to effectively incorporate standardized SaaS services into the enterprise's IT landscape. Their single-purpose scope can significantly reduce enterprise business and digital resilience and, consequently, composability. Business process adjustments in standardized SaaS applications are usually not perceived as the most viable options if business requirements change. They effectively solve fragmented business process problems while limiting enterprises to leveraging digital composability with an ever-increasing number of applications.

| Layer 4 | IT Legacy - systems | ERP platforms, CRM, mainframe, ... | Integrate & migrate |

The **IT legacy** layer does include the entire portfolio of legacy applications and systems. In digital composable transformations, the key focus is to effectively **integrate** IT legacy systems and execute appropriate **migration** efforts to prepare and adapt for digital readiness. This includes mitigating risks, securing compliance, and guaranteeing digital readiness on critical and prioritized legacy systems' application, development, and release levels.

To succeed in the digital economy, balancing competing objectives is critical and a concern when initiating cloud-enabled digital transformations. Enterprises must prioritize business resilience to operate effectively in the present, as they must continually transform to take advantage of continually evolving their business models and revenue streams. This approach will help organizations tackle both objectives by simultaneously running and transforming their business.

The book "The CIO's Dilemma: Balancing the Risks, Opportunities, and Investments of IT" (Colony, 2012) was written by George Colony, Forrester Research, addressing this fundamental dilemma of CIOs.

G. Colony discussed the challenges CIOs face in balancing the need to maintain existing systems while investing in new technology to drive innovation. With the capabilities and combinations possible, CIOs are finally finding support in solving this unsolvable dilemma if they only find the courage and CEO support to make those moves.

Those four layers of technology shall guide organizations to distinguish how architectural and investment decisions contribute to digital transformations and organizational and technology conversions. It is, therefore, critical to ensure consistency across all four investment layers to secure strategic and balanced utilization. This framework shall guide decision-makers better to understand digitally motivated investments' complexity and differentiation and make more informed and consistent interconnected decisions.

Technology layers of digital composable transformations	Select	Develop	Implement	Create value	Own	Maintain	Investment decisions
Digital capabilities - products	Business & IT	Business & IT	Business & IT	Business & IT	Business & IT	Business " IT	Development costs DevOps, projects and tools
Digital cloud applications - SaaS	Business & IT	Business	Business & IT	Business	Business	Business & IT	Application cost optimization
Digital foundational platforms - PaaS	IT	IT	IT	Business & IT	IT	IT	New platforms and technologies
IT legacy - systems	Business & or IT	Business & IT	Business & or IT	Business	Business	Business & IT	Modernize, replace, digital readiness

Figure 47 A reference framework guiding decision makers to make better informed and more consistent future interconnected investment decisions

Organizations that are often indistinct about ownership and responsibilities of their core technology layers can lead to incoherent decisions and ineffective utilization. Organizations may also experience major difficulties in delivering consistent value in a manageable and controllable complex new architectural landscape with new layers of technologies. Investing in digital foundational platforms in traditional ways may cause complications, as they are usually motivated by inappropriate reasons.

A typical miscalculation and example of inappropriate investments into those platforms is the "non-strategic" selection of lowcode platforms. This usually happens if organizations do not have a distinct understanding and strategy to utilize lowcode to transform the enterprise and build digital enterprise applications from the core of the business. To effectively apply distinct leadership across all four layers is critical for digital transformations to secure effective interoperability between those layers of technologies, solutions, and vendors. With those very different and purpose-driven layers of technologies, investment decisions require consistency and alignment with the digital composable architecture design and fundamental principles. Deciding on new technology investments presents a persistent challenge to CIOs, business leaders, and investment councils, demanding balanced investment strategies. Organizations that are not effectively guiding their investments and prioritizations may experience significant challenges to secure consistency with their complex technology investments in line with their transformational goals.

With those more distributed investment layers, organizations must apply a more balanced, adaptive, and adequate investment technology-savvy proficiency. Differentiating four kinds of technology investments is essential when designing the organization's digital foundation. And as initially addressed, both the macro and the micro perspectives play significant roles in the evolutionary transformation of traditional or digital compromises to effectively utilize loosely coupled services at scale.

Utilize loosely coupled services (and a microservice architecture)

A note from the author: This section is highly technical, emphasizing the criticality of microservices in composable architectures. It is good to understand why microservices are critical but not how they function. To the reader: This section is technical!

Loosely coupled services play a crucial role in digital composable transformations allowing for greater flexibility and scalability in digitalizing business processes. They enable different system components to interact without having a tight dependency on one another, allowing for the easy replacement or modification of individual components without affecting the overall system. They guarantee the creation of modular and reusable components that can be combined to achieve different business objectives.

Loosely coupled services also enable the composition of existing services to form new business capabilities, creating unique and differentiated solutions.

These services minimize dependencies on other components and have clearly defined inputs and outputs. They make it possible to update or replace individual components without affecting the rest of the system or business processes, which can reduce the risk of faults and downtime. They allow for implementing microservices architectures, increasing their scalability and ability to handle highly complex interoperability problems. Loosely coupled services can lead to more efficient and flexible development and deployment of digitally packaged business capabilities and greater scalability and adaptability in responding to changing business needs. A typical (but not widely adopted) use case is utilizing loosely coupled services and infinite modularity of modern enterprise lowcode application design.

Deploying and managing effective loosely coupled service architectures is a crucial differentiator to leverage leading-edge digital development in the cloud. Combined services can describe and execute a business capability and are the foundation to build and operate digitally packaged business capabilities. While this practice with fully autonomous loosely coupled services enables the digitalization of self-contained packages, their utilization is still rare in many enterprises. Microservices "backend" refers to the part of the architecture responsible for processing and managing data, logic, and functionality. It consists of autonomous services individually functioning for a specific aspect of the system. The backend includes basic services to handle data storage, processing, and retrieval, including API services for applications to communicate with those backend services.

Each backend service is loosely coupled and independently deployable, enabling developers to change or update a specific service without disrupting the entire system. The backend services are often connected using APIs and message queues, allowing them to communicate with one another in a decoupled and flexible way. Microservices communicate effectively with each other through well-defined APIs. They do not need to share internal information details, while another great advantage is that microservices utilize different technology stacks, libraries, or frameworks once they are designed and deployed correctly. This is an enormous advantage to developers, ensuring high flexibility, interoperability, reliability, and stability in operations.

Platform-enabled orchestration capabilities usually support microservices. They are responsible for managing and placing them on nodes, identifying failures, and rebalancing services across those nodes, as they are functioning as off-the-shelf technology rather than custom-built solutions.

In this architectural framework, the API gateway is the entry point for clients. Instead of calling services directly, clients call the API gateway, which forwards the call to the appropriate services on the back end. A client is a component or system consuming the services from a microservice. Clients and microservices communicate through interfaces or APIs and can do this with multiple microservices, where each microservice can have multiple clients. This concept of autonomy enables the decoupled nature of microservices, allowing clients and microservices to evolve separately, making it easier for developers to add new features or scale the system as needed. A key characteristic of microservices is that they carry their data or external state, which differs from traditional models, where a separate data layer manages data diligence. The concept of microservices is essential for designing and developing modern digital services in composable architectures, while CIOs shall not focus on rewriting the existing code of their IT legacy applications. Instead, CIOs may use microservices and API gateways by decoupling business logic from services as an essential step towards sustainable digital composable transformations.

Microservices can be changed and versioned without updating all the digital composable business capabilities (components). The API gateway can perform multiple activities such as logging, authentication in AD (Active Directory), SSL (Secure Sockets Layer) termination, and load balancing. At the same time, policies are important to validate or transform the microservices function without any issues with performance or stability.

Developers focus on solving business problems instead of compiling, optimizing, and deploying digitally developed and deployed independent services. This creates agility and makes it easier to identify, manage, and solve errors and simplify future releases. All applications using this service remain unaffected while service updates occur without requiring redeployment. Enforcing the reusability of services becomes possible as multiple applications can simultaneously consume digitally packaged business capabilities built out of numerous single services. Unlike traditional software deployment and release management, bugs do not block the entire application from functioning and would enable continuous deployment and release processes, while developers can release new features instantly.

Compared to monolithic development, coding applications in different languages implies risks of personal dependencies and difficulties in maintaining code. New development or adjustments require changes to existing code with up to thousands of lines of code, which are difficult, if not impossible, to manage and oversee.

The microservices architecture minimizes dependencies, which makes it easier to enable reusability, add new or change features, and amend existing applications. This helps to secure the stability of services deployed across applications, minimize risks for downtime, reduce complexity, and secure, controlled life-cycle management of products/applications/integrations.

Scalability is a key advantage of good architectural design, as services can be scaled independently, promoting greater agility to even scale out subsystems that demand more resources without scaling out the entire application. By orchestrating those services, a much higher density of services across multiple applications allows for more efficient utilization of such resources.

When using microservices and API gateways, the lean approach is to simplify the overall complexity of software development and brings new lean methods to development teams. This is a significant advantage for all application and integration development teams to apply lean principles and significantly reduce the need for coding. Another layer of productivity gain is achievable by utilizing enterprise lowcode development platforms, as they can take software development to another level than traditional software development teams can do. Lowcode will be further discussed in Chapter 7.

Implementing a microservices architecture requires advanced skills, experiences, and an in-depth understanding of effectively designing and implementing a solid architecture. There are risks of inadequate execution which adds another layer of complexity to organizations and teams when designing highly agile microservice-based architectures. The effective mitigation of such risks is critical to not jeopardize enterprise lowcode investments and to secure lasting, scalable, and robust platforms. Ideally, new microservices shall undergo a quality assurance process in successful environments before deployment and release. Making the microservices available in the underlying "microservice catalog" makes deploying them relentlessly across multiple applications simple. However, success in terms of stability depends on establishing the governance required to qualify, approve, and release new microservices.

Organizations must focus more on relentlessly following and executing governance and design principles to be effective. Highly effective lowcode development teams will be able to reinforce reusability, secure rapid development, design adaptive and highly flexible applications, assure inbuild quality measures, integrate security into their design, build at low costs, and minimize test efforts and complexity in the design process.

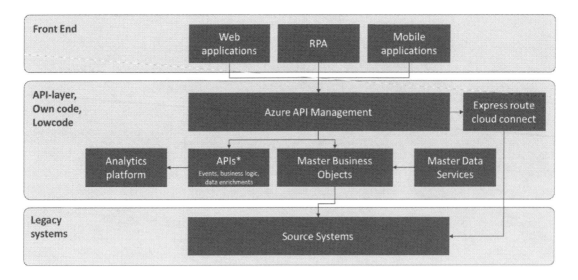

Figure 48 API-focused technology agnostic, services-based, loosely coupled, event-driven integration architecture

The proposed architecture is technology agnostic (generalized), designed to be service-based, with loosely coupled services, event-driven and API-enabled. This allows the architecture to construct systems out of services in many technologies. All are interconnected using modern event-driven patterns and exposed to the outside world as packaged, secured, and monitored APIs. With centralized communication, the architecture allows for monitoring, governance, access, and security for the applications to be built and managed in one coherent place.

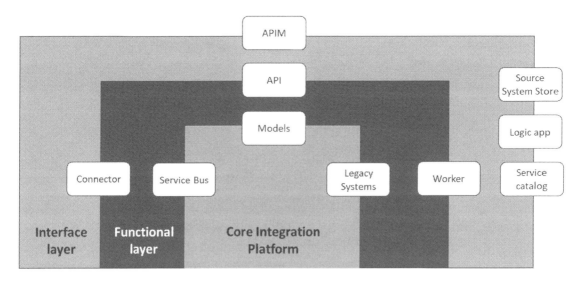

Figure 49 Three possible layers of modern Hybrid Integration Platforms

The main purpose is to allow loosely coupled services to orchestrate into custom solutions rapidly. With more autonomous in-house development and external expertise, this architecture significantly reduces development times to secure more sustainable and qualified results.

Enterprises can manage the complexity that arises as applications grow by breaking them up based on their responsibilities or concerns. This approach follows the principle of separation of concerns and can help keep applications and code organized and simplified. By organizing code into layers, common low-level functionality allows code reusability throughout the design and development of future applications. This is where reusability differentiates lowcode from Enterprise lowcode development.

Reusability is highly beneficial because it means less code is needed, as the code does allow the application to utilize existing standards. With this concept of layered architectures, applications enforce restrictions on which layers they can communicate with other layers to enable encapsulation and separation. Layers (and encapsulation) simplify the replacement of functionality within all applications built based on this layered design principle. In addition to the potential of scope changes in software development, application layers can make the development of future changes or new applications much easier. Logical layering is a common technique to effectively organize code in complex enterprise applications and utilize several ways code organizes into layers. There are great benefits to this architecture and principles once they are applied and fully governed.

The benefits already mentioned reduce traditional total isolation between functional blocks and replace or add new functionality in data processing, with no or minimal impact on the application performance and operations. Creating templates, increasing development speed, and combining your services with external services is easier, while parts of the flow or segmented coding can be written in different programming languages in different environments without impact. Orchestrating services across multiple applications minimizes the risks of application incidents, as a failure in an input component does not compromise the entire flow.

The above-described "good architecture" requires designing and implementing "loosely coupled services." Loosely coupled services increase flexibility, encourage multiple changes across multiple applications simultaneously, and allow for new solutions, especially in situations where the system should adapt rapidly to external changes.

The profound adoption of DevOps to operate in good, designed architectures, the right governance, and processes will lead to advantages in in-house software development, maintenance, and life-cycle management. As sustainability in software development is one of the last unresolved problems, organizations that choose this way will revolutionize how to design, develop, deploy, and effectively manage software, transforming organizations to new heights of software development.

By implementing and embedding enterprise lowcode platforms, any organization can transform into highly autonomous, world-class software factories, scaling software development in new ways. The design of a distinctive microservice architecture is essential for digital transformations to secure the maximum utilization of its core principles in every digital development project or activity. The effective combination of Lowcode development and practicing loosely coupled services will leverage the enterprise's capability. Organizations developing enterprise applications will apply similar principles beyond Lowcode development in their critical attempts to integrate the enterprise from the core of the business.

Integrate the Enterprise

Most traditional organizations faced huge complexity and disintegrated IT legacies, which causes enormous problems when organizations pursue digital transformations. In many cases, end-of-life integration tools or platforms introduce significant risks, and developers have few opportunities to mitigate those risks in other ways than replacing those legacy integration platforms.

Integration complexity usually is a major cost driver and challenge for traditional IT projects and programs, while complexity increases to operate in highly segmented environments. Solving the integration challenge is a key undertaking that organizations must address right from the beginning of their digital transformations. The challenges to establishing enterprise-wide integration capabilities are complex, and it is not seldom that IT organizations fail to develop EHIP capabilities embedded into their fragmented architectures.

Those difficulties include activities such as:

- Integrate various systems and applications,

- Manage distributed data layers and sources of origin,

- Update and maintain data from multiple data sources,

- Maintain the complexity of data integrity and access,

- Implement data management and data governance,

- Address data ownership and quality,

- Interconnect with various stakeholders in digital ecosystems,

- Advance into real-time and event-driven digital processes,

- Migrate away from IT legacy systems and legacy integration platforms.

As integration complexity is a growing concern, traditional IT organizations maintain and manage different integration technologies, so-called middleware, or integration platforms, which usually drive costs, risks, and complexity. Organizations sometimes must implement industry-specific integration platforms to serve industry-related digital ecosystems with complex standardized integration requirements and communication standards. Enterprise integration is a central capability of digital composable transformations, enabling different systems, applications, and data sources within and outside an organization to communicate and work together seamlessly. This allows for the efficient sharing and processing of information, seamless integration, and automation of core business processes.

Enterprise hybrid integration platforms (EHIP) also allow for the creation of new digital services and capabilities to combine existing ones, enabling more agile responses to change business needs when applying modular principles. Enterprise integration is key to realizing the full potential of digital composable transformations by allowing organizations to create new value from their existing IT assets and better leverage the data they collect.

Hybrid enterprise integration platforms are PaaS services that enable enterprises to integrate their on-premises and cloud-based systems, applications, and data sources. They provide unified ways to manage and monitor all integrations. They come with a wide range of pre-built connectors and integration templates to reduce the time and effort required to connect various systems and technologies. EHIPs also provide effective ways to integrate cloud services with existing on-premises systems, allowing developers to take advantage of cloud-based platforms' full scalability, cost-effectiveness, and flexibility.

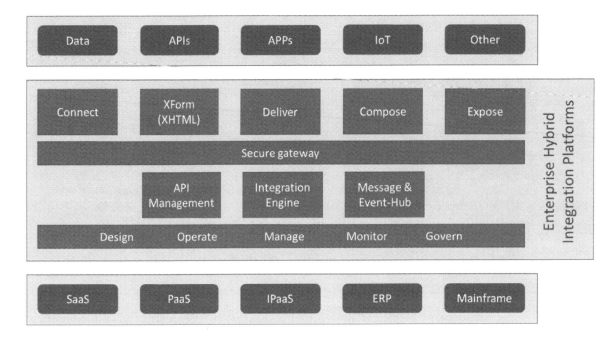

Figure 50 Enterprise Hybrid Integration Platforms (EHIP) are at the center of every digital composable transformation

EHIPs also provide a unified way to manage and monitor all integrations, regardless of where they reside, which can help to simplify and streamline integration management. EHIPs often offer a wide range of pre-built connectors and easily configure integration templates, reducing the time and effort required to connect systems. They also leverage security, compliance, and control of on-premises systems and secure overall interoperability without increasing risks. EHIPs function for various types of integration, such as application integration, data integration, API management, and B2B/EDI integration. EHIPs create a seamless, end-to-end integration infrastructure to support their digital composable transformation efforts.

Hybrid integration platforms deliver significant value for digital composable transformations by enabling organizations to integrate their on-premises and cloud-based systems, applications, and data sources. Organizations can continually improve interoperability by utilizing cloud-based systems' scalability, cost-effectiveness, and flexibility. EHIPs facilitate the creation of seamless, end-to-end integration infrastructure, which supports digital composable transformation efforts. These platforms enable full-scale interoperability between existing IT legacy and new digital platforms, systems, and applications developed in lowcode across the entire enterprise.

APIs (Application Programming Interfaces) suggest new and smarter options to manage enterprise integrations' complexity effectively. API strategies are vital and critical for positioning traditional organizations at the core of their composable strategy. With the highest possible grades of flexibility, this requires implementing enterprise hybrid integration platforms as digital foundational platforms at the center of every digital transformation to solve the integration challenges of composable architectures.

It is a key task for CxOs to define API strategies to set guidelines and principles to effectively manage and leverage its application programming interfaces (APIs) to achieve its business goals. Tools are highly important, and making the right choice is difficult. APIs are essential to improve their digital operations, automate workflows, and enhance their customer experience. Effective strategies help to improve enterprise-wide agility, scalability, and innovation capabilities by enabling them to integrate easily with other systems, automate processes, and create new products and services.

API strategies are essential for digital composable transformations for several reasons. They allow for integrating different systems, applications, and data sources within an organization to share and process information and automate business processes. APIs enable organizations to create new digital services by combining existing ones, increasing agility and responsiveness to changing business needs. They allow for the creation of external-facing interfaces that enable partners, customers, and other third-party developers to access and use the organization's assets in a controlled and secure way. APIs also allow organizations to improve their ability to leverage data by making it available to other systems and applications. They provide flexible and scalable ways to connect systems and enable organizations to respond more to changing business needs. API strategies are key to realizing the full potential of digital composable transformations, creating new value from existing IT assets, leveraging data, and opening new business opportunities.

APIs can also expose events/functions of the IT legacy system to simplify and streamline integration and to reduce risks with integration complexity. With general APIs connecting with existing IT legacy systems, they realize integrations in modernized and highly effective ways.

APIs will support the extension and modernization of the organization's IT legacy systems as a crucial capability to deliver performance while they increase flexibility.

Service layers can serve as middleware between a legacy system and new applications by translating or transforming information before it is sent to a new system or received by the existing system. With the adoption of new service layers, new options are available to extend single functions from the legacy systems to reduce pressure on those or provide more features. Developers can easily add new service layers to modernize existing systems, leveraging integration capabilities with greater flexibility, lower costs, and reduced maintenance efforts.

Implementing API management and connecting with core information assets and functionality is possible without involving the IT legacy systems. To achieve such organizational decoupling using APIs, organizations must consider the business demand, including its underlying information assets and business capabilities, to be exposed as APIs and to enable consumption with those APIs. Smart API strategies also reduce complexity and could minimize the burden of migrating away from ERP platforms with inbuild integration engines, such as SAP PO (Process Orchestration). With multi-disciplinary teams supporting the integration of the IT legacy, the new digital platforms, and digital capabilities, the IT and digital landscapes can be incrementally API-enabled, supporting critical business development initiatives.

As the demand and expectations for integration technologies and cloud computing intensify rapidly, managers, analysts, and executives require real-time, reliable, and instant access to critical business data at any time on any device and at every level of granularity. Data integration capabilities must satisfy this demand across various systems, technologies, and computing environments. They must be able to perform complicated queries across disparate sources while orchestrating the data objects event-driven and in real-time. Data integration tools must seamlessly work across multiple technologies and platforms over various networks to achieve a high level of integration between modern applications and the organization's IT legacy systems. Distinct prioritization and allocation of development resources are critical, considering the overflow of business integration needs.

Designing and implementing more holistic, comprehensive, and adaptive integration strategies is not new but may increase relevance in the shadow of digital composable transformations.

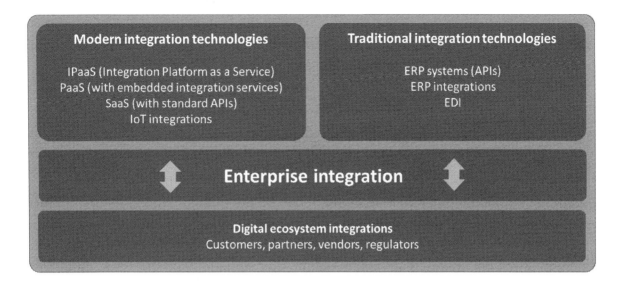

Figure 51 Enterprise integrations are at the core of digital transformations

Integration strategies and the implementation of modern hybrid enterprise integration platforms are critical to controlling and scaling digital composable transformations. This is essential for traditional organizations to secure fundamental capabilities across the enterprise, especially addressing interconnectivity and digital ecosystem integrations and API strategies.

As integration complexity is a significant challenge for most organizations, modern integration strategies consider different integration perspectives and apply smart principles while they utilize their EHIP as the engine for dynamic and controlled integration development. The options or scope areas of integration strategies vary, requiring strong governance for effective deployment.

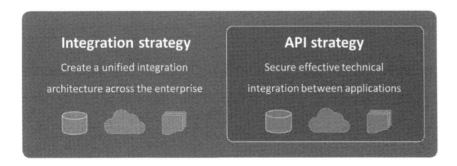

Figure 52 Integration strategies encompass API strategies, as both are critical for achieving digital composability

An API strategy and an enterprise integration strategy are important components of an organization's overall technology strategy, but they focus on different aspects of its technology architecture.

API strategies secure to expose functionality and data from different systems within the organization or to third-party systems. It is a business-driven strategy to ensure the APIs needed to support the organization's goals and objectives. Those strategies include designing and building APIs and managing and optimizing their usage over time. Even though API development and utilization is business driven, it is typically more focused on the technical aspects of integrating different systems and services and ensuring they can communicate effectively.

Enterprise integration strategies focus on integrating different systems and services across the organization by utilizing a unified technology architecture, ideally in the cloud. To develop those strategies, one needs to identify the systems and services that require integration, design and implement the integration architecture, and ensure seamless sharing of data and functionality across various systems. They include API strategies to support business aspects of integrating the enterprise internally and externally.

Both strategies have different focuses and goals. API strategies focus more on the technical aspects of integrating different systems and services through APIs, while enterprise integration strategies focus more on the broader goal of creating foundational integration technology architecture across the enterprise.

Integration strategies must include the following domains:

- **API development** developed and deployed on iPaaS platforms secures to utilize standards, processes, architecture, principles, service catalogs, and more.
- **ERP integration tools** (specialized integration tools incorporated into ERP systems) can cause issues with ERP legacy systems (flexibility, costs, complexity, risks), especially as they are complicated, expensive to maintain, and may bring service and volume restrictions in modern integration environments.
- **SaaS** integrations must utilize standardized integration capabilities (APIs) or SaaS without API standards causing issues when integrating those services (flexibility, costs, complexity, risks, standardization).

- **PaaS** (Platform Software as a Service) integrations are instantly available or only require minor adaptions and come with strategic choices of platforms (such as Microsoft Azure or Dynamics) that offer highly integrated services with tremendous advantages across the composable architecture. Some platforms (such as lowcode and automation) include complementary integration tools but do not replace the need for EHIPs and API strategies in more complex business environments.

- **Investments in external integration platforms** (industry specific) can be avoided in regulated industries with modern EHIPs if there is a demand for external integration platforms.

- **IoT integrations,** services provided as IoT platforms in the cloud, integrate IoT Hubs with other services to act as a central messaging hub for communication between IoT applications and their attached devices (connecting and managing millions of devices and their backend solutions reliably and securely).

Integration strategies must be effectively governed and embedded at the core of digital platform strategies to avoid complexity and minimize strategic risks. Organizations must be very clear on how they approach integration complexity, not just from a development perspective but, even more importantly, from a business perspective. As integration is the most central part of digital transformations in composable architectures, this is the core discipline every organization must get right.

Since integrations are recognized as one of the most critical bottlenecks of digital transformations, developing effective integration strategies and architectures requires utilizing resources efficiently and scaling skills while working within given budgets and potential constraints. The demand for integration development will remain at an all-time high, and enterprises must address those concerns in financial planning and forecasting.

Organizations must prepare to design and collaborate effectively across digital ecosystems with their customers, partners, and regulators. They must significantly increase their efforts to share and utilize data to seamlessly integrate and interoperate with complex, dynamic, and rapidly changing digital collaboration across digital ecosystems. Those increasing demands of infinite connectivity require integration capabilities enabling inter-company connectivity and communications. The need for increased levels of digital collaboration will force data integration teams and architects to develop more robust, cloud-based innovative, and scalable integration capabilities and capacities (technology, processes, and resources).

Cloud-based platforms will become the engines of multidisciplinary ecosystems at ever-increasing speed, with increasing complexity, variety, and velocity.

The challenge for traditional IT organizations is to stay on top of technology developments, constantly review market developments, and extend, adapt, and adjust their integration strategies. Enterprises that will not invest in modern integration strategies, architectures, and integration development capabilities, will introduce serious risks to their digital and digital composable transformations.

The best architectures for integration combine principles such as portability, agility, scalability, reusability, simplicity, and cloud compatibility in a single-cloud, multi-cloud, or hybrid-cloud environment. Those capabilities are already implemented across many organizations but still not fully utilized to enable seamless enterprise-wide digital transformations. As digital transformation strategies become more sophisticated and systemic, it can be challenging to identify and select the most appropriate integration architecture and digital foundational platforms.

"Boards and CEOs MUST secure long-term investments (platforms) and costs (developers) into the execution of integration strategies to secure composability and digital resilience at the center of their digital transformation efforts."

Ingo Paas

Investments into integration capabilities are foundational and critical to secure successful business-driven and technology-enabled digital transformations. With integration at the core of digital foundational technologies, organizations must ensure the right approach to enterprise-wide integration as one of their most critical, if not the single most critical, undertaking of digital transformations.

As most organizations already consider API-enabled architectures, the concept of loosely coupled services and the relentless orchestration of those microservices across multiple environments and applications demand high-performance EHIP platforms. With the integration strategy at the core of new digital foundational platforms, the transformational aspect requires exponentially rethinking and utilizing digital foundational technologies.

Utilize foundational technologies "exponentially."

Organizations that understand and appropriately apply foundational capabilities will relentlessly increase their chances of delivering business value. Understanding investments in digital foundational platforms is necessary to industrialize and automate business processes at a scale and foster a culture of continual problem-solving and innovation. One particular dilemma and generally missed opportunity with the majority of digital transformations is the inability to gain advantages of developing digital assets beyond their initial purpose and scope. This is usually the case if reusability is not a core principle in the design of digital architectures. Only a few enterprises seem to realize the enormous potential of reusability, interoperability, and scalability, to leverage unforeseeable levels of innovation and continual problem-solving capabilities.

Organizations that master collaborative utilization of digital foundational technologies will be able to accelerate improvements at the core of the business, align the organization on commonalities, and minimize risks with failed design and development. Enterprises with such foundational capabilities will, over time, make better collaborative decisions to make more effective use of their digital investments in new and "exponential" ways. They do this based on collaborative efforts to leverage their skills, processes, tools, and leadership to prosper and strengthen their abilities to reuse already-built digital assets. Successful enterprises continually develop, construct, offer, and orchestrate new digital reusable products (objects) that are qualified, accessible, and ready to **reuse**. Those digital products (objects) include APIs, algorithms, data models, application features (loosely coupled services), and more. Digital-developed reusable, interoperable assets are valuable for future development, problem-solving, and innovation, as they are the accelerators and enablers of superior digital transformations.

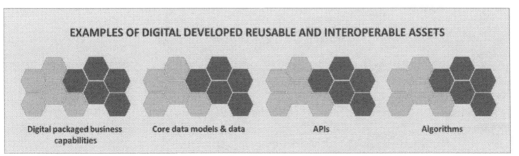

*Figure 53 Digital developed and reusable assets function as the digital **base** of digital transformations*

Those modular digital assets constantly add business value by guaranteeing full interoperability and compatibility, while this approach leads to a continuous increase of options as digital objects are accessible to developers and teams. They can reuse those qualified digital objects, saving time and streamlining development by constantly increasing their abilities to accelerate innovation and solve business problems.

Most digital transformations do not envision the reusability of digital assets at scale, while enterprises leveraging their digitally developed assets will ensure consistency, sustainability, and quality. The positive effects of reusability are comparable with exponential development, even though this comparison is more symbolic than practically applicable.

Rapid digital development based on foundational principles, such as reusability, scalability, and interoperability, realized on digital foundational platforms, does bring new and unexplored advantages to enterprises comparable with accelerated and exponential developments.

If the base of an exponential growth model continues to increase, it can lead to rapid and sustained growth. This is because the base of the exponential function represents the growth rate, and a larger base means a faster growth rate. In the case of Airbnb, the number of high-quality images improved significantly as the company grew faster and faster. This led to increased available listings on the platform, growth of customers, more rentals, more social notifications, and a positive feedback loop, where more high-quality images and more listings led to more customers, which in turn led to more listings. As a result, the base of the exponential growth model for Airbnb continued to increase, leading to rapid and sustained growth for the company.

The same applies to enterprises, where reusability and interoperability of their digital assets open up new opportunities. The "exponential" curve does not mean enterprises will experience exponential growth, but they will realize unique and significantly accelerated opportunities to drive digital development at higher growth rates, at least far better than linear developments.

The next figure explains this phenomenon that can occur when the number of digitally developed reusable and interoperable assets grows is applied.

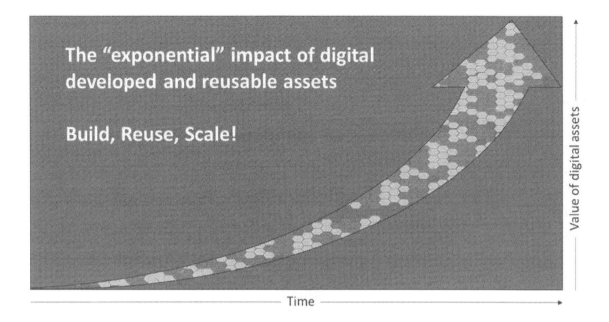

Figure 54 The exponential impact of reusability in digital development

The design of digital foundational architectures must enable and promote reusability and interoperability at scale. This creates unrestricted development opportunities with higher growth potential over time. This new way to build digital capabilities is a key differentiator and game changer compared to traditional software development and digital transformations. Instead, it enables digital leaders to accelerate digital transformations and problem-solving abilities exceptionally.

Enterprises can enhance business logic in distinctive ways and resolve any insufficiencies. They can create new business opportunities, increase quality, eliminate non-value activities, and make data instantly available across digital ecosystems. They enrich customer processes in new ways and improve KPIs and customer satisfaction with optimized business decisions. Reusing those digital assets even across multiple digital ecosystems will allow customers to use the same digital assets to participate and collaborate within new digital ecosystems.

This new digitalization approach offers new collaborative business development and improvement opportunities to assume ownership, engage, and evolve with those new opportunities. Successful organizations will consider those new openings and build a sustainable digital transformation and digital future from the core of their business.

This approach will differentiate organizations that implement isolated digital solutions (such as SaaS rigorous strategies) from those that master unconstrained digital development from the core of their business.

Digital foundational technologies can make the difference between digital masters and digital superiority with open architectures to foster and embrace continual digital technology-enabled innovation. With appropriate and balanced strategic investments into digital foundational platforms, organizations must leverage their agile development capabilities.

Leverage agile development

Enterprises can leverage agile development to secure digital transformations because it allows flexibility and adaptability in changing requirements and technologies. It provides several benefits for enterprises undergoing digital transformations.

This allows for a more flexible and adaptive approach to development, which is important in the rapidly changing digital landscape. It also promotes collaboration between teams and stakeholders, which can improve communication and increase the chances of success. Agile development emphasizes regular testing and iteration, which can help identify and fix problems at the beginning of the development process, reducing the risk of costly delays or failures. Agile methodologies prioritize customer needs, which can improve customer satisfaction and increase the chances of successfully adopting new digital systems. It takes time for organizations to embrace agile working methods and to adjust their methodologies and ways of working.

Collaboration can encourage and improve unified ways of working between business and IT by fostering a culture of open communication and shared responsibility. When business and IT work together closely, they can develop a shared understanding of the organization's goals and priorities and align their efforts and resources accordingly. This can lead to more effective decision-making and better alignment between IT initiatives and business needs. The collaborative power of developing and innovating business processes is bringing traditionally isolated parts and functions of the organization closer together. The power of interdisciplinary prioritization, resource utilization, and cross-functional business development will leverage traditional silo thinking and accelerate the digitalization of the business.

The key advantages will accelerate collaborative learning and increase business process optimization. Incremental and experimental innovation will encourage continual improvements in addressing real business problems at the core of the business.

Collaboration can help to break down silos between IT and the business, promoting a more holistic view of the organization's operations. Such attempts can lead to a more integrated and cohesive approach to digital transformation, with IT and business working together to identify and implement new technologies and processes to drive the organization forward. Unified working can also improve collaboration, engagement, and the user experience by ensuring that the design of digital solutions focuses on the end user. By involving the business in the development process, IT can better understand the needs and perspectives of the people using the new digital systems and design solutions that are more likely to be adopted and used effectively.

DevOps (Development Operations) is a set of practices and principles to bring development and operations teams together to increase digital development's speed and quality. They play a vital role in digital transformations, quickly adopting new technologies and exploring the most effective utilization to help to achieve prioritized business goals. They play a critical role by enabling faster and more efficient development and deployment of new digital systems. One key aspect of DevOps is automation and continuous integration/continuous delivery (CI/CD) pipelines. These tools allow for faster and more reliable code deployment, which can help to speed up the development and deployment of new digital systems. DevOps teams emphasize clearly defining the scope of their development work, delivering high-quality small packages, and finalizing development bundles. They secure quality through monitoring and testing, which can improve the quality and stability of the solutions deployed.

DevOps also promote collaboration and communication between different parts of the organization, which can help to break down silos and increase alignment between business and IT. This can be especially important in digital transformations, where organizations rapidly implement and improve digital solutions and processes.

Agile development methodologies and DevOps practices are often combined and referred to as "Agile DevOps," which allows for faster delivery of features, frequent feedback, and continuous improvement. Those best practices help the organization to increase responsiveness to changing business demands and customer needs.

Most organizations recognize the necessity to increase their in-house agile development capabilities within today's hypercompetitive business environments and mediocre technology-enabled business innovation. With this ever-growing challenge, the DevOps (Development Operations) concept has become crucial to IT, tech teams, and businesses. DevOps can help increase reliability and minimize disruption risks while they promise greater flexibility, higher speed, and agility to support prioritized business demand rapidly. Those multidisciplinary teams bring new capabilities to organizations and facilitate collaborative alignment from ideation to production, realizing improvement after deployment.

Besides more agile development capabilities and immediate responses to business demand, the real benefit is DevOps's ability to secure continuous delivery of the developed digital assets and features. DevOps are the most effective concept of in-house development and operations. DevOps are part of the agile framework, and its ability to collaborate seamlessly with the business is key to successful development, deployment, and operations. At the same time, DevOps readiness is a wide field of processes, responsibilities, activities, tools, and responses. It refers to an organization's ability to adopt and implement DevOps principles and ways of working. This includes having the necessary infrastructure, tools, processes, and culture to enable collaboration and communication between development and operations teams and the ability to quickly and efficiently release and update software.

Some of the key components of DevOps readiness include:

- Automated infrastructure and configuration management,
- Continuous integration and continuous deliveries (CI/CD),
- Monitoring and logging tools,
- Collaboration and communication tools,
- A culture of experimentation and continuous improvement,
- Agile methodologies and fast-paced development cycles,
- Continual and incremental problem-solving,
- Reuse and scale existing digital products,
- Embed innovation and secure value creation,
- Apply strong security practices.

DevOps readiness involves having the right tools, processes, and skills to enable collaboration and the ability to quickly and efficiently release and update software and other developed digital assets.

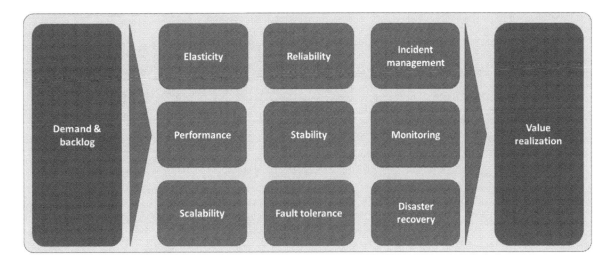

Figure 55 Core elements of successful DevOps frameworks

DevOps (Development Operations) includes several key elements, such as:

1. **Value realization**

   DevOps helps organizations increase the speed and efficiency of software delivery and improve collaboration and communication. It allows for faster time-to-market, greater agility, and cost savings. They can significantly enhance organizations' ability to integrate innovation into agile thinking, prioritization, design, and development. They can incorporate innovation into the new ways of working, utilizing innovation from data, technologies, and skills by promoting and creating a continuous improvement and modernization culture.

2. **Reliability**

   DevOps improve reliability by implementing automation, testing, and monitoring throughout the software delivery. DevOps promote collaboration between development and operations teams, allowing for early detection and resolution of issues and promoting the use of industry best practices such as configuration management and continuous integration.

   Their focus on collaboration, processes, and the willingness to deliver the right quality and finalize their development will increase reliability before and after deployment.

3. **Stability**

    DevOps improves software system stability by implementing automation and testing throughout the delivery process, promoting collaboration and communication between development and operations teams, and utilizing continuous integration and monitoring to detect and resolve issues quickly. It also encourages using industry best practices such as infrastructure as code and configuration management to maintain consistency and stability in the system.

4. **Performance**

    Secure high-performance applications are key for every business environment, as application performance has a direct negative impact on user satisfaction and usage of the applications or services. Performance optimization is the set of best practices and standards developers must apply to ensure that an application runs effectively by consuming fewer resources and avoiding costly technical debt. Application performance monitoring tools can decrease the challenges for development teams by providing real-time, proactive monitoring for common problems like infrastructure overload and downtime. This may also include error logging to allow teams to identify where coding issues might occur.

5. **Scalability**

    Scalability of software is the ability to process a higher workload on the given hardware resources without compromising the application's service and avoiding service interruptions. In digital composable enterprises, scalability is critical to ensure that any development is done based on this core principle. Scalability is essential to effectively deploy digital assets and products in multi-cloud and multi-platform composable architectures. The design of digital foundational platforms is also a question of scalability, as wrongly designed platforms will restrict digital composable development rather than enable unconstrained scalability.

    Applications scalability is critical with deploying new applications, especially when reusing micro-services effectively. Scalability must address cost issues and the risk of costs triggered by third-party software.

    The quality and scalability of an application are equally dependent on effective traffic management, capacity planning, and performance evaluations.

6. **Elasticity**

Elasticity is the capacity of the hardware and platform layer, which ideally would be running on a usual cloud infrastructure. It should allow for an increase or decrease in the computing infrastructure resources to satisfy the application's processing demand in operations effectively. The variations in increase and decrease generated by business demand and rules must be defined in advance, while the actual shift of demand with rapid changes in demand can increase or decrease significantly and be managed carefully to avoid service interruption.

7. **Fault tolerance**

Fault tolerance is becoming increasingly important to software developers, which might include higher demands on backup systems in case of system failure. The relentless compliance with the agreed foundational principles and design patterns is critical to be applied by all DevOps teams across all technologies and platforms. Only by using those principles will the microservice-enabled architecture enable the highest possible level of fault tolerance in operations.

8. **Monitoring**

Monitoring of digitally developed applications is vital to detect and avoid greater problems. It includes various KPIs, such as monitoring the application performance, ideally managed through a single dashboard across the various applications deployed. Automating manual tasks when monitoring application performance is vital to inform about important deviations from agreed service levels or detecting problems requiring immediate attention.

9. **Incident management**

DevOps teams are responsible for implementing incident management processes to quickly detect, diagnose, and resolve issues that arise within software systems. This responsibility includes implementing monitoring and logging tools, creating incident response plans, and promoting a culture of collaboration and communication between development and operations teams to minimize downtime and ensure system availability.

The role of incident management in composable architectures is increasingly important, as downtime in IT legacy systems may cause problems and downtime in digital applications.

10. **Disaster recovery**

DevOps teams play a crucial role in disaster recovery by implementing automation, testing, and monitoring throughout the software delivery process to ensure that systems are robust and quickly restored in case of an outage. They also promote using industry best practices such as infrastructure as code and configuration management to maintain consistency and stability in the system. DevOps teams ensure that disaster recovery plans are updated and tested regularly.

Applied Technology Leadership
Thomas Wickman, Head of IT Development, Green Cargo

"Green Cargo started to apply agile development in 2020, utilizing the OutSystems lowcode platform to verify and learn about agile development. The organization began to engage in integration development and used PMO budgets to start agile development of APIs and integrations on Green Cargos' new enterprise hybrid integration platform. Another project was developing core analytics capabilities in our new Google Cloud Platform. Those activities were uncoordinated but essential to verify the implementation of agile development at Green Cargo. After organizing those resources in the PMO and Applications department, we established the new IT Development department in early 2022.

The focus was on reorganizing and strengthening our agile transformation and applying similar ways of working across our DevOps teams for integration, lowcode development, and analytics. By sharing those resources with funding limitations, we utilized investment budgets from our PMO to finance the rapid growth of those teams, wherever applicable.

Our DevOps teams are all educated in SAFe5.0, and we apply Microsoft DevOps and other tools. Our teams enable our composable interoperable approach, where we put our integration development team into the center of all five teams. They are usually very constrained, as enterprise integration is at the core of our digital transformation. They all work collaboratively, are highly integrated, and apply best practices in a balanced mixture between employees and consultants.

The strengths of our DevOps teams are their access and utilization of our digital foundational platforms and applied foundational principles. Our teams continually improve collaboration with our business and strengthen cooperative work. The next step is introducing agile budgeting and engaging our business in prioritizing our features, epics, and backlog. Our value-driven focus integrates into every aspect of our work. We will continue transforming Green Cargo into a product-driven business where digitally developed products are embedded into the core of our business model and processes. Our increased focus on value-driven digital development further strengthens our ability to innovate our business collaboratively and engage in value-driven utilization of resources.

We continue leveraging our focus on finalizing work packages with acceptable levels of quality (and avoid being perfect) and as packaged business capabilities. We can see great efforts in different parts of the business where digital leaders and product owners are arising, primarily within Marketing & Sales, Network Management, and Operations.

Our modular thinking is applied everywhere, and the main reason why the outcome of our work is the core foundation for turning Green Cargo into a leading digital composable enterprise".

Written by Thomas Wickman, Head of IT Development, Green Cargo, Consultant & Agile Coach

There are several different types of DevOps teams that organizations can implement, each with its unique structure and focus.

Some of the most popular DevOps team types include:

- **Centralized DevOps teams**

  They oversee and manage the entire DevOps process across the organization. Those teams typically include members from development, operations, and other relevant departments.

- **Embedded DevOps teams**

  They usually integrate practices and principles into individual development teams. This type promotes collaboration and communication between development and operations teams at the team level.

- **Hybrid DevOps teams**

  They combine elements of both centralized and embedded DevOps models. Those teams typically include a central DevOps team responsible for overseeing and managing the DevOps process across the organization and embedded DevOps teams integrated into individual development teams.

- **Distributed DevOps teams**

  They are effective when spread across different locations, often in other countries and time zones.

The chosen approach depends on the organization's size, the complexity of its systems, and the level of collaboration and communication desired by the organization. Agile development is essential to succeed with digital transformations because it promotes a flexible, adaptive approach to software and digital development. It allows organizations to quickly respond to changing business requirements and market conditions and to assume greater responsibility to leverage and integrate existing IT legacy systems and new digital capabilities and development.

AGILE DEVELOPMENT FRAMEWORKS			
	SAFe 5.0	**Scrum**	**Kanban**
Definition	A framework for implementing agile at scale.	A framework for agile software development focused on iterative and incremental delivery.	An agile methodology that emphasizes continuous flow and delivery.
Key Principles	Lean, agile, and systems thinking.	Empirical process control, transparency, inspection, and adaptation.	Visualize workflow, limit work in progress, manage flow, make process policies explicit.
Roles	Product Owner, Scrum Master, Development Team, and others.	Product Owner, Scrum Master, Development Team, and stakeholders.	No specific roles, but typically includes a team lead and team members.
Ceremonies	Program Increment (PI) planning, iteration planning, daily stand-up, iteration review, and retrospective.	Sprint planning, daily Scrum, Sprint review, and Sprint retrospective.	Daily stand-up and regular retrospectives.
Artifacts	Program Backlog, Team Backlog, Feature, Epic, and Story.	Product Backlog, Sprint Backlog, and Increment.	Kanban board, Work-in-Progress (WIP) limits, and Cumulative Flow Diagram.
Scale	Designed for mid and large-sized enterprises and complex systems.	Designed for small to medium-sized teams.	Can be applied to teams of any size.
Benefits	Helps organizations achieve alignment, visibility, and predictability at scale.	Provides a simple, flexible framework for iterative delivery.	Emphasizes continuous flow, reduces waste, and improves efficiency.

Figure 56 Comparison of agile development frameworks

Agile methodologies, such as SAFe 5.0, Scrum, and Kanban, support continuous improvement, which is crucial when organizations undergo digital transformations. Agile development focuses on delivering small, incremental changes to software systems and digitally developed assets. This is beneficial when organizations want to modernize legacy systems or introduce new technologies, especially if they implement composability and interoperability.

Agile development also encourages collaboration and communication between development teams, which is crucial when organizations try to implement new digital technologies and services. Agile working methods allow teams to identify and resolve issues quickly and constantly adapt to business priorities and process changes. Effective cooperation between modern architecture teams and DevOps teams is crucial, especially if agile teams support agile projects, such as developing a customer portal in B2B or an eCommerce platform in B2C.

Agile development enables organizations to respond quickly to changing business requirements and market conditions, prioritize customer feedback, and continuously improve products and services. This allows organizations to more effectively implement digital transformations, modernize legacy systems and introduce new technologies. Successful transformations may introduce the need to leverage digital development with DevOps teams toward more product-driven organizations.

Evolve into a product-driven organization

Organizations that drive their digital transformations most likely evolve from the traditional development of applications, tools, models, and algorithms towards more product-focused and product-driven organizations.

Product-driven digital development teams contribute to designing, developing, and maintaining digital products, such as mobile applications, integrations, or analytics. They work closely with product managers, users, developers, process owners, and other stakeholders to understand the requirements and goals of a digital product and use their technical and business expertise. Product owners support the entire process, from design to production and life-cycle-management.

They prioritize new development and backlog, allocate resources, and identify value generation and business cases to inform and engage with end-users. They must also realize the estimated benefits of their digital products and support or driven implementations and roll out of changes (if required). A product-driven digital development team plays a key role in creating and delivering high-quality digital products that meet the needs of users and stakeholders and, most importantly, deliver and sustain value generation with a well-grounded purpose and business case realization.

Organizations must reconsider the business owners of their new digitally developed assets and applications to leverage the maximum value of digital transformations. They should therefore foster a climate of empowerment where product owners can make independent decisions guided by their vision, strategy, goals, and business priorities.

Applied Technology Leadership
Jörgen Lindholm, Green Cargo, Consultant MaxiTech

"At Green Cargo, there has been a big change in recent years where IT development has shifted from uncontrolled and completely outsourced to almost completely transformed inhouse ownership. The system landscape dominates by highly complex IT legacy systems that cannot create new business offerings. Many processes included manual steps, and those systems had little integration.

The outsourced development mainly focused on sustaining the business. The business and IT development gap were too big for radical changes. To realize the evolutionary IT strategy established by the new CIO, it was necessary to take control of development and bring the business and IT much closer. The focus is to modernize the system landscape to enable digital transformation and establish a climate encouraging embedded, continual, business-driven, technology-encouraged innovation.

With well-defined teams working closely with the business, we have created a new culture where innovation sees as a competitive edge. With established processes and tools for requirements, prioritization, and planning, we utilize collaborative, agile methodologies to ensure value is constantly delivered.

> *The business digitalizes to a much higher degree, and there is a constant dialogue on further improving processes from the core. The encouragement to be innovative has led to IT can show the business the possibilities with new technology and platforms, tradition and legacy are constantly challenged. New and unthinkable solutions and product offerings constantly develop where innovation is embedded daily. And most notably, we develop enterprise applications in lowcode highly integrated and interoperable with our legacy systems.*
>
> *We still have many things to improve, but looking back, one can only realize that we have accomplished a paradigm shift. It is no longer a necessary support function but a muscle that gives a competitive advantage. Key factors to the success have been a clear IT strategy, skilled resources, and dedicated and supportive leadership."*
>
> *Written by Jörgen Lindholm, Green Cargo, Consultant MaxiTech*

Evolving traditional organizations into product-driven organizations takes time. To overcome digital transformation issues and increase user acceptance, enterprises can create distinct digital business product ownership within the line organization. This is achievable by identifying individual business owners of new or existing digital products or applications. They are typically decision-makers and represent their business unit or department in agile prioritization, planning, and development processes. They have full control over their products, as they seek empowerment and distinct decision rights, alternatively to align with other appropriate decision-makers or key stakeholders, such as information owners, system owners, process owners, data owners, and users. They will ensure compliance with policies, laws, regulations, and access rights.

Product owners will secure the required communication and information/training on why and how to use the product most effectively. They will provide or organize support and address any issues that can help build end-users' trust and confidence in the product.

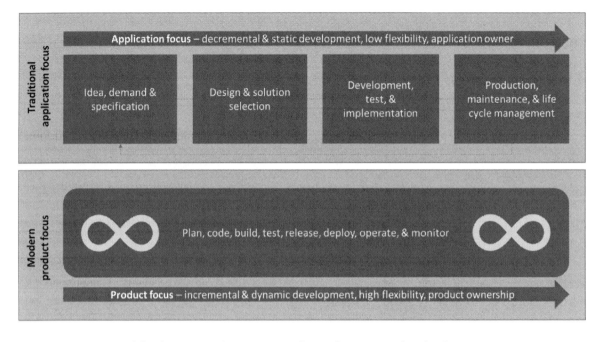

Figure 57 Organizational development requires a transition from software to product development

Mature digital transformations manage to evolve strong product management and ownership with shared but clear responsibilities.

Implementing product-driven organizations with collaborative business and tech teams will help to overcome conventional problems such as resource allocations, master data management, product ownership, backlog management, and more. Those complications may diminish or disappear over time, as distinct product ownership enables effective collaboration with clear responsibilities.

TYPICAL ROLES IN AGILE DEVELOPMENT TEAMS (overview)

Role	Responsibilities	Skills	Organizational Belonging
Product Owner	Represents the voice of the customer and prioritizes the product backlog based on business value.	Product management, customer empathy, backlog management, stakeholder management.	Business and development.
Scrum Master	ManAges actual work facilitates collaboration and cooperation manages workloads and helps achieve development goals.	Facilitation, coaching, conflict resolution, agile methodology expertise.	Development.
Developer	Develops (Lowcode), writes code, tests, and deploys software iteratively and incrementally.	Programming, testing, continuous integration and deployment, version control.	Development or engineering.
Operations Engineer	Deploys and manages infrastructure and applications, ensuring high availability, scalability, and performance.	Infrastructure management, cloud computing, automation, monitoring and logging.	Operations or IT.
Quality Assurance Engineer	Tests software to ensure that it meets quality standards and customer requirements.	Test automation, manual testing, exploratory testing, test planning, defect management.	QA or testing.
Security Engineer	Ensures that the software is secure and compliant with regulatory and industry standards.	Security testing, threat modeling, vulnerability management, compliance.	Security or operations.

Figure 58 Typical roles in agile development teams

Product ownership is value-driven and may help organizations to solve inefficiencies they have been struggling with for decades. It is a new way to foster an unprecedented new climate of trust, accountabilities, and autonomy across organizations. Value-driven product teams will flourish ineffective routines, making traditional governance models inadequate and obsolete.

To leverage product ownership, organizations must constantly increase business value through product development in self-regulated and autonomous ways. Organizations that leverage agility, flexibility, and adaptability will develop a climate and culture where innovation embeds into routines and daily business operations.

In particular, enterprises with the ambition to transform their business into composable enterprises must embrace the opportunities of product-driven organizations. Those who master this development will secure greater business benefits, more satisfied users and customers, more effective utilization of resources, aligned changes in interoperable digital applications, and greater success of digital composable transformations.

Distinct product ownership will lead to optimized costs and monetization of investments, drive collaboration, and increase innovation capabilities across organizations. Besides the efforts of always doing the right things, product ownership and agile teams shall not be afraid of experimental approaches. Where applicable, understanding and motivating imperfectness in digital development efforts is a critical capability of digital transformations.

Motivate imperfectness - where applicable

Motivating imperfectness is a critical ability of high-performing digital transformations. They constantly consider external and internal requirements to utilize new tech and data to maximize business benefits without risking compliance or safety.

Highly regulated industries are typically subject to strict rules and regulations imposed by governments or other regulatory bodies. Those demands that enterprises comply with various regulations, laws, and industry standards, such as safety, quality, data security, environmental protection, and other areas. They are applying risk management, facing various operational, financial, reputational, and compliance risks.

Regulated enterprises have strong processes to identify, qualify, mitigate, and report on their risk programs. They make their leaders accountable for their actions and decisions while maintaining records and providing regular reports to regulatory bodies, shareholders, and other stakeholders. They must secure transparency in highly regulated industries to build trust and maintain public confidence. In other cases, enterprises must disclose information about their operations, financial performance, and compliance efforts to stakeholders. They often focus on programs supporting continuous improvement and have recently learned to utilize data and intelligence to continuously improve their operations, products, and services to meet changing regulatory requirements and customer expectations.

Highly regulated industries may, at first hand, see significant risks with imperfectness. At the same time, they must embrace how to utilize digital composability to increase compliance while adjusting their risk perception levels significantly to allow greater adherence to more experimental and incremental practices. They must reconstruct their often rigid and archaic demand with high proportional degrees of diligence, attention to detail, and sometimes overinterpreted levels of commitment to meeting regulatory requirements while delivering quality products and services.

Traditionally, tech and development organizations establish processes, methodologies, and routines to become the perfect business partner and deliver the right IT solutions to the business and users. Technological development and acceleration reinforce new thinking to empower organizations with agile development on their digital foundational platforms, increasingly succeeding with sustainable in-house development. CIOs and IT leaders started to adjust their expectations of digitally developed products, opening up for greater failure tolerance and incompleteness of digitally created products (applications).

IT development teams focus on the quality of their development, as products must deliver on the expectations and agreed levels of quality. Digital product development differs from traditional product development in that it often involves a more iterative and flexible approach, focusing on continual development and the ability to quickly pivot or make changes based on user feedback and data. This approach also often emphasizes failure tolerance, as digital products can be updated and improved more easily than physical products. Digital products are released as an outcome of minimal viable products (MVPs), allowing for testing and iteration before a full release. This allows for a more agile and responsive development process, where identified failures get addressed more quickly.

As imperfectness is a key differentiator in agile development, it is most likely inappropriate in traditional projects (if not run agile and in sprints), traditional deliveries, or the design of new foundational platforms or other digital tools and capabilities (such SaaS, PaaS). The argument and reasoning behind imperfectness shall not be confused with higher failure tolerance, which must be applied in the right context and appropriately. Imperfectness will accelerate digital product development and help solve larger problems in smaller steps in digital development environments. By doing so, organizations will eliminate the fear of failure to encourage experimental thinking and execution. Imperfectness is a key element in digital evolutions to promote and enable incremental and experimental development.

With increased failure tolerance, development teams take appropriate measures, take corrective actions, and learn from mistakes. However, it is important to distinguish between tolerated and non-tolerated imperfections in digital development.

There are two different scenarios:

1. **Tolerate the imperfectness of digital development**

   Imperfectness results from agreed deviation from a perfect product, as digital products may never reach a final stage and are subject to constant change and continual development. One of the general obstructions to speed is the traditional way of looking at IT, processes, and the concern of overdeveloping specifications. Applying user stories is a strong tool within innovation and design thinking (from Stanford University d.school). This traditional behavior is a well-recognized hindrance for agile IT organizations to rapidly evolve and shift their focus towards value creation, not perfectness. Instead of striving for perfectionism, IT organizations shall adjust their efforts towards speed and value and build modular and small digital business capabilities for unlimited orchestration and reuse. Development policies must support elasticity, variability, failure tolerance, and learning rather than follow traditional approaches to software development. Modern agile development teams allow every user to directly provide feedback, automated and integrated into their DevOps tools, such as Microsoft DevOps.

2. **Ensure the perfectness of foundational technologies/platforms**

   Designing digital foundational architectures and platforms is critical to securing a sustainable, effective digital foundational architecture. Small missteps, wrong intentions, or wrong technology design can lead to major problems concerning the long-term effectiveness of such platforms. lowcode platforms designed for orchestration, reusability, interoperability, modularity, reliability, and flexibility must secure digital development aligned with the guiding principles as discussed.

   Organizations shall never compromise on their universal architectural principles to secure the holistic implementation of core digital foundational platforms. There is no room for inadequate governance and the absence or ignorance of those principles. Small mistakes in initial platform design can cause long-term problems and, in worst-case scenarios, lead to an inadequate design with severe failure and performance/stability problems.

Technology Leadership
Kasem Chahrour, Executive Digital Leader I Author I Advisor I at Digital Vibrations AB & Lowcodi AB

The Powerful Synergy of Composable Architecture and Low-Code Platforms: Accelerating Digital Innovation and Success!

"Composable architecture, as a key part of composable business, combined with modern digital foundational platforms enables easier, faster, better, and more cost-efficient development of digital solutions, which align with the essence of digitalization. This approach should not be overlooked by today's leaders, considering the high frequency of failed digital initiatives and the increasing need for digital solutions. The combination of composable architecture with enterprise Low-Code platforms brings several advantages to digital development:

Rapid Application Development: Using modular and reusable components, visual development tools, and pre-built components enable accelerated application development. This allows organizations to create and iterate on applications, quickly reducing time-to-market.

Flexibility and Agility: Flexible and modular construction of applications, together with visual configuration, component building, and customization capabilities, makes it easy for reusability and modifications or extensions of applications as business needs or market conditions evolve.

Cost-Effective Development: Component reusability and less redundant coding with rapid application development resulting in more cost-effective development.

Collaboration and Innovation: Business stakeholders actively participate in the development process while development teams rapidly prototype and iterate on features promoting innovation.

Enhanced User Experience: User-friendly interfaces and tools for designing intuitive user experiences combined with the flexible composition of user interface components makes it easier to create engaging and customized user experiences with improved user satisfaction.

Scalability and Maintainability: Loosely coupled components that can be independently developed, deployed, and scaled with unified development and solution environments result in better components and scalable, maintainable applications with reduced complexity and technical debt.

In summary - Combining composable architecture with Low-Code platforms is a powerful approach. It has numerous benefits for modern application development, empowering organizations to achieve their digitalization goals and innovation efficiently and effectively."
Written by Kasem Chahrour, Executive Digital Leader I Author I Advisor at Digital Vibrations AB
& Lowcodi AB

The right principles determine the overall direction and appropriateness of foundational principles. They will be the guiding force to ensure that principles and approaches to failure tolerance are critical and may vary from situation to situation.

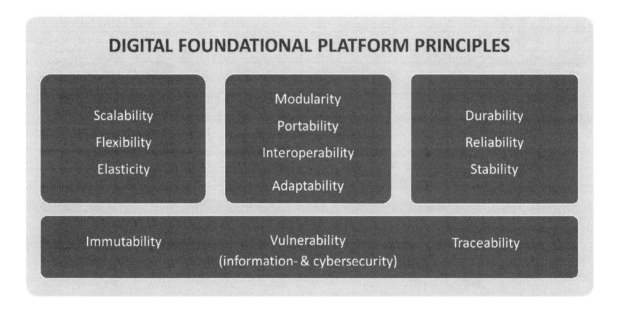

Figure 59 Digital foundational platform principles (simplified)

Digital transforming organizations must understand why, how, and when to focus on perfection and when to allow imperfectness.

When or when not to be perfect is essential to do digital work and must be understood and applied distinctively:

- **PERFECTNESS**

  Perfectness is critical for designing agile architectures and a prerequisite to building scalable and interoperable systems, platforms, and technologies. Insufficient design and mistakes during the initial platform establishment may cause long-term and significant problems regarding stability, multi-service orchestration, scalability, and reusability.

- **IMPERFECTNESS**

  Applying agile ways of working and failure-tolerant development is critical for digital development. Communicating and aligning with users about the agreed level of incompleteness is critical, as imperfections are important factors in continual development.

Successful organizations may realize large-scale benefits from their situational approaches to imperfections, as they most likely have invested in the skills required.

In this context, leading IT organizations offer unprecedented digital transformational opportunities to business leaders. Leading organizations know when to apply imperfectness and when not. They utilize and scale foundational technologies and platforms with their distinct approach to building the future digital enterprise.

Key conclusions and takeaways

The key conclusions and takeaways from the chapter "**INDISPENSABLE CAPABILITIES**" are:

1. Enterprises must apply distinct technology layers in their strategies, including their IT legacy, PaaS, SaaS/IaaS, and digitally developed products.

2. Enterprises must utilize loosely coupled services as a concept and principle for all digital development at the core of the design and utilization of digital composable architectures.

3. Enterprises must secure successful and sustainable digital composable enterprise transformations without establishing a new digital legacy.

4. Enterprises must reflect the high demand for integration development in financial planning and forecasting.

5. Enterprises must secure enterprise-wide integration utilizing digital foundational technologies as one of their most critical digital capabilities!

6. Enterprises must secure the reusability of their developed digital assets to solve problems limitlessly, create new opportunities, and foster infinite innovation.

7. Enterprises must encourage and adapt the culture of agile thinking, not only in terms of agile development.

8. Enterprises must introduce digital product-driven ownership to capitalize and monetize on their digital investments.

9. Enterprises must motivate imperfections where applicable but never compromise compliance, operational safety, or platform design.

SEVEN – DIGITAL FOUNDATIONAL PLATFORMS

THOUGHT DIGITAL LEADERSHIP

Tiago B. Azevedo, Chief Information Officer (CIO), OutSystems

"Your business future lies in the hands of Digital Foundational Platforms (DFP). Modern, business-enable technology capabilities characterize these platforms. And they include data and analytics (D&A) platforms, interoperability frameworks (APIs, microservices, integration protocols), and low code. What DFPs can do for you and your business is revolutionary. Here is why.

Time to market has decreased exponentially. Every company requires a dramatic increase in productivity while releasing new products faster—or managing agility internally. Backlogs fed by dozens of business areas produce an insurmountable list of often conflicting to-dos. Competition or other external pressures drive business change at a breakneck pace. Your capacity to prototype, adapt, change, and constantly iterate (and rapidly) is critical to winning. With the Great Resignation and talent shortages, businesses need an effortless way to get work done. Low-code platforms can cut timelines, from one-half to tenfold, across the full software lifecycle—from a kernel of an idea through customer development, deployment, and use.

Low code is here to stay. With it, the path to convert your IT team into a lean software factory, benefiting from visual development environments and Continuous Integration, Delivery & Deployment (CI/CD) automation that covers from frontends to databases, from business rules to notifications, and from integrations to user-friendly operations.

Make a seismic shift—break down the software monoliths. Please do this by adopting a composable business architecture based on the keystones of modularity, autonomy, orchestration, and their underlying digital architecture principles. This shift of perspective from systems to services will give you the freedom and adaptability to personalize your company, with the benefit of smaller team sizes and lower skill set requirements."

Written by Tiago B. Azevedo, Chief Information Officer (CIO), OutSystems

Adopt digital foundational platforms

IT needs to adapt more rapidly to changing business requirements by adopting new technologies and redefining the role that technologies play in business and digital transformations.

The role of IT is changing in several ways, mainly because of enterprise-wide digital foundational platforms, which are innovative strategic technologies that most enterprises oversee. These technologies enable organizations to become more agile and responsive to changing business needs. They also allow for increased collaboration and interoperability, meaning that IT needs to manage and maintain these systems holistically and represent broader goals, such as enterprise-wide composability. Another key opportunity is utilizing these technologies to enable enterprise-wide innovation capabilities and foster cultural adaptation and development. They also allow the provisioning of embedded information security and data protection, helping IT to implement and maintain such capabilities embedded into ready-to-deploy and robust security measures.

Digital foundational platforms are the core differentiating technologies, making the difference between digital and digital composable transformations. They are offering core components of technologies that are vital to:

- Interconnect any systems and technologies,
- Collect and redistribute any data from any source,
- Allow building any application interoperating with any application,
- Interconnect internal and external digital ecosystems,
- Allow embedded collaboration between employees, customers, and partners,
- Integrate information security and data protection capabilities.

Defining a digital foundational platform strategy and considering and architecting the enterprise's approach to those services in the cloud must be at the core of every digital composable strategy. Enterprises that disregard wide-ranging platform strategies and platform thinking may certainly not find ways to transform their organizations to the next level and achieve enterprise-wide inter compatibility and composability. Another advantage is that their availability, utilization, and scalability come at affordable costs and with highly scalable and configurable services.

Those platforms enable enterprises to rapidly test, verify and scale enterprise-wide composable technologies in unprecedented ways. Their immense innovative capacity and scalability also include unique interoperable capabilities, enabling entirely new strategies for bringing evolutionary technology innovation even to the most traditional enterprises. They are creating multiple opportunities and rapidly integrating new digital products and services with various essential capabilities and services, such as application development, enterprise integration, API management, enterprise analytics, data storage and management, and computing power.

One of the primary benefits of digital foundational platforms is to enable organizations to develop and iterate new digital products and services rapidly. Businesses can create new offerings more efficiently and flexibly by breaking down applications into smaller, more modular components. This enables organizations to respond more quickly to changing customer offerings, market conditions, and emerging technologies. Besides those advantages, they guarantee agility and flexibility, as digital foundational platforms allow organizations to scale their digital products and services quickly, cost-effectively, rapidly, and on demand.

Digital foundational platforms are key differentiators in digital composable transformations because they provide all the core capabilities required to realize composability at scale. Therefore, traditional, and digital enterprises will benefit from such undertakings and strategic considerations to create new digital products and services more quickly, flexibly, and cost-effectively than ever before. They will raise their level of autonomy and can utilize those platforms to transform their organizations.

The key challenges for most enterprises will be finding the skills and digital architects to understand what is required to make those platforms work in the enterprise context. As those talents are rare, CIOs should focus on architects and ambassadors who tried to implement service-oriented architectures (SOA) about 20 years ago. Those early attempts failed as IT perceived those concepts as too complex and costly, missing standardization, and difficult to align with the business. However, the most significant hinder was the absence of suitable technologies and their readiness to realize effective architectures deploying the good patterns of SOA. Those fundamentally well-equipped skills might still be part of IT organizations and could be motivated by getting a second chance to realize their passion for SOA by strategizing and designing future enterprise digital foundational strategies and architectures.

This has profound implications for the changing role of IT and how enterprise-wide foundational strategic technology decisions and how to manage those on an enterprise level. The consequences are huge as the role of IT is changing in several ways:

1. **IT is a critical business capability** and is no longer a support function but proactively contributing with technology leadership to transform or contribute to strategy and business development as a key enabler of business transformations. CIOs must take advantage and assume full responsibility and accountability to encourage and enable innovation and strategy enhancements by leading and deploying enterprise technologies at scale.

2. **IT drives enterprise composability and platform strategies**

   Composability requires enterprise-wide capabilities and distinct approaches to platform strategies, guaranteeing interoperability inside and outside enterprises. Siloed technology implementations and distributed decision-making in functional units require either enormous discipline or clear mandates with a full understanding of the consequences of distributed ITIf distributed IT organizations do not address those consequences from a composable enterprise perspective and jeopardize platform strategies, and they will increase complexity, costs, and risks instead. Without setting strategic goals to secure enterprise composability, distributed IT organizations will significantly hinder the development of composable enterprises.

3. **IT enables and pushes data-driven business models** to access data and technologies to provide insights that businesses can utilize and explore, to drive, optimize, and automate business decisions and utilize data to inform executives about strategic choices. IT shall make data accessible and ensure compliance, security, and proper access rights, while the business shall be enabled and empowered to utilize data for appropriate analysis and decision-making.

4. **IT supports the rise of customer-centricity from the core of the business** by ensuring relentless opportunities to develop critical business capabilities from the core of the business. Due to unconstrained access to multiple digital foundational platforms and critical IT legacy systems, development teams can secure seamless customer centricity, while business development and new features will ensure interoperability between relevant technologies.

5. **IT enables enterprise collaboration** by introducing new collaborative digitally enabled agile processes and prioritization. The continuity and continual involvement of business and IT will shape and create new opportunities to improve and enable collaboration at scale.

6. **IT establishes autonomy and flexibility** to reduce the dependencies of IT development from external resources and partners. Modern IT organizations will instead assume full in-house responsibility to utilize internal resources once their availability is secured. Both business and IT are constantly learning and growing their level of independence with increased knowledge about technologies and processes.

7. **IT influences cultural development** through agile methods to help enterprises quickly adapt to new technologies and changing business needs. The capabilities are innovative as such and enable the business to apply innovation from the core of the business. New collaborative ways of working will engage everyone, removing silos and fostering a culture of evolutionary, continual, and scalable innovation from the core of the business.

8. **IT drives automation** to automate repetitive tasks to increase efficiency and reduce costs by making platforms and easy-to-use capabilities.

9. **IT integrates enterprise-wide information security and data protection** to ensure that data, assets, people, systems, and processes are secure and capable of effectively detecting risks and responding when needed. IT supports the organization to constantly increase its understanding and awareness to avoid incidents or inappropriate actions. This will include compliance to secure the enterprise's duties and obligations to adjust to external requirements.

This list gives an overall impression of the changing role of IT in the context of digitally transforming enterprises and the risks of making inappropriate and uninformed choices.

"Interoperable digital foundational platforms must be selected, implemented, and owned by the CIO or CTO, as enterprise composability will never be achievable without strategically architecting and scaling those fundamental and strategic investments."

Ingo Paas

Traditional IT Manage the IT systems	Future IT Transform with technologies
Support technology choices Support the business strategy Support crisis on demand Support business processes Deliver IT services Integrate IT systems Develop the business Fulfill business demand	Drive and make technology choices Reshape the business strategy Build the composable enterprise Create business capabilities Innovate the business Integrate the enterprise Explore digital opportunities Shape business demand
Focus on system IT as a support function	Focus on IT as a business innovator

Figure 60 The shift of focus of IT organizations from "Manage the IT systems" to "Transform with Technologies"

Traditionally, IT organizations should avoid making technology decisions and running tech projects without involving the business. However, this has changed during the last few years, especially as digital platforms provided by global tech vendors constantly become dominating factors in selecting and utilizing digital foundation technologies. This has significantly changed how IT organizations respond to foundational enterprise-wide composable demand.

IT organizations must be mandated or assume accountability to make effective strategic technology decisions that business representatives could ever accomplish or demand. This implies a major shift in the perceptions and responsibilities of IT organizations. Leveraging digital foundational platforms requires a different approach and new thinking to redefine the role and responsibilities of IT. As business functions usually think in silos, processes, and problems motivated by clearly defined goals, they cannot assume enterprise-wide responsibilities to develop strategies that secure coherent, systemic, and holistic approaches to enterprise-wide technology strategies and deployment.

IT organizations must proactively shift their strategic focus to analyze and understand the most critical enterprise's business capabilities. They must design and promote platform technology investments for the enterprise rather than supporting traditional business demand. They must assume responsibility and accountability to make strategic investment decisions, establish digital foundational architectures, and compose the existing IT legacy with the enterprise's future digital foundational technologies.

IT organizations must evolve and facilitate those strategic changes aligned with the enterprise's purpose, vision, strategy, goals, and business priorities. IT organizations must offer the business a multiverse of cloud-native-enabled digital foundational capabilities by utilizing digital foundational platform architectures.

Successful organizations allow businesses to build their strategies around multi-purpose technologies, ready to access, use, scale, and adapt. They reinforce new approaches to solving unsolvable business problems by strategically utilizing the enormous power of underlying digital foundational platforms. They promote relentless and unlimited problem-solving capabilities and create dynamic business demands and continuous improvements in collaboration. They enable businesses and IT to effectively utilize platforms to digitalize customer relationships and to optimize and innovate their core business models. They support the business to advance into new business models or revenue streams, integrate into digital ecosystems, and increase the digitalization of products and services. Those organizations ensure that business ownership is understood as an asset and fully applied to support new and future digitalized processes.

Applied Technology Leadership
Ingo Paas, CIO & CDO Green Cargo

"At Green Cargo, we faced enormous complexity, IT debts, and other challenges without any chance to consider any digital investments. We initiated a digital foundational platform strategy and architecture to create interoperability and enterprise-wide IT and digital resilience. Our objectives were to:

- *modernize and utilize our IT legacy,*

- *integrate and compose our IT legacy and digital platforms,*

- *engage the organization in collaborative development,*

- *increase business agility and IT and digital resilience,*

- *enable business development from the core of the business,*

- *promote a data-driven business,*

- *increase our digital autonomy at scale, and*

- *foster a culture of inclusive and embedded innovation.*

Three years later, we can confirm that our strategy executes with a high grade of completeness. Green Cargos' fast-evolving ability to leverage unique technologies at scale allows us to support those significant transformational business changes. Our capabilities are constantly improving, with constrained access to resources and funding to continue eliminating the backlog of more than ten years without decent IT investments and business development with IT. Our greatest challenge is not to develop but to solve the right problems with the right business requirements and scope.

We implemented five fundamental platforms, including our lowcode platform (OutSystems), our analytics platform (Google Cloud Platform & Microsoft Power Platform), our hybrid integration and analytics platform (Microsoft Azure), our automation platform (UIPath), and our workplace platform (Microsoft). Besides our digital foundational architecture's flexibility, scalability, and instant composability, we build full composability and interoperability into the design of our new and future digital foundational platforms.

We have further advanced our strategy and leveraged Microsoft's digital platforms at the core of our comprehensive platform strategy, with a strong focus on Microsoft's Dynamics services. Our advanced strategy will secure a fully composable transformation from traditional ERP to cloud-based platforms (on Microsoft Azure) by deploying Microsoft SaaS solutions in our MS tenant. This strategy will unite core capabilities, secure interoperability, flexibility, and full-scale collaborative capabilities (eco-systems, workplace, data analytics, development, APIs, security, access rights, and more).

Although intensive SaaS usage will be part of our future, we have fully integrated our critical SaaS capabilities based on our principles (similar to those already discussed in this book) to facilitate enterprise-wide interoperability and composability. Our digital foundational platforms and assets are reusable and scalable without limitations and ready for multipurpose orchestration. To summarize our achievements, we delivered on all the above strategic business concerns and needs and have further advanced our initial strategy."

Written by Ingo Paas, CIO & CDO Green Cargo

The main role of cloud-native digital foundational platforms is to provide a set of technologies and tools that enable organizations to build, deploy, and manage applications in a cloud environment. These platforms offer various features to make it easier for organizations to utilize the cloud's scalability, elasticity, and cost-effectiveness. Some of the key features of cloud-native platforms include the following:

1. **Containerization and modularity**

   Cloud-native platforms use containerization for packaging applications and their dependencies, making them portable and easy to deploy across different environments. With this in mind, we relentlessly strive for modular capabilities.

2. **Microservices architecture**

   Cloud-native platforms support a microservices architecture, allowing organizations to build applications out of small, loosely coupled services independently developed, deployed, and scaled.

3. **Automated scaling**

   Cloud-native platforms provide automated scaling, enabling applications to automatically scale up or down based on demand and changing volumes instantly.

4. **Self-healing**

   Self-healing is an automated feature in cloud-native platforms providing self-healing capabilities to detect and recover from failures automatically, used to automate the detection and resolution of issues that may occur in an application through automated monitoring, diagnostics, and remediation.

5. **Automated deployment**

   Cloud-native platforms provide automated deployment, which enables organizations to deploy and orchestrate new versions of their applications across multiple platforms. Cloud computing platforms automate deploying applications and services to the cloud to quickly and easily provision new resources, deploy applications, and manage updates and changes effectively.

6. **Cloud agnostic**

   Cloud-native platforms are cloud agnostic, meaning they can run on any cloud infrastructure (AWS, Azure, GCP). In a cloud-agnostic architecture, the application logic and data are separated from the underlying infrastructure, which is a strategy to allow the application to be deployed and run on hybrid

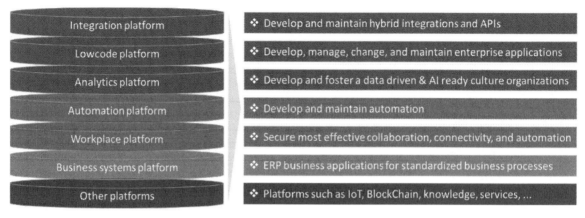

Integration platform	❖ Develop and maintain hybrid integrations and APIs
Lowcode platform	❖ Develop, manage, change, and maintain enterprise applications
Analytics platform	❖ Develop and foster a data driven & AI ready culture organizations
Automation platform	❖ Develop and maintain automation
Workplace platform	❖ Secure most effective collaboration, connectivity, and automation
Business systems platform	❖ ERP business applications for standardized business processes
Other platforms	❖ Platforms such as IoT, BlockChain, knowledge, services, …

or multi-cloud environments.

Figure 61 Digital foundational platforms build the core of digital transformations similar to the strategy as applied at Green Cargo)

Business benefits of utilizing digital foundational platforms in composable transformations

- Improve overall business performance from the core,
- Foster the development of a data, tech, and intelligence-driven culture,
- Accelerate the integration into and the development of digital ecosystems,
- Support acceleration and innovation of business strategies,
- Enable process and data-driven business model innovation,
- Increase overall business and digital/technology resilience,
- Enable organic business growth through superior digital customer services,
- Reinforce and accelerate collaborative, effective, and sustainable business development,
- Mitigate significant and prioritized business and IT risks,
- Digitalize, automate, and simplify processes,
- Generate new and advanced data from digitalized processes and IoT devices,
- Build customized preventive and predictive models and techniques,
- Improve customer satisfaction through a unique customer B2B experience,
- React to ever-faster changes in external digital eco-system demands,
- Secure enterprise-wide interoperability and utilize the composable digital architecture,
- Establish autonomy in digital development,

- Embed and automate information and cyber security measures (detect & respond),

- Accomplish a realistic, profitable, controlled, and sustainable digital transformation.

IT benefits of utilizing digital foundational platforms in composable transformations

- Create greater digital and IT autonomy (sourcing, cloud, IT development, …),

- Establish a software factory for lowcode application development,

- Reuse innovation capabilities to utilize innovation power from global CSPs,

- Implement a collaborative development culture with incremental and experimental capabilities,

- Establish a collaborative workspace for office workers and personnel in the field,

- Establish effective, flexible, and dynamic composable architectures to secure interoperability.

In summary, cloud-native platforms make it easier for organizations to rapidly test, verify and scale the advantages of cloud platforms, such as scalability, elasticity, and cost-effectiveness. They provide a set of technologies and tools that simplify cloud-based applications' development, deployment, and management. Enterprises must reevaluate their strategies, architectures, and technology if they do not leverage digital foundational platforms at the core of their digital composable transformations.

Design a composable platform architecture

Traditional enterprises should consider adapting to the design of composable architectures to increase flexibility and digital resilience, leverage competitive advantage, drive and embed innovation, improve customer experience, drive business improvements, enable digital transformations, and create agile, collaborative cultures.

Some architecture-related advantages of composable enterprises are:

- Increase flexibility and digital to respond to a crisis effectively and rapidly,

- Leverage competitive advantages,

- Secure continuity and discipline in digital investments,

- Minimize risks of investing in new digital legacy,

- Secure enterprise-wide interoperability,

- Ease implementation of new technologies and digital services,

- Revitalize unleashed data and value from IT legacy systems,

- Simplify buy versus build decisions,

- Motivate to complement missing functionality with lowcode development,

- Increase digital resilience,

- Allow the business to own and drive continual innovation,

- Engage the organization in incremental learning and improvements,

- Enable cost savings to reduce costs and increase operational efficiency,

- Accelerate ecosystem adaptation and development.

Enterprises select multiple hypersacler platform vendors, such as Google, Microsoft, and Amazon, as PaaS providers. Core business capabilities (such as integrating analytics, integrations, AI, and the workplace) suggest a more strategic consideration of current and future business needs. Such business capabilities require integrated processes as highly integrated domains that benefit organizations long term, primarily when capabilities are used dynamically and cross-functionally. Building those capabilities on different platforms can cause interoperability problems and drive complexity, costs, and user-friendliness. Such strategic choices are essential to consider as early as possible and to capture those risks in designing composable architectures. This approach and strategy require that IT defines and applies distinct guiding principles to leverage those platforms' opportunities.

Organizations must avoid compromising on those principles and only approve divergences if principles must be reviewed or adjusted based on learnings, changes in conditions, or business requirements. A strong digital foundational platform strategy and architecture can avoid misalignment with business objectives, scalability issues, high costs, increased technical debt, security vulnerabilities, and restricted flexibility. Enterprises must invest in those technologies to not risk their digital composable transformations.

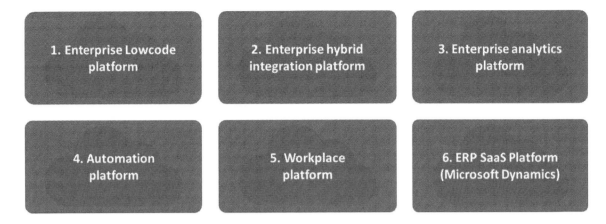

Figure 62 Cloud-native platforms are at the core of digital composable transformations

A brief explanation of those platforms shall help better understand their purpose and readiness. The digital foundational platforms include but are not limited to:

Introducing enterprise lowcode platforms is a fundamental change for every company, whether they develop their software with DevOps teams or start with in-house application development. The choice and implementation of lowcode platforms have strategic consequences that must be understood and managed. The long-term benefits of enterprise lowcode platforms are unprecedented and include rapid development, reusability, simplicity, transparency, interoperability, cost savings, continuous development, reduced risks of new coded legacy, and more.

Enterprise lowcode platform developers can develop enterprise applications supporting multi-purpose needs, such as replacing ERP functionality and developing new apps with real-time and event-driven capabilities. Developers and businesses can jointly solve any business problem effectively with rapid development and deployment.

The opportunities are unrestricted, and the right platform will be an accelerator for building the digital composable enterprise in the cloud. Leading enterprise Lowcode platforms are not just another way of developing applications! Such platforms are a foundational and revolutionary approach to making traditional software development obsolete while leveraging while revolutionizing the conventional method of coding.

They are at the core of digital composable strategies and transformations to realize and scale those advantages, enabling autonomous software development from the core of the business in unprecedented ways. Without significant investments into enterprise lowcode, composability will eventually be unreasonable to achieve in digital transformations.

2. Enterprise hybrid integration platform

Enterprise hybrid integration platforms (EHIP) are Over the past few years, integration has emerged as a significant hurdle and limitation for IT organizations. The demand for new integrations has increased rapidly, outpacing the ability of IT organizations to keep up. Adopting an enterprise-wide integration approach that is flexible, scalable, and platform-based is critical to achieving digital composable transformations.

Developing an agile integration strategy is essential for building interoperability and creating digital composable enterprises. These platform-based solutions provide organizations with the necessary integration capabilities to integrate data and applications across IT legacy systems, multi-cloud services, foundational enterprise platforms, and digital assets.

The core components of enterprise hybrid integration platforms include:

- API lifecycle management to create, secure, manage, and share APIs across different environments fast and effectively, the application and data integration, and to use and synchronize data across applications to address various issues, including data formats and standards.

- Messaging and event-driven architecture to synchronize and standardize data in real-time, including effective integrations and exchange to securely exchange data across ecosystems from and between any cloud-based to on-premise applications.

- High-speed data transfer can effectively manage vast data volumes without any performance issues. Enterprise hybrid integration platforms must unify traditional and state-of-the-art integration capabilities within a containerized platform. Those platforms are essential investments for any digital transformation as they secure modern and scalable enterprise-wide integration capabilities internally and externally.

Those platforms are foundational for seamless interoperability and the agile development of digital transformations. Enterprises will never achieve true composability and interoperability without these two critical digital foundational platforms.

3. Enterprise analytics platform

The role of analytics platforms in digital composable transformations is to provide the ability to collect, store, process, and analyze large amounts of data to gain insights that can drive business decisions and actions. They offer a variety of critical domains to guide and facilitate data-driven evolutions on the enterprise level. They contribute with various critical capabilities, such as data collection, data processing, data visualization, predictive analytics, automation of data processing and tasks, and more. Those platforms can be used to develop enterprise-wide core data models, host critical business data and reports, and act as the engine for data analytics and ML capabilities.

They support and facilitate a more democratized utilization of data-driven transformations, allowing end-users access to qualified data for individual analysis leveraging data-driven cultures.

The benefits empower businesses to optimize and/or automate their decision-making processes. Business insights in dynamic business processes will outperform any traditional way of analyzing data, while embedded AI capabilities will help enterprises understand patterns in data to increase predictive and other data-driven capabilities. Analytics platforms play an essential role in digital composable transformations as they provide the ability to collect, process, and analyze large amounts of data to gain insights that can drive business decisions and actions in real-time.

They engage organizations in data-driven business, democratizing the utilization of data across the core domains of data use cases, such as

- Integrated guided analytics
- Trusted and accessible self-service analysis
- Predictive & prescriptive analytics
- Intelligent AI analytics & automation

4. Automation platform

Automation will reduce or replace unnecessary human intervention in business processes at a maximum. The main purpose of investing in automation platforms is the effect those investments can realize to replace manual work. This can lead to reduced costs, better quality, faster processing, minimized business risks, and often new data points to measure and further improve business outcomes.

Effective automation processes help organizations decrease or eliminate ineffective data processing. Automation platforms help to drive efficiencies, while their ability to scale is restricted compared with highly scalable lowcode platforms.

Automation platforms can manage multiple bots processing multiple processes and multiple data sources in the most effective ways with strong ROI and effective TCO.

5. Workplace platform

Digital workplaces are common platforms utilized and implemented broadly with prioritized investments in the shadow of the global pandemic. Not only that those platforms effectively contribute to greater resilience, but they are also the core enabler of collaborative capabilities for enterprises.

Organizations often undervalue the role of workplace platforms in digital transformations and consider their contribution to composability irrelevant. They make digital transformations more comprehensive and contribute various features to digitalization efforts. Those include mobile workplaces, remote working, onboarding and off-boarding, user access rights, automation of controls, CRM, and more. They help to manage B2B (Business to Business) or B2C (Business to Consumer) access rights with Active Directories of partners to simplify authorized access to multiple applications.

6. ERP SaaS Platform (Microsoft Dynamics)

The cloud offers new strategies and responses to secure future ERP generations exclusively in the cloud. Enterprises can select major vendor cloud solutions such as SAP, Oracle, or similar offerings. They could likewise buy best-of-breed or prioritize a PaaS-enabled multi-SaaS implementation by utilizing capabilities such as Microsoft Dynamics for small to midsize enterprises. This third example of using the cloud and its PaaS capabilities offers new opportunities to leverage it for future ERP.

In summary, Digital Foundational Platforms significantly impact digital transformations and CxOs' priorities. They provide the infrastructure and tools organizations need to deliver their digital initiatives to leverage business-driven digital transformations. Those platforms can include the above-discussed platforms like data analytics, lowcode, automation, and more.

Digital foundational platforms can help organizations to more easily and effectively implement new technologies and processes and solve traditionally unresolvable problems on the enterprise level. They provide solid foundational and uncompromisable effects for digital composable transformations.

They can also help reduce the complexity and costs associated with digital transformations, making it easier for CxOs to prioritize and implement the most important organizational changes.

Digital foundational platforms also enable CxOs to focus on more strategic initiatives, such as digital innovation and customer engagement, rather than spending time on maintaining and upgrading legacy systems. Digital foundational platforms are important in enabling digital transformations and can help CxOs prioritize and implement changes more effectively by providing the underlying infrastructure and tools needed to support these initiatives.

"Foundational platforms strategies are critical and indispensable for enterprises to enable composability and full-scale interoperability. CIOs are responsible for securing enterprise-wide capabilities as innovative and scalable investments."

Ingo Paas

Applied Technology Leadership
Christian Eriksson, Head of Architecture, Green Cargo

"Green Cargo was in a situation where a large-scale investment program to replace the most critical legacy systems had failed to get approval, and the new strategy was to go for Evolution rather than Revolution.

There was a great need for business development and changed ways of working, and with that, improved application support for the core processes at Green Cargo which was severely hampered by the decision not to invest in replacing major legacy systems.

The decision to start building a composable architecture was very much constraints based.

Because large-scale investments were impossible, Green Cargo had to take a different approach. Instead of changing major systems, Green Cargo tried implementing various cloud-based platforms, Lowcode Platform, a Process Automation Platform, an Analytics Platform, and an integration platform, all built in the cloud.

With the new platforms and the technology made available in the cloud, Green Cargo started digitalization, building applications to augment and improve functionalities in the old legacy system using a composable approach. This has been a very successful strategy where we have been able to build new functionalities incrementally and, at the same time, build the capabilities of the IT organization with new tech competencies.

The result is that Green Cargo has delivered new and improved application support with significant business benefits to the organization without large-scale investments.

At the same time, this has enabled Green Cargo to build organizational capabilities and add new tech competencies and new and modern agile ways of working with fusion teams to include business and tech competencies in the same team to be able to design, develop and deploy new business capabilities with unprecedented speed.

The key takeaway is that Green Cargo found a way to improve and augment old legacy systems and add new business capabilities without large-scale investment programs due to the composable approach and by implementing cloud platforms that enables and provides new technologies and new ways to consume these services available in the cloud."

Written by Christian Eriksson, Head of Architecture, Green Cargo

Enterprises may consider cloud-only digital foundational platform strategies at the core of their digital transformations to streamline and optimize the realization of sustainable and effective digital composable transformations.

Develop high-performance Lowcode applications

Enterprises of various sizes and industries are increasingly adopting low-code platforms for application development, and the adoption rate of low-code development platforms will continue to grow in the coming years.

With a varying adoption rate of low-code platforms across different industries, industries such as finance, insurance, and healthcare are early adopters of Lowcode platforms.

Lowcode development enables creating applications using a visual interface instead of writing code. Enterprise lowcode platforms (ELPs) are used for high-performance lowcode development to develop enterprise-level applications that meet the business's specific needs. Those platforms provide a drag-and-drop interface for building applications, pre-built components, and integrations, making it easier for non-technical users to create integrated, powerful, and custom applications without writing traditional code. This approach allows for faster and more efficient development and greater accessibility for non-technical users.

Enterprise Lowcode development can help organizations build applications faster and less dependent on external vendors or highly qualified developers with special programming skills. They are typically used to build business-critical applications and to enable effective application development in complex and multi-technology enterprise environments. Enterprise lowcode platforms can handle the specific needs and requirements of larger and more complex organizations with complex IT legacy systems and interoperability requirements. They typically offer a wide range of features and functionalities tailored to support the development of business-critical applications and are critical to accomplishing enterprise-wide composability and interoperability. They include built-in security and compliance features able to handle large amounts of data and up to millions of users.

The key difference is the ability of those platforms to create complex applications with minimum coding while securing high performance, flexibility, and scalability.

DIGITAL FOUNDATIONAL ENTERPRISE LOWCODE PLATFORMS		
VENDORS	**KEY FEATURES**	**INDUTRIES & SCOPE**
OutSystems	Visual high-performance enterprise development, drag-and-drop interface, AI/ML, integration, security, mobile apps, large number of application users.	Most businesses of all sizes and industries
Mendix	Visual enterprise development, drag-and-drop interface, AI/ML, integration, security.	Most businesses of all sizes and industries
Salesforce	Visual app development, drag-and-drop interface, AI/ML, integration, security.	Most businesses of all sizes and industries
Appian	Visual app development, drag-and-drop interface, AI/ML, integration, security, with focus on business process management, robotic process automation.	Most businesses of all sizes and industries
Microsoft	Visual app development, drag-and-drop interface, AI/ML, integration, security, workflow automation, data integration.	Most businesses of all sizes and industries

Figure 63 Digital foundational enterprise Lowcode platforms overview

The following vendors are market leaders in enterprise lowcode development platforms, including:

- **OutSystems**

  OutSystems is the leading enterprise lowcode platform capable of rapidly developing high-performance enterprise applications. It allows for web, mobile, and API-based applications, modular development, relentless orchestration, and built-in support for security and scalability. It is eventually the most capable lowcode platform for developing digital composable enterprises.

- **Mendix**

  Mendix is an enterprise lowcode platform designed to build complex enterprise applications. It offers a wide range of pre-built components and a visual development environment that makes it easy for non-technical users to create and deploy applications. Mendix is another lowcode platform capable of developing digital composable enterprises.

- **Salesforce**

  Salesforce's lowcode platform allows users to create custom applications using a drag-and-drop interface and pre-built components. It is a popular choice among businesses looking to build customer-facing applications.

- **Appian**

  Appian is a lowcode platform designed for building process-driven applications. It offers a visual development environment, pre-built components, and built-in support for security and scalability.

- **Microsoft PowerApps**

  Microsoft PowerApps is a lowcode platform that allows users to create custom business applications using a drag-and-drop interface and pre-built components. Power Apps comes fully integrated with other Microsoft products and services, such as Azure and Dynamics 365.

These are some of the most popular and widely used enterprise lowcode platforms, but many other companies offer lowcode platforms with certain individual capabilities but rarely address enterprise high-performance capabilities to develop digital composable enterprises. OutSystems is the distinguished market leader and the most recognized vendor in enabling enterprise lowcode development. Enterprise lowcode platforms promise enormous innovation to traditional software development, while the lowcode market is highly fragmented, with great discrepancies and variations of development capabilities. The current utilization level of enterprise lowcode platforms at the core of digital composable transformations is rather low.

> *"High-performance enterprise lowcode platforms seem to be one of the most underrated platform technologies, where maturity, market knowledge, and strategic awareness irrationally despair while lowcode promises enormous scalable potential."*

> *Ingo Paas*

Foundational knowledge about the potential of lowcode development among CxOs is a rare skill, leading to fundamental misalignment of their attempts to understand the role, market, and strategic choices concerning enterprise lowcode platforms and individual vendors. As most enterprises are still uncertain about lowcode, they miss out on the substantial opportunities to utilize lowcode at the core of their digital and digital composable transformations. By doing so, they are creating risks to their corporations, as they may be unable to leverage their enterprise's level of composability.

CIOs often do not consider implementing enterprise lowcode platforms as a strategic investment. The utilization of lowcode platforms varies across all industries, ranging from single workflow development to large-scale, highly integrated enterprise application development. The crucial lesson to learn is that the effective implementation of lowcode platforms depends on the strategic choices made by CxOs. Lowcode platforms are often categorized as technology platforms allowing Citizen Developers to leverage and develop simplified workflows or simple apps. This limited view of lowcode that emphasizes citizen development is a critical issue that requires rethinking and redesigning a large majority of digital transformations.

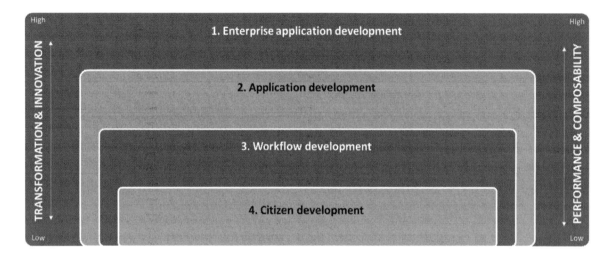

Figure 64 Lowcode development strategies offer different levels of transformation & innovation

Four major variations of lowcode development strategies are fundamentally different in terms of their relevance to enable digital composable enterprises. They include:

1. **Enterprise application development**

   Enterprise lowcode platforms allow the development of high-performance enterprise applications in a complex environment. They let developers build real-time, event-driven, resilient, flexible, and scalable applications (products). They meet all requirements for complex business processes at the core of every business, with deployment capabilities to develop and orchestrate external customer-facing applications for millions of users. Enterprise lowcode platforms enable exclusively to build and effectively maintain full-scale composable enterprise architecture.

They can be integrated with existing IT legacy systems (such as ERP and mainframe), allowing the developers to build "Packaged Business Capabilities" on those platforms. Those platforms can replace functionality in existing IT legacy systems such as ERP, mainframe systems, and AS/400 functionality. They are fundamental to digital composable transformations and must be part of any composable strategy. The number of lowcode vendors in this category of lowcode development is small, simplifying the selection of appropriate lowcode development platforms for enterprise-wide digital composable transformations. Enterprise lowcode platforms are critical at the core of developing digital composable enterprises. Without those platforms at the core, digital resilience may be impossible to achieve!

2. **Application development**

   Application development lowcode platforms mainly support the development of less complex applications, more difficult than workflows but with much less complexity than enterprise lowcode development. The number of lowcode vendors in this category of lowcode development is larger, more competitive, and more diversified in focus, scope, and capabilities. Those lowcode platforms utilize application development integrated with IT systems, such as major global platforms like SAP, Oracle, SalesForce, ServiceNow, and Siemens. They provide increased application development capabilities but may not be able to leverage and scale enterprise application development. Developers using those platforms can develop applications, but they will find restrictions or limitations when developing and scaling enterprise applications, while enterprise composability and digital resilience are difficult to achieve.

3. **Workflow development**

   Workflow development does enable developers to develop workflows at the process and automation levels. CxOs should try to understand the limitations and how they may impact business processes when selecting platforms in this category. The possibilities for application development on workflow lowcode platforms are unconstrained. Developers can leverage these platforms to create individual workflows that automate tasks, such as document approvals, purchase orders, onboarding, ordering, mail collaboration, and customer service requests. Security and compliance are not to forget, to not expose the organization to security and compliance risks. Performance and scalability can become a concern with complex and resource-intensive workflows.

4. **Citizen development**

   Organizations are increasingly democratizing digital development, enabling end-users to develop simple applications in lowcode while most vendors support this capability to empower Citizen Developers to automate their business processes. Democratization of software development mainly considers simple applications, while it still requires effective educational governance to minimize risks with intensive and distributed development. Developers should collaborate and seek aligned methods and processes, securing effective development, deployment, and application management, depending on the criticality of their applications.

   Organizations should provide governance and guidance for application classification and different approaches to application maintenance, life-cycle-management, ownership, and documentation.

Those four different strategies significantly impact the ability of enterprises to leverage digital transformations and innovation through modern application development. While many lowcode vendors are out in the market, enterprises with complex digital transformations and the need to integrate IT legacy systems must consider utilizing enterprise lowcode platforms.

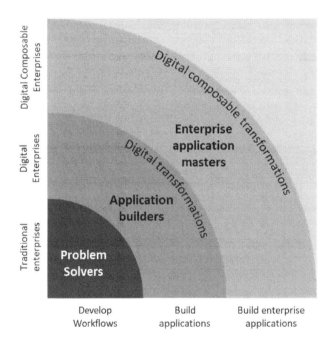

Figure 65 Three types of organizations to utilize enterprise lowcode development

1. **Enterprise application masters**

   Significance: Lowcode enterprise application masters utilize their platforms to build coherent high-performance enterprise applications with high modularity, reusability, and interoperability grades. They position enterprise lowcode development at the core of their digital composable transformations. They have an incremental but systemic approach to lowcode development and strategically utilize lowcode to build high-performance enterprise applications and outperform traditional application development processes at scale. They develop products (rather than applications) with multipurpose capabilities and use fundamental principles in distinct and coherent ways to revolutionize application development. Enterprises can build any application they need but focus on those that promise the greatest possible business value and help to create competitive and innovative advantages where standard software is rarely available. They accelerate incremental and radical business model development and innovation, differentiating themselves significantly from their peers. By applying the outstanding platform capabilities, they focus on modularity to develop digitally packaged business objects and digital composable transformations at the core of their business. They utilize lowcode platforms as the core enabler to scale and build digitalized capabilities for multi-purpose orchestration, simultaneously reusing the same digitally packaged business capability in various applications. lowcode allows the creation of flexible, reusable, stable, scalable, reliable, failure-tolerant, scalable, and durable products.

   Recommendation: Enterprises must invest in high-performance enterprise lowcode platforms!

2. **Application builders**

   Significance: Application builders utilize their lowcode platform to build applications but may not have applied a strategic approach to long-term strategic application development. They have no visionary enterprise-wide approach to lowcode and intend to develop single-purpose applications with limited flexibility, reusability, and scalability. They use lowcode platforms as a tool rather than a strategic capability. They partly support digital transformations while they may experience performance issues, such as limited flexibility, reusability, scalability, and stability issues during orchestration.

   They support digital transformations but do not have systemic and dynamic capabilities, to utilize application development on an enterprise level and the driver of digital or digital composable transformations.

Therefore, they will experience limitations in using and scaling digitally packaged business capabilities in their lowcode platforms as they build non-reusable single-purpose applications and create isolated value and ROIs for their business. lowcode investments and their total cost of ownership are higher in comparison due to limited reusability. This leads to missed opportunities, as enterprises are underperforming and not utilizing their investments compared with enterprise lowcode application masters.

Recommendation: Enterprises shall avoid this strategy if the goal is to become digitally resilient and evolve towards digital composability at scale.

3. **Problem solvers**

Significance: They usually implement enterprise lowcode platforms to solve limited, isolated problems and to build one new application on their lowcode platforms. Platforms are not utilized, not scalable, and only implemented as tactical tools with a single purpose, low ROI, and TCO.

Recommendation: Enterprises shall avoid this strategy if the goal is to become digitally resilient and evolve towards digital composability at scale.

Those three fundamentally different strategies for utilizing enterprise lowcode platforms must reflect and support the enterprise's strategic objectives. Decision-makers must know lowcode platforms' role in helping enterprises get there. Depending on the chosen strategy, lowcode investments contribute significantly differently with their strategic value, return on investments, and total cost of ownership. CxOs must understand and decide on their development strategy before getting started.

Organizations that apply ELP can make quantum leap progress in software development in a very short time. They can shift their focus from traditional coding and application development towards continual and universal product development with DevOps teams. This will allow enterprises and development organizations to increase their level of autonomy and enable the enterprise to make more effective buy versus build decisions. They can integrate and embed business logic across business processes, IT systems, and digital ecosystems to connect enterprises with their customers, partners, and vendors. They will, over time, be capable of solving nearly any business problem to develop and maintain complex enterprise applications without coding.

They will collaboratively engage with the business to accelerate the entire process from design to development, testing, and deployment and leverage unrecognized opportunities to drive innovation and continuous improvements at the core of the business. They will lower the barriers to implementing agile development teams while considerably increasing their abilities in digital product development.

Many enterprises have a huge potential to leverage Enterprise lowcode Platforms at the core of their strategies and digital composable transformations. Leveraging large-scale and multiple DevOps teams is challenging, while the learning curve for effectively utilizing ELP is highly intuitive, effective, and fast.

Effective ELP DevOps teams can build a full-scale application on their lowcode in just weeks, better, more adopted, and more integrated into the enterprise's specific technologies than SaaS applications. They can do this because they start from the core of their business, accelerate innovation, and help create highly competitive business processes. Those DevOps teams can establish full-scale in-house development capabilities within a few months once the platform is ready to scale.

The iterative process will engage businesspeople and developers in fusion teams to design and develop new applications rapidly and jointly. They will realize the enormous shift of autonomous decision-making in product development. Those teams can utilize their composable architecture and build enterprise-wide applications that traditional organizations could not even consider as a theoretical option before.

Effective lowcode DevOps teams develop composable applications to support Packaged Business Capabilities to secure full interoperability between the existing IT legacy systems and the new digital foundational technologies and architecture. They can replace business logic and functionality in their ERP or mainframe systems with the help of lowcode development. Such abilities will also support efforts to replace inflexible IT legacy systems functionality, to move critical business capabilities into their lowcode platforms. They can harmonize inconsistent business logic between different systems and remove business logic from their integration layers and middleware. They can remove ERP code and functionality from monolithic systems, minimize business logic inconsistencies, build applications to solve complex problems and build portals or apps for customers, partners, employees, and more. They can build every type of application thinkable. They can build applications on top of algorithms to monetize the outcome of Machine Learning algorithms, utilizing the indicators from identified patterns as input for their development.

Experiences from best practice and effective enterprise lowcode deployments include examples such as:

- Rapid application development,
- Enterprise high-performance application,
- Real-time and event-driven applications,
- Flexible redesign of applications,
- Continual development and deployment,
- Modular digital application design,
- Multi-purpose digital packaged business capabilities development
- High-performance orchestration capabilities,
- Stable production environments with high failure tolerance,
- Automated applications operations,
- Embedded security and compliance,
- Separation of concerns and modular business logic.

Lowcode platforms are critical digital foundational capabilities to overcome one of organizations' and CxOs' most important and difficult problems. With the right strategy and design of Enterprise lowcode Platforms, lowcode DevOps teams can become highly autonomous with the ability to:

- Develop, deploy, and maintain sustainable in-house developed applications,
- Integrate digital applications with the IT legacy,
- Interact relentlessly with other applications across various business processes,
- Run processes between applications and solve unsolvable data quality and integrity problems,
- Accelerate the digital transformation, build digital applications, and features effectively integrated with IT legacy systems,
- Develop complex customer applications and portals,
- Scale packaged business capabilities event-driven and in real-time,
- Automate or optimize decision-making processes,
- Build applications on top of algorithms,
- Digitize and simplify business processes,
- Secure compliance with policies, rules, and regulations.

Enterprise Lowcode development can rapidly change the traditional deployment and operations of code to leverage platform-managed enterprise-wide digital applications. ELPs (if applied correctly) will be the most important capability for traditional enterprises to evolve and migrate their business into digital composable enterprises. They will enable a never-before-possible transformation of business processes, highly integrated with the underlying IT legacy applications and systems.

On a micro level, lowcode will have implications as well. The reusability of correctly implemented loosely coupled services will accelerate and simplify new application development. Developers can easily change and completely redesign low-code applications while utilizing or merging them with other applications whenever necessary. Lowcode platforms will give the business enormous flexibility to solve problems in unprecedented ways at low costs and in a short time. The focus will shift from processes and applications toward digital business capabilities.

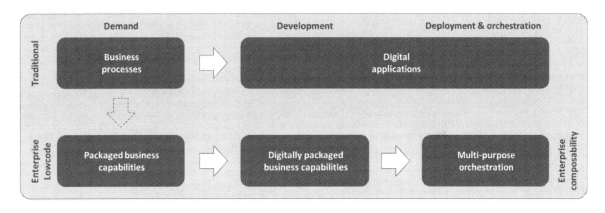

Figure 66 Enterprise lowcode will shift the focus away from application development towards digital packaged business capabilities

This new approach of digitally packaged business capabilities utilized in modern development is a game changer for "application" development. The key differentiator is the revolutionary shift from developing applications towards the development of "digitally packaged business capabilities" orchestrated for multi-purpose consumption/use simultaneously in various "applications" or "role-based dynamic combinations" of DPBCs. This new concept of utilizing DPBCs is explained in chapter EIGHT, Innovate application development.

Enterprise lowcode platforms will allow business users to practice incremental and experimental development jointly with their developers, ideally organized in fusion teams.

They will utilize more data, reuse already-built business logic, and combine existing digital assets and knowledge with innovative and new digital insights to master superior digital product development. Organizations capable of utilizing this unlimited power of continual improvement and innovation will empower their business development at exceptional levels.

OutSystems is the undisputed global leading vendor in this segment, with astonishing capabilities (AI-enabled development and more). As a vendor, they have proven, in reality, and at Green Cargo, to have the most innovative comprehensive enterprise lowcode platform available.

Applied Technology Leadership
Filip Mood, Product Owner OutSystems, Green Cargo

"As Green Cargos Product Owner for our OutSystems platform, I handle the platform's life cycle and road map together with our backlog, responsible for the overall design and usage of the platform in line with our architectural principles.

Green Cargo was incapable of in-house software development and needed an approach to mitigate major business risks and aggressively attack a backlog of more than ten years without IT development. Our OutSystems lowcode platform helped us industrialize software development, become independent, and make better choices about buying and building. With lowcode at the core of our business and digital transformation, we started gradually and managed to establish our first DevOps teams within less than a year, soon followed by a second team.

Lowcode is our most foundational digital platform at the core of our digital transformation. Enterprise lowcode development's speed allows us to fulfill more business needs than we ever could have done with traditional development. We enable unconstrained digital development as we secure the highest possible levels of speed, flexibility, and responsiveness to fulfill our new and changing business needs instantly and consistently.

OutSystems is a great foundational digital platform helping us overcome composable challenges with large and complex IT legacy systems integrated with our digital transformation. The platform allows a composable approach to speed our development with innovative solutions. As we continually strengthen our collaboration with the business, we have enabled and embedded innovation with our platform-based digital composable architecture. Our shift toward shared business and IT product management teams supports our approach to continually expanding our level of enterprise composability.

Our new thinking with composability allows us to reuse the packaged business capabilities that we build in different apps for different parts of the organization, which increases the possibility of bringing out more business value with a higher development speed. It is also an enabler for our brand-new approach to developing various types of applications with different methodologies, such as function- and role-based solutions.

With composable components, we can continuously expand our library of functionality. With our high-quality library of digital package business capabilities, such as pricing, or damage reporting, we are taking software development to another level. We are deliberately moving towards full-scale enterprise composability on new digital development in the cloud with our lowcode platform from OutSystems. We leverage our architecture in unanticipated innovative ways to maximize enterprise-wide interoperability, composability, and digital resilience. By full flexibility and reusability of our digital capabilities, we can satisfy every business need by reusing existing digitally packaged digital capabilities without any development or reconfiguration need. Instead, if new functionality is needed, we build a new digitally packaged capability ready for unconstrained reuse and orchestration.

By utilizing this new architectural software development concept in lowcode, we move away from applications and build the future of Green Cargo based on digitally packaged business capabilities. Those will be organized and available in our lowcode library, ready for deployment in a new context. Our approach to accelerate and transform traditional application development is the most significant change we can imagine. We are not only bringing innovation to the business, but we also innovate how to enable business innovation at scale."

Written by Filip Mood, Product Owner OutSystems, Green Cargo

Organizations that make this strategic move, such as Green Cargo, will embrace a never-before achievable level of autonomy in application development.

"Enterprises that plan to evolve into composable and digitally resilient organizations cannot disregard strategic investments in lowcode platforms. They must consider the power and capacity of enterprise lowcode at the core of their transformations and business innovation."

Ingo Paas

The foundational aspects of enterprise lowcode enable never-before-possible degrees of digital autonomy and enable businesses and IT collaboratively to solve unsolvable problems while they allow enterprises to navigate effectively with their existing IT legacy and digital transformational investments. They will empower their customer-focused initiatives to optimize their offerings and boost improvements concerning their cost of sales and margins. Organizations that profoundly understand the infinite business gains and future opportunities of enterprise lowcode strategies in action will experience significant advantages to become digital masters, as they will outperform their competitors at scale while they industrialize software development.

With OutSystems, combined with excellent architectural, technology, and business leadership, enterprises can leverage their business models from the core, succeed with their digital transformations, and finally realize the digital composable enterprises at scale.

As lowcode platforms are at the core of digital composable transformations, enterprises must leverage integrated systemic enterprise-wide integrations as an equally critical and essential digital foundational platform capability.

Integrate the enterprise

Enterprise hybrid integration platforms (EHIP) are PaaS enabling organizations to integrate and manage the flow of data and information between different systems and applications, both within the organization and with external partners. EHIPs connect various systems and applications, including on-premise systems, cloud-based services, and mobile devices.

EHIPs enable organizations to connect and integrate different technologies, platforms, and systems in digital composable transformations as they move towards a more agile, flexible, and composable digital architecture. This includes connecting legacy systems with newer technologies, such as cloud services and IoT devices, and integrating different data sources and applications to support existing and new business processes and use cases. EHIPs also provide a layer of abstraction that simplifies the complexity of connecting various IT legacy systems, applications, and cloud services. It enables integration teams to assume responsibility for enterprise-wide integration to deliver increased business value.

DIGITAL FOUNDATIONAL ENTERPRISE HYBRID INTEGRATION PLATFORMS		
VENDORS	**KEY FEATURES**	**INDUTRIES & SCOPE**
Microsoft	Cloud-based integration, data integration, API management	Most businesses of all sizes and industries
MuleSoft	API management, data integration, application integration	Most businesses of all sizes and industries
Dell Boomi	Cloud-native integration, API management, data management	Most businesses of all sizes and industries
IBM	API management, data integration, application integration	Most businesses of all sizes and industries
Informatica	Cloud-based integration, data management, API management	Most businesses of all sizes and industries

Figure 67 Comparison of enterprise hybrid integration platforms vendors

Microsoft Azure is a cloud-based platform that offers various integration services and tools, making it a hybrid integration platform. Azure provides a wide range of services for integration, such as event-driven features, API management, data factory, service bus, and more.

Microsoft Azure does include features such as:

- Azure Event Grid builds event-driven architecture to enable real-time data integration and processing. This allows organizations to build real-time applications that react to business events caused by transactions.
- Azure API Management publishes, manages, and secures API management, providing and including API gateways, developer portals, analytics, security, and access control features.
- Azure Logic Apps creates workflows and integration solutions using a visual designer, connecting various systems and applications, including cloud, on-premises, and third-party services.
- Azure Service Bus connects different systems and applications reliably and securely., supporting a variety of messaging patterns, including point-to-point, publish-subscribe, and request-response.
- Azure Data Factory creates, schedules, and manages data pipelines to move, transform, and integrate data from various sources and to orchestrate data integration workflows.

These services and tools available in Azure provide the necessary capabilities to build hybrid enterprise integration platforms. Platforms, such as Microsoft Azure, must be designed and configured to meet the needs of enterprises' IT integration strategies and business needs.

Integration Platforms as a Service (PaaS) provide crucial capabilities to enable and accelerate evolutionary digital transformation initiatives and digitize core business processes more systematically. The rise of cloud integration capabilities does allow rapid and modern responses to customer and external integration needs for distributed/connected hybrid applications, data, APIs, digital eco-systems, and real-time and event-driven processes. Other more specialized integration platforms and vendors enable streamlining and automating data flow across organizations. They use end-to-end, bi-directional, no-code data pipeline platforms to facilitate integration, allowing data teams to pull data from various sources into centralized data warehouses. They perform those transactions in near-real-time to easily set up their databases or data warehouses for analytics. Data teams can better focus on data analytics without worrying about data integration tasks constantly. Custom configurations of data flows are codeless and automated out-of-the-box, simplifying how users manage future changes like adding tables and columns and changing data types.

Platform vendors offer ready-to-use integrations for databases, cloud storage, and streaming services and are compatible with data warehouses such as BigQuery and Snowflake. Cloud storage (such as Amazon S3 and Google Drive) and various analytics platforms/tools are supported (such as Google Analytics, Power BI, and Looker). Platform vendors offering this service include Fivetran, Hevo, Integrate.io, Workato, and Supermetrics.

Enterprise hybrid integration platforms in the cloud offer several key advantages, including scalability of resources and services, which is important for enterprise integration platforms that handle large amounts of data and processing. They provide great flexibility, can be accessed from anywhere, and can be customized to meet specific business needs. Those platforms can be more cost-effective than on-premise solutions, as they do not require a significant upfront investment in hardware and infrastructure. They promise great cost-savings with time reduction in development.

Cloud Service Providers (CSPs) typically increase reliability with robust infrastructure and disaster recovery plans, which can help ensure that enterprise integration platforms are highly available and can quickly recover from outages. They often have advanced security measures to protect data from unauthorized access and breaches. Their cloud integration platforms offer the best of both worlds, where sensitive and critical data leverages on-premise with highly sensitive and non-sensitive data in the cloud.

Enterprises aiming for composability by leveraging those platforms at the core of their digital transformations do this in favor of digital foundational platform strategies. Those who disregard or overlook such critical investments may not experience significant problems instantly but will most likely cause substantial business problems and risks for their enterprise's long term.

Enterprise hybrid integration platforms are critical in digital composable transformations as they connect and integrate various systems and data sources. They enable organizations to create a unified view of their data and processes and to automate and streamline business operations.

There are several critical domains covered by those platforms, such as:

- **Data integration**

  Data integration is a core capability of those platforms to integrate data from various systems and sources, such as ERP, CRM, and IoT devices, and to make that data available for use in other applications and systems.

- **API management**

  API management is the most significant capability to provide a central point of control, which is important to expose and consume data and services across different systems and applications internally and externally. API management is at the core of digital transformations and is critical in transforming toward enterprise composability.

- **Application integration**

  Application integration enables the integration of different applications and services, such as cloud and on-premise applications, and allows them to work together seamlessly.

- **Event-driven architectures**

  Event-driven architectures allow systems and applications to respond to real-time events, such as changes in data or the status of business processes.

Enterprise hybrid integration platforms play the single most critical role in digital composable transformations as they enable enterprises to connect and integrate their IT legacy systems, applications, and data sources across different environments, such as on-premise, cloud, and edge. Enterprises must invest in modern cloud-enabled enterprise-wide integration capabilities to secure enterprise-wide interoperability and composability, both internal and external. This allows organizations to create unified, multi-connected digital ecosystems which can be composed and reconfigured to support new business processes and services. Organizations can leverage the benefits of the cloud by using enterprise hybrid integration platforms while controlling their sensitive data and creating a composable architecture that can adapt to changing business requirements.

Enterprise hybrid integration platforms are the most critical enablers of digital composable transformations. They provide the connectivity, integration, and orchestration capabilities necessary to create a unified digital ecosystem that can be easily composed and reconfigured to support new or changing business processes and services.

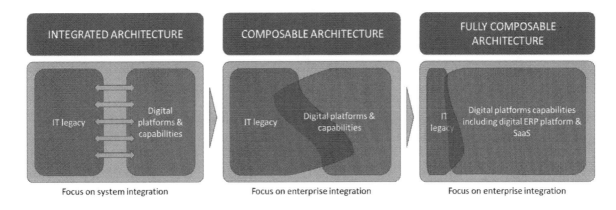

Figure 68 Enterprise integration strategies may have to differentiate between traditional system integration and more comprehensive strategies toward enterprise integration

Modern approaches to integration strategies require holistic enterprise-wide integration approaches, including data, processes, and applications, both inside and outside the enterprise and position purpose-driven initiatives at the core of their composable architecture and platform strategies. They will utilize modern integration capabilities as the key accelerator of business and digital transformations, allowing simplifications of business processes (traditionally, integrations often included business logic), accelerating digital transformations, and utilizing data across the enterprises (internally and externally).

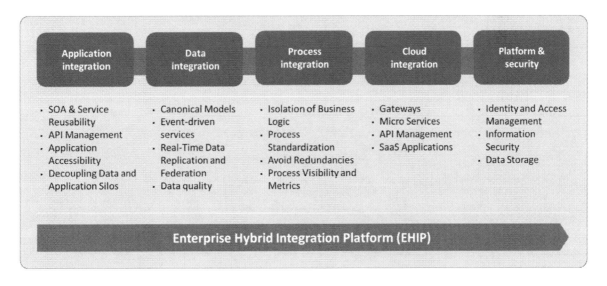

Figure 69 Enterprise hybrid integration platforms contain at least five distinct domains

Those critical capabilities describe the aspects of composable enterprises, which continuously must integrate entire organizations. The integration strategy and architecture are foundational to composable transformations, with benefits such as **adaptability** with change data requirements or internal or external IT landscape changes, **interoperability** across various technology platforms and digital ecosystems, and **extensibility**. They will consider future growth and changes as fundamental software engineering and systems design principles.

The core domains of enterprise hybrid integration platforms allow to:

- Integrate applications and systems to communicate effectively,
- Integrate with multiple digital ecosystems (internally and externally),
- Enable and simplify the development of responsive apps with messaging services (Lowcode),
- Expose traditional enterprise solutions as API,
- Manage the platform as a product designed for scalability and reusability,
- Rapidly integrate SaaS and other applications,
- Create secured gateways for access to on-prem API and data,
- Enable future growth predictions while ensuring systemic scalability.

Applied Technology Leadership
Per Jalmelid, Enterprise Architect, Green Cargo

"The challenge of adapting an old IT landscape to support the ever-growing need for rapid business change is a reality for companies today, and Green Cargo is no different. We have a plethora of critical legacy applications that are excellent at what they do but are difficult to change and add new capabilities to. Building integrations for these applications is often difficult since they use old technologies and often insecure communication protocols.

By designing and implementing our own Enterprise Hybrid Integration Platform in the cloud, we have created an efficient central platform for secure information exchange that bridges the technology differences between our core on-premises legacy applications and our more fast-paced modern development platforms.

> *Our platform allows us to connect to various applications and digital ecosystems surrounding us and replace our legacy applications in a controlled fashion.*
>
> *Our goal is to enable integration between applications through loosely coupled services exposed in the Enterprise Hybrid Integration Platform with well-defined and documented APIs. This concept will allow the integration platform to provide an ever-growing amount of reusable services, enabling us to quickly build new solutions and connect internal and external applications by combining the exposed API:s in different setups. Using the platform as a product allows us to continue swiftly and quickly to answer any business needs or requirements. Since the platform is cloud-native, we can easily expand it with new capabilities and solutions on demand and thus let individual projects finance the IT change.*
>
> *In short, our cloud-based Enterprise Hybrid Integration Platform allows us to connect any applications, microservices, mobile devices, or IoT devices in a secured and monitored way, thus enabling a composable architecture at Green Cargo."*
>
> *Written by Per Jalmelid, Enterprise Architect, Green Cargo*

As applied in the Green cargo case, those capabilities suggest various benefits organizations may experience from utilizing cloud-native integration platforms. Those benefits include the reusability of integrations, scalability, stability, and reliability, combined with continual performance monitoring.

Digital foundational platform strategies must fully embed hybrid integration platform architectures at their core. Those platforms shall not be confused with integration capabilities embedded in other platforms, such as lowcode or Automation. Those embedded integration capabilities offer great and rich functionalities but can usually not support extensive enterprise-wide integrations. With the introduction of EHIP, enterprises must define clear architectural design principles that specify why, how, and for what reasons they will use or not use embedded integration capabilities and other legacy integration platforms (ERP). EHIPs are also called IPaaS (Integration Platform as a Service) platforms.

Enterprises implementing other platforms, such as Lowcode or Automation, often find competing integration capabilities when harmonizing their integration strategies.

In the case of Lowcode platforms, they often include integration capabilities, where architects may distinguish when and why to choose embedded integration features and strategy. To support developers with distinct models, architects must consider the advantages and disadvantages of their integration frameworks for enterprise integration, guiding developers in selecting the right integration capabilities for the right project. Architects must consider the advantages and disadvantages in the full context, not just from the needs of a project:

- **Advantages of lowcode integration capabilities**

  These capabilities are designed for ease of use and require minimal coding or technical expertise to create integrations. lowcode platforms provide visual development tools, such as drag-and-drop interfaces, to facilitate the creation of integrations, speeding up development times. They often offer pre-built connectors and integrations with popular third-party applications and services, which can reduce development time and increase productivity.

- **Disadvantages of lowcode integration capabilities**

  These platforms may limit the development of certain integration types and may not be suitable for complex or highly customized integrations that require specialized tools or advanced development skills. Organizations with large or complex integration needs may be concerned about these platforms' limited scalability and performance, which could conflict with their enterprise integrations and API-centric strategies.

- **Advantages of EHIP integration platforms**

  They offer more advanced integration capabilities, such as support for advanced data mapping and transformation, process orchestration, and more advanced security features. They include more customization options and flexibility, allowing organizations to create more complex and highly tailored integrations. In addition, they allow for better scalability and performance than lowcode platforms, which can be important for large-scale or mission-critical integrations.

- **Disadvantages of EHIP integration capabilities**

  They require more technical expertise and development skills to create integrations. They have a steeper learning curve than lowcode platforms, which can increase development time, reduce productivity, and require more resources and infrastructure, which can be a concern for smaller organizations with limited budgets or resources.

Enterprise lowcode platforms offer ease of use, visual development tools, and pre-built connectors but may be less customizable and less well-suited for complex or highly customized integrations. Enterprise Hybrid Integration Platforms offer more advanced integration capabilities, customization options, and better scalability and performance but may require more technical expertise and resources. Enterprise hybrid integration platforms are composability engines critical for securing enterprise-wide interoperability and sustainable integration development efforts. The choice between lowcode platforms and enterprise hybrid integration platforms is a strategic decision that enterprise architects must guide and govern based on their organization's integration needs and available resources.

Typical integration scenarios include:

- Application-to-application (A2A) integration
- Cloud service integration (CSI)
- Mobile application integration (MAI)
- Business-to-business (B2B) integration
- Internet of Things (IoT) integration

The selected Hybrid Integration Platform shall operate as the nerve center of "every" digital foundational platform strategy. Those choices and the right design are foundational when enterprises foster and accelerate digital transformations from the core of their businesses. With the ability to support various integration needs, organizations can utilize those platforms at the center of their digital foundational platform architecture.

Those platforms will support users to:

- Utilize the data of the IT legacy,
- Integrate digital capabilities with the underlying legacy applications,
- Relentlessly share data across various business processes,
- Integrate between applications and solve unsolvable data quality and integrity problems,
- Accelerate the digital transformation, build digital applications and features while harmonizing data with underlying legacy applications,
- Inform digital applications about events in real time,
- Collect new digital business-critical data points from new digital applications,

- Automate data flow and provide data to perform algorithmic analysis and simulations,
- Automate decisions,
- Optimize decision-making processes through recommendation engines or automated decisions,
- Gather data from various assets (such as IoT platforms) and provide data for further analysis.

Enterprise hybrid integration platforms include services such as API policy management & enforcement, file transfer and file movement, messaging services, and event broker, data interchange standards, protocol mapping, data mapping, data transformation, data quality features, routing, orchestration, EDI support, and tools such as an integrator workbench.

Those platforms strengthen the development of APIs and system integrations on an enterprise level. They will help reduce costs for integration development and establish integration DevOps teams while effectively orchestrating, monitoring, and managing integrations.

Potential integration development scope may include activities such as:

- Develop APIs in-house (for internal integrations, customer integrations, digital eco-systems)
- Develop in-house integrations (integrations between legacy, SaaS, and lowcode platforms),
- Rebuild integrations of on-premise ERP integration platforms to facilitate stepwise consolidation of end-of-life platforms (life-cycle-management) proactively,
- Reduce costs for integration development significantly (shorten the time, reduce complexity, simplify specifications),
- Establish Integration DevOps with fully dedicated teams to support any integrations and to interconnect with other DevOps teams (such as lowcode),
- Inbuild platform management features (monitoring),
- Orchestration of integration objects.

Integration strategies are at the core of digital composable transformations and must promote fundamental principles (similar to lowcode platform principles) to secure seamless integrations on an enterprise level. Those strategies will enable organizations to build and maintain faster, smarter, better, and cost-effective integration capabilities compared with traditional approaches.

It will accelerate organizations' advancements and adaptation into composable enterprises and digital transformations at unmatched speed, quality, and autonomy levels.

"Enterprises must invest in hybrid integration platforms, preferably in the cloud. Without this approach to seamless interoperability and readiness to integrate and evolve into digital ecosystems at scale, digital composability will not be achievable on an enterprise level."

Ingo Paas

The role of unconstrained utilization of APIs (Application Programming Interfaces) will bring enormous efficiency to simplify and automate business processes with partners and customers. Developing such capabilities will determine any organization's ability to rapidly integrate, navigate, and make necessary adoptions in existing and future digital ecosystems. Traditional organizations may be experiencing major limitations in utilizing their enterprise-wide data to establish and foster a data-driven business culture.

API capabilities are critical for digital composable enterprise transformations because they enable businesses to break down complex systems into smaller, more manageable components for quick assembling or disassembling as needed. They serve as the building blocks of modern software development and enable developers to easily create, integrate, and extend applications. They provide standardized interfaces for communication between different applications and their component, allowing the exchange of data and functionality without any knowledge of functionality, the application, and business logic.

APIs enable different systems and applications to connect and communicate seamlessly. They facilitate the integration of third-party software (such as SaaS) and other services to leverage and integrate technologies and innovations faster and with little or no effort. They enable businesses to expose their services and data to external developers, partners, and customers in various ways (such as offering APIs in a customer portal).

API capabilities are critical for digital composable enterprise transformations, enabling businesses to increase agility, responsiveness, and innovation. With this strategy in place, enterprises break down complex systems into smaller, more manageable components and facilitate the integration of compliant third-party software and services. They allow businesses to expose their services and data to external partners, fostering seamless collaboration and overtime opportunities for co-creation.

Enterprises must establish agile integration DevOps teams. They must operate seamlessly and integrate with Lowcode and analytics teams into agile development. Those agile integration development teams (Integration DevOps) are at the core of any digital composable transformation and are responsible for effective digital composable interoperability and enterprise integrations. This does include integrating their IT legacy with the digital foundational platforms seamlessly embedded as the core of composable architectures. Integration platforms and enterprise lowcode platforms are the most important technologies and capabilities for organizations to overcome and master the challenges of enterprise-wide interoperability and composability.

Organizations applying such thinking in execution will evolve their digital composability at scale, enabling and accelerating enterprise-wide data-driven business culture.

Evolve data-driven cultures

Data is the most critical asset for and at the core of digitally transforming enterprises! It is crucial for digitally transforming enterprises and introducing data-driven cultures at scale. Data-driven cultures are:

- Providing insights for better decision-making,
- Automating business decisions,
- Enhancing customer experiences,
- Optimizing the output and design of business processes and capabilities,
- Innovating incrementally from the core.

Data-driven culture needs digital foundational analytics platforms to transform composable enterprises digitally. They enable enterprises to collect, analyze, and utilize data more effectively, leading to better decision-making, enhanced customer service and satisfaction, business growth, increased innovation, and improved operational efficiency. There is no doubt that data is the most critical asset for enterprises undergoing a digital transformation because it is the basis for driving business growth and profitability.

With the right data, enterprises gain valuable insights into customer behavior, market trends, and internal operations.

Instead, organizations can use internal and external data to automate processes, improve decision-making, and leverage existing or create new revenue streams. Data analytics helps monitor and measure enterprise performances, providing intelligent feedback and insights.

Future successful composable enterprises depend on their ability to utilize their data at scale. In future composable enterprises, data management processes and advanced analytics capabilities create a seamless version of the truth that enables different teams and parts of the organization to work together and make or automate better-informed decisions without risking utilizing incoherent data sources and data. Different teams can collaborate to make decisions confidently, enabling organizations to be more responsive and agile to changing business conditions.

Data-driven platforms are essential foundational capabilities for digital composable transformations as they provide a basis for collecting, analyzing, and utilizing data to drive business growth and innovation. Such platforms enable the provisioning of a centralized location for storing and managing data from various sources. Data-driven platforms will be a comprehensive and critical source for business analysts with secure and unconstrained access to data, such as customer interactions, sales transactions, and operational metrics. Utilizing Data-driven platforms allows enterprises to access, analyze, and use data more efficiently, improving decision-making and reducing duplication of effort. Those platforms will provide real-time insights into collected and analyzed data, important insights into business operations, and customer behavior. They allow analysts and business functions to quickly identify areas for improvement and respond rapidly to market or customer needs changes. They can handle data effectively and collect, share, and organize to continue leveraging data insights on demand.

Enterprises can create predictive models and capabilities to anticipate trends and make or automate decisions. Predictive models can improve customer experiences and asset utilization or minimize operations risks by providing personalized and situational even-driven recommendations to automate decisions wherever valuable.

The burden on cloud-native analytic platforms is relatively low. Organizations can initially implement leading Enterprise Analytics Platforms (EAP) at low costs. Organizations should embed those platforms at the core of digital and digital composable transformations. They are fundamental and critical to leverage intelligence embedded in the organization's culture, proving those platforms' ability to substantially leverage data-driven improvements.

Analytics platforms automate many data-related tasks, such as data cleaning, integration, and analysis, freeing employees to focus on more strategic tasks. Those platforms will improve efficiency and reduce errors and risks with data security and operational implications on running IT systems. Making the most optimal choices to define critical technologies and architectures to support short- and long-term business needs effectively is a huge challenge.

The core advantages of utilizing enterprise-wide architectures for analytics embedded into the digital composable platform architecture are:

- Ready to use and prepare data for business users and analytics (ad-hoc and standards),
- Identification of patterns in reliable data to optimize and automate decisions,
- Utilize data to prepare for storytelling, explaining complex data insights into understandable context,
- Secure deeper and learning insights with artificial intelligence,
- Share and collaborate around accessible business intelligence and insights,
- Protect the enterprise data and support users in being compliant and acting responsibly.

DIGITAL FOUNDATIONAL ENTERPRISE ANALYTICS PLATFORMS		
VENDORS	KEY FEATURES	INDUTRIES & SCOPE
Google	Offers a wide range of analytics services in the cloud, with strengths on web analytics and centralized data management. Drag-and-drop interface, AI/ML integration, cloud integration.	Most businesses of all sizes and industries
Microsoft	Offers a wide range of integrated analytics services in the cloud, with strengths on democratized data management. Visual development, workflow automation, data integration.	Most businesses of all sizes and industries
Amazon	Offers a wide range of analytics services in the cloud, with strengths on high-volume data management. Low-code development, data integration, API management.	Most businesses of all sizes and industries
IBM	Offers a analytics services in the cloud, with strengths on AI analytics. Visual development, AI/ML integration, application lifecycle.	Most businesses of all sizes and industries
SAP	Offers analytics services in the cloud, with strengths on its own platform and embedded data management. Low-code development, data integration, workflow automation.	Most businesses of all sizes and industries

Figure 70 Overview of enterprise analytics platforms vendors

Some of the most popular platforms that also include the most advanced analytics capabilities include:

- **Google Cloud Platform (GCP)**

  Google includes various analytics services, including BigQuery, Cloud Dataflow, and Cloud SQL, to perform big data analytics, real-time stream processing, manage relational databases, and advanced AI (Artificial Intelligence) capabilities.

- **Microsoft Azure & Power platform**

  Microsoft includes different analytics services, which include Azure Synapse Analytics, Azure Data Factory, and Power BI, which create and manage data pipelines, perform advanced analytics, create interactive visualizations, and advanced AI (Artificial Intelligence) capabilities (such as OpenAI).

- **Amazon Web Services (AWS)**

  Amazon includes many analytics services, including Amazon Redshift, Amazon QuickSight, and Amazon Kinesis, which collect, store, and analyze large amounts of data.

- **IBM Cloud**

  IBM offers various analytics services, including IBM Watson Studio, IBM Cloud SQL Query, and IBM Cloud Object Storage for data preparation, machine learning, and storage.

- **SAP Cloud Platform**

  SAP includes several analytics services, including SAP BusinessObjects Cloud, SAP Data Intelligence, and SAP HANA Cloud, for data warehousing, real-time analytics, and machine learning.

The Enterprise Analytics Platforms (EAP) market is complex, and enterprises must thoroughly decide how their strategies fit most effectively with the available platforms and their foundational philosophies on managing and consuming data. There is no simple answer to finding the ultimate platform, as different vendors have built different architectures supporting the diverse needs of various enterprises. Critical evaluation criteria include strategic fit, data storage, processing power, scalability, and TCO. The following figure indicates potential differences and the necessity to agree on the enterprise's needs of their data-driven transformation.

CONCEPTUAL DIFFERENCES	GOOGLE CLOUD PLATFORM	MICROSOFT POWER ANALYTICS PLATFORM
Focus	Provides infrastructure and platform services for building, deploying, and scaling cloud-based applications and services	Enables users to build data-driven solutions that can analyze, visualize, and share data
Architecture	Built on top of Google's proprietary infrastructure, which includes its global network of data centers, servers, and other resources	Built on top of Microsoft Azure, which is a more general-purpose cloud computing platform that offers a wide range of services and features
Target audience	Primarily designed for developers and IT professionals who want to build, deploy, and manage cloud-based applications and services	Designed for business users who want to create, analyze, and share data visualizations and insights without requiring extensive technical skills
Services and Features	Offers a wide range of services and features, including compute, storage, networking, databases, machine learning, and analytics	Offers services and features such as Power BI, which is a cloud-based business intelligence and analytics service that allows users to create interactive visualizations, reports, and dashboards
Integration	Integrates with a wide range of third-party tools and services, including popular development tools, such as GitHub and Jenkins, as well as other cloud-based services, such as Salesforce and SAP	Integrates with Microsoft's other productivity tools, such as Office 365 and Dynamics 365, as well as other third-party tools and services, such as Salesforce and Dropbox

Figure 71 High-level indicative comparison of Google Cloud Platform and Microsoft Power Analytics Platforms vendor overview

To foster a data-driven culture, enterprises must invest in several areas, such as data infrastructure, to guarantee robust data infrastructures that can collect, store, and process large amounts of data. Those investments may include data governance practices and tools, including data quality management, and security. Data skills are another important investment area in training and development for employees to ensure they have the skills and knowledge to work with data. Data access and collaboration tools must be accessible to all employees with access rights. Appropriate data access is a key prerequisite for data-driven organizations and may include data portals, catalogs, and self-service analytics tools. Investments are not a one-time effort, as data analytics capabilities and technologies will continue to evolve and change.

They foster a climate of collaboration across an organization to collaborate and share data insights more easily, facilitating a more cohesive and data-driven culture and leading to increased innovation and more effective decision-making.

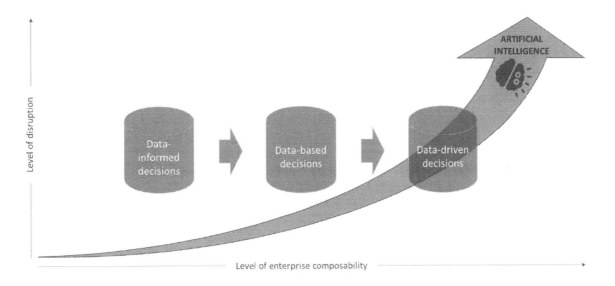

Figure 72 Data-driven decisions do require evolving data-driven cultures and fundamental skills

A general question for all enterprises is the strategy they want to choose when investing in enterprise analytics platforms. A common approach to defining an enterprise-wide data analytics strategy is the consideration of data mesh as an underlying theory.

Data mesh is a different modern approach to data management and architecture that is different from traditional business intelligence (BI) capabilities in several ways:

- **Decentralized ownership**

  Data mesh approaches prioritize decentralized data ownership, meaning that different teams and business units own and are responsible for the data they use. Decentralized ownership differs from traditional BI approaches, where a central team or department manages and maintains all data.

- **Microservices architecture**

  In data mesh approaches, organizations use a microservices architecture that breaks down data into small, independent services that we can manage and scale independently.

- **Product-centric approach**

  Data mesh approaches take a product-centric approach, which means that data services are built and managed as products with a clear set of customers and use cases. This varies from traditional BI, where data services are typically organized as projects.

- **Prioritize self-services**

  Data mesh approaches prioritize self-services with access to data. Teams and individuals can access the needed data without relying on a centralized team or department. Data mesh differs from traditional BI, where access to data is often restricted and requires approval from a central unit.

- **Incremental and experimental ways of working**

  Data mesh approaches prioritize incremental and experimental ways of working. They try out new data services and features without going through a long and complex development process. Data mesh diverges from traditional BI, where changes to data services are often slow and difficult.

Data mesh prioritizes decentralization, autonomy, and self-services, which allows teams and individuals to experiment and iterate rapidly. The key advantage is that data is decentralized but managed and accessible in consistent and secure ways, processes are standardized, and data consumes flexibly to satisfy ad-hoc analytics, standardized reports, and dashboards. It is most suitable for organizations in digital transformation journeys, where agility and innovation are key. They shape the prerequisites for data-driven enterprises in collaborative ways, evolving their culture to embrace the advantages and opportunities of their technologies.

Figure 73 A data-driven culture can only evolve if critical capabilities are in place (varying from organization to organization)

A data-driven culture is one where decisions are made based on data and analysis rather than gut feelings or intuition. There are a few key steps that organizations can take to improve ownership of data management, data quality, and data integrity:

- **Define data ownership**

  Defined data ownership means identifying who collects, manages, and maintains the enterprise data. It is important to have clear ownership so that there is accountability and a clear understanding of who is responsible for each aspect of data management.

- **Invest in skills and talents**

  Such investments are important to provide employees with the required skills and knowledge to work effectively with data to encourage a data-driven culture, which might include training in data analysis, data visualization, or data management best practices.

- **Foster transparency & accountability**

  Creating a culture where data is a valuable, accessible, and trustful asset shared and used for the organization's benefit means fostering transparency around data, encouraging collaboration and knowledge sharing, and holding individuals accountable for data quality and integrity.

- **Leverage technologies**

  Many tools and technologies are available to support data management, from data governance platforms to data quality tools. Investing in these technologies can help ensure that data is accurate, consistent, and secure.

- **Establish policies and procedures**

  Establishing clear policies and procedures for data collection, storage, and management can help ensure consistency and accuracy across the organization.

By taking these steps, organizations can create a data-driven culture where data is utilized as a strategic asset, leading to better decision-making and improved business outcomes. From a strategic perspective, those organizations perform more informed and accurate analyses with optimized insights and input to their business strategies. This helps enterprises make better decisions, optimize business plans, and anchor financial forecasts with better predictive models and simulation capabilities.

> ### *Applied Technology Leadership*
> *Per Jalmelid, Enterprise Architect, Green Cargo*
>
> *"We have a huge amount of data on which to base our decisions at Green Cargo. With the IT legacy landscape, a large part of the data is often difficult to access and interpret or sometimes suffers from poor data quality. Moreover, the IT landscape has not been able to support the need for swiftness regarding data analytics, leading to the business resorting to developing its business-critical analytics solutions. Many of these have shown themselves to be difficult to maintain.*

Our solution to these challenges was twofold. The first step was introducing a cloud-based Enterprise Analytics Platform to support the different analytics capabilities needed. This modern and secure analytics environment has enabled the organizational functions to focus on the right things, with the business being able to independently do analyses and create reports while allowing the IT department to provide quality assured data. This separation of responsibilities is a key success factor as it allows the business to gain new insights from the available data without involving IT. New insights lead to smarter decisions, giving the business functions control of achieving these insights and allowing them to react to, adapt to, and steer business change.

The second step was introducing a data council since the platform does not solve data quality issues or the data used for decision-making. The data council aims to build a data-driven culture by focusing on processes, tools, education, and knowledge sharing surrounding data and information management. The council includes IT and business side members, who act as ambassadors for a data-driven mindset throughout the organization.

The combination of an Enterprise Analytics Platform and the focus on a cultural shift in the decision-making process throughout all functions have set Green Cargo on the path of becoming a truly data-driven organization."

Written by Per Jalmelid, Enterprise Architect, Green Cargo

Data skills are important to leverage business outcomes in reliable, structured, and sustainable ways. They include data collection and management, which requires technical skills in database management, data warehousing, and data engineering. Data-driven organizations demand educated data analysis and interpretation skills in statistics, data science, and machine learning. Another required skill is data visualization and communication; sharing data insights with stakeholders and decision-makers requires data visualization, storytelling, and effective communication skills. Different skills are needed to encourage data-driven innovation, such as ideation, experimentation, and design thinking. Without identifying and implementing competence development strategies in data-driven evolutions, enterprises will experience significant issues utilizing those capabilities at scale.

Figure 74 The four capabilities four digital data-driven organizations

Investing in critical capabilities such as data ownership and stewardship is crucial for data-driven organizations. Data governance fosters a data-driven culture that ensures data quality, accuracy, and security. Data stewards manage and maintain data throughout its lifecycle, while data owners are legally and ethically responsible for specific data sets. To define responsibilities across the enterprise, structures, role descriptions, and data governance policies must be in place, which include collaboration with various roles such as Data Protection Officers (DPOs), Chief Information Security Officers (CISOs), juridical staff, and other security specialists and functions. With data ownership and stewardship supported by enterprise analytics platforms in the cloud, enterprises can leverage those capabilities effectively and effectively.

Data-driven cultures usually change or improve business using data and analytics as they change or impact decision-making processes, giving more weight to data and evidence rather than relying solely on intuition or experience. Using durable technologies and platforms is essential to liberate access to data in controlled and governed ways, to ensure secure and effective ways of sharing, and to access internal and external data. Enterprises that establish those technologies and capabilities will empower their organizations, driving digital composable transformations while continually evolving their digital foundational platform capabilities. The preferred data strategy to support digital transformations in line with the proposed platform architecture combines the centralized approach and a more democratized approach when fostering a data-driven business culture (see next figure).

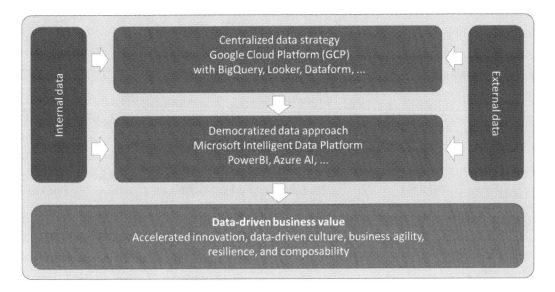

Figure 75 A simplified model of establishing a data-driven culture with a centralized and decentralized platform support

Those who strive for data literacy must understand and compensate for potential disparities and inconsistencies in their data and develop and implement more cohesive strategies. This will have implications on existing processes, as data-driven enterprises will make more informed, consistent, automated, and optimized decisions, as enterprises must embed data-driven innovation at the core of their digital composable transformations. They will increase their ability to act responsive to changing business conditions if analytics is designed and implemented based on similar foundational principles. They may include principles such as modularity, flexibility, reusability, interoperability, scalability, stability, accessibility, and sustainability.

They will be better prepared to utilize and evolve new opportunities with Artificial Intelligence (AI) to further innovate from the core of the business. They will be more effective in aligning execution in their digital composable transformations with their daily business priorities, united with their visions, strategies, objectives, and priorities.

Applied Technology Leadership

Steve Binning, Consultant at Green Cargo, Business Intelligence Specialist, Atea

The implementation of a successful Analytics strategy 2.0 at Green Cargo!

"In today's digitalized world, many organizations struggle to capitalize on the vast amount of data they produce daily. Almost every company recognizes analytics as a crucial "tool" to be competitive, but years of investment in business intelligence technology do not seem to deliver real business value fast enough. The data produced in different operational IT systems increase exponentially, leading to a bottleneck of IT- and analytics experts trying to keep up with new business requirements on delivering new reports and dashboards. The initial success with IT providing breakthrough development and decision support to the business will not engage and democratize Green Cargos' data-driven transformation. Therefore, a decentralized data-driven approach is now under implementation with an evolution of the successful and initial Google enabled analytics strategy. In our initiative Analytics 2.0, business and IT jointly address this challenge based on three equally important cornerstones.

Business value: Every analytics initiative should be based on its potential business value. In general, traditional reporting to answer questions like "What happened?" has relatively low business value because it has already happened, while predictive analysis answering "What will happen?" has potentially high business value given the actions taken based on the prediction. The first step to a more efficient and data-driven organization is implementing self-service analysis capability for the business. This will significantly reduce time spent on manual work to collect data and create reports, which can be used for value-added analysis to learn and distribute new insights for more proactive actions. It will increase the reliability and quality of data, provide one single version of the truth, and prevent the risks of data breaches, security issues, database incidents, and related problems with uncontrolled data management.

People: This approach requires new working methods and skill sets throughout the organization. It is also an opportunity to attract and engage people who demand interesting job assignments in a modern work environment.

New roles include Business Analysts who serve their organization with insights through self-service tools such as reports, dashboards, and other analysis output. On the other hand, the IT organization will be more of a data provider and develop enterprise-wide core analytics capabilities. Rather than developing reports and dashboards, centralized data engineers work with data management to extract and transform data from several operational systems to enable the business to access relevant and quality-assured data.

Technology: The development of analytics technology is unbelievably fast, and foreseeing coming innovations is almost impossible. Therefore, when choosing an analytics platform, there are some fundamentals to consider. The analytics platform must support different analytics capabilities used by the business, such as guided analysis (reporting), self-service analysis, predictive analysis, and AI applications such as Machine Learning. In other words, no "one size fits all" tool fulfills all analytics requirements, it is rather a combination of several analytics tools required. Furthermore, and perhaps most important, the analytics platform must have effective and scalable data management capabilities such as data integration, data lake storage, data transformation, and tool-independent data access only, to mention a few. Given the above requirements and other important factors, Green Cargo selected the cloud architecture from Google Cloud Platform, which is now being complemented with Microsoft Azure enabling the democratization of our data-driven approach.

The journey to a more efficient, data-driven, proactive organization has just started!"

Written by Steve Binning, Consultant at Green Cargo, Business Intelligence Specialist, Atea

But with the rise of AI, such as OpenAI, enterprises must focus on providing data, not just for in-depth analysis by business functions. Data is essential for evolving and enabling enterprises to utilize machine learning (ML) effectively. Algorithms rely heavily on high-quality, diverse data to learn and make accurate predictions or decisions. Machine learning models require a large amount of data to learn and improve their accuracy over time, while more data can increase the accuracy and relevance of AI output and predictions. Data is critical to improving machine learning models and reducing bias by training ML models on diverse datasets.

The right quality and amount of data allow enterprises to customize machine learning models to their specific business needs and improve their relevance significantly, identifying patterns, trends, and insights that may not be possible through traditional analysis. By investing in data quality and availability, enterprises can leverage the power of machine learning to drive innovation, efficiency, and growth.

Leadership is another critical investment to secure the right skills and ensure that data-driven organizations evolve collaboratively, considering different disciplines, such as business, technologies, business capabilities, processes, leadership, data privacy, security, and more. Developing and encouraging organizations to evolve into data-driven businesses, border user acceptance with deep-rooted cultural adaptations are indispensable.

A data-driven culture will benefit from enterprise-wide integrations to leverage the collaborative power of organizations, technologies, and data.

While data-driven organizations transform sequentially, they still have to meet the challenges of ineffective and repetitive processes, often faced with ineffective manual or poorly automated data management processes/activities. Enterprise Automation Platforms (EAP) promise to address these problems differently, by offering effective solutions that can eliminate inefficient manual work and drive focused automation at scale.

Automate business processes

Business process automation (BPA) uses cloud-enabled technologies to automate repetitive, manual, and time-consuming tasks in business processes. BPA typically involves using digital foundational platforms specialized in specific business processes. BPA can include tasks such as data entry, document management, workflow management, report generation, sorting and grouping of tasks, automated order processing, or eliminating the manual input of the same data into different systems.

Organizations can implement BPA in various ways, such as using robotic process automation (RPA) software that mimics the activities of a human worker. They use artificial intelligence (AI) and machine learning capabilities to learn, make decisions, and perform tasks without human intervention. BPA is used in many industries and processes, such as human resources, finance, marketing, sales, and customer service.

BPA can help enterprises to improve efficiency, reduce errors, and save time and money. It is a supportive platform for enterprises undergoing digital transformation, while they are not critical for achieving enterprise composability. Though it usually promises fast ROI and appropriate TCO, it can help automate and streamline processes, allowing them to reduce errors, improve speed, and reduce costs.

For several reasons, automation is important for enterprises undergoing an enterprise-wide digital composable transformation. Automation does leverage several critical improvements, such as:

- Streamline and automate repetitive or time-consuming tasks to significantly improve efficiency and reduce the need for human intervention.
- Reduce costs by reducing the need for labor costs and errors, especially in highly repetitive and data/transaction-intensive processes with fewer faults and higher productivity (24/7).
- Scale operations eliminate the need to add or reduce human resources and may help overcome resource constraints.
- Ensure that tasks are performed consistently and to a high standard, which can improve quality and speed, often leading to cost savings with reduced failure costs and higher customer satisfaction.
- Handling large volumes of data faster and more accurately than humans to increase quality also enables identification and automation responses to patterns in data and transactions.
- Operate unconstrained, which can be an advantage for companies operating 24/7 or running 24/7 processes.

Automation offers great opportunities for enterprise-wide during their digital transformations, as it enables companies to improve efficiency, reduce costs, and scale their operations while enhancing the quality and data processing and being available all the time.

Digital composable transformations may gain significant advantages from the effective deployment and utilization of BPA platforms. However, different technologies and platforms are available to better align business needs with technology choices. As BPA is one core approach to automation, there are different platforms and automation technologies that enterprises may utilize in their digital transformations.

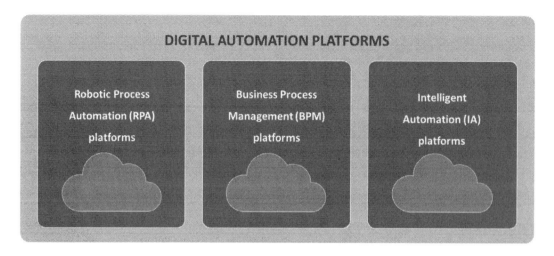

Figure 76 Digital automation platforms

Different automation platform models are grouped based on purpose and may fill special gaps in digital transformations. Some of the most popular platforms are:

1. **Robotic Process Automation (RPA) platforms**

   UiPath, Automation Anywhere, Blue Prism, and WorkFusion are platforms that allow companies to automate repetitive, manual tasks by mimicking the actions of a human worker.

2. **Business Process Management (BPM) platforms**

   Pega, Appian, and IBM BPM are platforms that provide a comprehensive set of tools to automate and manage business processes, including workflow management, process modeling, and analytics.

3. **Intelligent Automation (IA) platforms**

   Cognizant UiPath, AutomationEdge, and OpenConnect combine RPA and AI capabilities to enable more advanced automation and decision-making capabilities.

These platforms have strengths and weaknesses, and choosing the one that best fits the enterprise's needs is important. They can but must not have a significant impact on digital transformations. They will support a variety of tasks, of which BPA platforms are most known for automating inefficient processes with promising ROI and acceptable TCO calculations. Many of these platforms offer a range of services, and an organization might need to use a combination of platforms to achieve its automation goals.

The great advantage of Digital Foundation Platforms with multi-purpose capabilities is their flexibility and ability to test and verify new development rapidly. Examples are Googles Cloud Platform and Microsoft Azure, which include various innovative digital tools and features that can instantly be tested and verified. Those platforms will further support and encourage incremental and experimental development and enhancements within enterprises' Digital Composable Transformations but should be selected wisely.

Applied Technology Leadership
Åsa Blom, Head of Applications, Green Cargo

"At Green Cargo, we have a mix of legacy systems, such as SAP and Mainframe, and modern platforms, such as OutSystems and Azure. We have implemented Robotic Process Automation (RPA) to streamline repetitive processes in our legacy systems using the UiPath platform.

The UiPath platform uses an orchestrator to manage the autonomous robots that run processes triggered by schedules or events. Three robots are in operation, hosting eleven live processes, with more under development. The orchestrator ensures the smooth operation of the robots and processes, providing traceability of transactions and notifications in case of unexpected events.

RPA has been successfully implemented in various areas, such as HR/Payroll processes and Customer Service, resulting in significant time savings for our employees. For instance, automating invoice checks for wagons and locomotives has reduced manual checks and improved accuracy, leading to yearly savings of several million Swedish crowns.

Adopting RPA has brought numerous benefits to Green Cargo, including reduced manual labor costs and increased data input and output accuracy. Overall, RPA has proven to be an effective complement to our legacy systems and a valuable addition to our modern technology.

Using RPA is a complementary approach to our enterprise lowcode development platform. We are utilizing the special strengths of our vendor's platform to introduce effective, controlled, and manageable robotic services. By doing so, we gain significant advantages and business process improvements with good ROIs and acceptable TCOs. Robotics is a complementary element of our digital transformation, with a strong focus on improving business outcomes, with little implications on our approach of enterprise-wide composability."

Written by Åsa Blom, Head of Applications, Green Cargo

In some cases, decision-makers may confuse lowcode with RPA platforms, as both seem to address similar, if not the same, problems. Enterprises differentiate between enterprise lowcode platforms and RPA platforms because they primarily use enterprise lowcode platforms to develop and orchestrate complex enterprise application development. They are used to digitalize processes, such as to rebuild functionality within IT legacy systems or to build complex integrated enterprise applications or any mobile application.

RPA platforms primarily focus on automating business processes and tasks and provide tools and technologies to automate and streamline business processes and tasks. In summary, Low-code platforms enable application development, while automation platforms focus on automating business processes and tasks. RPA platforms support enterprise digital composable transformation journey, while they play a less important role in developing the digital composable enterprise. However, they can help solve critical business problems with often impressive ROI and acceptable TCO. They also increase acceptance of digital transformations and help organizations reallocate resources from nonvalue add, towards more value add activities.

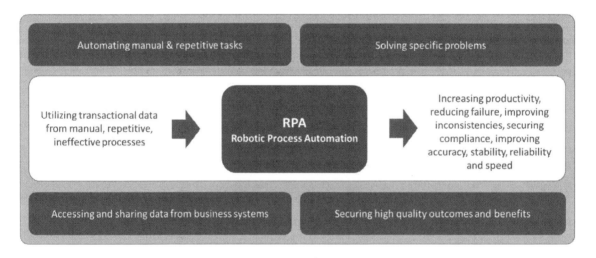

Figure 77 RPA (Robotic Process Automation) guarantees consistent monetization of investments

Distinct ownership, maintenance, and overall controls are necessary to ensure that automated business-critical processes operate consistently and run without interruptions, including life cycle management and continual monitoring.

Even though those platforms play a vital role in terms of efficiencies and effectiveness, they are not necessarily strategic. Bots replace human interaction and reduce the dependency on human workers while integrating workplace capabilities will remain critical for most digital transformations.

Encourage enterprise collaboration

The global Covid-19 pandemic has significantly impacted office workers and digital workplaces. Many businesses and organizations shut down physical offices and encourage or require employees to work from home. Remote work and digital collaboration tools have found global acceptance and were critical to most office workers during the global pandemic. The rapid adaptation of enterprises worldwide and end-users' ability to adapt to new working methods happened nearly overnight.

This change has increased the use of video conferencing, collaboration software, and cloud-based systems. The pandemic has accelerated the digital transformation as companies adapted to remote workforce strategies and new ways to stay productive and connected.

A digital workplace is a digital work environment that utilizes digital technologies to enhance communication, collaboration, and productivity for employees, consultants, and partners. New collaborative platforms include a range of tools, such as cloud-based storage and file-sharing platforms, digital communication and messaging platforms, automation and workflow tools, digital project management tools, virtual training, and development resources, employee self-service portals, analytics and reporting tools, mobile access to information and tools, and cybersecurity measures to protect sensitive data.

The goal of a digital workplace is to enable employees to work more efficiently and effectively, regardless of location or device. Organizations of all sizes and industries can use digital workplaces, from small businesses to large corporations, supported by various platforms.

Figure 78 Leading digital workplace platforms

Leading digital workplace platforms:

1. **Microsoft 365**

   Microsoft's cloud-based platform includes remote work and collaboration tools like Office 365, Teams, and SharePoint.

2. **Google Workspace**

   Google's cloud-based platform includes remote work and collaboration tools like Gmail, Google Drive, and Google Meet.

3. **Slack**

   Slack's popular communication and collaboration platform allows team members to chat, share files, and make audio and video calls.

Digital workplaces have grown in popularity and become business-critical capabilities to enable effective remote communications and collaboration for organizations of any size and scale. They are supposed to be part of every digital transformation and are vital to utilize effective automation tools to manage access rights, onboarding, off-boarding, mobile devices, and much more.

Enterprise Workplace Platforms (EWP) have a much wider scope and include various products and services. An enterprise workplace platform typically includes multiple tools and services to support different aspects of an employee's work life.

The specific components of a digital workplace platform can vary depending on the organization's needs and goals, but generally, it includes:

- **Collaboration and communication tools**

  Those tools share information and collaborate on projects in real-time, regardless of their location. Examples include instant messaging, video conferencing, and collaboration tools.

- **Mobile and device management (MDM)**

  MDM allows employees to access work resources from any device and enables the organization to manage and secure those devices. Organizations gain better control over their devices and data and better protect the enterprise.

- **Cloud-based productivity tools**

  Many tools help employees to create, edit and share documents, spreadsheets, and presentations. Examples include Microsoft Office 365 and Google Workspace. They are widely available on different end-user devices and highly configurable.

- **Social intranet and knowledge management**

  Those capabilities and tools allow employees to share and access knowledge and information within the organization and find the right people to collaborate with.

- **Workflow automation**

  This component allows organizations to automate repetitive tasks and processes, such as expense reporting or time-off requests, to improve efficiency and reduce errors.

- **Digital identity and access management**

  Those tools allow organizations to manage and secure access to digital resources and provide Single Sign-On capabilities for employees.

- **Training and development**

  This component allows employees to access online training resources and e-learning courses to improve their skills and knowledge.

Workplace platforms are configurable, but stringent and simplified usage and administration of those platforms suggest single vendor solutions instead of combining different platforms. Their main goal is to provide an integrated and cohesive environment that supports the needs of employees and the organization.

Active Directory (AD) is a technology developed by Microsoft, embedded in the Azure Active Directory (Azure AD) service. Azure AD Microsoft's cloud-based identity and access management service provide similar functionality to on-premises Active Directory but with additional features and capabilities specific to cloud-based environments. AD manages and organizes user and computer accounts and provides authentication and authorization services. AD can be deployed on-premises, in a hybrid environment, or in the cloud using Azure Active Directory (Azure AD), Microsoft's cloud-based version. Azure AD can authenticate users to access cloud-based resources and manage user and device identity for on-premises resources in a hybrid scenario.

Utilizing Active Directories in the cloud is not just the platform to create world-class collaborative digital workplaces. It is a strategic capability to integrate different perspectives of modern workforces as much as those platforms enable controlled and secure collaboration across various external groups of customers, partners, and stakeholders (such as owners, advisors, and revisors).

Workplace platforms are often linked to the digital workplace of office workers but have, over time, also remote working personnel. They include core functionality such as mail, chat, videoconferencing, file sharing, social media, and mobility. The global and rapid introduction of digital workplaces implies various benefits, such as increased productivity and efficiency, as collaboration allows team members to share ideas, expertise, and resources, leading to faster problem-solving and decision-making. It improves communication and teamwork because collaboration promotes simplified communication and optimizing working hours.

Digital workplace helps to provide greater flexibility and increase convenience while contributing to increased and improved work-life balance. Cooperation allows for a broader range of input and perspectives, leading to more informed decision-making and encouraging diverse perspectives and the chance to significantly reduce traveling, time, and efforts and lower CO_2 creation. Diversity increases and new recruitments are not constrained to office locations.

One of the most effective improvements is consistency in data and information sharing and collaborative work in shared files and documents. Knowledge sharing and learning have increased, and employees found sharing information and file more appealing. Instead of using file servers, the cloud manages and stores corporate data and information.

Collaboration allows teams to respond quickly to changes and adapt to new situations and challenges. Collaboration has increased workplace resilience and helps enterprises handle and recover from crises or unplanned events.

Those features embedded in digital workplaces foster digital collaboration inside organizations and enable effective digital collaboration across digital ecosystems. Digital workplaces are a core capability necessary to manage access rights even in collaborative B2B (Business to Business) and B2C (Business to Consumer) environments. This includes B2B collaboration with other organizations while they can review cross-tenant access settings to ensure professionally managed inbound and outbound B2B collaboration and scope accessing specific users, groups, and applications.

Organizations that drive their digital transformations must secure digital workplace initiatives as an integrative part, including Mobile Device Management applications, to effectively manage and control mobile workplaces across the organization and beyond (partners, customers).

Microsoft Azure Active Directory (Azure AD) B2B collaboration is a fully embedded feature within External Identities inviting guest users to collaborate across selected business processes inside and outside the enterprise. This is managed effectively through modern workplaces in the cloud to secure compliance, security, and access rights in line with policies and external requirements.

With B2B collaboration, organizations can securely share applications and services with guest users from other organizations while maintaining control over their corporate data. This feature enables effective, controlled, and secure digital working relationships with external partners, large or small, even if they do not have a Microsoft Azure AD or an IT department. Organizations can easily design attractive and simple maintain, share, and utilize digital capabilities embedded into digital workplace platforms. They can also integrate different platforms and applications into collaborative workplace environments. The Dynamics of digital workplaces are about to explode, as their maximum collaborative capacity utilizes not to its full extent.

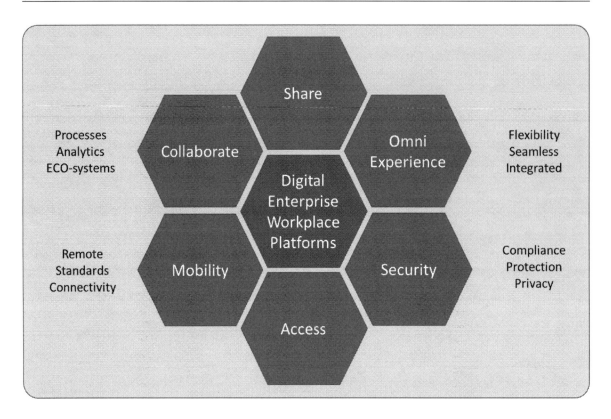

Figure 79 Digital workplace is a central and highly integrated element of digital transformations

Highly integrated workplaces support greater digital enrichment of collaborative ways of working. They embed collaboration into business application layers, automated through predefined and ready-to-use APIs, limitless utilization of data and information, digital interaction in event-driven and real-time business processes, simplified sharing, and utilization of analytics capabilities as utilization of advanced ready-to-use Machine Learning algorithms and services.

Applied Technology Leadership
Dennis Eklöf Lundin, Head of IT Operations, Green Cargo

"At Green Cargo, most of our business users are operational staff who drive locomotives around the Nordic region, manage wagons in the railway yards, or control and plan the marshaling of train compositions 24/7. Such business conditions highly demand mobile and durable devices for effective communication services. Our lowcode applications and analytics capabilities are provided as mobile services and are business-critical services integrated with our mainframe system and other critical systems.

Our administrative staff uses mainly laptops, but even here, the needs and requirements for mobility are growing due to increased remotely connected workforces. The integrated collaboration capabilities of our different Microsoft platforms will further simplify the utilization of future Microsoft products, such as Dynamics, Power, and Azure services.

Another critical element is utilizing our Active Directory, securing controlled and roles-based access to applications and services for internal and external users of our digital services. By introducing role-based access rights, on-and offboarding, as well as internal changes, are being automated. This is a prerequisite for the planned roll-out of digital services to our partners and customers.

Our future focus on information and cybersecurity will continue to evolve, and our Microsoft centricity is further increasing our level of protection concerning Green Cargos workplaces, assets, and data. We have implemented advanced security measures to quickly identify and remedy risks, vulnerabilities, and threats that appear, preferably automated, with established detection and response capabilities.

All this makes us choose to build and implement our Workplace strategy based on Microsoft products, which are the building blocks we need across all areas today.

Our workplace strategy is under continual review to implement and succeed with our digital transformation and further accelerates through the roll-out of additional embedded Microsoft capabilities.

We prioritize secure communication and enablement of business services. We must extend our scope to access and utilize information, services, and data through mobile means, empowering our operational and administrative personnel to work seamlessly regardless of location, time, or tools.

One of the most significant changes is how we have transformed from buying packaged IT services into an IT Operations organization where autonomy is one of our guiding principles. Our approach has changed to leverage environmental improvements by utilizing effective services from leading sustainable vendors, while we are shifting our focus on running infrastructure as a code wherever beneficial."

Written by Dennis Eklöf Lundin, Head of IT Operations, Green Cargo

A key argument for enterprises utilizing Microsoft Dynamics is the appreciation of collaboration capabilities with other Microsoft products, such as Dynamic 365. Sales is seamlessly integrated into the workplace capabilities, as much as into other MS products. The future of digital workplaces is more than just a file-sharing and conversation platform, while truly developing into a strategic user-centric and business process-enabling platform for relentless collaboration, inside and outside organizations. Those services are enriched with embedded mobility management and integrated information- and cybersecurity and are vital for the effective execution of digital transformations. Modern Digital Workplace platforms in the cloud will accelerate the digital conversion of traditional ERP and complex IT legacy systems towards cloud-based digital foundational platforms.

Evolve composable ERP in the cloud

Cloud ERP systems are becoming increasingly popular among organizations because of their scalability, accessibility, and cost-effectiveness. As more and more enterprises move their ERP and systems of records to the cloud, the demand for cloud-based ERP systems is likely to increase. The future of ERP (Enterprise Resource Planning) will significantly shift from on-premise to cloud-enabled platforms, forcing enterprises to discontinue their on-premise ERP platforms in the coming decade.

Enterprises have two very different and distinct choices amongst various vendors operating their ERP cloud under other circumstances:

1. **Bundled cloud ERP vendors**

   These vendors are migrating from on-premise ERP offerings towards bundled ERP cloud offerings, such as SAP S/4HANA, Oracle cloud ERP, and Unit4 ERP.

2. **Modular cloud ERP vendors**

   These vendors mainly have modular platform-based ERP offerings in the cloud, such as Microsoft Dynamics, Oracle Netsuite, and Infor CloudSuite.

Enterprises migrating from on-premise to cloud ERP often prefer a conventional cloud ERP vendor. They even consider modular and more flexible cloud ERP vendor strategies during this period, while this strategic choice has significant implications for those enterprises, in terms of costs, resources, times, and risks, because of complexity. Firstly, there are fewer concerns about the perceived ease of migration and continuation of a trusted on-premise vendor relationship. Secondly, these strategic choices must support future business demands to secure digital resilience through end-to-end enterprise-wide digital composability.

Uninformed decisions without considering and evaluating cloud ERP vendors might limit the ability of enterprises to customize their digital business capabilities to meet their specific business needs, leading to reduced flexibility and limited abilities to respond effectively to crises and rapidly changing business needs. Dependencies on a single vendor can increase the risk of vendor lock-in and limit the digital responsiveness of enterprises. To mitigate potential risks, enterprises must plan their ERP migration strategies to the cloud by ensuring appropriate requirements embedded in their selection criteria, such as flexibility, agility, modularity, interoperability, and digital resilience. Modular, open, and interoperable architectures allow unconstrained integration of innovative technologies. In today's rapidly evolving technological landscape, achieving effective open architectures and standards is increasingly important. Those architectures can include multiple technologies from different vendors for seamless integration without requiring major modifications to the underlying architecture.

Modular ERP platforms offer a key advantage by allowing the integration of transactional and regulatory processes and data into cohesive and digitally integrated technologies. Companies can leverage ERP systems managed by CCoEs (Cloud Centers of Competence) in their cloud environments to enhance and expedite the composability of future ERP platforms. These systems promote unrestricted collaboration, rejuvenate data-driven business processes, and seamlessly integrate the transactional core digitally into the enterprise's overall digital architecture. Composable enterprises utilize their ERP systems as fully embedded digital architectures and technologies, ensuring the highest levels of digital collaboration and business innovation. Traditional back-office transactions will diminish in significance within the enterprise's digital foundational architecture as they become the core of its digital operations. The future of cloud-based ERP architectures will enable and accelerate the deployment and scalability of innovative capabilities and technologies like generative AI, IoT, advanced analytics, blockchain, workplace collaboration, and more.

Future modular and composable ERP systems will facilitate digitally-enabled ecosystems that integrate front-end digital customer interactions with the core of the business. Overseeing this trend and developing unconstrained modularity and digital ERP autonomy are crucial capabilities for digital composable enterprises. These enterprises can leverage their ERP investments to transform into data-driven, digitally enhanced, customer-centric, cost-effective, resilient, and innovative organizations. In enterprises with complex technology environments, it is essential that cloud ERP vendors and their platforms guarantee and actively support digital composability in line with the enterprise's risks and strategic choices. Bundled ERP cloud offerings may compromise enterprise composability, introduce major risks, and hinder enterprise-wide digital resilience in worst-case scenarios. Enterprises that choose modular cloud ERP platforms can combine different digital foundational platforms and variations of SaaS services. They can manage those services in the scope of cloud operations in their CCoE (Cloud Center of Excellence).

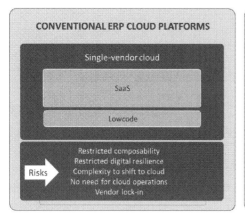 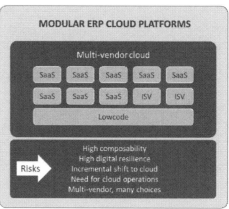

Figure 80 Comparison of single vendor & platform strategy with multi-vendor, -platform, and -SaaS strategy

HIGH LEVEL COMPARISON OF TRADITIONAL ERP CLOUD VENDORS WITH MODULAR ERP CLOUD VENDORS		
Core Domains	**CONVENTIONAL ERP CLOUD OFFERINGS**	**MODULAR ERP CLOUD OFFERINGS**
VENDORS	SAP, Oracle Cloud ERP, Unit4 ERP, IFS Applications	Microsoft, Oracle Netsuite, Infor CloudSuite, Epicor ERP, Acumatica
Enterprise composability	• Supports ERP composability with risks of limited enterprise composability. • Decreases composability depending on the vendor's ERP strategies and technologies and overall design patterns.	• Requires composable strategies, architectures, investments, and overall systemic thinking. • Shifts accountability to customers to design and implement complex technologies to secure enterprise composability at scale.
Digital flexibility	• Offers a modular structure allowing customization and flexibility in deployment options.	• Offers a modular architecture allowing more advanced customization and flexible deployment options. • Requires higher grades of architectural design and accountability. • Requires cloud operations skills and Cloud Center of Excellence.
Digital resilience	• Has built-in redundancy and disaster recovery capabilities for business continuity but might come with restrictions in terms of responsiveness	• Offers built-in resilience and disaster recovery options for business continuity.
Digital autonomy	• Causes risks with vendor lock-in effects in technology choices. • Causes dependencies on the vendor's roadmap. • Can limiting innovation and technology choices. • Platforms, such as S/4HANA are customizable and configurable.	• Comes with a highly adjustable technology stack and unconstrained choices of technologies. • Provides autonomous services for database management, security, and compliance.
Enterprise interoperability	• Offers integration with third-party applications and cloud platforms through APIs and standard interfaces. • Secures interoperability with a highly modular design.	• Provides seamless integration with other Microsoft applications and third-party systems through APIs and standard interfaces. • Some vendors offer digital foundational platforms critical for digital composability on an enterprise level.
Digital Transformations	• Provides a roadmap for digital transformation with SAP's Intelligent Enterprise Framework. • Creates vendor dependency on transformative technologies roadmap.	• Enables digital foundational platform strategies with embedded ERP by vendors such as Microsoft. • Offers integrated cloud services for digital transformation, including Dynamics 365 and Power Platform, MS365, and MS Azure. • Platforms, such as MS Dynamics, are customizable and configurable.
Data Analytics	• Utilizes in-memory computing and machine learning to enable real-time analysis and insights. • Offers SAP Analytics Cloud for business intelligence and data visualization with inbuild AI capabilties. • Reduces analytics capabilities with high integration complexity.	• Utilizes data analytics tools for business intelligence and data visualization on an enterprise level, not the ERP system level. • Offers integrations with Azure services for data warehousing and big data processing. • Encourages unconstrained democratization of data consumption.
Integration	• Offers integration with third-party applications and cloud platforms through APIs and standard interfaces. • Supports open standards and offers pre-built connectors for common integrations. • Real-time integration of large amounts of data (S/4HANA)..	• Provides integration with other Microsoft applications and third-party systems through APIs and standard interfaces. • Offers integration Services for advanced integration scenarios. • Comes with a full enterprise composable platform architecture. • Provides seamless integration with other Microsoft applications and third-party systems through APIs and standard interfaces.
Complexity	• Makes implementations and transformations more complex and time-consuming. • Results in significant costs and risks associated with the ERP migration.	• Allows for incremental and systemic migration from existing platforms towards cloud-based services. • Allows enterprises to pay as they go, consuming services driven by business needs with more advanced digital resilience.

Figure 81 High-level comparison of traditional ERP cloud vendors with modular ERP cloud vendors

This high-level comparison of bundled cloud ERP vendor offerings with modular ERP cloud vendor offerings indicates the need for overseeing cloud ERP vendor selection strategies and criteria, as some low-weighted selection criteria may have greater influence and impact during vendor selection than traditional ones.

Organizations utilizing digital foundational platforms should embrace alternative opportunities when overseeing their ERP strategies, especially for standardized and commodity business processes. To replace existing IT legacy systems, including processes such as finance, HR, marketing, commerce, logistics, and customer services, is a new approach towards more agile digital ERP by applying a platform-centric approach to replace those systems with SaaS on its own PaaS, managed by CCoE (Cloud Center of Excellence).

Leveraging intelligent cloud-only strategies to modernize, shift, and replace on-premise ERP platforms is crucial to simplify, integrate, and rationalize modern, composable, and autonomous ERP modernization programs. Incremental and systemic approaches, driven by business priorities, will generate more business-driven roadmaps without overprioritizing necessary ERP investments at the disadvantage of digital composable transformations.

Independent Software Vendors (ISVs) offer easy-to-integrate complementary business capabilities. They can effectively support platform and cloud-based ERP strategies with multiple SaaS portfolios. ISV solutions can bring several benefits when utilized in composable digital transformations and increase flexibility to advance standard SaaS applications with specific business capabilities quickly. They can help to avoid or reduce costs, but they must be implemented in controlled ways, securing compliance, security, and other critical criteria.

Organizations that prioritize composable and interoperable enterprise ERP transformations ensure greater and more flexible business and digital resilience. CIOs must consider potential risks and benefits, largely driven by the enterprise's visions, strategies, goals, business priorities, and overall approach to composability, interoperability, autonomy, and digital resilience.

Boards, CEOs, and CIOs MUST consider those strategic criteria when deciding cloud ERP vendor selections. All vendors can satisfy strategic business requirements concerning digital resilience and interoperability. However, those decisions require in-depth analysis and understanding before making final decisions. Ignoring those options may put enterprises at risk, not achieving composability while risking long-term complications and irreversible difficulties.

New leadership is required to transform organizations into digital composable enterprises. Those transformations will only materialize if risk-tolerance leadership overcomes traditional thinking and decision-making burdens. Successful strategies and actions must foster and encourage new leadership to increase organizational and individual autonomy by assuming accountability and establishing trust.

The right and informed choices of cloud ERP transformations have a significant role in designing and realizing digital composable enterprises. Making technology choices is complex, requiring consistency, discipline, and holistic and systemic thinking.

Embrace complementary digital platforms

The number of digital platforms enterprises can utilize is enormous. The most known example of visualizing tools and platforms of the "DATA & AI LANDSCAPE" by Matt Turck indicates the infinite opportunities for technology choices. The following examples of additional platforms indicate the variety of options enterprises must conduct when selecting new platforms and technologies.

"TO EVERY BUSINESS LEADER: Selecting new technologies must start with identifying the business opportunities or problems, not by finding a technology. Instead, business and architects must first identify and define business capabilities to find and select the right approach or technologies, and not vice versa."

Ingo Paas

Enterprises need to engage with partners during their transition from traditional ERP towards modern composable ERP platforms in the cloud. Those migrating away from traditional ERP vendors may find support in financing and driving this transition with experienced partners, such as RiminiStreet. Financing the digitalization and modernization of ERP transformations through significantly lower maintenance costs during the legacy ERP system transformation is one of several key benefits, CxOs must consider in their business cases and business modernization roadmap. Not considering such options before making any strategic decisions reduces options in making strategic choices and securing a smooth path toward composability at scale.

Additional examples of platforms capabilities:

ENTERPRISE SALESFORCE AUTOMATION PLATFORMS		
VENDORS	**KEY FEATURES**	**INDUTRIES & SCOPE**
Salesforce	Customizable sales automation and CRM tools, marketing automation, AI-powered sales forecasting, and sales analytics.	All industries.
ubSpot	Lead management, email marketing, live chat, web forms, social media integration, and analytics.	B2B, B2C, and E-commerce.
Zoho CRM	Sales automation, lead generation, pipeline management, email marketing, and analytics.	Small and medium-sized businesses.
Pipedrive	Sales pipeline management, sales reporting and forecasting, email integration, and mobile app.	Small and medium-sized businesses.
Freshsales	Sales automation, lead management, deal management, analytics, and AI-powered lead scoring.	B2B and E-commerce.

Figure 82 Overview of Enterprise Sales Force Automation Platforms cloud vendors

ENTERPRISE INTERNET OF THINGS PLATFORMS (IoT)		
VENDORS	**KEY FEATURES**	**INDUTRIES & SCOPE**
AWS IoT	Device management, data management, security, and analytics services	All industries, with a focus on manufacturing, smart cities, and healthcare
Microsoft Azure IoT	Device management, data management, security, and analytics services	All industries, with a focus on manufacturing, smart cities, and healthcare
IBM Watson IoT	Device management, data management, security, analytics, and cognitive services	All industries, with a focus on manufacturing, smart cities, and healthcare
Google Cloud IoT	Device management, data management, security, and analytics services	All industries, with a focus on manufacturing, smart cities, and healthcare
Salesforce IoT	Device management, data management, security, and analytics services, with a focus on customer engagement and marketing	All industries, with a focus on retail, hospitality, and transportation

Figure 83 Overview of Enterprise Internet of Things (IoT) Platforms in the cloud

ENTERPRISE BLOCKCHAIN PLATFORMS		
VENDORS	KEY FEATURES	INDUTRIES & SCOPE
IBM Blockchain	Hyperledger Fabric-based blockchain platform, smart contract support, scalability, and security	All industries, with a focus on financial services, supply chain management, and healthcare
Microsoft Azure	Blockchain-as-a-service (BaaS), multiple blockchain protocols support, low-code development, and enterprise-grade security	All industries, with a focus on financial services, supply chain management, and healthcare
Amazon Web Services	Blockchain-as-a-service (BaaS), multiple blockchain protocols support, low-code development, and enterprise-grade security	All industries, with a focus on financial services, supply chain management, and healthcare
Oracle Blockchain	Enterprise-grade blockchain platform, multiple blockchain protocols support, integration with enterprise systems, and secure identity management	All industries, with a focus on supply chain management, financial services, and government
R3 Corda	Distributed ledger technology (DLT) platform, secure smart contracts, interoperability, and scalability	Financial services, supply chain management, and healthcare

Figure 84 Overview of Enterprise BlockChain Platforms in the cloud

ENTERPRISE BLOCKCHAIN PLATFORMS		
VENDORS	KEY FEATURES	INDUTRIES & SCOPE
IBM Blockchain	Hyperledger Fabric-based blockchain platform, smart contract support, scalability, and security	All industries, with a focus on financial services, supply chain management, and healthcare
Microsoft Azure	Blockchain-as-a-service (BaaS), multiple blockchain protocols support, low-code development, and enterprise-grade security	All industries, with a focus on financial services, supply chain management, and healthcare
Amazon Web Services	Blockchain-as-a-service (BaaS), multiple blockchain protocols support, low-code development, and enterprise-grade security	All industries, with a focus on financial services, supply chain management, and healthcare
Oracle Blockchain	Enterprise-grade blockchain platform, multiple blockchain protocols support, integration with enterprise systems, and secure identity management	All industries, with a focus on supply chain management, financial services, and government
R3 Corda	Distributed ledger technology (DLT) platform, secure smart contracts, interoperability, and scalability	Financial services, supply chain management, and healthcare

Figure 85 Overview of Enterprise Cybersecurity Platforms in the cloud

Key conclusions and takeaways

The key conclusions and takeaways from the chapter "**DIGITAL FOUNDATIONAL PLATFORMS**" are:

1. Enterprises must empower CxOs to make foundational tech decisions without formal business demands.

2. Enterprises must invest in core digital foundational platforms, such as enterprise lowcode, enterprise integration, and enterprise analytics.

3. Enterprises must identify additional critical digital foundational platforms, such as workplace, collaboration, and artificial intelligence.

4. Enterprises must application development into highly effective software factories, literally capable of solving any business problem, based on PBCs (Packaged Business Capabilities).

5. Enterprises must invest in continually developing those platforms to secure further adaptations and technology innovation by utilizing or completing existing technologies with changing business demands.

6. Enterprises must select future platforms by balancing business needs and the technical conditions of those platforms in terms of composability and interoperability.

7. Enterprises must consider their desired autonomy and enterprise composability when making decisions concerning their future ERP systems.

EIGHT – INNOVATION FROM THE CORE

THOUGHT DIGITAL LEADERSHIP

David Logg, Vice President Global Business Engineering, CGI

"The question of whether innovation should be open or closed recurs in various aspects of innovation. Opening/inviting the entire business into the work that innovation should not be managed by an external unit or thanks to an own budget is a shift away from traditional thinking. The level of innovation is often linked to a company's culture, and companies might leverage innovation as part of their digital transformations at the core of the business.

That we have an elaborate framework for assessing the level of innovation is a matter of course for most businesses I have met. The big challenge is often to dare to bet big in the square where disruptive and radical ends up. And to stay relevant, companies need to have in-depth knowledge of their client's expectations and future demands.

Managers also need to proactively look outside their industry to find solutions and innovations that can be used to strengthen their future market position.

To quote Gunnar Gurra Krantz, one of Sweden's sail tycoons' leaders with years of global experience, "You will not win the race if you currently are the second runner up in a sailing race and if you do the same things as the leader". Innovation could be about designing a new race boat or making a difference in the middle of the race.

Innovation can be defined as the process of generating ideas, solving problems, and generating value. The concept of incremental and embedded innovation through dynamic levels of engagement at the core of the business is opening for continual innovation.

Industrializing innovation at the core of digital transformations is a promising, unconventional way of "innovating" innovation processes. To embed innovation in collaborative ways to utilize digital foundational platforms might be sustainable new ways of evolving future digital composable enterprises."

Written by David Logg, Vice President Global Business Engineering, CGI

Understand the innovation obstacle

Innovation is not natural, and most enterprises are struggling significantly while leading tech giants continually utilize innovation at the core of their enterprises. While rigid innovation still is doomed to fail in most enterprises, CEOs continue believing that conventional innovation processes and frameworks are the solutions to their problems to deliver on the promises of enterprise innovation.

The book "Alphabet/Google, Amazon, Apple, Facebook, and Microsoft" by Matthew C. Le Merle and Alison Davis (Matthew C. Le Merle, 2017) shows that successful corporate innovation requires a combination of entrepreneurial thinking and disciplined execution. The authors argue that the most successful innovation companies, such as the five giants (Alphabet/Google, Amazon, Apple, Facebook, and Microsoft) studied in the book, share a common approach that balances experimentation and risk-taking with rigorous measurement and data analysis. They also emphasize the importance of leadership, culture, and organizational structure in fostering innovation and provide specific examples and case studies to illustrate their points. The book provides a valuable roadmap for companies seeking to innovate in today's fast-paced and rapidly changing business environment.

Global research reveals a large difference between executives' innovative ambitions and their organizations' ability to execute. CEOs have high expectations for digital transformation, but the outcomes often fall short. While they expect digital transformation to drive significant improvements in key business metrics, such as revenue growth and profitability, the results are often dissatisfying and much less impactful than the business cases promised. Some reasons for this gap include a lack of clear strategy, insufficient investment in technology and skills, and challenges in effectively implementing and scaling new digital capabilities.

Organizations can fail with their innovation strategies for several reasons, including:

- **Ineffective utilization of technologies**
  Organizations are over-trusting the benefits of technologies without clearly defining why and how to apply those in foundational interoperable platform architectures. It is often not about the technologies enterprises are investing in. Instead, enterprises implement technologies in fragmented and isolated ways without leveraging their innovation potential. With this approach, technologies often solve individual problems, while their potential to bring innovation at scale becomes impractical.

Such technology investments may lead to non-scalable or non-reusable design during implementation, the absence of foundational principles, or insufficient adherence to the utilization of both during execution. Ineffective technology implementations do not support innovation, leaving few opportunities to encourage technology-inspired and scalable innovation.

- **Missing collaboration and cultural evolvement**

  Organizations struggle to collaborate effectively across departments and with external partners, which can limit the sharing of ideas and resources. Corporate innovation processes reinforce and create silo-thinking, limiting collaboration and cross-functional innovation. The disconnection of the organization from traditional innovation frameworks will hinder the cultural evolution and adaption of a more common approach to innovation across organizations.

- **Lacking the ability to solve business problems**

  Innovation generated in organized workshops may be counterproductive to the burning needs of organizations solving their actual business problems with new innovative thinking and rapid responses. The ignorance of daily business problems in traditional corporate innovation processes is leading to poor execution in problem-solving. The frustration reduces overall participation in corporate innovation, diminishing trust and confidence, and will not resolve burning business problems. Resources are difficult to allocate, as dynamic prioritization processes (such as SAFe 5.0) in agile organizations will be difficult to align with rigid and sporadic corporate innovation processes. Organizations may not clearly understand what they want to achieve with their innovation strategy, leading to a lack of focus and direction, creating distance to the need for daily innovation from the core of the business.

- **Hierarchical and overregulated innovation processes**

  Large organizations suffer from risk-averse cultures, strict governance, and overregulated and hierarchical processes. They create problems caused by bureaucracy and decision-making processes that slow innovation. Organizations often apply such principles and top-down management approaches to overregulate and manage innovation frameworks. Such complexity contradicts the idea and principles of innovation, where innovation expects to encourage and evolve the organization's culture, conditions, and collaborative engagement.

  This can result in missed opportunities and a lack of agility when organizations experience major discrepancies between principled innovation processes and selected prioritized initiatives.

Organizations may experience processes, selection criteria, and execution capabilities as theoretical and impractical. Another restriction occurs as organizations tend to behave risk-averse to minimize risks.

- **Organizational resistance to change**

  Employees and other stakeholders may resist innovation-related changes, which can obstruct and delay innovative behavior due to the "not-invented-here syndrome". Change can be difficult, and corporate cultures that resist change can restrain innovation attempts. Organizations may experience a lack of willingness to take risks and try innovations outside the approved and governed framework. The absence of solving real and burning business problems is another reason organizations may be reluctant to reinforce innovation programs.

Enterprises can solve the lessons learned from decades of unsuccessful attempts to bring innovation to life. This chapter will reveal the hidden advantages of successful digital transformations to foster a culture of innovation integrated with the enterprise's approach to cultivating evolutionary digital composable transformations.

Corporate innovation frameworks are having difficulties finding and bringing real innovation and breakthrough ideas to life. Instead of leveraging innovation from the core of the business, innovation is usually an overdeveloped process not integrated into daily operations and problem-solving efforts. Those processes are typically disconnected and not aligned with organizational priorities. When applied corporate innovation processes, the main problems may include resistance to change, lack of resources, disconnection from digital transformations, and difficulties integrating new innovative solutions with given conditions (such as processes, business logic, systems, or organizational structures). Due to potentially counterproductive corporate innovation frameworks, organizations struggle to implement and scale dynamic incremental and experimental innovation initiatives, resulting in poor outcomes and non-scalable investments. The true purpose of innovation is to improve the organization's efficiency (do things smarter), increase effectiveness (secure better results/outcomes), and enhance the organization's competitive advantage (apply to learn and continually innovate and improve). Even though this seems logical, most organizations use innovation processes and models to identify and prioritize finding rare but innovative breakthrough ideas. They interpret innovation as the search for the holy grail, while most prioritized innovation attempts permanently struggle to reach those objectives.

It seems to be an unsolvable problem for organizations to add innovation to their business agenda, monetize the potential of creativity and technologies, and turn ideas into sustainable benefits, as organizations may be uncertain about the true definition of innovation. They may hope to achieve a kind of "Aurora" effect, to identify and capitalize on the golden innovation idea as an outcome of the firm well-organized innovation processes. In reality, this moment rarely happens, and investments into martial innovation processes and organizations (such as corporate x-teams) are most likely doomed to fail.

The ability to utilize innovation is therefore limited, and to hope for one big IDEA, is not perceived as a good management practice. Instead, CEOs should accelerate their organization's innovation capacity while the opposite effect is revealed. Most organizations still prefer to organize innovation as a process outside the organization's daily business. Those innovation programs are often well-financed, supported by the CEOs, and reasonably well-organized (with innovation processes and models). However, they still seem to underdeliver and may not create the value and outcome expected from CEOs.

Innovation initiatives repeatedly fail to deliver sustainable improvements and benefits because of the nature of those restrained archaic frameworks and processes. The more or less inappropriate structure and embedded rigid processes force organizations and their employees into inflexible and ineffective governed innovation work. Selected participants contribute to innovation workshops where they are supposed to produce ideas on demand. Those organizations evaluate and rate ideas, then choose the ones that will receive support to advance further and demonstrate their first proof of concept before releasing further funding.

The disadvantages of traditional innovation processes include the following:

- **Slow speed**
  Traditional innovation processes can be slow and bureaucratic, leading to missed opportunities and a slower time-to-market. Bureaucratic processes can take a long time, and speed is not the focus of most innovation frameworks.
- **Rigidity**
  Traditional innovation processes may be rigid and resistant to change, making it difficult for organizations to pivot and respond to new opportunities or threats. Their rigidity comes from their nature and over trust in traditional assessments in linear and controlled processes.

- **Lack of flexibility**

  Traditional innovation processes may not be flexible enough to accommodate new ideas and approaches, limiting the innovation potential. They often discourage innovation and cause frustration, as they cannot solve real-life problems.

- **Limited collaboration**

  Traditional innovation processes may not encourage collaboration and cross-functional teamwork, limiting the sharing of ideas and resources. Due to the nature of those frameworks, initiatives that may proceed through the different phases cannot utilize the power of collaborative networks and tools, already building digital assets and skills and effectively utilizing capabilities.

- **Lack of experimentation**

  Traditional innovation processes may not allow experimentation and risk-taking, which can be important for fostering a culture of innovation. Experimentation neglects as MVPs must deliver strong business cases, which may lead to issues of innovating around the right problems.

- **Insufficient feedback**

  Traditional innovation processes may not provide real-time feedback, making it difficult for organizations to adjust their approaches and refine their strategies quickly. Feedback not coming from learning and failure may lead to early exclusion.

- **Poor engagement**

  Traditional innovation processes do not consider the burning problems of the organization, are not contributing to continual improvements, and do not prove to work from the core of the business. In competitive situations, engagement may reduce engagement rather than motivate teams to take further risks and start t scale.

- **Incoherent outcome**

  Traditional innovation processes rarely provide scalable business value embedded into business processes, producing measurable outcomes and financial improvements improving the enterprise's profitability. Securing coherent results from innovation processes is more difficult, if not impossible, especially if innovation ignores the fundamental principles of creating interoperability and composability and the inability to utilize existing platforms.

Traditional innovation processes can limit an organization's ability to boost and utilize innovation. Corporate innovation frameworks must find new ways to absorb their disintegrated working methods from ideation to monetization. Organizations may reconsider their innovation efforts and align those seamlessly with their digital transformations. Separating those two indistinguishable approaches could minimize misalignment and eliminate incoherent investments and similar conflicts. Instead of causing irritation and competitive situations, enterprises could bring innovation and digital transformations closer together.

To come up with a reasonable conclusion and approach, enterprises must understand the forces of powerful and sustainable innovation in the context of disruptive radical and incremental sustainable approaches to innovation

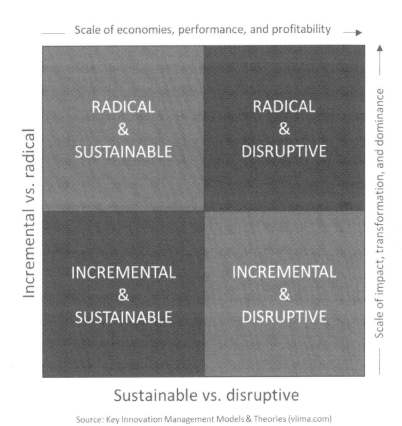

Source: Key Innovation Management Models & Theories (viima.com)

Figure 86 Incremental and radical innovation leading to sustainable or disruptive transformations (Source: Key Innovation Management Models & Theories (viima.com)) (Viima.com, 2018)

Innovation initiatives and purposes classify in terms of their magnitude and potential level of change. Innovation can be **disruptive** or **sustaining (durable)**, depending on the innovation and its overall impact. Clayton Christensen was the first to introduce the disruptive innovation model, referring to a concept, product, or service that creates a new value model by establishing or disrupting existing markets. He introduced the idea of disruptive innovation in his 1997 book "The Innovator's Dilemma" (Christensen, 2015). In this book, he argued that established companies often struggle to respond to disruptive innovations because they restrict their existing processes, structures, and business models.

The findings of Christensen's research showed that disruptive innovations often emerge from small, niche players and eventually overtake established ones in the market. This dynamic development is disruptive, as innovations usually start by addressing underserved or overlooked customer segments and then gradually improve and expand to displace the dominant players in the market eventually. Christensen's findings also showed that established companies often fail to respond to disruptive innovations because they are focused on optimizing their existing business models and cannot pivot quickly enough to respond to new opportunities or threats. Since its inception, enterprises have widely used the concept of disruptive innovation as a framework to understand innovation and its impact on businesses.

Traditional innovation processes may not solve the findings from Christensen, but he indicated the necessity of leveraging innovation from the core of the business to improve the overall ability to respond to disruptive innovation. Those often inconsistent approaches are major obstacles for traditional organizations in their attempts to apply and scale innovation. This fundamental issue does hinder enterprises from adopting innovation principles in their day-to-day business because they obstruct opportunities to embed incremental innovation integrated and rooted into the culture of their organizations.

"Radical and incremental innovation are indispensable from each other. They cannot exist in isolation and require fundamental incremental innovation capabilities, to ensure that radical innovation can connect with or evolve from the core of the business."

Ingo Paas

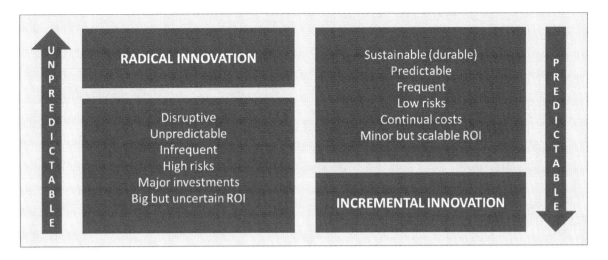

Figure 87 Incremental innovation ingests a more predictable way of embedding innovation at the center of agile development and digital transformations

Disruptive and sustainable innovation models have significantly different purposes and consequences:

- **Radical innovation** - revolutionary

  It occurs when new technology disrupts existing businesses or industries. Based on global research, only 10% of innovations are disruptive because of their dignity, high investment burden, lack of great ideas, and because they are the most difficult ones to execute. They are often initiated by start-ups or digitally transforming companies, applying early digital innovation in their industry segments.

- **Incremental innovation** - evolutionary

  It refers to the organizations' ability to deliver small, reusable, and scalable improvements experimentally, gradually, and continually innovate their products, services, processes, and methods, gaining and sustaining innovations concerning their products/services, business models, customer relationships, and working methods. Incremental innovation refers to continuous improvement by applying experimental approaches and principles of continual learning. Incremental innovation often enhances or modifies existing services/products, processes, or business models, while evolutionary approaches to innovation encourage small, gradual, reusable, and scalable improvements.

This kind of innovation comes at low risk and cost and typically requires smaller investments and efforts, especially if it can reuse existing scalable foundational technologies or digitally developed assets. Such investments have a higher probability of success than radical or disruptive innovation. This approach can help enterprises to respond more effectively to customer needs, inspired and driven by real-time customer feedback and demands. Incremental innovation enables continuous improvement, especially if scalable digital foundational technologies and platforms allow innovation.

There is a massive issue of ineffective innovation applied across most organizations in their attempts to utilize best practices and introduce sustainable innovation. Instead, enterprises repeatedly fail with their innovation processes due to incoherent decisions (investments, architectures), non-integrated prioritizations (innovation funnel vs. agile and portfolio management) and missing foundational technology readiness and capabilities. Continual, implanted, and sustainable innovation, embedded into digital transformations and realized from the core of the business, is a more compelling alternative to traditional ineffective innovation processes.

Incremental innovation requires a normalized and higher frequency of innovation, with continual attempts across organizations to let employees experience innovation incrementally and sustainably. Instead of dealing with innovation in isolation, it is more favorable to empower teams and individuals. They should continually contribute to business innovation by utilizing existing structures, processes, and technologies. They should ensure a strong alignment and integration with other critical undertakings, such as digital transformations.

Digital foundational platforms and digital transformations play a crucial role in modern innovation, especially for organizations where innovation is at the core of their business. These technologies and approaches can provide significant benefits to leverage innovation from the core of the business.

- **Increased efficiency and speed**
  Digital foundational platforms and digital transformations can automate and streamline processes, reducing the time and resources required to develop and launch new products and services. They make new technologies instantly available, shorten lead time, inspire innovation, and minimize risks. They also consider embedded principles and key requirements, such as security, compliance, and data protection.

- **Improved collaboration and knowledge sharing**

  Digital technologies can facilitate collaboration between departments and external partners, enabling sharing ideas, resources, and feedback. Tech, fusion, and DevOps teams can utilize and reuse existing solutions collaboratively and continually empower, strengthen, and elevate new ideas embedded in their agile processes. They inspire and invite everyone to solve business problems with a high sense of urgency, as they often find innovation in problem-solving.

- **Enhanced customer and business insights**

  Digital technologies can provide real-time data and insights into customer needs and preferences, which can inform and guide innovation efforts. Besides enhanced customer understanding, data will be at the core of every innovation, relentlessly implementing innovation pragmatically and focusing on rapid and sustainable value creation.

- **Increased experimentation and verification**

  Digital technologies and applied data-driven insights and intelligence (such as ever-advancing AI innovations) can enable organizations to experiment quickly and test new ideas, reducing the risk associated with innovation and increasing the potential for breakthroughs. With unlimited access to innovative technologies, experimentation will be motivated during ideation and design, rapidly verifying data and technologies' appropriateness.

- **Improved scalability**

  Digital technologies can enable organizations to quickly and efficiently scale innovations to meet market demand, improving the potential for success and growth. Platforms' nature is scalability, but the innovation is incremental, supporting digital evolutionary transformations. They will be scalable without being constrained by costs, resources, investments, or similar innovation obstacles. Given the availability and access to those digital foundational platforms, resources, and funding, innovation will happen at the core of the business in unprecedented ways, both sustainable and value driven.

- **Architectural interoperability**

  Enterprises can accelerate innovation by seamlessly integrating capabilities through the decisive utilization of architectural interoperability. The foundational architectural design guides investment and integration strategies, ensuring new components can integrate into the existing architecture and its services without compromising data security or reducing functionality.

With architectural interoperability, businesses can add new technologies, services, and platforms without worrying about compatibility issues or complex integration processes.

Digital foundational platforms and transformations are essential for modern innovation, providing organizations with the tools, data, and capabilities they need to stay competitive and drive growth.

Organizations will empower themselves to leverage sustainable innovation to be responsive to external digital disruptive or radical innovations by seamlessly integrating innovation and digital transformations. They may create the foundation to start digital disruptive or radical innovations from the core of their business by applying such capabilities.

Rather than making isolated attempts and taking huge financial risks, organizations may accelerate sustainable (durable) innovation, identify new strengths, intensify incremental innovations, and leverage disruptive or radical innovation on the baseline of their innovation success. Those attempts may lead to more competitive advantages and leadership in their industries, developing from their successful incremental and sustainable innovation attempts.

Leveraging incorporated innovation and digitalization strategies should be reconsidered by boards, CEOs, and CxOs. It is important to overcome and solve the great innovation dilemma in traditional organizations, to minimize risks of insufficient utilization of resources with overinvesting, and to utilize and scale innovation opportunities.

As Christensen argued, for disruptive innovation, most organizations must rethink their approach to innovation, build sustainable digital foundational platform architectures, and evolve their culture. They should utilize digital foundational technologies to engage themselves in search of radical and disruptive innovations. Those could embrace new revenue streams, new or modified business models, and innovative digital ecosystems. They leverage a data-driven visionary approach to innovation rather than gathering innovation wishes from their markets and customers.

Organizations that outperform their competitors will utilize their innovation outcome to generate better, if not outstanding, results, shifting their innovation potential towards radical and disruptive innovation. Amazon did this to leverage its incremental and disruptive concept of highly effective cloud and data center management and turned its core skills into disruptive global services known as Amazon Web Services (AWS).

With this approach in mind, innovation is not about searching for the big shots but rather the commitment and leadership of organizations to utilize incremental and sustainable innovation from a business value perspective. Digital foundational platforms inspire and enable sustainable innovation.

Understanding the innovation obstacle and dilemma is a critical first step to utilizing effective and sustainable innovation from the core of the business. This fundamental and inclusive approach may help traditional or digital enterprises to adopt the principles and opportunities of incremental and embedded innovation into their culture.

Embrace cultural embedded innovation

Organizations are not only struggling to get innovation to work and to deliver on the CEO's expectations. They are also incapable of fostering a cultural adaptation to innovation, as they too often promote innovation as a rigid quarterly process rather than a core value and capability of their enterprises. This is even more surprising, as innovation can significantly affect the organization's cultural development and could lead to superior and sustainable improvements.

The following patterns briefly describe the potential impact of incremental and experimental innovation on organizations:

- **Encourage a culture of collaboration**
  Innovation embedded into the design, development, and deployment of digital processes enabled by technologies encourages cross-functional collaboration and fosters teamwork and cooperation, eliminating silo-thinking and isolated problem-solving.

- **Promote a culture of creativity**
  Effective innovation can inspire and promote creativity, leading to a more dynamic and adaptive corporate culture, as digital enterprise-wide access to existing data and solutions will simplify ideation and creativity. They will rapidly develop solutions to deliver initial.

- **Enable a culture of digital transformation**
  With the increasing emphasis on digital technologies, effective innovation can drive the adoption and integration of these technologies, leading to a culture of digital transformation within the enterprise.

- **Embrace a culture of change**

  Effective innovation can change a company's culture to encourage a mindset of continuous improvement and a willingness to embrace change.

- **Foster a culture of learning**

  Effective innovation can create a continuous learning and improvement culture by encouraging experimentation and learning from failures.

Organizations must utilize innovation to adapt, gradually evolve their culture, and involve the organization in collaborative practices. They could achieve those learnings and changes by embedding innovation into the core of digital evolutionary transformations. They can encourage diversity and leverage cultural change by embracing diversity in their workforce, leading to more diverse perspectives and ideas. They can foster a culture of innovation to create encouraging environments to inspire innovation and drive cultural change within and from the core of the business. They encourage cross-functional collaboration with agile development teams to bring diverse perspectives and experiences together to drive innovation and cultural change. They do this at the core of their digital transformations, agile prioritization, and digital development. They use the same resources, budgets, platforms/technologies, and processes in their agile working methods as they do in their inclusive attempt at innovation.

They emphasize a culture of continual learning and improvements, where business priorities create engagement to drive cultural change and innovation. They lead by example with senior leaders to set the tone for cultural change by modeling the desired behavior and attitudes. They reinforce engagement and support innovative ideas, inspire each other, and share their knowledge. They will embrace failure and encourage a culture that accepts failures in digital development and innovation as opportunities for learning and growth to drive cultural change and innovation.

Most organizations do not succeed in establishing collaborative, democratized, and continual innovation embedded into their digital transformations.

As a result, most organizations never succeed in bringing innovation to life and helping evolve the organizational culture. Traditional innovation attempts do not prove effective, as organizations cascade their approaches without considering their organizations' cultural adaptation of innovation.

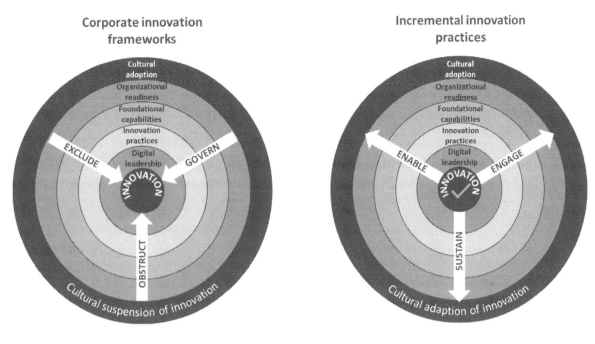

Figure 88 To overcome the innovation obstacles with the cultural adaption of innovation practices

Organizations evolving **incremental innovation** practices will likely succeed with their innovation growing a cultural adaptation rather than pursuing corporate innovation frameworks isolated from the organization. Those enterprises will embrace foundational digital platforms/technologies in collaborative attempts as their core enablers of innovative technology capabilities. They will embed innovation into their digital transformations and prioritize innovation continually integrated into their agile practices.

Applied Technology Leadership
Ingo Paas, CIO & CDO Green Cargo

"At Green Cargo, we apply incremental innovation in our digital transformation and continual agile development processes. Our evolutionary approach to innovation is inspired and motivated by the enormous urgency to solve daily business problems.

Innovation has not been a topic for Green Cargo since late 2019. Instead, we applied innovation embedded into our business prioritizations. We understand innovation as a capability that supports our three key priorities: safety, punctuality, and profitability. Business functions drive transformational innovation to reshape our core business model, while our digital foundational technologies are key enablers to make that transition possible.

As part of our "innovation" work, we utilize and shape new opportunities by introducing a data-driven culture. Our digital foundational platforms accelerate innovation capabilities and utilize in all digital development. We do not separate decision processes, resources, development, budgets, and more when we do innovation at the core of our business model. We rather do innovation as a naturally embedded part of our digital transformation. As we never use the word innovation, we can see it happen everywhere, from predictive maintenance to advanced analytics, to never before granularity of business analytics capabilities, and our ability to innovate the customer interface with a revolutionary approach to offer digitalized services, even to customers that have no industry knowledge. We have implemented digital capabilities with leading-edge technologies to integrate into digital ecosystems in Europe instead of buying an outdated technology platform, as every other enterprise in our industry sector did.

With this approach in mind, we foster innovation as a core competence, accessible to everyone, with innovation as an integrated part of our collaborative approach to digital transformation.

- *Our digital leadership perspective promotes an egalitarian approach with distributed and shared responsibilities. We encourage innovation as everyone's genuine responsibility, engage everyone collaboratively, and are business driven.*

- *Our innovation practices are embedded into our agile processes and fully integrated into our agile methods and tools, including prioritizations embedded in our agile processes and collaborative attempts to make more aligned decisions.*

- *Our foundational capabilities are accessible to everyone. We safeguard and ensure consistencies during ideation, design, test, and deployment to ensure scalable innovations and reuse existing digital assets (APIs, data models, algorithms, apps, features).*

- *Our organizational readiness utilizes agile resources and funding to foster and motivate effective development and value generation.*

> - *Our cultural adaptation is uniform and unrecognized, as innovation is integral to our transformation.*
>
> *Change takes time, things go wrong, and conflicts may arise. We are on that journey but still have a long way to go. We have started to democratize decision-making with embedded innovation, wherever and whenever. We will continue to engage and encourage our business decision-makers to assume more responsibility and scale for more innovation from the core of the business."*
>
> *Written by Ingo Paas, CIO & CDO Green Cargo*

The most important recommendation for organizations to leverage cultural change as part of their innovation efforts is to foster a culture of innovation. Organizations can leverage cultural change by encouraging diverse perspectives, promoting cross-functional collaboration, emphasizing continuous learning, leading by example, and embracing failure as an opportunity for growth and learning. By creating an environment that supports and rewards innovation, organizations assume full responsibility for driving cultural change and their innovation efforts embedded into their digital transformations.

Cultivate embedded incremental innovation

Incremental innovation involves gradual improvements to existing products, processes, or services. Incremental innovation is less risky and expensive than disruptive innovation based on established products, processes, or services. The goal of incremental innovation is to incrementally improve the performance and functionality of existing capabilities incrementally, leading to increased efficiency and enhanced competition.

Enterprises can take advantage of incremental innovation to respond better to disruptive competition, making them more responsive and digitally resilient. Incremental innovation is not necessary to respond, but it helps organizations to learn faster, improve responsiveness, solve problems, and utilize their digital foundational technologies and processes to scale.

To embed incremental innovation, organizations can take several actions, such as encouraging a culture of continuous improvement while continually embracing change. They promote innovation and empower individuals and teams, encouraging cultural adaptations and continual evolvement to solve business challenges and problems with innovative solutions. Organizations may also change their ambitions and abilities, embrace failure and experimentation, adapt design thinking principles (if applicable), and encourage risk-tolerance behavior.

Incremental innovation helps organizations to respond better to any disruption. By fostering a culture of innovation, promoting collaboration with experimentation, and embracing change, organizations become more resilient and better prepared for future changes.

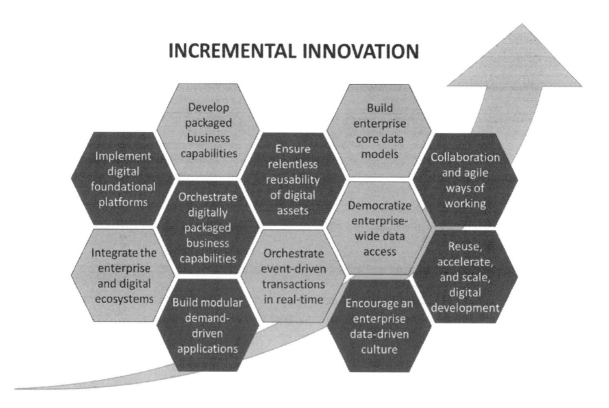

Figure 89 Important digital-enabled capabilities to develop innovation from the core of the business

Changing from corporate innovation frameworks and processes toward embedded incremental and experimental innovation is not a project but rather new thinking and cultural change. This change also requires new abilities trusting the organizations to leverage innovation in significantly different ways.

Defining appropriate conditions and environments for this incremental and experimental approach to innovation is achievable if enterprises with their digital transformations consider the proposed framework and strategies discussed in this book.

Cultivating autonomous enterprise-wide innovation requires new and adaptive integrated approaches. Realizing this transformation from corporate innovation work requires assimilating innovation with the organization's agile processes, digital foundational platforms, technologies, and data-driven abilities. Enterprises that are successfully enduring this change can accelerate and scale innovation from the core of their businesses. They can do this by collaboratively embedding innovation into their agile working methods, utilizing data and digital foundational platforms.

Incremental innovation does guarantee a more continual, conservative, evolutionary, experimental, and gradual change, seamlessly integrating innovation with the enterprises' digital composable transformations.

Enterprises should encourage more autonomous, collaborative, and integrated approaches to innovation. They can do this by leveraging and accelerating enterprise-wide innovation and digital composable transformations, such as:

- **Utilize digital foundational platforms**
  Innovation opportunity: The underlying digital foundational platform strategy secures full proficiency and autonomy of existing and future platforms from hyperscalers (such as Microsoft ad Google) and specific platform vendors (such as UIPath and OutSystems).
  Innovation impact: This enables enterprises to integrate new platforms and accelerate innovation easily.

- **Integrate the enterprise and digital ecosystems**
  Innovation opportunity: The organization has the full proficiency and autonomy to integrate existing and future applications seamlessly and easily, systems, services, data sources, platforms, or digital ecosystems.

Innovation impact: This enables enterprises to rapidly integrate the enterprise and digital ecosystems and accelerate or stimulate business innovation.

- **Digitalize packaged business capabilities**

Innovation opportunity: The organization has digitalized packaged business capabilities while defining and developing them from the core of the business.

Innovation impact: This enables enterprises to modularize their business processes and create greater agility, flexibility, and reusability in reconfiguring those DPBCs to enable and accelerate business process development and innovation.

- **Orchestrate digitally packaged business capabilities**

Innovation opportunity: The enterprise can design, build, and orchestrate digitally packaged business capabilities built out of autonomous, loosely coupled services, digitalizing its core business processes by dynamically combining DPBCs (mainly possible with enterprise lowcode developed applications and future modular designed applications).

Innovation impact: This enables enterprises to dynamically configure their business processes on demand to respond to radical innovation if required.

- **Build modular demand-driven applications**

Innovation opportunity: Reusability of digitally packaged business capabilities is possible by reusing DPBCs loosely. This flexibility allows enterprises to configure or build new applications by regrouping those components around user profiles (roles) or business processes.

Innovation impact: This enables developer teams to reconfigure those DPBCs rapidly to accelerate innovation at scale.

- **Ensure relentless reusability of digital assets**

Innovation opportunity: Through the unconstrained reusability of digitally developed assets and business capabilities, enterprises will inspire, enable and accelerate digital development in unprecedented ways.

Innovation impact: This enables enterprises to effectively reuse and orchestrate data models, algorithms, applications, and APIs on the organization's foundational platforms to foster scalable "exponential" innovation opportunities. They can leverage improvements or solve business problems using existing solutions rather than building everything from scratch.

- **Orchestrate and leverage event-driven transactions in real-time**

  Innovation opportunity: Developers can orchestrate applications in real-time by applying distinct digital foundational principles, enabling business process design with new automation and analytics capabilities.

  Innovation impact: This enables enterprises to utilize new real-time data to innovate their business by enhancing or developing processes, products, and services.

- **Build enterprise core data models**

  Innovation opportunity: By building core data models in enterprise-wide data analytics platforms (such as Google Cloud or Microsoft Power Platform), analytics teams can create and maintain enterprise-wide analytics capabilities related to core digital business capabilities owned by the business.

  Innovation impact: This enables enterprises to provide harmonized, trustful, and consistent data for various purposes with unlimited individual options to accelerate innovation through data access.

- **Democratize data access**

  Innovation opportunity: The organization has the full proficiency and autonomy to relentlessly orchestrate and use data from all systems and applications inside and from external sources and digital ecosystems ready for democratization and data distribution for citizen developer creation of individual analytics capabilities, algorithms, reports, and more.

  Innovation impact: This enables enterprises to accelerate innovation through the effective utilization of data significantly.

- **Encourage a data-driven culture**

  Innovation opportunity: The organization has the full proficiency and autonomy to master a culture of data-driven business processes with distinct data modeling and flexible ad-hoc critical data analytics abilities.

  Innovation impact: This enables enterprises to create data-driven innovation through foundational access to data and core data models when solving complex business problems, such as building innovative predictive capabilities, building data-driven applications to identify constraints in business processes, or innovating pricing.

- **Collaboration and agile ways of working**

  Innovation opportunity: Collaboration and agile ways of working can enable incremental and experimental innovation in enabling rapid iterations with agile cross-functional teams to allow for a more holistic approach to problem-solving and idea generation. This enables teams to experiment and iterate more quickly, embracing fail fast and learning fast while applying iteration. Agile methodologies and collaborative decision-making empower teams while encouraging creativity and experimentation to explore new ideas and approaches.

  Innovation impact: This enables organizations to embed innovation in agile prioritizations, utilization of development budgets and resources, technologies, and data, and already build digital assets/products with full access to the enterprise's technology stack and digital foundational capabilities in collaborative environments.

- **Reuse, accelerate, and scale digital development**

  Innovation opportunity: Utilizing digital development as a key opportunity to engage the organization in digital development will help organizations learn and apply new technologies and processes and think about solving real business problems rapidly in non-bureaucratic ways. They find inspiration to embrace genuine creativity and solution design by utilizing foundational digital capabilities aligned with the enterprise's digital composable transformation.

  Innovation impact: This enables enterprises to reuse, accelerate and scale innovation by solving real and urgent business problems from the core of their business in pioneering but durable/sustainable ways.

Incremental innovation allows enterprises to make small, gradual improvements that can result in significant cost savings and continual improvements. Improved efficiencies and continuously enhancing processes, with incremental innovation, can help organizations become more efficient and streamline their operations. They increase competitiveness, as they commit to incremental innovation may maintain competitive advantages. They focus on and enhance customer satisfaction by applying incremental innovation from the core of the business. This will increase responsiveness to changing customer needs and preferences, increase customer satisfaction and enhance their digital business reputation and brand image. Enterprises that apply this approach of democratized innovation will better support complex changes in their business models and core business processes to democratize innovation.

Democratized innovation

Democratized innovation refers to a systematic and scalable approach that leverages technology, data, and process optimization to drive efficiency and speed up the innovation process. It involves integrating technology and innovation into a company's core operations, enabling it to quickly and consistently generate new ideas and bring them to market. Democratized innovation typically involves using data-driven insights and advanced technologies, such as automation, lowcode, and artificial intelligence, to streamline the innovation process, reduce time to market, and increase the likelihood of success.

Democratization of innovation is also a metaphor for automated, technology-enabled, and infinite utilization of various capabilities, such as technologies, skills, processes, data, and human creativity, from ideation to execution. Democratizing innovation is the ability to effectively apply incremental, experimental, and sustainable development while embedding innovation into agile development processes makes it accessible to everyone. This approach includes ideation, prioritization, funding, resource allocation, technology selection, development, deployment, orchestration, rollout, scaling, and monetization.

The democratization of innovation refers to the organization's ability to leverage innovation constantly and repeatedly from ideation to monetization and to utilize the existing capabilities of organizations. This refers to the ability to embed innovation at the core of the business model and the business processes.

Applied Technology Leadership
Ingo Paas, CIO & CDO Green Cargo

"At Green Cargo, we foster an integrated and inclusive approach to innovation from the core of our business, mainly addressing incremental and sustainable innovation with the help of data, technologies, and processes. Green Cargo's approach to innovation is rooted in data and digital development. We innovate our business incrementally and sustainably, focusing on foundational technologies and data aligned with our business priorities and new opportunities. Our approach to innovation is experimental and incremental, allowing us to progress from the core of our business. We are not differentiating innovation from other activities and investments, as we see innovation as a fully integrated part of Green Cargos' digital transformation.

We are gradually applying incremental innovation embedded into our agile development processes to leverage our data, prioritize the usage of our platforms, reuse existing digital capabilities, and leverage our skills and continual improvements. Instead, the core idea is to provide technologies and offer the business core digital capabilities in our digital foundational platforms. Our standard decision-making processes fully integrate prioritizations and decisions about investments in innovation without being separated from our agile prioritization of epics, features, and backlogs. We are increasingly innovating incrementally at scale to solve nearly many unsolvable business problems and consider innovation as continual digital-enabled improvements. We are innovating our customer B2B platform by offering first and innovative new customer experiences. We support the innovation and optimization of our business model and innovate data utilization to foster a data-driven culture.

In practical terms, innovation is happening in all digital development activities. It is not an easy undertaking, and qualifying ideas is one of the most difficult tasks. But our businesspeople and developers regularly identify new business opportunities or improvements when discussing user stories during ideation and design. They can leverage new demand to demonstrate how existing data models, APIs, and features, may be reused in new and changed contexts. They can create better solutions far beyond what our business would be able to demand and define. In many discussions, we build solutions that outperform the scope and ROI of initial problem definitions. We easily identify larger improvements and innovation opportunities to leverage automation, intelligence, and simplification. Establishing innovation is only the first step, while the hard work comes with monetizing new and enriched technology and digital solutions.

We are constantly enriching existing applications and are fostering a climate of embedded innovation, where innovation is measurable but invisible! And the best is that most smaller innovation is reusable and scalable."

Written by Ingo Paas, CIO & CDO Green Cargo

Digital technologies are important for innovation and transformation. They include data analytics, low-code platforms, AI, and more. These technologies help organizations become leaner, more efficient, and more automated. They also enable collaboration and faster time-to-market for new products and services.

As these technologies evolve, they will continue to allow even more innovation. The next figure explains how technology-inspired innovation enables different layers and intensities of innovation. This figure explores organizations' potential development and maturity levels while they mature in realizing industrialized innovation.

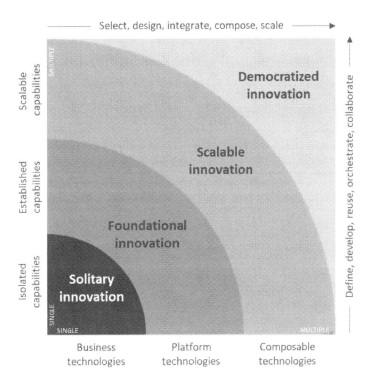

Figure 90 The four layers of technology-enabled innovation

The four layers of <u>technologies</u> and <u>capabilities</u>-enabled innovation illustrate the possible distinctions between different technology-enabled innovations. They distinguish between the impact on innovation from single to multiple abilities to, over time, industrialize enterprise innovation.

The four layers of technology and capability-enabled innovation demonstrate how one can differentiate various innovations based on their potential distinctions. These layers differentiate the impact of innovation from single to multiple abilities and the ability to industrialize enterprise innovation over time.

1. **Solitary innovation**

   Isolated and fragmented digital business technologies enable individual and isolated innovation. Business technologies enable business process optimization and may promise strong individual ROIs but may not be applicable or useful to allow systemic innovation. Business technologies do not enable enterprise innovation, but they can bring substantial innovation in isolated processes, such as pricing optimization engines.

2. **Foundational innovation**

   Isolated platform technologies enable innovation allowing the organization with restricted levels of scalability. Platform technologies enable integrated business process optimization capacity and flexibility. They may promise tactical scalable value and ROIs, while single isolated platform integrations (such as robotics/automation) may only contribute to restricted process innovation. They have a limited foundational impact on enterprise innovation.

3. **Scalable innovation**

   Multi-purpose enterprise-wide full-scale integrated digital foundational technologies and platforms enable scalable innovation. Business and foundational technologies secure interoperable business process optimization, access to data, and the ability to optimize business logic through continual improvements from the core of the business. Foundational platform technologies promise long-term strategic ROI while fully supporting universal innovation. Their scope is enterprise-wide, with a strong foundational impact on enterprise innovation. This innovation does fully enable composable and resilient enterprises. Examples of innovation are enterprise Lowcode development, data-driven analytics, predictive maintenance, and more.

4. **Democratized innovation**

   Democratized innovation encourages and pushes multiple levels of innovation by utilizing and scaling innovation across multiple purposes and integrated technologies to enable innovation on an enterprise level. Innovation is possible by addressing different domains from multiple business perspectives, while composable technologies ensure interoperable business process optimization and innovation at scale. They support radical innovation on the business model level with long-term strategic implications. These technologies have a foundational impact on enterprise and digital ecosystem innovation, extending beyond the enterprise. Composable and resilient enterprises can accelerate their competitive capabilities through this innovation.

Enterprises can evolve democratized innovation if they allow systemic adaptation and integration of their creativity and ideation processes to innovate and improve continually. Continual innovation can be achieved through seamless integration and adaptation of innovation efforts into digital composable transformations, making corporate innovation processes and frameworks unnecessary.

This approach to seamlessly democratize innovation does require the implementation of fully integrated digital foundational technologies. They must find support by utilizing clearly defined digital principles, skills (such as CCoE, developers, and security technicians), processes, and leadership in execution.

Making democratized innovation processes work is about the willingness and leadership to embed innovation into the enterprise's transformational efforts. Accelerating innovation at the core of business processes requires coherent digital foundational platform strategies.

Data-driven innovation and culture comes from innovating and democratizing enterprise data strategies. According to MIT Technology Review Insights, "Building high-performance data and AI organizations" (MIT Technology Review Insights & Databricks, 2021), less than 13% of enterprises excel in delivering on their data strategies. Those high achievers were not only focusing on democratizing data for seamless innovation, but most organizations ran half or more of their data services or infrastructure in a cloud environment.

Additional findings from this research indicated that wider adoption of cloud environments is at the core of their strategies. Enterprises are pursuing technology-enabled collaboration to establish data-driven cultures while they seek extensive utilization of cloud-native platforms, enabling data management, analytics, and AI uses cases. The rise of AI and Machine Learning models requires modern lake houses or similar architectures based on digital foundational platforms, ingesting unlimited innovation power and enterprise capabilities.

While the rise of new capabilities, such as generative AI, will increase significantly in the coming years, lowcode development platforms are necessary to encourage rapid, flexible, and scalable innovation. To accelerate innovation and utilize the enormous potential of digital transformations, its skills, data, and technologies will further accelerate innovation at scale.

Accelerate innovation

Traditional enterprises can accelerate innovation to leverage rapid digital prototyping through digital foundational platforms. The opportunities to combine Machine Learning and enterprise Lowcode capabilities are a unique capability to drive innovation with a focus on monetization with short ROI and effective TCO.

The innovator's dilemma of innovation driven by the search for solutions can result in fragmented choices when individual technologies are sought after, which can be time-consuming and complicated. Access to infinite digital foundational platforms, digital assets, and related knowledge, such as DevOps teams, can facilitate innovation. These resources can inspire human creativity to apply, leverage, and scale ready-to-use digital capabilities. This approach can increase the overall value of innovation, making it more realistic, deployable, and accessible without the need for major purchases or complicated processes.

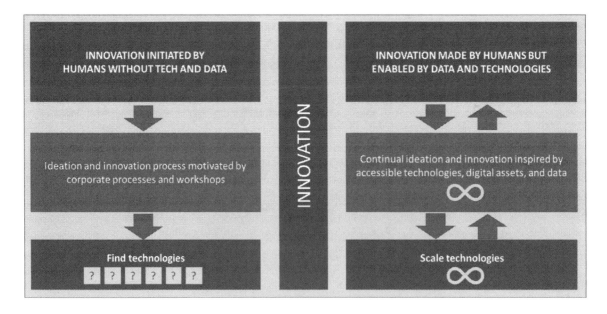

Figure 91 Innovation embedded into digital composable transformations will enable continual innovation inspired by assessable and scalable technologies

Traditional and digital enterprises can use digital foundational platforms to leverage significant innovation capabilities at scale. They will accelerate innovation by utilizing various platforms while utilizing the technology foundation of composable enterprises. The collaborative aspect of digital composable enterprises is indisputable and a core capability embedded into agile development.

Enterprises can scale their development by utilizing cloud-native platforms at the core of their transformations. They can access infinite innovation capabilities and new digital ecosystems inspired by leading-edge technologies from the most innovative organizations in the global tech industry. Organizations investing in those platforms do not have to build, configure, test, and implement innovative technologies; instead, they can choose between various capabilities ready for use and scale.

Lowcode platforms reinforce organizations' new digital sovereignty and ability to support business innovation at unprecedented levels. The reusability of those solutions will allow developers and business product owners to reorganize and rebuild applications constantly and at any time. Lowcode platforms encourage organizations to build their applications and to make better build or buy decisions. They will accelerate innovation as they constantly add needed digital assets for future reuse, accessible in the cloud. The innovative gain with enterprise Lowcode development is the ability to build digital capabilities in-house, without traditional coding. Solving nearly every business problem is a fundamental improvement in how software can help to inspire business innovation at a scale.

Leading Enterprise lowcode platforms enable organizations to rapidly build complex and fully integrated applications in interactive collaboration with the business. Those integrated development platforms safeguard cloud-native, enterprise-grade applications' security, resilience, and scalability. They foster innovation at a scale with unlimited development capabilities.

"Innovation in the digital composable transformation from the core of the business is only achievable when utilizing the immense power of high-performance lowcode platforms at scale. Scalable enterprise composability is unachievable with traditional software development."

Ingo Paas

Figure 92 Accelerate innovation with enterprise lowcode development

Modern high-end lowcode platforms offer a broad spectrum of functionality and capabilities and allow organizations to find new ways to transform traditional or even entirely new IT development organizations into highly effective software factories. By scaling lowcode development, organizations can become fully autonomous in software development, deployment, and management. The achievements of high-performance enterprise lowcode platforms accelerate business innovation with new and promising development opportunities.

Technology Leadership
Pekka Rinne, Enterprise Architect and Digital Strategist

"Wave surfing is not just a sport, and it's a lifestyle, a mindset. As a surfer, you follow a path, not a process. Surfing is about who and why you are. You do not become a surfer by reading a guide or buying an old VW van; you must change from the core. The same applies to organizations that want to transform to a higher state of digital readiness with an increased willingness and ability to embrace and act on change. They must transform from the core. Successful transformation requires, first and foremost, a clear vision and strong leadership. It also requires a foundation to build new ideas and innovations to enable and fuel the journey toward the vision. Ideas potentially delivering value do not just materialize from thin air. They build upon past ideas and innovations that form composable and reusable bricks from which an organization can build its foundation for innovation.

Incumbent businesses are usually searching for the perfect innovation that will change it all and will often try to find the Holy Grail by heavily investing in processes and structures for innovation, often set apart from the normal business. Instead of unleashing the collective innovational power of the whole organization from the core, this approach often restricts innovation and value creation by channeling investments to the few and making the processes and structures too rigid for innovation to grow. By developing and utilizing digital foundational technologies and reusable digital assets, combined with a culture of exploration and collaboration that permeates the whole organization, incumbent businesses can learn to see new opportunities and approach threats, tackling the innovator's dilemma. If not, they risk the same fate as one of the characters in Hemmingway's The sun also rises. When asked how he got bankrupt, he answered: "Two ways. Gradually, then suddenly". Here we see that S-curve again. It's not easy, and it requires much courage to build a surf tribe with innovation at its core. Ingo has shown me how to do it. A surf tribe around the same campfire, knowing the direction of the Pole star (or the Southern cross), seeing, listening, and feeling the smaller waves composed to a ridable one."

Written by Pekka Rinne, Enterprise Architect and Digital Strategist

With Artificial Intelligence and increased access to Machine Learning features in digital foundational platforms, AI capabilities drive innovation further to the edge. Embedded everywhere, they have two implications for digital development. First, they innovate using traditional development methods as they leverage the already breakthrough achievements of ELPs. Second, they bring unlimited innovation opportunities through new use cases and ready-to-use AI services embedded everywhere.

Those two powerful trends will further accelerate the utilization of digital foundational platforms at an unprecedented scale. The level of automation in future lowcode development enabled with ML will outperform every level of traditional innovation.

Organizations that utilize the power of enterprise Lowcode platforms and machine learning embedded into digital foundational platforms will not only be able to master innovation but will most likely enable, encourage, and accelerate innovation to innovate their business at scale. The future of enterprise innovation will further optimize interoperability and composability on an enterprise level.

Innovation is not only appropriate from a business perspective, as innovation can become a game changer in developing digital composable enterprises by utilizing innovative technologies in truly innovative and groundbreaking ways.

Innovate application development

The traditional approach to monolithic application development was about building a single, large, and encapsulated application that contained all the necessary components and business functionality. Development teams of monolithic systems would typically create comprehensive specifications before building composite system architectures. Development was done in a distinct framework with developers utilizing standardized technology stacks, ensuring all components and interfaces were integrated. This approach had many disadvantages, such as limited flexibility, scalability, interoperability, stability, performance, and digital sustainability, while those systems handle complex use cases and are challenging for developers to modify or adapt to changing business requirements.

According to "Research and Markets", the global low-code development platform market revenue is predicted to grow a 31.3% CAGR to reach up to $190 million by 2030.

The utilization of Lowcode is widely spread, with only a smaller percentage of organizations utilizing enterprise Lowcode development. Of those enterprises, most enterprises miss out on monetizing the enormous advantages of using Lowcode at the core of their digital transformations. Even fewer enterprises utilize Lowcode to innovate software development on leading enterprise Lowcode platforms. The following argument explains why Lowcode is used mainly on the low end of application development rather than on the development of enterprise applications.

According to "Research and Markets", there are other interesting facts explaining the low penetration of Lowcode across industries and enterprises. Lowcode has been widely adopted within the IT industry as the largest customer base of this technology to develop software to optimize productivity and reduce their reliance on expensive resources.

While organizations outside the IT industry increasingly adopt lowcode platforms, they still apply similar traditional approaches to software development rather than applying modern design best practices. Such best practices include modular thinking and microservices-based architectures. They enable greater scalability, flexibility, and resilience by breaking business processes into packaged business capabilities into smaller, independently deployable components.

Traditional coding can hardly guarantee the flexibility, agility, and reusability required to apply the best modular practices. The same goes for digitally developed applications on lowcode platforms when organizations use the same software development patterns, which remains a key problem for organizations to leverage the maximum value of enterprise Lowcode platforms. Many organizations developing applications on high-performance Lowcode platforms (a minority of all enterprises) are building on traditional applications on highly agile platforms. They have not yet achieved flexibility and composability by utilizing lowcode platforms to build traditional applications.

Lowcode is still a <u>rare</u> strategic investment across industries and is <u>not</u> utilized strategically at the core of digital composable transformations. Enterprises, such as Green Cargo, that optimize the utilization of Lowcode development and take this technology to the next level are exemptions. In the case of Green Cargo, the composable transformation with leading innovative Lowcode development at the core is drastically challenging traditional ways of traditional software development, including utilizing Lowcode platforms.

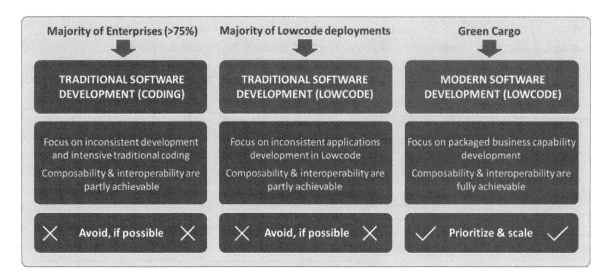

Figure 93 Software and application development on lowcode platforms is not necessarily leading to full-scale enterprise interoperability and composability

Traditional software development with coding or Lowcode platforms holds enterprises back from leveraging modern software development's potential and maximum value. Organizations that invest in Lowcode development to achieve enterprise-wide digital resilience must apply modern approaches to software development on Lowcode platforms. They must shift towards maximum modularity, overcoming the trenches of encapsulated traditional software development.

The future of composable application development is based on applying three core conceptual principles to achieve full-scale enterprise interoperability and composability.

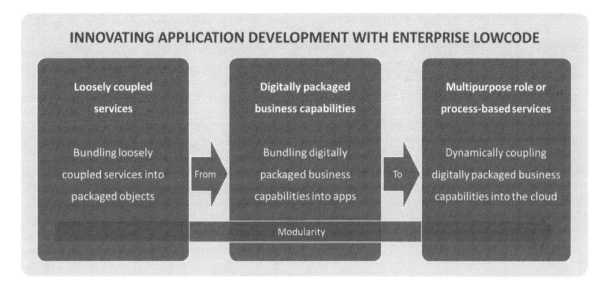

Figure 94 Innovating application development in Lowcode to orchestrate loosely coupled services bundled into digitally packaged business capabilities orchestrated as role- or process-based services

This next innovation in software development utilizes a modular concept of repacking loosely coupled services by bundling those into digitally packaged business capabilities, applied and under verification at Green Cargo. This is a ground-breaking innovative way of leveraging modern application development utilizing the enterprise Lowcode platform from OutSystems. This project will continue accelerating and innovating Green Cargos' approach to building Lowcode applications by orchestrating digitally packaged business capabilities 100% dynamically rather than building traditional applications.

Pricing is a typical example of a digitally packaged business capability. "Pricing" developed and deployed in Lowcode and orchestrated dynamically for consumption in various use cases. The same digitally packaged business capability orchestrates dynamically into the cloud on requests from three different sources, such as:

1. Customer portals or e-commerce (process-based),
2. Pricing simulators (role-based),
3. Customer proposals (role-based).

The future of application development is undergoing a revolution, with loosely coupled services configured to function as digitally packaged business capabilities. Those can be utilized and orchestrated dynamically in unlimited constellations. This innovative software development concept is the cornerstone of future digital application design and composable architectures.

Applied Technology Leadership
Jonathan Hammander, Tech Lead, Green Cargo

Innovating software development with Lowcode

"Composable architecture includes a distinct software design approach that emphasizes building complex systems by combining smaller, independent components or services. In a composable architecture, each service is designed to perform a specific function, and these services can be combined and orchestrated to create digital composable business capabilities or, if needed, larger applications.

At Green Cargo, we take our full-scale implementation in our lowcode OutSystems platform one step further. We use a new hierarchical block structure where a function block can be a singular function/service or a fully functional application. To make this concept work, we increasingly utilize reusable functions as components in our digital composable business capabilities, also called functional blocks. Utilizing the enormous advantages of this three-layer model with loosely coupled services, functional blocks, and modular applications, we are taking the application development with our loosely coupled services architecture to the next level.

To work together seamlessly and efficiently, we make this possible by integrating different information technology domains, such as networking, software development, data management, cybersecurity, and others. Doing so guarantees seamless interoperability and highly effective orchestration of our digitally developed assets and components on our foundational cloud platforms, integrated into real-time and event-driven with our critical and prioritized IT legacy systems.

At Green Cargo, we are developing different strategies to solve potential collaboration issues depending on where in the development sequence our teams are.

The domains of our library and concept do continually advance, functioning unified across the whole infrastructure and multiple business environments, which we continually enhance and update. We encourage effective communication between our developers, product owners, IT architects, service owners, super-users, and end-users, to ensure quality and strictness in development and operations.

The goal is to grow further our dynamic and modular digital foundational platform architecture capable of orchestrating digitally packaged business capabilities in two fundamentally different variants. The first variant is a role-based combination of digitally packaged business capabilities dynamically configured based on predefined roles in our active directory. The second variant is a function-based combination of digitally packaged business capabilities. Utilizing those two distinct variants to publish in-house built software, we are not limited to one specific user group or application with the design of our future highly composable software development.

Role-based applications focus on a specific role or group of employees, and function-based applications merge functional blocks with similar functions like traditional applications or web portals. This foundation can minimize the number of applications needed as employees until we have a single application providing all functionality required for the users' needs or purposes.

This is an innovative and progressive approach to in-house software development with lowcode development on our OutSystems platform, under implementation at Green Cargo."

Written by Jonathan Hammander, Tech Lead, Green Cargo

Digital composable architectures must enable innovation in the process of innovating the business. This is a prerequisite for architectural design utilizing and scaling on our digital foundational platforms and architecture, integrating our IT legacy and digital capabilities. Reusability, elasticity, interoperability, scalability, flexibility, stability, and scalability enables unbroken interoperability and consistency in using the Green cargo platform and technology design principles.

Those principles define a solid three-layer domain and holistic thinking while embedding those into technology-inspired business and IT development innovation. This is at the center of Green Cargos' strategy to continue and accelerate our composable digital transformation in unprecedented ways.

"Enterprises that will innovate their business through digital transformations must revolutionize how they utilize, deploy, and scale digital foundational technologies and platforms. Repeating traditional development patterns in the digital age without leveraging Lowcode at the core of digital transformations will certainly differentiate winners and losers."

Ingo Paas

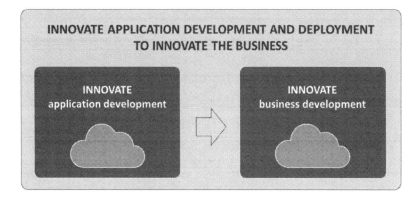

Figure 95 Business innovation enabled by IT innovation

Organizations planning to embrace future composable enterprises must evolve and transform by applying distinct principles, new intelligent design, and utilizing lowcode and integration platforms. Succeeding with this approach can make the ultimate difference between failure and success. Green Cargo is making solid achievements and enhancements utilizing the world's leading lowcode platform as one the first enterprises to move into this new era of digital development.

However, there are various challenges to overcome while organizations must ensure effective ideation, demand management, and realizing the maximum business value. Establishing a culture of innovation is a long-term undertaking with both failure and success during a learning and unstable process rather than a linear repetitive one.

Recognizing and accepting the importance of engaging in collaborative learning and improving how to bring innovation closer to the core of the business is essential. This will help businesses and IT overcome obstacles and problems as they engage in an evolving learning and innovative culture. Although it may not be a straightforward process, accepting the effort and learning from mistakes is worth it.

Innovating and utilizing technologies is a hard nut to crack, while establishing effective collaboration between development teams and business is an enormous challenge to overcome and sustain.

As Ericsson brought it to the point more than two decades ago, "It's about communication between people, the rest is technology! "

Key conclusions and takeaways

The key conclusions and takeaways from the chapter "**INNOVATION FROM THE CORE**" are:

1. Enterprises must embed innovation and digital transformations at the core of their business, avoiding separation.

2. Enterprises must realize incremental innovation with sustainable and monetizable results embedded into digital composable transformations.

3. Enterprises must embed prioritization of innovation investments in agile processes with democratized empowerment allowing decentralized prioritizations and decisions.

4. Enterprises must leverage innovation as an intuitive and integrated part of digital business development to encourage incremental and experimental innovation.

5. Enterprises must encourage technology and data-inspired innovation by utilizing digital foundational platforms.

6. Enterprises must industrialize innovation as the organizations institutionalize and adopt ability embedded into the culture, leadership, and values.

7. Enterprises must avoid separate innovation processes and frameworks.

NINE – DIGITAL COMPOSABLE ENTERPRISES

THOUGHT DIGITAL LEADERSHIP

Stefan Gustavsson, Managing Partner, Gartner

"In the ever-changing business environment, adaptability remains a key factor for survival. Regardless of whether Darwin said those famous words or not, the message is more relevant than ever.

Global events over the last few years have reinforced how volatile and unpredictable the operating environment is for businesses of all kinds. There are few safeguards available while navigating the change necessary to not only stay relevant but to emerge in a leading position. Acknowledgment of this is a key step towards the conversation and solutions required to respond effectively to this complexity and pace of change.

Now more than ever, there is a pressing need to build sustainable and resilient businesses, which has created an opportunity to re-think how we effectively compose IT and Business Technology to enable this.

Traditional structures and thinking about IT capabilities and organizations often constrain how successfully we can respond to change. Even with the best of intentions, legacy can leave us with challenges and barriers like rigid processes, monolithic technology landscapes, organizational risk aversion, and a high degree of central control.

Imagine a future where organizations are more successful because they re-think how to reduce friction, be more adaptable to change, and do more with less because they deliver the business based on a composable, modular foundation. This would involve a technical shift towards a modular business architecture designed with loosely coupled yet orchestrated services that align with business capabilities. Delivered by an empowered organization with the right degree of autonomy, clear accountability for business outcomes, and full product lifecycles. Over time, as the business becomes composable, the orchestrated re-use of capabilities provides an opportunity for business and IT to align and optimize cost/value from short- and long-term perspectives.

Creating a compelling digital strategy is like crafting a destination postcard. However, executing that strategy requires hard work and can be intimidating. It involves relinquishing control, introducing new types of risk management, changing people's needs, and making tough decisions. This book, particularly this chapter, provides thinking and guidance to these questions. It will help you set up for success.

Composable business goes beyond IT and Business Technology, but they play an instrumental role in making it real and successful."

Written by Stefan Gustavsson, Managing Partner, Gartner

Recalibrate business logic digitally

Digital transformations driven in incremental and experimental ways secure a much stronger base of technology and data-driven opportunities to recalibrate business logic. Packaged business capabilities can secure consistency and sustainability in digitally inspired and enabled business transformation, empowering enterprises' digitalization with foundational technology platforms and IT legacy systems.

Business process design is achievable with defined packaged business capabilities in composable and consistent business architectures. Organizations with digitally digital resilient capabilities applying this concept can recalibrate their business logic in systemic and responsive ways. Especially organizations with complex IT legacies will gain major benefits from this approach.

CxOs must understand and change their perception of how they should enable and encourage continual recalibration of business processes and business models. They must provide digital foundational platforms in evolutionary ways and discontinue waiting for the business to say what they want. Technology investments must avoid solving and addressing encapsulated and isolated business problems, as fragmented investments will hinder enterprises from establishing consistency in their transformations based on the fundamental principles discussed in this book.

Technologies will continue to reshape how enterprises must function as integrated digital players in varying and dynamically changing digital ecosystem constellations. CxOs must stop seeking solutions that can solve isolated problems. Instead, they must seek new conceptual and foundational thinking to identify technologies that eliminate or minimize fragmented investments. Building and designing the underlying architecture on digital platforms that serve as a foundation is essential. To continue challenging traditional IT responses, organizations should couple their efforts with new and innovative thinking, reconsidering technologies' role. CxOs must invest in multi-purpose technologies and build fundamental and dynamic interoperable architectures. Those shall inspire the business to solve the business problems that are their burning platforms. But this is not enough, as foundational platforms must encourage businesses to solve systemic, complex, and fundamental issues. Most enterprises are eventually unaware of the underlying and structural problems that inconsistencies in business logic and data may cause, which can have significant negative implications, such as inadequate analytics, missing insights, or inability to leverage their business processes to the next level.

They are often hidden in complex programs, modifications of standard software, add-ons, integrations with inbuild business logic, and other problem-solving techniques such as converting and translating data sets from one system to the other.

Digital foundational technologies must inspire business, accelerate innovation, and encourage new thinking beyond the fences of traditional technologies and limitations. With new platforms, technologies, and architectures, enterprises must not only become digitally resilient to better respond to crisis and change. They must become digitally resilient to foster and accelerate business innovation in collaboration.

Enterprises with a systemic approach to digital transformations can build the future digitally independent of their traditional, often insufficient design of irrational business logic and restrictions from their rigid IT legacy systems. They will replace information disorder with structure, workarounds with automation, and interpretation of data with knowledge with actionable trustful insights. They will enable significant business improvements to address new opportunities and allow the business to recalibrate its business logic continually.

It is important to consider whether many tech-savvy enterprises with business acumen can effectively leverage and articulate their IT needs. CxOs must rethink, cannot wait, and must reconsider their changing role as tech and business leaders. No one else will fill that space if they cannot understand this dilemma and assume full accountability.

Successful digital transformations are achievable, and they can foster digital and constant recalibration of business logic as long as they assume a systemic approach, to relentlessly recalibrate and optimize their business logic from the core of the business.

"The ability to constantly recalibrate business logic is critical to developing future digital resilient enterprises from the core of the business, enabled by its digital composable business architecture."

Ingo Paas

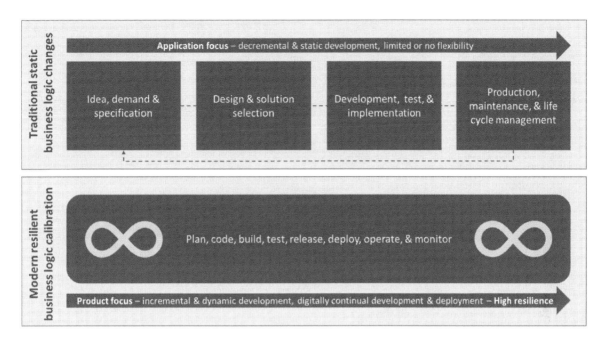

Figure 96 Successful digital transformations are to foster digital and constant recalibration of business logic

The proposed incremental and experimental approach to digital transformations allows organizations to optimize their entire spectrum of business processes and incoherent business logic. Enterprises that apply the concept of packaged business capabilities will create better pre-conditions for their digital transformations than organizations primarily focusing on business processes. Those enterprises will increase their opportunities to introduce fundamental improvements to their business, increase margins, make better customer offerings, or increase sales through improved customer relationships.

Based on robust composable and foundational architectures, applied universal principles, and foundational digital architectures, organizations can constantly adapt their IT and digital landscape with infinite changes enabled by their digital foundational platforms and integrated IT legacy systems. This structure will allow the greater exchange of data across business processes to utilize and integrate core business processes with highly integrated customer collaboration opportunities across various digital ecosystems and with all relevant external stakeholders.

With those capabilities, continual change can become the new normal at every level of modern composable enterprises. Everyone in the organization will be engaged to continually recalibrate and optimize business logic, utilize digital capabilities to their maximum potential, and constantly optimize business performance KPIs while understanding and exploring underlying structures and data models. KPIs become less important as the focus will shift towards optimized business outcomes, better understanding digital transparent patterns, and optimizing manual and automated decision-making processes.

Enterprises that continually recalibrate their business logic will improve their business performance by leveraging better insights and levels of control. Their digital resilience will produce more predictable and consistent business results. They will better prepare for future crises and business disruptions, recalibrate their business logic, and relentlessly drive innovation from the core of their business. With such capabilities, organizations can master the increasing complexity of constant change, further escalated by fast-evolving digital ecosystems. Organizations that want to adjust their business logic must leverage their technologies and encourage new digital leadership everywhere.

Encourage digital leadership

Encouraging digital leadership is recognizably central to evolutionary-driven transformations but a difficult undertaking for many senior leaders in IT.

CxOs may experience various difficulties in applying current and risk-tolerant leadership for several reasons:

- **Risk-averse thinking**
  Situation: CxOs must often live up to expectations driven by senior management and boards to deliver on business demands, as their main responsibility is to ensure stability, cost-effective IT services, and cost savings.
  Response: CxOs must become more risk-tolerant and engage in business strategy execution while accepting greater risks. They can apply incremental and experimental tactics to grow their confidence but must lead the digital composable transformation and take appropriate risks by thinking holistically and acting realistically.

- **Reluctance to find approvals**

  Situation: Innovative CxOs may encounter resistance from their boards, other senior leaders, departments, or employees uncomfortable with new and innovative approaches to technology and business operations. They may likewise experience restrictions because of risk-averse cultures, rigid processes, and inflexible governance that protects history rather than addressing future changes and risks.

  Response: They must assume technology ownership and shift from complicated annual planning, internal marketing, and overpromising strategy execution toward high execution modus operandi to demonstrate successful outcomes with simple but effective pilots. Nothing is more powerful than demonstrating a working proof of concept or minimum viable product compared with promising presentations.

- **Resistance to change**

  Situation: Innovative CxOs may encounter resistance from their boards, other senior leaders, departments, or employees uncomfortable with new and innovative approaches to technology and business operations. Change is introduced as traditional change management, applying traditional thinking and models, such as ADCAR (Awareness, Desire, Knowledge, Ability, and Reinforcement). There is nothing wrong with those models, but digital transformations must overcome those traditional waterfall concepts.

  Response: CxOs must utilize existing resources and act without asking for mandates. They must encourage change, engage in learning, and encourage collaborative change. They must bring technologies to business users who want to realize change with experimental approaches. CxOs must foster a culture of autonomy, accountability, and trust.

- **Shortage of willingness and lack of resources**

  Situation: Both willingness and lack of resources may stop them from assuming greater responsibility to drive change. Usually, CxOs demand resources and wait for the business to deliver; if there are no resources, they will not act.

  Response: CxOs must identify creative funding approaches to overcome shortages and build alliances with innovative but realistic business leaders to secure creative funding and affordable platform investments.

Planting a change can start with growing an idea, such as helping the business establish a new forum to develop a data-driven culture. By solving actual business problems rapidly, resources will join voluntarily or engage more.

- **Lack of transformational leadership**

Situation: Some CxOs may struggle to communicate new technologies' benefits and potential opportunities due to a lack of technical knowledge or an inability to connect technology-inspired business-driven innovation with key stakeholders.

Response: CxOs must collaborate with risk-tolerant leaders and build alliances with board members, other executives, or highly influential leaders. They must grow confidence and seek support if needed. They should find and promote new leaders with new visionary thinking and skills. Helping those leaders develop new technology skills and innovative platform thinking will help secure more sustainable investments in new projects. Increased transformational leadership will increase understanding and leverage foundational platform investments to improve utilization and scalability.

- **Budget constraints**

Situation: Limited budgets can prevent CxOs from taking risks or investing significantly in new technologies and solutions.

Response: They should identify and finance scalable investments or subscription-based costs without available scalable technologies. They most likely can simplify access to foundational platform technologies, get specialists on board, and support pilot investments. Identifying business sponsors with tactical investment opportunities and short-term ROI might help with the initial funding of digital foundational platforms and technologies (as already discussed before).

- **Legacy systems and processes**

Situation: Many organizations have legacy systems and processes that are difficult to replace, making it challenging for CxOs to implement new technologies and solutions.

Response: CxOs can finance initial readiness investments through smarter sourcing. They can prioritize and selectively identify activities for incremental changes to increase digital readiness rather than renovating entire systems.

By utilizing foundational digital platforms, CxOs could rebuild critical business functionality in lowcode platforms and minimize the need to replace business critical and complex systems.

They could also use integration platforms to diminish risks with IT legacy integration platforms by migrating integrations into cloud integration platforms.

Leadership is not about finding the perfect answers to questions but about growing people's comfort zone by creating new experiences. Both are helping CxOs to develop and encourage new creative thinking. Leadership facilitates cultural adaptation and engages the organization in collaborative but focused alignment. Digital leaders must attract, retain, and develop talent with the skills and mindset required for digital composable transformations. It will help to leverage and create environments that support diversity, equity, and inclusion to engage others in aligned evolutionary execution. Modern leadership is critical in driving digital composable transformations and ensuring their success. Leaders must be proactive, visionary, and collaborative to navigate the complexities of such transformations and create sustainable value and growth for their organizations.

Figure 97 Thought Digital Leadership is one of the if not the most critical capability in digital transformations

"Successful and sustainable digital transformations require thought leadership in establishing autonomy and encouraging a culture of accountability and trust to achieve greater levels of independence concerning digital composable transformations."

Ingo Paas

Autonomy, accountability, and trust are essential for digital transformations to help organizations evolve and adapt. CxOs must encourage modern digital leadership, critical for organizations fostering collaborative approaches and thinking to master digital composable transformations. Successful transformations are not just doing things right but demonstrating a strong focus and ability to deliver outstanding results relentlessly. They are constantly monetizing their digital investments while significantly influencing organizations' cultural adaptation and mastering digital autonomy at scale.

Master digital autonomy at scale

Mastering autonomy at scale in the digital age is a key differentiator for leading organizations, fostering a culture with embedded digital encouragement and empowerment. Empowering organizations to achieve digital autonomy is necessary to drive sustainable and effective digital transformations.

Digital foundational platforms and composable architectures will empower IT organizations to execute and scale. With the power of collaborative development teams, they encourage business owners and emphasize the need for autonomy, inspired by continual success, agility, and speed. Autonomy is achievable in different ways, such as:

Make balanced but sustainable investment decisions

- Conduct investment audits and identify the current enterprise investment focus and strategy.
- Evaluate and propose a more balanced investment strategy and adjusted governance to improve investment decisions covering sustainable tactical and strategic investments.

Embrace agile methodologies

- Adopt agile methodologies to become more agile and engage in collaborative fusion teams with the business.
- Assume greater responsibility and reinforce dynamic and systemic problem-solving.
- Focus on distinct and sustainable value creation and prioritize and embrace effective collaborative working processes and communication capabilities.
- Apply agile skills, thinking, processes, and tools to engage broader parts of the organization in agile ways of working, ideally from the core of the business.

Build digital products and services

- Learn and apply digital foundational platform strategies and technologies, such as lowcode and integration, to integrate the enterprise and apply modern API strategies.
- Become more independent even from traditional software vendors, and constantly increase the business knowledge and ability to develop their digital assets.
- Deploy new digital assets and products and never return to conventional application development.

Attract and keep digital talents

- Demonstrate attractiveness for tech specialists and digital talents by offering outstanding technology stacks built on top of best-in-class digital architectures.
- Demonstrate excellent leadership qualities and a commitment to learning.

Utilize a digital culture

- Leverage autonomy in the development process to foster a cultural adaptation to new continual digital development and deployment.
- Engage in ideation toward the effective realization of benefits and gradual cultural adaptations.
- Foster a culture of continual improvements and platform-inspired thinking and problem-solving capabilities.

Innovate the business

- Encourage employees to assume greater ownership of the scope of digital transformations, take more calculated risks, and secure continual innovative deployments.
- Create environments where employees feel comfortable proposing new ideas, testing and iterating on them while learning from their failures and successes.
- Leverage business innovation and utilize technologies without external dependencies or limitations because of hard-to-overcome vendor-lock-in contracts and dependencies.
- Encourage cross-functional collaboration as they work across different departments and functions.
- Promote leading-edge technologies, shift their focus on getting them to work in the bigger context, and constantly leverage and increase business value.

- Accept and adopt new technologies faster, such as artificial intelligence and machine learning, seamlessly integrated into the digital foundational composable architecture can help automate routine tasks and free up employees' time to focus on more creative work.

- Encourage using platform strategies, with innovation and experimentation supported by such systemic thinking.

Collaborate with partners

- Engage more distinctly in their external relationships, with greater expectations of tailored services and higher degrees of flexibility and adaptability than ever before.

- Take full ownership of their services and lead collaboration by default. Increase their dependency over time and become more and more independent from their traditional vendors.

- Eliminate obstructive and counterproductive outsourced services to digital transformations.

Relentless interactions across business functions with internal and external stakeholders, such as customers, partners, service providers, and regulators, are the basis for constantly leveraging intelligent and harmonized optimization capabilities in digitally unified organizations. Traditional outsourcing companies are eventually seeing and monitoring this incremental shift of power, driven by their fear of autonomous digital organizations, which are constantly diminishing and partly evaporating the role of traditional outsourcing partners.

"Digital autonomy is a compelling collaborative approach to drive continual change in complex environments where democratized decisions are encouraged by guiding vision and priorities and implemented through mutual accountability and trust."

Ingo Paas

Master autonomy at scale is a game changer for any organization, not only implementing new digital foundational platforms, agile ways of working, and establishing data-driven organizations. Organizations that shift their focus towards incremental and evolutionary digital transformations are examining and recalibrating their understanding and definition of digitally inspired autonomy.

Autonomous tech and data-driven organizations will likely assume greater responsibility and accountability with strong and clearly defined ownership of technologies, skills, data, and processes. They will develop more differentiated strategies for utilizing external partners and outsourcing as they accelerate their journey toward digital autonomy at scale.

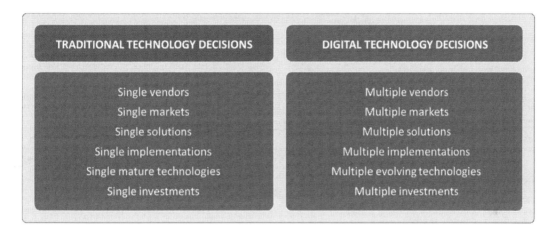

Figure 98 Less-autonomous as opposed to autonomous methods

The above figure shows the distinctions and discrepancies between traditional thinking and new digitally empowered and autonomous thinking. Developing and implementing composable enterprises do not exclusively require a new approach to digital transformations and establishing a composable business and digital architecture.

A composable architecture requires a fundamental rethinking of the use of the software at the core of the enterprise's business models and processes. After decades of ineffective software development, organizations are carefully experimenting with the ability to develop in-house world-class scalable and maintainable digital technologies and capabilities (such as applications, APIs, algorithms, and data models). This is increasing the autonomy of development organizations dramatically.

Enabled by digital foundational platforms, modern organizations can master this process by assuming full responsibility and accountability for their composable architecture and support technology platforms. They are most likely able to buy external development of applications, but on their premises, principles, and architecture, not on external cloud-enabled platforms owned and managed by external partners.

Autonomous and independent organizations are hosting most SaaS applications on their tenants instead of running their SaaS services externally. Autonomous organizations are exceptionally clear about their cloud strategies and principles, knowing exactly why, how, and what kind of services they want to run on their cloud tenants or which ones they want to be managed by SaaS vendors. They reduce their dependencies on external vendors when making new strategic choices. A typical example is when organizations shift and lift ERP platforms into their vendor's cloud platforms. They become highly dependent on their vendor without being able to manage or influence the development of their ERP platforms, infrastructure, and applications management. Instead, they accelerate their autonomy by establishing new skills and capabilities, such as CCoE (Cloud Center of Excellence), actively managing their cloud services and future cloud conversions.

Enterprise vendors fully govern and manage their ERP platforms, reinforcing traditional dependencies of classical ERP systems rather than supporting the development of a culture with increased levels of autonomy. Even if they may add ERP vendor-supported lowcode development platforms, they will most likely depend on their ERP vendors for most of their applications and digital services.

Autonomous organizations can selectively invest in cloud ERP portfolios to utilize and run selective SaaS on platforms such as Microsoft Dynamics. They can adjust their SaaS portfolio of applications at any time while selecting their individual SaaS services per their business priorities and needs. This platform thinking and much higher grade of flexibility reduce the risk of strategic dependencies when selecting cloud and platform-based ERP strategies.

Organizations are managing more cloud autonomously and assuming full responsibility for cloud operations, hosting SaaS applications on their cloud environments. This approach reaffirms the simplicity and autonomy that organizations may have these days. Through clarity on their desired composable business architecture, they may be increasing their level of autonomy, given that those organizations are gaining competitive advantages of building dynamic, flexible, and adaptive ERP capabilities embedded into their future composable architectures.

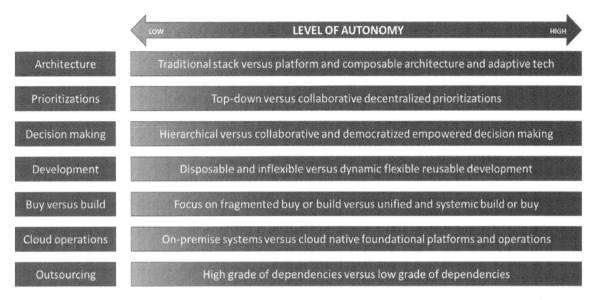

Figure 99 Selected characteristics of autonomous organizations

The level of autonomy is defined by various capabilities, which are the building blocks of autonomous organizations in the digital age. Therefore, achieving a higher level of autonomy is necessary while individually determining the appropriate level. Building autonomous organizations and teams is a fundamental statement and capability, distinguishing future digital masters from those organizations that apply digital technologies without taking clear ownership of their ability to continue to leverage their digital transformations independently and at scale.

Those organizations instead promote modern leadership, encourage more democratized and empowered decision-making, and support collaborative new ways of working. They are advancing existing governance and decision-making frameworks, allowing more decentralized and distributed prioritizations.

To align vision, strategy, goals, and business priorities with more decentral prioritizations and decisions, they empower leaders on every level and deliver on the maximum of the organization's capacities. Creating autonomous teams and leaders is essential for more autonomous organizations to utilize necessary changes. They must utilize powerful digital foundational platforms and agnostic architectures to continuously deliver sustainable improvements and changes without being constrained or limited by complicated and hierarchical governance models.

The decision to leverage the power of autonomous organizations and teams is necessary for determining the ability of organizations to drive sustainable, scalable, and systemic digital transformations. They will leverage technologies, data, processes, and skills in evolutionary ways to understand how they migrate and future onboard innovation while keeping control of their costs and business value-driven investments.

Establishing truly autonomous organizations is never-ending and requires substantial leadership efforts, starting small but growing big. Striving toward a new digital normal while promoting the collaborative execution of digital transformation is complex. Digital transformations enable greater autonomy and are most likely shifting their collective energy into collaborative ways of working and organizations and encourage the ability of systemic thinking.

Embrace systemic thinking

The theory of systemic thinking in digital transformations highlights the importance of holistic approaches to understanding and implementing digital transformation in organizations and their internal and external ecosystems. This approach recognizes that digital transformation is not just about technology but also the organization's complex interactions between people, processes, and technologies. Systemic thinking involves analyzing and addressing the interdependencies and feedback loops between various elements of the organization to create sustainable and effective digital transformations.

Systemic thinking theory helps secure cross-functional engagement in digital transformations, recognizing the need for effective interoperability of complex interconnected processes, people, and technologies. With those preconceptions, any change in one enterprise area can have far-reaching impacts on other parts.

Systemic thinking considers the relationships and interdependencies between critical parts of the organization. The system refers to the impact of digital transformation initiatives on the entire system rather than just isolated problems.

It will also help combine and utilize digitally packaged business capabilities dynamically, using systemic thinking in the execution and orchestration of those components across various digital foundational platforms. This allows organizations to identify issues to improve the design of digital transformation initiatives aligned with overall business goals and priorities.

The theory of systemic thinking in digital transformations also emphasizes the importance of considering the various perspectives and needs of important stakeholders involved, including customers, employees, partners, and digital ecosystems. This helps ensure that digital transformation initiatives are designed from the core of the business with the end user in mind to deliver the desired outcomes. Those organizations that embrace systemic thinking are better prepared to realize complicated transformations to realize sustainable and incremental, step-by-step enhancements, where the focus is on complementary enhancements rather than building isolated systems in fragmented ways.

Systemic thinking and execution is an adaptive approach to digital transformations, allowing highly dynamic and effective utilization of resources to secure a relentless focus on incremental and experimental progress. It does require a different mindset and effective execution capabilities compared with traditional approaches to drive change. This benefits deliberate, cautious, motivated, and transformational movers (see Chapter 1).

Systemic thinking and execution are foundational to the successful and empirical execution of modern digital transformations. Systemic thinking is a powerful method to solve contractionary, interlinked, and complex problems sustainably and effectively while requiring collaborative capabilities and the willingness of teams to work on bigger and broader questions and concerns. Their ability to effectively deal with conflicts, give feedback, and solve problems together is key to success.

The key characteristic of successful teams is their ability to jointly navigate complex changes while embracing and welcoming the positive and negative dynamics of systemic transformations. They must focus on solving critical but small business problems rather than trying to solve large and complex ones simultaneously.

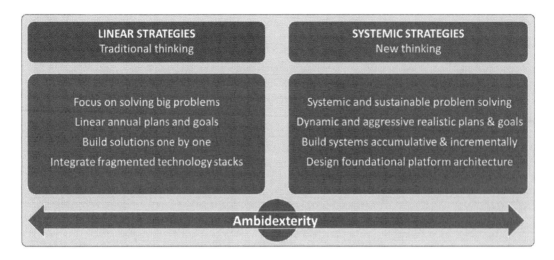

Figure 100 Linear strategies as opposed to systemic strategies in execution

"Systemic thinking is a powerful alternative problem-solving approach to break down and simplify complex and cross-functional issues by incrementally and experimentally executing digital composable transformations. Successful collaborative teams persistently focus on systems rather than just parts of them while continually solving smaller but related problems."

Ingo Paas

System thinking involves a shift from observing events or data to identifying the elements of primary systems required to build complex structures or architectures. Systemic thinking will break down complex problems into many small components to help understand causes and actions better as the choices may become more complex and interdependent. This method expands the choices applicable to solving foundational problems, especially in digital composable transformation, where interoperability and reusability require such approaches.

Characteristics of systemic thinking interventions are continual efforts, not one-time events, often well-known, and having a history that others have unsuccessfully tried to solve.

In the case of ambidexterity, applying the concept of systemic thinking (ideally in teams) will help define practical but sustainable solutions to incremental problems of larger systems. Ambidexterity will help enterprises focus on exploitation and routine while continuing to focus on exploration and innovation.

Digital transformations inspired and encouraged by systemic strategies and new thinking are more capable of overcoming high complexity and delivering on their promises, plans, investments, and business benefits. Teams must have a positive mindset and appreciate continually solving problems, while they must be willing to support each other constantly. They must appreciate collaborative work and elevate learning rapidly. Only teams with high levels of integrity and profound leadership skills can oppose and deal with frustration during this challenging journey.

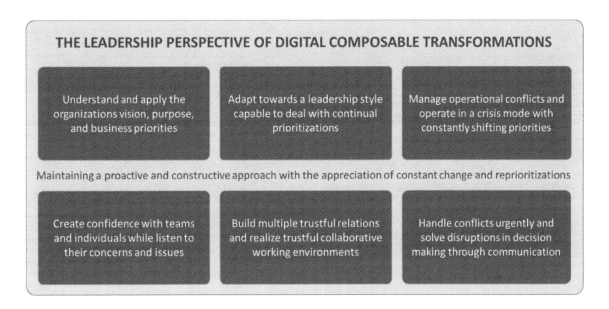

Figure 101 Systemic execution demands adaptive and collaborative leadership qualities

Adopting systemic thinking is not necessarily demanding that the entire organization engage in this demanding process. Introducing systemic thinking and execution may introduce new challenges and complications. Those are most likely related to individual leadership and the ability to deal with the enormous dynamics of systemic thinking during execution. Organizations that embrace this approach will most likely experience high-stress levels caused by huge dynamics with high workloads and a sense of constant problem-solving. They will recognize a shift from strategic and long-term planning towards more reactive, continual prioritizations, focusing on problem-solving and priority-driven execution. Independent of those challenges, systemic thinking can leverage digital transformations and especially support evolving collaborative organizations.

Evolve collaboration everywhere

Collaboration is imperative for digital composable transformations with incremental and experimental approaches. Collaborative efforts align multiple perspectives, promote collective decision-making, foster a culture of continuous improvement and innovation, and ensure that all stakeholders have a shared understanding of the goals and outcomes of the transformation. Collaborative organizations increase the success rates of their digital transformations at scale, becoming more relevant and inclusive. They prioritize and solve daily business problems, drive changes from the core of the business, and engage employees from the start. Working together, teams can more effectively identify and mitigate risks, prioritize their agile processes, solve complex problems, and allocate resources effectively.

Collaboration ensures that the transformations align with business strategies, objectives, and priorities. It informs strategies about identified changes and new opportunities inspired by more innovation enabled through digital foundational platforms and the reusability of digitally developed assets. Collaboration also helps build trust and foster a sense of shared ownership on a broader scale, increasing employee engagement and commitment to the transformation effort.

Establishing collaborative organizations is a mandatory approach to anchor a shared commitment and level of engagement in digital transformations across organizations. Achieving sustainable success with digital transformations increases acceptance, engagement, and willingness to adapt to change. Without engaging organizations in collaborative working, even the smartest capabilities and technologies will end up as fragmented and non-scalable investments. Building collaborative organizations is necessary to empower businesses to engage in foundational learning and cultural adoption.

"Collaborative culture in digital transformations is the shared and committed approach to align different key stakeholders during digital transformations, informed and guided by mutual vision, purpose, objectives, and clear business priorities, to secure cooperative tactics from ideation to monetization with collaborative learning."

Ingo Paas

Organizations that understand the strengths of collaborative transformations should encourage the incorporation of product ownership in digital development. Those organizations will prioritize their undertakings with data-driven insights, new learnings, and greater awareness of traditional problems that have remained unsolved for decades (such as data ownership and quality).

Figure 102 Building collaborative organizations and culture is a long but unavoidable element of digital transformations

Collaborative organizations can foster and encourage discussions and actions to identify clear digital responsibilities, such as owners of information, business capabilities, digital products, processes, systems, and core-data models. Such responsibilities may include data management, demand management, testing of new functionality, information ownership, process ownership, compliance, security, privacy, and systems control.

Collaborative organizations play a critical role in securing the long-term success of digital evolutionary transformations by encouraging new, digitally inspired leadership. Collaboration is essential to adapt to continual learning and to learn from failures.

Effective collaboration aligns individual stakeholders' efforts, including business units, IT departments, customers, partners, and vendors, which helps to break down silos, improve communication, and accelerate aligned decision-making. Evolutionary transformations, in collaborative ways, will advance the adaptation of digital culture across the organization in unprecedented ways, to even leverage traditional organizations into the status of "tech companies".

Advance the digital culture

Enterprises must advance their organizational culture to support successful digital transformations collaboratively. They must embrace cultural changes as the outcome of collaborative new working methods and create learning organizations.

Culture deeply affects how organizations approach and adopt new technologies, processes, and working methods. A culture that values innovation, agility, collaboration, and continuous learning will better enable enterprises to effectively implement and adopt digital technologies, whereas a rigid, hierarchical, and resistant culture may impede progress.

The collaborative approach to cultural change inspired by digital transformations is a prerequisite to making change last, relevant, and valuable to employees, customers, and partners. Only digital transformations that allow the culture to evolve incrementally will explore new opportunities, embed innovation into their daily prioritizations, and improve business performance through relentless problem-solving.

The key factors in digital transformation that will drive organizational cultural change are:

- **Customer expectations**
  Situation: Digital transformation must satisfy customers' evolving and changing needs and expectations, with changes developing from the core of the business, and must adapt their culture to prioritize customer-centricity.

Response: Customer expectations shall be a driving force, but enterprises shall secure full integration of customer-facing digital solutions integrated with the core of their business.

- **Developing technologies**

Situation: Rapid technological innovation and access to new digital capabilities transform traditional work methods.

Response: Tech-savvy organizations must adapt to new technologies embedded in their culture. Enterprises must accept continuous learning to keep up with the latest technologies and continually embrace with tech teams how to further utilize tech and data to transform their enterprises collectively.

- **Data-driven enterprises**

Situation: Most enterprises heavily invest in data analytics, utilizing the power of data, while others are missing clear strategies and purposes, technologies, skills and talents, and an integrated approach to data analytics embedded into digital transformations.

Response: With the increased availability of analytics tools and access to data, data-driven organizations must improve the utilization of data at the core of their transformations. Those changes profoundly impact enterprises' cultural adaptation to evolve and collectively utilize data-driven decision-making. Data-driven cultures do not prosper using advanced algorithms and significant investments in data science teams.

A data-driven culture requires enterprises to have clear strategies, prioritize data quality, skilled talents, and advanced foundational scalable technologies. At the same time, they foster a data-driven culture throughout the organization in collaborative ways, driven by the desire to increase business performance and value.

- **Collaboration and cross-functional teams**

Situation: Most organizations are still organized in silos and have not practiced collaborative working in a broader context. Therefore, an organizational culture that enables collaboration and cross-functional teamwork requires common processes, tools, roles, and agile standards.

Response: Digital transformation requires collaboration across functional silos shall be encouraged, especially as composability and interoperability demand new thinking and design of packaged business capabilities. Their impact on multiple processes requires collaborative teamwork, applying the principles of agile fusion teams.

The positive effects of those efforts will consequently lead to cultural change, profoundly different than KPIs (Key Performance Indicators) could ever do. Learning and common processes, including collaborative prioritization of new development and backlog handling, are essential for success.

- **Agility and elasticity**

  Situation: Digital transformation is an iterative process that requires an agile and flexible approach. Enterprises must develop a culture that values and encourages agility, experimentation, and continuous improvement.

  Response: Agile capabilities require collaborative fusion teams with commonly agreed, transparent, and dynamic processes. Risks with agile prioritization and issues with rigidity and stiff prioritizations with 100% development resource allocation undermine the necessary elasticity of development resources to support unplanned agile development needs.

By embracing these key factors, enterprises can foster a culture that supports and drives successful digital transformation. Cultural development is not only inspired and affected by the consequences and opportunities of collaboration. There are other key factors, such as risk-tolerant leadership, that organizations must consider in their cultural development.

Modern risk-tolerance leadership has significant implications for digital transformations. In the context of digital transformations, modern risk-tolerance leadership refers to leaders willing to embrace change, take calculated risks, and are comfortable with uncertainty.

Risk-tolerant leadership style allows organizations to embrace and encourage experimentation, innovation, and new ideas, which are essential to successful digital transformation. They encourage agility and change as they are comfortable with uncertainty and change. They enable their organizations to be more agile, adapt quickly to changing conditions, and encourage decisive and faster decision-making in rapidly evolving digital environments. They also promote continuous improvement, which is crucial for scalable success in the rapidly evolving digital landscape.

Positively recognized and welcomed digital transformations attract and develop new skills, most likely attracting and retaining new top talents easier. If digital technologies find acceptance and adaptation, digital foundational technologies, such as analytic platforms and strategies, may create the environment that makes enterprises become attractive tech brands and employers.

Those organizations foster a culture that values and encourages accountability combined with risk-taking, where successful innovation will more likely motivate less risk-tolerant employees and teams, to engage, challenge, and innovate. Doing so inspires confidence in others to continually learn and increase their comfort zones and approach to risk tolerance. Modern risk-tolerant leaders usually engage organizations in collaborative, dynamic changes, increasing engagement across teams as they open up traditional silos. Modern risk-tolerance leadership is a critical component of successful digital transformations, as it fosters an environment that values innovation, agility, and continuous improvement and enables organizations to navigate the uncertainties and risks associated with digital transformation effectively. Risk-tolerant leadership approach can help change the culture of organizations as they promote innovation, experimentation, agility, and trust as critical components of successful digital transformation.

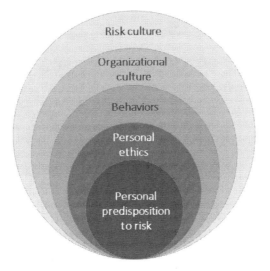

Source: Institute of Risk Management – The Risk Culture Framework

Figure 103 Institute of Risk Management – The Risk Culture Framework (The Institute of Risk Management, 2012)

Risk-management frameworks of enterprises usually emphasize identification, mitigation, control, and reporting of the risks of enterprises. With digital transformation and a modern risk-tolerant leadership approach, new and major tensions may arise with traditional enterprise risk management frameworks. They could cause problems with cultural resistance, lack of agility, lack of expertise, and inability to adjust external regulatory compliance requirements. Such challenges require better alignment and in-depth discussions to find appropriate and acceptable common approaches to balance traditional and modern risk leadership.

This could include areas such as:

- **Risk perception**

  Situation: Traditional enterprise risk management frameworks often focus on avoiding risk, whereas risk-tolerant leadership is willing to embrace calculated risk to drive innovation and progress.

  Response: Enterprises must make risk management frameworks more adaptive to change, apply risks driven compliance, and allow the business to accept risks and assume responsibilities for risk mitigation activities.

- **Accountability and transparency**

  Situation: Insufficient support of individual accountability and transparency in the overall approach often results in bureaucratic decision-making. Decisions made in slow, hierarchical processes, and senior managers reluctant to delegate decision-making power to lower levels, can hinder increased accountability.

  Response: Accountability must find support from incentive systems that reward accountability and risk-taking differently, even in the case of failure. To encourage leaders to assume accountability, risk-taking into uncertainty and risk of failure must find acceptance and support from senior management.

- **Decision making**

  Situation: Traditional risk management frameworks can slow decision-making by requiring extensive analysis and approvals, while risk-tolerant leaders value agility and quick decision-making.

  Response: Enterprises must build capabilities into risk management frameworks to speed up decisions and ensure that risk appetite and risk-culture support individual and more risk-tolerance leadership.

- **Experimentation**

  Situation: Traditional risk management frameworks can resist experimentation and change and slow down the positive effects of evolutionary transformations.

  Response: Risk-tolerant leaders utilizing experimental development must find support from senior management to adjust rigid governance, support risk-averse thinking, and allow the democratization of decisions and risk-taking. Experimentation does also require greater tolerance and new thinking with experimental investments. Late requests must find support from administrative functions due to experimental development instead of accusing those leaders of insufficient planning.

- **Incremental innovation**

  Situation: Traditional risk management frameworks can stifle innovation by promoting a culture of caution and conservatism, while risk-tolerant leadership encourages experimentation and creativity. Enterprises and CxOs must eliminate or adjust those barriers to innovation because they prioritize minimizing risks over maximizing opportunities.

  Response: Empower agile and collaborative teams to make more decentral decisions to increase throughput and output from ideation and innovation without restricting development through administrative burdens. Innovation will grow with a combination of more empowered individuals and teams with more flexible decision-making.

Addressing these examples is critical, as they can create tension within organizations and may significantly limit the ability of enterprises to pursue digital transformation and achieve their goals. Organizations must balance traditional risk management frameworks and risk-tolerant leadership to overcome these conflicts, considering each situation's specific risks and objectives. This approach is achievable by renewing and evolving risk management frameworks or by simply encouraging modern risk-tolerance leadership in transparent ways. Risk levels will diminish or become insignificant due to incremental and experimental working methods.

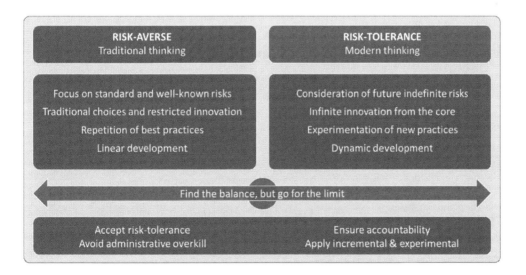

Figure 104 Risk-averse as opposed to risk-tolerance decisions

Numerous factors, such as competition, industry, geography, technology, history, ethics, religion, and economic and political developments, shape the risk culture of organizations. An organization's history potentially influences risk cultures. Other factors can be implied or reinforced by owners, laws, rules, and regulations, but likewise through dominating and ruling leaders who can strongly influence risk cultures.

Roles such as Data Protection Officers, Chief Information Security Officers, Chief Information Officers, Chief Financial Officers, and Chief Operating Officers usually promote a risk-averse rather than a risk-tolerance culture. Their fear of non-compliance is usually dominant, overruling even larger "potential future" risks. They most likely promote zero to low-risk approaches rather than support a more progressive risk-tolerance thinking.

Other executives with significant influence on strategies may have a greater tendency towards risk-tolerance leadership but often seem to ignore their distinct responsibilities. Risk-tolerance cultures do not necessarily exclude risk-averse decision-making, but they most likely continue to promote, prioritize, encourage, and liberate risk-averse leadership in coexistence.

Where shall organizations find those profiles willing to assume accountability and motivate risk-tolerance decisions in digital transformations? Enterprises must understand that an unproportionate balance in risk-taking will slow down or even out digital transformations at high risk.

"Risk-tolerance cultures must embrace uncertainties and encourage technology-inspired innovation with collaborative, agile thinking. They must mitigate and minimize future risks through incremental and experimental ways of working, as they encourage individuals and teams to take suitable risks in a self-directed but governed manner supporting and motivating appropriate approaches and incentives."

Ingo Paas

Transforming organizations from a risk-averse culture towards a risk-tolerance culture will require major efforts from decision-makers and influencers. The ability to make better strategic risk-tolerance decisions and engage individuals and teams will significantly impact more balanced and risk-tolerance investments.

Evolving the culture of organizations towards increased risk tolerance are fundamental undertakings enterprises must consider in the shadow of digital transformations.

Minimizing risk levels is important to leverage and optimize the ability to execute while monetizing digital investments is critical to secure the necessary funding.

Monetize digital investments

Digital transformations must improve business KPIs and objectives, contribute to business model innovation, improve critical business capabilities, and enable sustainable improvements. Generating positive returns and securing sustainable business benefits is necessary to justify the resources and investments for digital composable transformations. ROI (Return on Investment) and TCO (Total Cost of Ownership) are important tools for measuring investments and assessing digital transformations' overall impact and success or failure.

However, solely focusing on ROI-driven investments can have long-term consequences and determine the success or failure of digital transformations. Organizations must consider several risk factors with increased investments in digital technologies, such as unclear investment strategies, insufficient architectural governance, siloed departments, vendor lock-in issues, and other challenges. In addition, fragmented digital investments may introduce new strategic risks despite promising individual benefits. To avoid fragmented digital investments, enterprises must have clear digital strategies, holistic views, and architectural guidelines qualifying balanced technology investments.

The following three long-term risks of non-interoperable digital investments are important for enterprises while overseeing such risks as ineffective digital investments. Those risks may:

1. **Cause fragmentation**

    Enterprises must avoid fragmented technology investments is critical to prevent the decoupling of technologies, causing problems with interoperability and poor architectural alignment.

2. **Increase the overall cost base**

    Enterprises must avoid fragmented investments with the risk of unnecessary high or preventable TCO when operating and integrating those technologies into the enterprise architecture.

3. **End up as the new digital legacy**

    Enterprises must avoid technological investments that might become obsolete with changing business requirements or future technology investments.

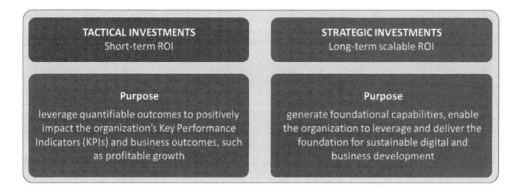

Figure 105 Primary and secondary effects of monetization of digital investments

Tactical and strategic investments serve different purposes and have different priorities, so it is important to achieve a better balance between those two options:

- **Tactical investments**

  Situation: Tactical investments drive distinct but fragmented business benefits. Examples are Customer B2B portals, e-commerce solutions, development projects, and SaaS applications (such as HR, CRM, and pricing optimization). Those investments aim to leverage rapid and quantifiable outcomes in solitary projects. They are usually not scalable, have a single purpose, and classifies as tactical investments. They have sufficient ROIs but may produce ineffective TCOs if investments are not scalable.

  Response: Tactical investments shall minimize risks with interoperability and must comply with core and foundational architectural design principles. Business owners must have additional accountability and incentives for delivering on their business cases with rapid ROI while ensuring long-term sustainability and interoperability with acceptable TCO.

- **Strategic investments**

  Situation: Strategic investments have no initial direct, distinct, measurable, or traceable business benefit. Digital foundational platforms are typical strategic investments with multi-purpose capabilities and high grades of scalability. Enterprises undergoing cost-cutting programs and focusing on short-term ROI mainly approve tactical investments and down-prioritize strategic investments.

Response: CxOs must assume greater accountabilities for initiating and executing strategic investments to secure the evolutionary development of digital composable architectures. By defining and implementing core digital foundational platform technologies, they must engage the business when further developing those platforms after initial investments. CxOs must timely engage with business and governing bodies to inform and educate those stakeholders about the purpose and reasoning concerning strategic investments. Data-driven organizations will become more effective with ready-to-scale enterprise-wide platforms, while they must be involved to influence future prioritizations and technology investments. CxOs must intensify their partnerships with influential leaders to ensure that strategic investments will find acceptance on all levels. Investments must be addressed and embedded into the enterprise's investment strategy.

The dilemma between those two perspectives does cause difficulties for organizations to motivate and prioritize strategic investments. The absence of strong ROI and TCO scenarios burdens many organizations only to prioritize tactical investments with short-term ROI. This introduces major risks for organizations to find the right balance between investment scenarios.

The most significant measures that enterprises can apply are:

1. Establish clear and realistic objectives and restrict the scope
2. Define distinct business ownership for investments
3. Implement standardized processes to qualify business cases, including ROI and TCO
4. Support business owners to measure and follow up on business cases
5. Identify risks that could hinder the realization of business cases
6. Implement agile measures to mitigate those risks
7. Create transparency and apply relentless learning considering of failure and success

The spectrum of tactical and strategic investments requires a sure instinct to identify and follow up on ROIs and TCOs and monetize digital investments. Enterprises should consider the arguments of those investment scenarios to make better informed and balanced investment decisions. They will also minimize risks with weak ROIs and new piles of incompatible digital legacy technologies.

Deal with increasing complexity

Challenges have only grown since, as choices are exponentially growing, far beyond the limit, even the most tech-savvy digital leaders and CxOs may comprehend. The acceleration of technology development can complicate CxOs' selection of technologies to solve business problems because it leads to a large and rapidly growing number of available options. With so many technologies emerging and evolving rapidly, it can be challenging for CxOs to keep up with the latest trends, evaluate each option's potential benefits and risks, and determine which technologies are most appropriate for their organization's specific needs. Additionally, the rapid pace of technological change means that CxOs and enterprise architects must continually reassess their technology choices and adapt to new developments, creating ongoing challenges for architectural design, planning, and implementation.

To minimize the risk of having to reassess their technology choices and adapt to new developments constantly, CxOs could consider the following recommendations:

1. **Develop a long-term technology roadmap**

   CxOs can create a roadmap that outlines their organization's technology goals and priorities over a multi-year period to help guide technology investments and ensure that the organization is moving towards its desired technology state.

2. **Focus on technologies that are adaptable, interoperable, and scalable**

   CxOs can prioritize technologies designed to be flexible and adaptable to changing business needs, which can scale to support future growth.

3. **Emphasize on composability**

   CxOs can prioritize technologies designed to integrate with other systems to reduce the risk of creating technology silos that are difficult to integrate or replace.

4. **Foster a culture of innovation**

   CxOs can create an environment where innovation is encouraged and rewarded, and employees are empowered to experiment with new technologies and approaches.

5. **Stay up to date on technology trends**

   CxOs can invest in ongoing education and stay informed about emerging technologies and industry trends to ensure they are well-equipped to make informed decisions about technology investments.

6. Secure resilient digital architectures

CxOs and architects must secure that they are building scalable but foremost resilient digital architectures to secure the continual adaptation and integration of ever-faster developing technologies for many years. If CxOs fail, enterprises will fail to achieve digital resilience!

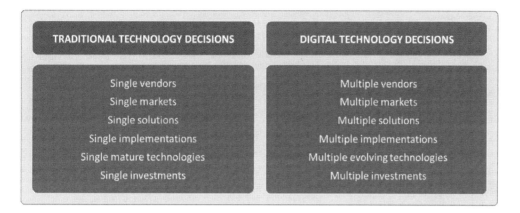

Figure 106 Digital technology investments, compared to traditional ones, introduce new layers of complexity, including interoperability, scalability, reusability, and adaptability for CxOs, architects, and business leaders

Traditional technology investments typically refer to a specific technology or product. These investments can be beneficial if the technology or product in question proves successful, has a high demand, and helps enterprises solve identified problems.

"CxOs and architects must invest in scalable and resilient digital architectures to secure the continual adaptation and integration of ever faster-developing technologies for many years to come. If CxOs fail, enterprises will fail to leverage innovation and secure digital resilience!"

Ingo Paas

Digital technology investments must secure divergence to optimize the total business value through increased interoperability, scalability, reusability, and short- and long-term adaptability. The choice between both options will depend on an enterprise's investment strategies, goals, risk tolerance, and overall culture, such as the desire to increase digital autonomy, interoperability, and improved digital resilience on the enterprise level.

Enterprises must consider multiple choices from multiple vendors and with multiple technologies in multiple combinations. This increased complexity makes simple traditional comparisons and traditional sourcing processes nearly impossible. Wrong or insufficient choices of technologies can either drive costs, delay projects, drive complexity, or in worst cases, grow the pile of enterprises' new digital technology legacy. Instead, digital technology-driven strategies and architectures must pave the way for projects and support decision-makers to be guided by strong business-driven technology roadmaps.

The numerous perspectives of recognized pitfalls of digital transformations are a key learning from the last decade and the endless attempts of digital transformations. It is noticeable that there are great variations in how organizations leverage their digital transformations and encourage innovative opportunities for their enterprises. Enterprises are still struggling and increasing their investments into digital transformations, while they are eventually not delivering on their promises and introducing new risks with uncontrolled deployment with ineffective digital investments. Effectively initiating, driving, and assimilating digital transformations depends largely on the organization's ability to understand and adapt to new opportunities driving digital transformations. Effective business and IT strategies and execution must embed and consider those learnings.

Organizations that consider those recommendations may rethink their approaches while considering new ways to build future composable enterprises enabled by their digital transformations. They should create a broader and more substantial foundation for long-term success with innovative digital leadership at the core of their business models. They should avoid major transformative programs (whenever possible) and understand digital transformations as one-time change initiatives.

Digitalization of traditional enterprises, with effective monetization of their investments, is usually overshadowed by various traditional risk-averse behaviors, complications, and challenges. It is crucial for organizations willing to adjust their approach and find new responses to avoid the potential pitfalls of their digital transformations.

Avoid the pitfalls of digital composable transformations

The synthesis of this book and the arguments to reconsider traditional approaches to digital transformations were manifested in the first chapter, introducing eight new-articulated, and organized comprehensive characteristics of successful digital transformations.

The following figure and reflection on the eight pitfalls of digital transformations include several suggestions in this book, providing a comprehensive "as complete as possible" framework to succeed. Enterprises that are applying the lessons learned from failed digital transformations will increase their chances of success significantly and may avoid and mitigate high-risk exposure with traditional approaches to traditional digital transformations.

OVERCOMING THE PITFALLS OF DIGITAL TRANSFORMATIONS		
#	**The eight pitfalls of digital composable transformations**	**The eight characteristics of successful digital composable transformations**
1	Enterprises prioritize large-scale waterfall programs	Embrace evolutionary and incremental development and value-driven investments with the empowerment of teams
2	Enterprises invest in digital readiness initiatives	Encourage demand-driven focused iterations to enable IT legacy readiness during transformations
3	Enterprises follow inconsistent ROI-driven investment strategies	Align investment strategies with business strategies and secure a balance between tactical and strategic investments
4	Enterprises disregard transformations from the core of the business	Secure that digital development and transformations are originating from the core of the business
5	Enterprises invest in fragmented non-scalable architectures	Design and invest in foundational and composable platform strategies and architectures
6	Enterprises trust in traditional change management	Involve the organization in continual collaboration to adapt and explore cultural adoption and new ways of working
7	Enterprises promote incapsulated innovation frameworks	Entrench and adapt inherent collaborative innovation work in agile processes and prioritizations
8	Enterprises prefer disconnected and isolated data analytics programs	Consider data analytics strategies as core capabilities of any digital transformation

Figure 107 The eight characteristics of successful digital composable transformations

The eight characteristics of successful digital composable transformations are indisputable and should be considered in every digital transformation to avoid traditional pitfalls and risks. They will help enterprises make better choices, maximize the outcome of their investments, and transform their enterprises across the spectrum from organizational culture to shareholder value. Considering those eight characteristics, digital transformations will significantly increase their chances of achieving digital resilience and responsiveness, laying the ground for transforming "traditional and digital enterprises" into "digital composable enterprises".

1. Embrace evolutionary and incremental development and value-driven investments with the empowerment of teams

- Embrace experimental and incremental development with liberation and empowerment.
- Postpone major programs and prefer investments into digital transformations, wherever possible.
- Reconsider lift and shift investments from data centers into the cloud if avoidable but consider an evolutionary approach if feasible.
- Avoid migrating IT legacy systems towards micros-services architectures if avoidable but consider an evolutionary approach if feasible.

2. Encourage demand-driven focused iterations to enable IT legacy readiness during transformations

- Embrace composable and interoperable capabilities to adjust digital readiness on demand.
- Utilize digital foundational platforms to minimize IT legacy complexity.
- Optimize balanced tactical and strategic investments to secure and accelerate digital transformations.
- Identify critical strategic issues and secure timely but evolutionary mitigating activities.
- Embrace and scale digital ERP in the cloud and integrate future ERP from the core of the business.
- **Encourage incremental migrations transforming from traditional towards future digital ERP whenever possible and utilize partners such as Rimini Street to maximize value, ERP investments, reduce running costs, and partly finance ERP transformations.**

3. Align investment strategies with business strategies and secure a balance between tactical and strategic investments

- Continuously align investment decisions with the overall business direction.
- Utilize learnings from insufficient ROIs and TCOs and inform the investment strategy.
- Reconsider investment strategies and apply more balanced approaches between tactical and strategic investments.
- Utilize investments to satisfy tactical ROI-driven business needs and secure compatibility between investments to the extent.
- Educate decision-makers and inform them about investment performance continually.
- Apply guiding and distinct architectural governance embedded into the design and execution of investment strategies.

4. Secure that digital development and transformations are originating from the core of the business

- Identify the core business processes to design and elevate digitally packaged business capabilities.
- Prioritize digital development from the core without ignoring significant investments into customer-facing processes.
- Build and design for relentless reusability and scale from the core rather than solving inconsistent business logic in traditional ways by building redundancy and complexity in various systems, integrations, and software.
- Scale from the core and identify the key business, customer, and digital success capabilities.
- Embed innovation and continual improvements with collaborative digital development at the core of the business. And then scale!

5. Design and invest in foundational and composable platform strategies and architectures

- Design and implement scalable architectures with digital foundational platforms.
- Define and consequently apply the core principles for enterprise-wide interoperability from the core of the business.
- Define the most business-critical packaged business capabilities.
- Secure maximum levels of digital resilience for packaged business capabilities.
- Design for core principles such as scalability, interoperability, flexibility, agility, adaptability, and sustainability.

6. Involve the organization in continual collaboration to adapt and explore cultural adoption and new ways of working

- Create a culture of engagement by utilizing agile development fusion teams.
- Involve employees and customers to give feedback and increase the value of digitally developed new capabilities.
- Establish well-functioning processes within IT first but involve business in prioritizations and overall utilization of resources as early as possible.
- Encourage greater federated decision rights and empower teams and individuals aligned with business priorities and overall direction.
- Secure that digital development continually and effectively contributes to solving fundamental problems.
- Follow up on deployed improvements' success or failure continually and identify how to leverage those or how to make further improvements.
- Communicate and celebrate success and apply learnings from failures or ineffective initiatives.
- Secure active involvement of employees during design, development, and testing to create greater acceptance and appreciation of changes with better loyalty and a positive mindset.

7. Entrench and adapt inherent collaborative innovation work in agile processes and prioritizations

- Secure embedded innovation processes integrated into agile ways of working.
- Ensure effective utilization of innovation integrated into existing development budgets, prioritization processes, and distributed mandates.
- Integrate innovation into agile and collaborative ways of working, AVOID separating innovation from the line organization and collaborative, agile development.
- Empower teams and employees to innovate by solving real-business problems and continually increase their ability to scale and rationalize from the core.
- Identify and experiment with breakthrough innovation (eventually but not necessarily enabled by breakthrough technologies) at all enterprise levels without disregarding continual innovation from the core of the business.

8. Consider data analytics strategies as core capabilities of any digital transformation

- Ensure integrated analytics entrenches into the core of digital transformations.
- Leverage insights and data in digital, agile development projects and collaborate about new digital data points, especially in real-time and event-driven business processes.
- Reinforce the integration of data-driven businesses into the collaborative implementation of digital transformations.
- Encourage cultural adaptation in parallel to digital composable transformations.
- Build core data modeling and analytics capabilities into and around new digital products.

Organizations that master those **eight characteristics of successful digital transformations into composable enterprises** have greater chances to successfully design, implement, and adapt to sustainable digital evolutionary change. Considering those actionable insights, organizations will significantly increase their chances of establishing substantially more robust, adaptive, resilient, and successful digital transformations.

The new digital normal requires hard work, immense discipline, and a collaborative and evolutionary approach, truly leveraging the unrestricted innovation capacity of digital transformations, engaging entire organizations, and securing achievements of business goals guided by clear visions and business priorities.

Enterprises evolve into digitally mature organizations from the core of their business models and processes. They must relentlessly adopt change in their culture and utilize collaborative ways of working, where new leadership supports the organizations to motivate through empowerment and liberation at scale.

Mastering the eight essential characteristics of digital composable transformations will help traditional and digital enterprises leverage their abilities to evolve into digital composable enterprises.

Scale composable business value

Enterprises must reconsider their strategies and digital leadership to scale business value from investments into digital composability. Examples of key considerations are digital foundational platform strategies, with modularity, interoperability, scalability, and other critical capabilities, all essential to ensuring end-to-end digital composability. Still, there is no meaning if those investments are not leading to digital autonomy, digital resilience, and sustainable business value.

The following core domains of composable business value exemplify the potential outcomes of digital investments into composable transformations and the value generated by related relevant investments.

The four most significant domains of business value include:

- Customers,
- Operations and productions,
- Digital products and services,
- Digital ecosystems.

Figure 108 Business value from digital composable transformations

Business value from customer relationships

Investments in customer relationships often dominate digital transformations, as digital customer solutions significantly impact the organization's ability to maintain, grow, and scale its customer relationships in the digital age. This is not a new focus domain of digital composable enterprises but in direct comparison with digital enterprises, significantly different, integrated, and embedded with the core of the business.

The importance of digital composability comes into play when customer processes are fully embedded into the organization's core processes, systems, and capabilities. The perceived customer value of integrated business processes with the core of the business will leverage and optimize digital customer relationships by creating enormous customer value. This will enable organizations to quickly adapt to changing customer demands and increase flexibility in operations, market conditions, and technological advancements.

This suggests that organizations can respond faster to new opportunities or challenges to stay ahead of their competitors or to enter new markets or segments.

Digital composability can help enterprises customize and evolve their digital customer relationships (in B2B and B2C) and, if successful, reuse and scale digitally developed individual customer solutions without major efforts across other or all customer segments. This will help to scale initial investments in new digital features and products/services across other customers and segments. This does also help to connect customers with more personalized marketing campaigns and promotions, enabling the digital customer journey that is especially important in multi-retail offerings to customers.

Business value from operations and productions

Digital composable organizations can improve their business operations and production by implementing digital composability across the entire enterprise and its digital ecosystems in multiple ways. One key advantage is to improve their agility by creating digital transparency and connecting all the critical business processes inside and outside the enterprise. They can optimize production capacities and resources and better prepare for variations in demand. Digitalization of core business processes will help to improve collaboration and tear down silos in traditional organizations.

Other critical improvements are to advance efficiency by automating processes and workflows, reducing manual intervention, and improving operational efficiency. This can help significantly improve the flow of goods by optimizing supply chain management aligned with fluctuations in customer demands and production capacities. It can reduce costs, prevent production from interruption, minimize capital employed, and increase the accuracy of production plans and customer commitments. Operations can better align capacity constraints with customer services, sales organizations, and their customers by creating seamless visibility of their production volumes. This leads to more satisfied customers with more accurate and reliable information concerning deliveries, offering greater flexibility and changes in ongoing customer order processes and more. Employees will experience greater quality and satisfaction in their day-to-day operations as digital capabilities simplify work, increase collaboration, solve problems, and improve work-life balance and quality. Role-based services will simplify work, eliminating non-valuable tasks.

Data is the core asset to secure transparency and seamless interpretations of business performances. At the same time, digital solutions and products will digitalize and automate processes, and developing software is no longer a hindrance, as the digitalization of business processes, even from the core of the business, is not a Utopia anymore. Optimizing production and operations will lead to lower costs, improved utilization of assets and resources, more effective planning and consumption of raw materials/products, and reduced stock, leading to higher profitability and increased productivity with improved customer experiences.

The business value of digital products and services,

Additional benefits come from digitally integrating core business processes with the organization's products and services. Digital composable enterprises can easily add new abilities, such as predictive analytics enabled by Industry 4.0 investments. Connecting products and services digitally with the core of the business and its embedded customer services does bring significant advantages to every organization. Examples are predictive maintenance, embedded service automation, and spare part or maintenance activities to avoid failure or problems in production processes or the use of products. Such digital connections are widely used remotely, even in B2C, such as connecting cars to centralized platforms, updating critical software, calling vehicles for service, or predicting engine failure. Integrated products and services provide organizations with valuable data to improve existing and develop new products and services. Improved and dynamic pricing is another compelling advantage and rising business capability enabled by digital composable enterprises. Intelligent and automated pricing usually enhances the organization's ability to drive profitability and improve margins.

Business value from ecosystems

Digital ecosystems will dominate the future of enterprises as multiple connectivities in constantly changing digital ecosystems is a critical necessity. Traditional or digital enterprises have no or limited capabilities to operate in those dynamic and digital-first environments if they do not transform into composable enterprises. Enterprises must invest in digital composability to integrate into digital ecosystems interchanging large amounts of data in multiple connections and formats. They must easily integrate and operate across and with digital ecosystems independent of their complexity, dynamics, and interconnectivity with increased complexity connecting larger networks of customers, partners, suppliers, and other stakeholders.

Investments in digital ecosystems are critical as they increasingly require seamless integration of constantly changing and diverse systems and applications. In addition, the future is not only about participating in digital ecosystems but rather about creating and growing those abilities to secure profitable digital growth.

The ability to effectively operate any business by driving and enabling unrestricted integrations into digital ecosystems allows enterprises to improve their agility, efficiency, and innovation capabilities. Enterprises can reduce the complexity of business operations and enable faster and more reliable connections with their external networks of stakeholders. Enterprises that cannot operate across various digital ecosystems may experience significant challenges and shortcomings in the digital age.

All four domains will lead to significant business improvements, such as:

- Higher customer satisfaction and improved customer focus.
- Digital branding and market secure digital enabled leadership.
- Improve costs with automated controls and pricing with increased margins.
- Improved product/service leadership and strengthened competition.
- Continual growth across existing and new segments and customers.
- Improved value through digitally connected or enabled products and services.
- Improved employee satisfaction and effectiveness.
- Increased productivity and utilization of assets and resources.
- Improved profitability and shareholder/owner value.
- Increased incremental and disruptive innovation.

Digital composable enterprises will first accelerate their improvements, then scale their capabilities, innovate from the core, and finally sustain and further evolve from the core of their businesses. In the digital age, evolving into digital composable enterprises is not a question of choice. It is a question of relevance and long-term business success. Those embedding composability into their business strategies may have much greater chances to succeed as they are exploiting and exploring the digital future of their enterprises, customers, partners, and digital ecosystems.

Digital composable enterprises can benefit strongly from M&A (mergers and acquisitions) undertakings. Benefits include improved IT and digital adaptation and integration to make M&A projects cheaper and more effective by utilizing the interoperability and scalability of their technologies. Streamlined IT operations will simplify due-diligence work and increase the value of enterprises. They have better data management and analytics capabilities to provide improved and deeper insights into business operations and facilitate more effective decision-making during and after M&A activities.

As this entire chapter is a book summary, the section "Key conclusions and takeaways" is not considered necessary in Chapter NINE.

TEN – EXPLOIT AND EXPLORE THE FUTURE

Explore technologies continually

Implicit strategic technology innovation is a core discipline organizations must embed into their DNA. Technology-driven innovation is essential for economic success, sustainability, and greater resilience, distinguishing valuable strategic from fragmented tactical technology investments.

Decision makers must feel overwhelmed due to the limitless array of investment options available, driven by advancements in breakthrough technologies and especially the accelerating development and continued deployment of AI inventions. Within months, new digital capabilities, such as OpenAI from Microsoft or Bard from Google (Alphabet), started revolutionizing how enterprise users consume and apply the latest AI developments to innovate their business.

The exponential development of AI and the enormous acceleration of unlimited publicly accessible use cases and applications in early 2023 is only the first sign of the revolution coming. Goldman Sachs Predicts that about 300 million jobs will be lost or degraded by artificial intelligence by 2030.

Goldman Sachs has stated that generative artificial intelligence (AI) can increase global GDP by 7% over ten years. This increase in GDP could be equivalent to a $7 trillion boost to the global economy. The report highlights the potential impact of generative AI on various industries, including enterprise software, healthcare, and financial services.

If generative AI lives up to its hype, the United States and European workforces will see significant changes in the shadow of the unstoppable rise of AI-enabled business improvements. On the other hand, there is hope that this wave of AI may generate new jobs to compensate for this significant change from labor costs to intelligent and automated business operations on every level. This estimate excludes larger parts of the world, meaning that the global impact potential is much larger, considering the rising dominance of AI globally.

Generative AI has shown its transformative potential, proven by the rapid global adoption of generative AI tools and applications. As those become more widespread, traditional services will experience disruptive examples of AI replacing such services in content production, now served by AI instead of humans. Public investors believe generative AI has the potential to transform various aspects of enterprise and consumer experiences, but there are concerns about the current hype surrounding AI technology and its actual capabilities.

Gary Marcus (a cognitive scientist, author, and professor) is an expert in psychology and neural science who argues that current AI systems lack human brains' intelligence and reasoning abilities. Marcus highlights that although progress toward artificial general intelligence may continue to grow, significant investment alone is unlikely to bring about such a transformation of the human brain, like AI.

This development is unstoppable, forcing enterprises to establish solid digital foundations to embed new disruptive technologies in controlled and sustainable ways. They must likewise prepare for changing consumer behaviors and new services demanded due to the disruptive creation and editing of content with generative AI. Implementing digital composable enterprises is the right approach to addressing this implication of new disruptive technologies, particularly the exponential rise of AI. But there are challenges with why and how enterprises must or should invest in innovative AI capabilities such as generative AI in the complex context of digital transformations. This development challenges enterprises to rethink their readiness to invest in and integrate AI strategically.

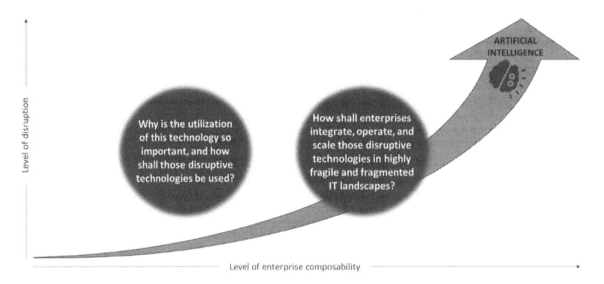

Figure 109 The disruptive rise of AI is bringing new opportunities and challenges to all industries

Enterprises must consider those two fundamental questions:

1. Why is the utilization of this technology so important, and how shall disruptive technologies be used?
2. How shall enterprises integrate, operate, and scale those disruptive technologies in highly fragile and fragmented IT landscapes?

Organizations face significant challenges when they lack AI-ready digital foundational architectures. This impacts their ability to incorporate AI and other disruptive technologies into their often fragile, fragmented IT systems and infrastructures. As powerful AI opportunities continue to emerge, disruptions caused by them will intensify the urgency for organizations to integrate AI from the core of their business. The ability to integrate and scale with supreme interoperability will distinguish enterprises with high composability and digital resilience from those that struggle to expand, maximize, and scale the value of their investments while they instead mainly increase costs and complexity. The prediction of the rise of composable enterprises is closely tied to the insights from this book and the accelerating need for organizations to reassess their digital readiness in light of these transformative challenges.

This is a concluding call for boards and CEOs to consider those revolutionary changes in evolutionary ways combined with the necessity to leverage enterprises in their ability to augment and embed new disruptive technologies seamlessly and unconstrained. They must secure effective monetization of technology and AI investments, realizing each investment's distinct advantages while keeping track of their strategic investment portfolio. Short-term benefits are critical to finance transformations to improve financial and business performance but require balanced strategic investments to secure scalable ROIs with strategic platform investments, founding resilient and scalable technologies.

Enterprises must rethink their current digital transformations to cope with the changes ahead. There is no reason to panic, fear, or ignore disruptive trends, as this book suggests a realistic and comprehensive strategy to prepare for and cope with this change. Instead, enterprises must continually add revolutionary digital technologies and build a foundation to augment and embed new technologies driven by emerging demands. CIOs and architecture teams must secure a layered, open architecture to add and integrate emerging technologies to scale digital investments more effectively without disrupting existing systems and services. The right architectures must handle such complex demands without overhauling their entire technology stack. Instead, they must build on their layered and digital foundational architecture that provides unconstrained scalability, flexibility, cost-efficiency, and unlimited augmentation capacity.

AI will ultimately surpass other major forces enterprises must consider in future disruptive digital scenarios. Although AI will continue to dominate in driving disruptive transformations for years, it is important to recognize that the most disruptive forces will emerge from various factors rather than solely relying on isolated innovative technologies or innovations, such as generative AI.

To create maximum value and optimize total ROIs and TCOs, enterprises should prioritize systemic design and adopt a foundational platform-oriented approach when making investments and undertaking digital composable transformations. They must integrate their legacy and future digital ERP into the new digital architecture to build data-driven businesses from their core. By doing so, they can effectively scale their operations and capitalize on the benefits that arise. Boards, executives, and digital decision-makers must continue to explore future disruptive technologies and prepare for their integration and exploitation by staying informed about those disruptive forces.

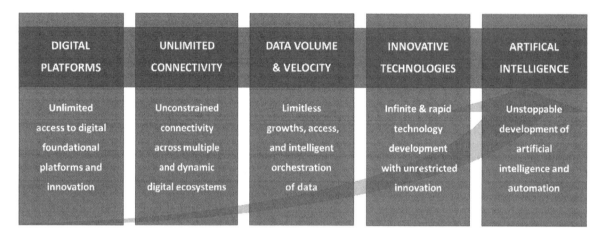

Figure 110 Five disruptive forces that are disrupting traditional leaders and organizations across multiple industries

Those five major forces with individual and combined potential to disrupt traditional enterprises will face high demands on future enterprise digital composability and resilience.

Those five major disruptive and major forces include:

1. **DIGITAL PLATFORMS**

   Situation: Only a few enterprises have implemented strategies and architectures to support digital evolutionary transformations to establish digital composable enterprises.

   Response: To establish enterprise-wide digital foundational platforms is the most effective response to the challenges of enterprises to secure sustainable digital composable transformations.

2. **UNLIMITED CONNECTIVITY**

Situation: Unlimited connectivity in digital transformations is one of the major forces challenging enterprises with ever-increasing digital communication demands and collaboration between individuals, organizations, and digital ecosystems. The increased use of digital devices and the widespread adoption of cloud computing, 5G networks, and the Internet of Things (IoT) are leading to unprecedented interconnectivity, making it easier to share information and work together in real-time.

Response: Enterprises must consider this mega-trend and disruptive force by securing unlimited connectivity with its profound impact on every aspect of automation, enabling new business models, and facilitating the creation and continual change of digital ecosystems. Enterprises must secure unlimited connectivity and data processing capabilities, including the design of digital twins as digital representations of physical objects and systems.

3. **DATA VOLUME & VELOCITY**

Situation: Unlimited data volume and growth with unconstrained access and data orchestration are forcing enterprises to invest in digital analytics platforms while enterprise struggles to manage as data volumes and velocity increase continually. They are confronted with challenges concerning effective data management due to the data volume and velocity increase, dealing with the information overload and data explosion.

Response: Transforming enterprises into data-driven businesses is not an option but a must-do to stay competitive and relevant. Every industry and enterprise will be affected by ever-increasing data volumes and velocity in the future. They must implement scalable processes, technologies, skills, governance, and analytics capabilities to manage unprecedented future data volumes and velocity effectively, controlled, and securely.

4. **INNOVATIVE TECHNOLOGIES**

Situation: Infinite technological advancements with unrestricted processing capabilities will further ingest their innovation and encourage unprecedented advances and levels of radical invention enabled by exponential technologies. With unrealistic attempts to embrace and use these new technologies to transform their core business models, traditional enterprises struggle to generate satisfying investment returns. Quantum computing is a game-changing technology revolutionizing and breaking computational limitations at scale, opening new and highly scalable innovation.

Response: They must invest in the technology infrastructure to assimilate and embrace innovative technologies by embedding their future technology investments at scale by onboarding those technologies in their digital foundational architectures. They must develop data-driven cultures to leverage future technologies to drive innovation effectively. They should partner or establish strategic relations with tech companies to build partnerships and access the latest and most innovative technologies and skills to improve their technology investment decisions. They must relentlessly invest in developing skills and recruiting while retaining business and tech talent.

5. **ARTIFICIAL INTELLIGENCE**

Situation: The extent to which traditional enterprises effectively apply artificial intelligence (AI) and machine learning (ML) varies widely. While some enterprises have significantly progressed in incorporating AI and ML into their operations, others are in the early stages of adoption. One of the biggest challenges for enterprises is understanding why and how to utilize AI and ML by monetizing their investments. The extent to which enterprises effectively apply AI and ML depends on several factors, including their ability and readiness to invest and utilize data effectively and monetize from new insights from recommendations or patterns. While adaptive enterprises are leading the way in adopting AI and ML, others still have long ways to go. The promises of AI must not compromise on its risks, such as ungoverned AI, including the potential for unintended consequences, biased decision-making, and loss of privacy and security.

Response: Develop a clear strategy and define the main objectives with AI and ML investments. Enterprises must carefully consider the need for large-scale data scientist teams and how to utilize data in more intelligent ways with the ability to execute and monetize those investments.

To improve business outcomes, traditional enterprises shall set clear goals and objectives for using AI and ML science. They also require a data-driven culture to leverage decision-making and automation effectively. Collaboration with technology partners or vendors will likely boost outcomes and value. With the latest prediction from Goldman and Sachs, the outlook for disruptions with AI is only getting more certain than ever before. Setting business goals and objectives is important for enterprises to effectively embed AI and ML into their strategies and improve business transformations and outcomes.

Goal setting involves identifying areas where AI can provide instant value, establishing measurable targets for implementation and performance, developing a plan for acquiring the necessary data and technology, and ensuring that the organizations have the required skills and resources to execute their strategies.

It is vital to ensure that the goals and objectives align with the overall business strategies and that there is a clear understanding of the potential benefits, limitations, and risks of accelerating the utilization of AI and ML. While strategies and business priorities inform AI investment decisions and transformations, AI will inform strategies and business models to adjust and constantly evolve.

Secure scalable business value with AI

AI technology has made remarkable progress across various domains, including machine learning, natural language processing, computer vision, and robotics. In some cases, advancements in computing power and quantum computing have driven this growth, large-scale dataset availability, and algorithm development breakthroughs. As the hype around AI generally focuses on innovations and new AI features, this book will focus on the effective adoption and monetization of AI in enterprises. The increased adoption of AI in healthcare, finance, manufacturing, and customer service has propelled its growth, enabling organizations to leverage AI for automation, decision-making, and improved efficiency.

Artificial intelligence (AI) has experienced significant progression and growth in recent years while the global public adaptation rate is accelerating at an unforeseeable, nearly exponential speed, with ChatGPT reporting 200 million users just a few weeks after going public. AI has experienced significant progression and growth in recent years while the global public adaptation rate is accelerating at an unforeseeable, nearly exponential speed. The recent (2023) developments around a much broader utilization and consumption of generative AI are the most remarkable game-changer in democratizing and exponentially orchestrating publicly available AI platforms and services. AI is transforming the landscape of content creation and intelligent analytics on a large scale, simultaneously causing significant disruptions to traditional search engines. Google's revolutionary approach aims to enhance further its already optimized search engine, boosted by the power of AI. The business impact of new applications of AI is causing a great level of indistinct and uncoordinated actions among enterprises, forcing decision-makers to respond to market trends without the ability to consider the strategic value of those investments aligned with the significant impact of AI on future strategies, business models, and organizations. The urgency of early adoption of AI increases the pressure on tech teams to leverage AI at any cost, only not to miss the new tsunami of AI opportunities.

As companies seek to harness the power of AI, they must learn to address key societal concerns. These concerns include ethical considerations, transparency, privacy, preference, and the potential replacement of jobs. Organizations must design and deploy AI systems responsibly, considering these concerns to mitigate any negative impacts on individuals, society, and the workforce. Ethical frameworks, guidelines, and regulations govern AI usage, emphasizing values and governing effective principles such as fairness, accountability, transparency, and privacy. Organizations must navigate these concerns effectively to gain or not lose public trust, avoid legal issues, and ensure the responsible and beneficial deployment of AI use cases. Organizations must continually reinforce their existing strategies and business priorities by ensuring the reasons for adopting AI and defining success align with their overall strategic goals. At the same time, new AI scenarios and predictions must inform strategies about new opportunities and business model innovation. The business value of AI is immense, as proven and future business cases promise substantial business improvements across various industries. Examples of business value enabled or improved through AI does include advantages such as:

- **General business**: Serve customers better, provide chatbots for automated customer service, reduce repetitive tasks, make data-driven decisions, identify business opportunities, optimize processes and assets, cost reduction and resource optimization, improve and automate product design, marketing, and automated content creation.

- **Business analytics**: Perform automated business analytics, utilize Graph databases for complex data and business logic analysis, provide accurate predictions and recommendations, empower decision-makers, automate repetitive tasks (beyond traditional automation), automate pricing and campaign management, innovate product design, replace traditional business analysis from reactive to predictive and prescriptive actions and more.

- **Manufacturing**: Revolutionize and enable Industry 4.0 through supply chain optimization, production automation, automated processes, and decision making, real-time monitoring and optimizations, increased utilization of multitasking robots in warehouses and factories, increase safety and compliance, with optimized prediction and prescription to raw materials and components needed in automated production lines.

- **Transportation**: Reduce carbon dioxide emissions, optimize fleet planning and utilization, optimize network and capacity planning, optimization of tour planning, predictive planning and execution, reduce incidents, predictive maintenance, traffic management, delay prediction, and safer transportation.

- **Finance and insurance**: Advance data analysis, risk assessment, automation, personalized customer experiences, fraud detection, assessing creditworthiness, evaluating loan risks, and predict market fluctuations, regulatory compliance, real-time customer support, enhanced investment strategies, and algorithmic trading.

- **Entertainment and media**: Target advertising, content recommendation, content optimization, deep fake and automated languages and mimics of actors, deep fake age, creation, fraud detection, script creation, automated journalism, automated routine tasks, and improved retention rates. In the future, AI will demonstrate its ability to generate and recreate digital content to replace human creativity and originality in content production.

- **Software coding and IT**: Increase code generation and testing, automation of digitalized processes, code optimization, and, finally, replace manual coding for more use cases.

- **Legal and law**: Automate legal processes, save time, improve client service, automate contract analysis, enable computer vision for document classification, and automate information interpretation.

- **Healthcare**: Improving patient outcomes, reducing costs, faster, more accurate medical diagnoses, and improving diagnosis and high precision data-driven but individualized treatments and prescriptions.

- **Security**: Threat detection and prevention, malware detection, real-time incident response, enhanced authentication and access control, insider threat detection, vulnerability assessment, patch management, removing malicious code, decrypting, and encrypting content autonomously.

Enterprises utilize AI differently across industries, while generic AI improvements demonstrate key enhancements and strong business cases on particular use cases. The utilization of AI across industries is progressing, while most enterprises may lack the ability to scale, as most AI implementations suffer from fragmentation, complex one-time integrations, complex data processing, and insufficient general management.

Scale AI in composable enterprises

As the development and utilization of AI continue to accelerate with popular and publicly accessible use cases and applications (such as ChatGPT and similar AI platforms), AI has made a quantum leap from conceptual use cases and integrated product-driven AI (such as Siri and similar tools), to applied mainstream innovation, reaching out to millions of users and early adopters. In contrast, enterprises still make little progress or advancements in applying use cases generated from generative AI platforms.

New technologies and AI-enabled capabilities come with opportunities and risks that require careful consideration and mitigation in the future. Uncontrolled deployment of generative AI can risks, forcing enterprises to adopt more resilient and responsive strategies for effective response and adaptation. Embracing AI is not a matter of right or wrong; it involves more than just generative AI applications and encompasses various formats, from small use cases to large-scale investments. To lead effectively, enterprises should categorize their AI initiatives across core domains, enabling them to make distinct and differentiated decisions regarding their often fragmented AI investments.

These four domains are the cornerstones of applied AI and can help better understand the criteria to select and invest effectively. While it may seem simpler to make investments in isolation, there is a bigger risk of neglecting the enterprise architectural design, data modeling, data orchestration, data management, digital foundational technologies, delivery models, security, privacy, compliance, and other critical domains of digital foundational business architecture. This strongly emphasizes the need for enterprise composability to scale AI's core and different domains by utilizing the enterprise's foundational digital architecture and platforms. To understand the role and needs of those most important business domains when applying AI, CXOs and digital leaders must differentiate those domains within the design of their evolving digital composable enterprises.

Those four main domains involve:

1. **AI developed and deployed internally** (such as algorithmic exploration and modeling)
   This domain includes developing and deploying AI solutions within an organization and includes algorithmic exploration and modeling, where the organization builds AI models and applications tailored to its specific needs.

2. **AI utilized as a platform capability** (such as generative AI)

    This domain includes the utilization of AI as a foundational capability or platform that enables the development of less complex AI applications. Generative AI (such as ChatGPT) can automate content production or analytics tasks and generate intelligent outputs.

3. **AI as pre-built and ready-to-adopt** (industrialized AI models or tools, such as DataRobot)

    This domain encompasses pre-built and ready-to-adopt AI models or tools for individual use case development. This domain includes industrialized AI models, solutions, or tools/platforms like DataRobot, which provide less advanced pre-built AI capabilities replacing the need for in-house labor-intensive data scientists and developers, accelerating the adaption of less advanced and not fully custom-made models.

4. **AI integrated into third-vendor products** (such as pricing engines)

    This domain includes black-box AI integrated into products or services offered by third-party vendors. Examples are AI-powered pricing engines incorporated into products to provide dynamic and optimized pricing strategies.

Those four domains of AI utilization require responsive, agile, and interoperable enterprise technology adaptive frameworks, architectures, and integration capabilities. Individually building those capabilities may become irresponsible, uncertain, cost-intensive, and unscalable while driving digital complexity and redundant digital investments. Their impact on composability and digital resilience varies, while the risk of fragmented investments, integrations, and technologies, may cause new significant long-term problems and risks.

To ensure effective collaboration and cultural adoption, enterprises must actively secure consistent architectural design for future AI capabilities across the four domains of AI in practice. Digital composable enterprises provide the entire spectrum of architectural principles, design, and platforms and facilitate cultural and collaborative synchronization. This approach enables enterprise-wide deployment and adoption of AI, fostering seamless integration of AI capabilities throughout the organization.

Composable enterprises utilize and integrate AI investments differently, as they avoid complexity, reduce costs, reuse existing technologies, augment new capabilities, reuse complementary investments (such as graph databases from Neo4J), and make required adjustments to their existing digital foundational platforms rather than building a separate data lake specifically for a new AI capability.

Instead, digital composable enterprises augment AI on their platforms and add selective technologies to solve a particularly new problem. In contrast, those technologies have a greater purpose to be reused with future projects to maximize investments and make them reusable and scalable. Digital foundational platforms provide sophisticated capabilities to comprehend the value of AI investments with rapid realization and deployment in production. They help to keep costs down, make better-informed technology decisions, minimize complexity by avoiding designing single-purpose solutions, automate operations (ideally in the cloud), and secure high-performing applications of AI.

The art of adoption of new groundbreaking and disruptive AI capabilities also shifts the power back to decision-makers when making buy or build decisions. More controlled conditions increase the chances of more realistic business cases, less focus on technologies, and a greater focus on the realization and scalability of business value. As data is another critical element, analytics platform architectures will ensure that data is reusable, consistent across many use cases, and accessible on demand.

The level of autonomy will likewise reduce the bias of introducing new individual solutions within the tech organizations, as existing roles, skills, processes, tools, and operations already exist or enhances. It is easier to make distinct and isolated changes in the existing composable framework instead of reinventing new capabilities when implementing new disruptive technologies, and composable enterprises will provide a more advanced portfolio and spectrum of digital composability over time.

While developing digital foundational platforms, organizations must address the need to evolve the culture, shift from risk-averse to more risk-tolerance leadership and oversee and advance enterprise governance and strategies. Developing new skills is essential, and technology-savvy business executives and leaders must grow with those new capabilities while developing product management organizations over time. This is critical to absorb technologies into the organization and ensure proper ownership by evolving product ownership with mature enough business leaders.

Those proposed four main domains of applied AI require different approaches, while most of their needs can be satisfied by simply deploying existing frameworks, architectures, and overall capabilities of digital composable enterprises. Besides those four main domains, there are additional variations of AI, while those four provide sufficient insight into the prospects of massive enterprise-wide AI investments. Concentrating on those four main domains will provide effective guidance and greater clarity about why and how AI requires digital augmentation capabilities

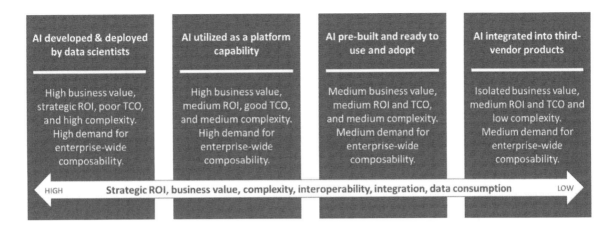

Figure 111 The four main domains of applied enterprise AI

Those four domains have different impacts on enterprises when making investments in AI. The most complex approach is the long-term strategic investment into AI developed and deployed by data scientists within the enterprise. Investments developed & deployed by data scientists promise long-term and powerful competitive advantages and unique business innovation and value once those investments generate effective monetization.

As complexity is high, ROIs of more strategic character, and TCO significantly higher than other AI domains, this option is not always the first and natural choice for organizations. Instead, other options may satisfy getting along with AI, address urgent needs to get started, and generate value with AI investment while the organization is learning and adapting. There is no exclusivity or need to select one of those four domains. At the same time, uncontrolled investments may cause additional complexity, a higher risk for failure, and greater difficulties integrating and operating various and fragmented use cases across those domains.

Specialized consulting firms help to develop or adjust predefined models for focused and rapid development and deployment while simultaneously creating greater and long-term dependencies with no or little insights and learning.

OVERVIEW OF THE FOUR MAJOR DOMAINS OF AI ENTERPRISE PROFICIENCIES

DOMAINS	OVERVIEW	EXAMPLES
AI developed and deployed by data scientists	▪ Large and long-term investments into own resources and tools with potential for powerful applications	▪ Inhouse development teams with data scientists and tools (such as open source, analytics, data lake, …) with selective tools from various vendors
AI utilized as a platform capability	▪ Foundational strategic investments into architecture with lower costs but less powerful application	▪ Microsoft generative AI integrated AI across various products/platforms such as Azure, Power, Dynamics, 365 and other vendors
AI pre-built and ready to use and adopt	▪ Ready to use AI models to ease adoption and rapid utilization of AI capabilities	▪ DataRobot, Dataiku.com, Microsoft Azure, and other vendors
AI integrated into third-vendor products	▪ Ready to use fragmented AI capabilities but unscalable investments with problem-focused	▪ OutSystems lowcode platform with integrated AI for high-performance software development ▪ Wiser retail price optimization and other vendors

Figure 112 Overview of the four major domains of AI enterprise proficiencies

Understanding the overall impact on traditional and digital organizations of those domains is important to building digital composable enterprises and securing scalable and fully integrated AI investments.

In all four domains, composable enterprises are foundational and necessary for long-term success and effective investments in business transformation enabled by AI, while their impact and level of necessity vary between high and medium.

Digital composable enterprises will gain greater outcomes, with unmatched opportunities for faster, better, more effective, and valuable AI investments, while each domain requires a different approach to successful deployment. Decision-makers must understand and consider the implications and lessons learned to augment new AI capabilities by utilizing ready-to-scale digital foundational architecture and its systemic approach to systemic AI augmentation.

"Effectively implementing AI investment strategies poses significant challenges, and the long-term success of AI investment strategies will primarily rely on the ability of enterprises to augment, scale, and monetize their total investments."

Ingo Paas

KEY CAPABILITIES OF AI DOMAINS IN DIGITAL COMPOSABLE ENTERPRISES	
DOMAINS	**EXAMPLES OF KEY CAPABILITIES**
AI developed and deployed by data scientists	▪ Predictive analytics to analyze historical and other data to predict future outcomes ▪ Optimize complex systems and processes with a high grade of uniqueness to gain competitive advantages ▪ Develop complex anomaly detection to identify unusual patterns or outliers in datasets ▪ Solve individual problems of complex data and models and turn those into actionable decisions ▪ Invest in data scientists etc to engage in collaborative innovation and develop personalized applications
AI utilized as a platform capability	▪ Produce incremental innovation and inventive outputs with ready-to-use integrated AI (hyperscaler platforms) ▪ Focus on systems to engage in human-like conversations to enable data-driven intelligent business ▪ Train AI agents to learn through trial and error and make decisions in dynamic environments ▪ Embed intelligent collaborative analytics with predefined AI features to foster incremental innovation and culture
AI pre-built and ready to use and adopt	▪ Use pre-built ready-to-use platforms and models to adapt AI without the need to develop and deploy in-house ▪ Utilize pre-built industry-specific models and use case-specific AI for fast deployment ▪ Embrace basic innovation capabilities with non-competitive but short ROI promising deployment ▪ Increase speed with limited customization of AI models utilizing underlying platforms (such as DataRobot)
AI integrated into third-vendor products	▪ Use integrated AI capabilities in SaaS applications and platforms to focus on end-to-end problem solving ▪ Enable pre-build industry-specific embedded AI to develop complex processes, such as intelligent pricing ▪ Focus on process implementation and optimization capabilities, embedded as key features into vendor products that never need to or can be touched/changed/modified

Figure 113 Key capabilities of AI domains in digital composable enterprises

The key capabilities of enterprise AI capabilities must guide decision-makers and investment strategies. Successfully applying and growing those domains of applied AI in enterprises requires IT and tech teams to build individual capabilities, satisfying the enormous need for scalable and innovative foundational AI capabilities. Those foundational AI capabilities include critical capabilities such as:

Data Management and integration

▪ Drive complexity with complex integrations from various data sources,

▪ Secure consistency of and access to data through data pipelines in data-intensive real-time applications,

▪ Distribute data distributed across multiple systems and formats, making it challenging to harmonize and aggregate, especially for complex AI purposes.

Scalability and performance of AI algorithms and models

▪ Provide computational resources,

▪ Manage large datasets or complex deep learning architectures,

▪ Scale AI architectures to control and process high volumes of data and changing user demands,

▪ Design reusable, scalable, and flexible high-performance computing infrastructure,

▪ Optimize algorithms to achieve scalability and responsiveness.

Infrastructure and technology stacks

- Build robust, scalable infrastructure for effective operations,
- Ensure that the technology stack is capable of scaling and optimizing,
- Choose the right infrastructure (as a code), software frameworks, libraries, and deployment tools,
- Avoid the design of one-time solutions and fragmentation of AI investments,
- Integrate with existing systems, compatibility issues,
- Reduce the complexity of the technology stack through applied platform strategies,
- Augment and scale new technologies or concepts, such as demanding enterprise AI capabilities.

Deployment of AI models

- Standardize and reuse integration capabilities and APIs,
- Orchestrate AI models with seamless integration with other applications, databases, and APIs,
- Maintain reliability, security, and performance,
- Secure real-time inference, model versioning, and scalability of model serving systems.

Management of sensitive and valuable data

- Make security and privacy crucial for various enterprise-wide data sources with high demand on data confidentiality, integrity, and availability,
- Protect AI capabilities against attacks or data breaches with robust security measures and policies,
- Architect and deploy standardized data models and information modeling,
- Secure compliance with data protection regulations and ethical considerations,
- Implement effective and balanced information governance with dedicated business ownership,
- Implement data management through collaborative information ownership within the line organization.

AI operating models (often operate as black boxes)

- Challenge the reasoning behind modeling of predictions or decisions,
- Ensure transparency and knowledge about applied AI models, not only in regulated industries or when ethical considerations are involved,
- Develop interpretable AI models or integrate interpretability techniques with enterprise-wide policies owned and anchored within the business.

Evolving culture and governance requires adopting changes motivated by new AI applications, addressing resistance to change, and ensuring cross-functional collaboration. Aligning AI initiatives with business goals drives more coordinated organizational change to absorb, embed, and scale AI.

Fostering a climate of collaborative AI innovation requires discipline and cooperation between different disciplines. Keeping the balance between too harsh interpretations of external rules and regulations can be equally devastating as the ignorance of those requirements. As risk-averse and risk-tolerance components are most likely causing difficulties in agreeing on a balanced approach to keep risks under control while maximizing business opportunities, it is most likely one of the greatest challenges for CEOs in judging the most effective approaches and systems of compliance. In addition, business ownership is critical to monetizing AI investments to ensure that data, business logic, and the outcome of algorithmic processing will not harm but enrich the business and drive business value.

KEY CAPABILITIES OF THOSE FOUR MAJOR AI DOMAINS IN PRACTICE

DOMAINS	EXAMPLES OF KEY CAPABILITIES IN PRACTICE
AI developed and deployed by data scientists	▪ Predictive analytics to analyze historical and other data to predict future outcomes ▪ Optimize complex systems and processes with a high grade of uniqueness to gain competitive advantages ▪ Develop complex anomaly detection to identify unusual patterns or outliers in datasets ▪ Solve individual problems of complex data and models and turn those into actionable decisions ▪ Invest in data scientists etc to engage in collaborative innovation and develop personalized applications
AI utilized as a platform capability	▪ Produce incremental innovation and inventive outputs with ready-to-use integrated AI (hyperscaler platforms) ▪ Focus on systems to engage in human-like conversations to enable data-driven intelligent business ▪ Train AI agents to learn through trial and error and make decisions in dynamic environments ▪ Embed intelligent collaborative analytics with predefined AI features to foster incremental innovation and culture
AI pre-built and ready to use and adopt	▪ Use pre-built ready-to-use platforms and models to adapt AI without the need to develop and deploy in-house ▪ Utilize pre-built industry-specific models and use case-specific AI for fast deployment ▪ Embrace basic innovation capabilities with non-competitive but short ROI promising deployment ▪ Increase speed with limited customization of AI models utilizing underlying platforms (such as DataRobot)
AI integrated into third-vendor products	▪ Use integrated AI capabilities in SaaS applications and platforms to focus on end-to-end problem solving ▪ Enable pre-build industry-specific embedded AI to develop complex processes, such as intelligent pricing ▪ Focus on process implementation and optimization capabilities, embedded as key features into vendor products that never need to or can be touched/changed/modified

Figure 114 Key capabilities of those four core domains in practice

The difficulties of establishing AI in enterprises vary depending on the choices and strategies concerning AI investments. As enterprises may choose different approaches to secure benefits with AI, they must consider the impact on their digital composable transformation to maximize returns.

The key differentiators in a balanced approach may include and consider:

- Short ROI versus scalable ROI,

- High TCO versus lower TCO and lower autonomy,

- Ability to achieve optimized interoperability,

- Integration and data management,

- Long-term scalability strategic ROI,

- Required level of digital resilience,

- Digital interoperability, reusability, scalability, and more.

The insight and understanding of those differentiators shall secure optimized value creation for enterprises. Important factors are the state of enterprise composability, the level of digital resilience, the ability to innovate from the core of the business, and the urgency and value generation (short versus long-term).

Without digital foundational platforms, the augmentation of the AI core domains drives complexity and costs while reducing AI investments' strategic value and scalability. The criticality of those platforms requires enterprise-wide digital composability to implement and scale AI from the core of the business, not the other way around.

CRITICALITY OF DIGITAL FOUNDATIONAL PLATFORMS ON EFFECTIVE AUGMENTATION OF AI CORE DOMAINS					
DOMAINS OF AI	INTEGRATION	ANALYTICS	LOWCODE	DIGITAL ERP	CRITICALITY TO SCALE AI
AI developed and deployed by data scientists	High demand	High demand	Medium demand	Medium demand	High criticality of digital foundational platforms to scale AI
AI utilized as a platform capability	High demand	High demand	Low demand	High demand	High criticality of digital foundational platforms to scale AI
AI pre-built and ready to use and adopt	Medium demand	Medium demand	Low demand	Medium demand	Medium criticality of digital foundational platforms to scale AI
AI integrated into third-vendor products	High demand	Low demand	Low demand	Medium demand	Medium criticality of digital foundational platforms to scale AI

Figure 115 Criticality of digital foundational platforms on effective augmentation of AI core domains

The criticality of digital foundational platforms on the effective augmentation of AI core domains is not exclusively about the AI capability to solve particular problems but rather about the essential need of enterprises to utilize their digital foundational platforms to support any AI integration from the core effectively. Instead of reinventing and rebuilding new integration capabilities and applications and developing data models, enterprises must prepare their operations for relentless AI augmentation.

The three major problems of AI augmentation include data compatibility and integration, scalability and performance, and real-time data processing.

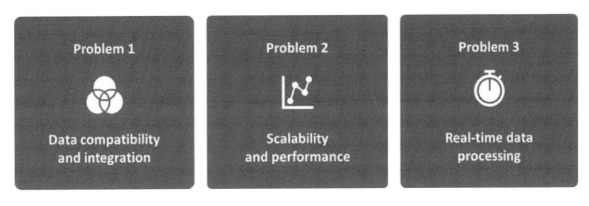

Figure 116 The three major problems of AI augmentation

1. **Data compatibility and integration**: Integrating and harmonizing data from different systems, databases, or file formats into AI applications is a key challenge. Incompatibilities in data structures, naming conventions, or data representations can hinder the seamless integration of data into AI systems. Utilizing digital foundational data integration pipelines and adopting standardized data formats or protocols is critical to effective augmentation.

2. **Scalability and performance**: AI applications require automated management of massive datasets, often demanding high-end computational resources and infrastructures. To effectively handle larger amounts of data without compromising performance, scaling AI systems imposes the utilization of flexible hardware infrastructure (ideally as-a-code), distributed computing frameworks, and optimization techniques. These capabilities are crucial for minimizing processing time and optimizing resource utilization in transactional and data-intensive processing.

3. **Real-time data processing**: AI applications with real-time decision-making or monitoring (such as predictive maintenance) require continuous and instant access to data, while real-time implies technological challenges compared to normal batch processing. Real-time applications of AI require technologies like stream processing, event-driven architectures, and low-latency data ingestion mechanisms, ideally provided as ready for scale.

Addressing these technology and integration problems is one of the key advantages of digital composable enterprises to leverage scalable and performant computing infrastructure and implement real-time data processing solutions if needed. Digital composable enterprises create optimized conditions to implement core AI domains profoundly and effectively.

Adopting this transformative mindset and harnessing AI's tactical and strategic potential is crucial to effectively building and operating AI solutions. The importance of skills varies depending on how AI is applied and which of the discussed core domains of AI are involved. Executives and digital leaders must recognize that AI must not become the sole focus of organizations but rather be utilized as a strategic and crucial area of business innovation that requires effective strategies to ensure robust returns on investment (ROIs) and effective total cost of ownership (TCOs). AI exerts a powerful and dominant influence on all industries. However, it is important to recognize that AI alone is not the sole solution for enterprise evolution and innovation.

"To fully leverage AI's strategic potential, it is crucial to acknowledge its complexity and important but not absolute role. Digital composable enterprises must adopt a resilient approach to integrate disruptive technologies at the core of their business, maximize their investment's value, and evolve innovation holistically."

Ingo Paas

Considerations for successful implementation include establishing teams, fostering collaboration between data scientists and domain experts, and promoting a culture of continuous learning. Highly skilled teams with AI expertise are critical but not guaranteeing business success. Addressing these challenges requires careful planning and effective collaboration between data, development, tech, and business teams, including a holistic approach to digital foundational architectural design.

Successful AI strategies and deployments require enterprise-wide understanding and separation of AI domains seamlessly supported by and incorporated into the foundational architecture of digital composable enterprises. AI investments with new technology and integration requirements must benefit from the augmentation of the existing digital foundational architecture to avoid fragmented design and utilization of special-purpose and ineffective technologies.

This is where digital resilience becomes important, differentiating digital composable enterprises from digital enterprises that master augmentation, integration, and scalability of their AI investments to overcome barriers to effective monetization.

Overcome barriers to AI monetization

AI is a disruptive and investment-intensive game changer, causing difficulties for boards and CxOs on where to start and how to embed AI into their business and investment strategies effectively. This must not discourage organizations from investing in AI, even though the anticipated outcomes and actual effects of these AI investments may differ greatly regarding perceived impact, ROIs (Return on Investments) and TCOs (Total Cost of Ownership).

The often disappointing reality is not just about insufficient ROIs and TCOs, as fragmented implementations and operations drive unexpected complexity and costs. In addition, AI projects often do not deliver on the promises to scale benefits to enhance the initial investments beyond initial investments. Irrationally investing in major disruptive AI projects ending up in fragmented and complex technology disorder must be avoided.

AI comes with known and new risks, forcing cross-functional leadership teams to establish ethical principles and guidelines for generative AI use and thoroughly assess risks for each use case. Implementing risk-management practices, and staying informed about generative AI regulations, helps organizations manage and comply with evolving regulatory environments and risks effectively. Consequently, organizations must prioritize non-technical requirements to develop and deploy ethically aligned AI systems to guarantee value from responsible AI growth.

This includes new and developing practices, such as;

- Establish robust data governance practices to protect privacy and mitigate risks,
- Develop AI models capable of providing explanations for their decisions,
- Promote collaboration between humans and AI systems,
- Stay updated with evolving regulations and standards related to AI usage,
- Secure automated processes to measure and control data-intensive processes.

Getting busy with those essential questions and important principles is not the only burden to overcoming initial barriers with AI and generating business value in scalable and resilient ways.

AI is a substantial challenge for traditional and digital enterprises to find the right strategies to utilize the opportunities and strengths of AI integrated with their business strategies and culture. Enterprises must understand those barriers to secure successful AI investments and innovation from the core.

The majority of enterprises face challenges in finding effective and consistent responses to the following concerns:

- The difficulties in defining the strategic purpose, impact, and investments strategies,
- The high complexity and fragmented development of AI applications,
- The inability to effectively augment new AI applications from the core of the business,
- The necessity to invest in digital foundational technologies, architectures, and skills,
- The inability to manage data quality, access, availability, velocity, volumes, and more,
- The missing organizational readiness and maturity to adapt to changes driven by AI,
- The inability of organizations to scale AI investments in digitally resilient architectures.

Not having sufficient responses to those key challenges will increase the risk of failure of AI investments, as poor outcomes of deficient implementations decrease the enterprise's ability to monetize its investments. Compared with non-composable enterprises, digital composable enterprises provide comprehensive and adaptive pre-conditions for successful AI adoption, scalability, and monetization. They can seamlessly integrate and embed AI by viewing it as a complementary and enhancing digital feature rather than treating it as the sole priority in digital enterprise transformation.

Master digital disruptive forces

Enterprises must explore new ways to effectively respond to transformational forces, including digital platforms, unlimited connectivity, data volumes and velocity, innovative technologies, and the accelerating growth of AI. To effectively respond to those challenges is a significant change in strategic thinking and digital transformation that organizations must undertake to augment AI and other game-changing technologies from the core of their businesses. This augmentation goes beyond digital foundational technologies and does require holistic responses with balanced investments, the attraction of technology-savvy leaders, cultural adaptation, and the rise of data-driven enterprises.

The future of organizations is dependent on their ability to invest in AI, whit the strategic business value of depends heavily on the ability to scale those investments, and AI has turned into a disruptive game changer. AI can only deliver on its promises if it naturally evolves with the enterprise. Implicit technological innovation is not following a single formula or activity but is a holistic approach embedded into the evolutionary thinking and realization of digital composable transformations. Creating a foundation for seamless and effective integration of future technologies at scale is the core advantage of digital composable transformations to avoid investments into fragmented and non-scalable breakthrough technologies. Even the most revolutionary technologies cannot deliver expected returns and fulfill their promises of business cases if the enterprise cannot assimilate and integrate them effectively and at scale at acceptable costs and guaranteed positive returns.

Evolutionary and systemic approaches can better facilitate incoherent dynamics of future breakthrough innovations, leveraging foundational capabilities to contribute to the four objectives of digital composable enterprises effectively. The earlier discussed four objectives summarize how enterprises must position AI correctly in their strategic and tactical investment strategies and invest in evolving digital composable enterprises.

Enterprises that successfully embrace and accomplish the four strategic objectives of composable enterprises can expect to experience the highest Return on Investment (ROI) and most effective Total Cost of Ownership (TCO). By forming collaborative organizations to evolve like digitally developing organisms, they can enhance and expand their investments in technology and data. This advantage ensures they will gain a significant competitive edge, allowing them to lead or dominate in their markets and capitalize on their enduring ability to innovate at scale.

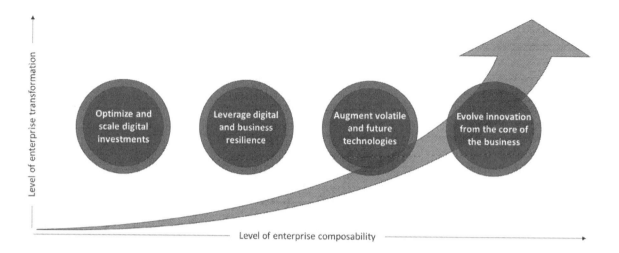

Figure 117 The four strategic objectives of composable enterprises

Balancing those four strategic objectives is fundamental for establishing digital composable enterprises. These objectives serve as the foundation and hold equal importance, as their combined influence stems from the core, enabling the evolution of composable organizations. They affirm the alignment of digital composability with the enterprise's strategic direction and emphasize learning and advancements. When applied wisely, these objectives provide clear direction on achieving enterprise-wide interoperability by seamlessly balancing the competing purposes of exploitation and exploration.

They contribute to the successful rise of digitally resilient enterprises by reinforcing strategic investments and making more balanced and better-informed technology choices while strengthening the overall vision and direction.

In the case of digital composability, ambidexterity refers to the organization's capacity to simultaneously pursue and excel at two seemingly conflicting strategies or approaches. The significance of adopting this suggested approach and theory of ambidexterity lies in the ability to seamlessly integrate and collaborate legacy and digital technologies and achieve relentless interoperability in unprecedented ways.

Embracing this thinking in practice enables organizations to effectively leverage the power of incremental innovation, maximizing their potential for growth and success. As accentuated throughout this book, the ability and continual focus to innovate from the core of the business is not a question of choice but a necessity.

THE FOUR OBJECTIVES OF DIGITAL ENTERPRISE COMPOSABILITY	
OBJECTIVES	**KEY MEASURES OF DIGITAL COMPOSABLE READINESS**
To optimize and scale digital investments	▪ Tactical and strategic digital investment strategies are composed ▪ Digital platforms and data are utilized and scaled for business success
To leverage digital and business resilience	▪ Critical business capabilities are modularized and digitized from the core ▪ New and changing business demands are managed rapidly and consistently
To augment volatile and future technologies	▪ Digital disruptive and critical technologies are embedded and integrated ▪ Technology investments are interoperable, scalable, and evolve over time
To evolve innovation from the core of the business	▪ Innovation is democratized and embedded into the organization's culture ▪ Innovation is empowered and scaled from the core of the business

Figure 118 The four strategic objectives of composable enterprises

CEOs, CxOs, tech leaders, and business leaders must fundamentally rethink their roles and skills and educate themselves about rising technologies' opportunities, the cloud's purpose, and data. They must consider risks but rather explore the future risks of not investing in digital composability before drawing their conclusions solely on general and traditional risk assumptions.

"Mastering those disruptive forces and challenges with AI is conceivable when organizations understand their digital transformation as continued evolution where people, intelligence, technologies, and data evolve into collaborative, learning, and self-regulated organisms."

Ingo Paas

One of the key challenges enterprises need to overcome is the risk of not fully understanding the potential of disruptive technologies to drive innovation and their central role in shaping future business strategies.

"Enterprises that successfully embrace and accomplish the four strategic objectives of composable enterprises can expect to experience the highest Return on Investment (ROI) and most effective Total Cost of Ownership (TCO). By forming collaborative organizations to evolve like digitally developing organisms, they can enhance and expand their investments in technology and data. This advantage ensures they gain a significant competitive edge, allowing them to lead or dominate in their markets and capitalize on their enduring ability to innovate at scale."

Ingo Paas

Boards and CEOs must reconsider their perception and understanding of the true purpose of digital transformations, digitalizing the as/is, while they must ensure digital enterprise resilience to augment future disruptive technologies effectively. At the same time, they must maximize the business value of their investments in their current state of digital transformations.

Transformational recommendations to decision-makers

Digital composable enterprises are not only a shared responsibility, where distinct leaders have distinct responsibilities, as they most likely require new thinking and adjustments in traditional and digital organizations, including their culture, leadership, and governance. The Board of Directors, the CEOs, The CxOs, and the Business Executives must considerably change their approaches to develop digital composable businesses to scale their enterprises further collaboratively.

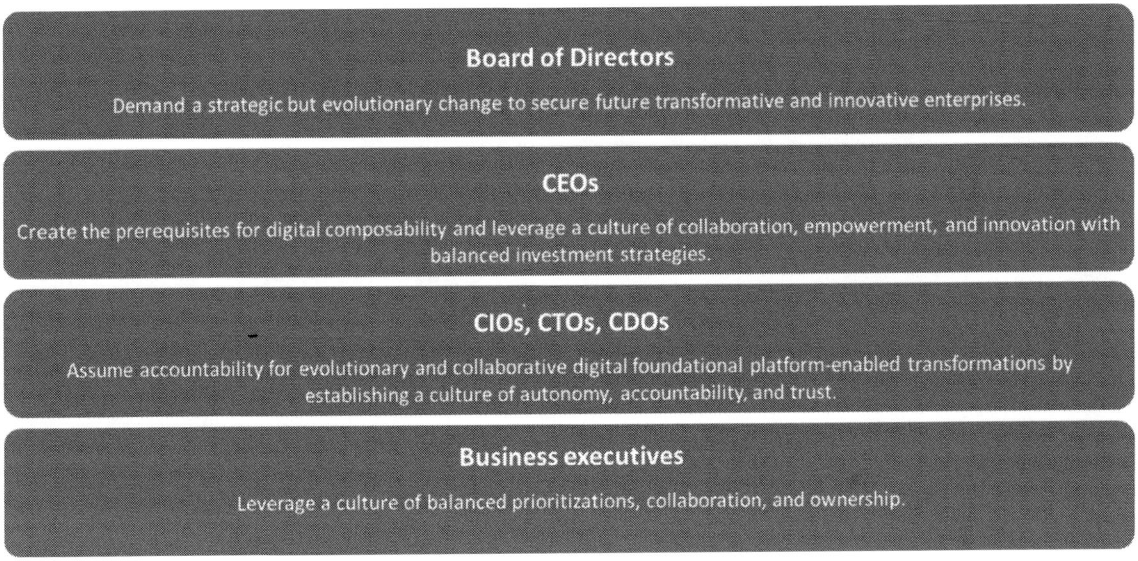

Board of Directors

Demand a strategic but evolutionary change to secure future transformative and innovative enterprises.

CEOs

Create the prerequisites for digital composability and leverage a culture of collaboration, empowerment, and innovation with balanced investment strategies.

CIOs, CTOs, CDOs

Assume accountability for evolutionary and collaborative digital foundational platform-enabled transformations by establishing a culture of autonomy, accountability, and trust.

Business executives

Leverage a culture of balanced prioritizations, collaboration, and ownership.

Figure 119 The roles and core responsibilities to ensure the effective execution of digital composable transformations

"Implementing digital composable enterprises is a collaborative approach involving every stakeholder inside and outside the enterprises. Only those who understand their transformations as the new normal and realize those changes from the core of their business will succeed. Culture is essential to everything, as a culture will eat strategies and technologies for breakfast."

Ingo Paas

Organizations must migrate into digital organisms, overcoming traditional management practices and investment strategies. CxOs and decision-makers will find explicit recommendations on the following pages.

Board of Directors

Recommendation: demand a strategic but evolutionary change to secure future transformative and innovative enterprises.

- Demand innovation and digitalization from the core of the business,
- Demand technology and data-inspired strategies,
- Demand digital resilience and composability,
- Demand data-driven transformations,
- Demand enterprise-wide competence development strategies,
- Demand balanced strategic & tactical investment strategies,
- Set goals that encourage strategic transformations, such as composability,
- Demand a shift toward a risk-tolerance culture,
- Demand incremental approaches rather than large-scale programs (if possible),
- Provide necessary resources and funding.

Boards of Directors must demand digital evolutionary transformations by financing interoperable enterprise-wide foundational technologies, supporting business transformations, promoting collaboration, and securing balanced investments into digital transformations from the core of the business. They must set the overall framework for the enterprise to navigate inside without defining the framework. They must demand the organizational prerequisites to successfully align purpose, mission, vision, and strategy with the ultimate goal of digital composable enterprises.

CEOs

Recommendation: create the prerequisites for digital composability and leverage a culture of collaboration, empowerment, and innovation with balanced investment strategies.

- Promote a culture of continual innovation from the core of the business,
- Encourage a risk-tolerance culture,
- Secure preconditions to innovate and digitalize from the core of the business,
- Encourage decentralized decision-making and empowerment,
- Minimize bureaucracy and adjust governance frameworks,
- Oversee balanced tactical and strategic investments,
- Follow up on investment strategies and their effectiveness.

CEOs must impact digital evolutionary transformations by financing interoperable enterprise-wide foundational technologies, supporting business and digital transformations, promoting collaboration, and securing balanced investments into digital transformations from the core of the business. By doing so, they can create the organizational prerequisites to successfully navigate the challenges and opportunities toward the ultimate goal of digital composable enterprises by optimizing resources and investments with business outcomes.

CIOs, CTOs, CDOs

Recommendation: assume accountability for evolutionary and collaborative digital foundational platform-enabled transformations by establishing a culture of autonomy, accountability, and trust.

- Become a technology-driven business leader,
- Drive business strategies with tech and platforms from the core,
- Make strategic tech and platform decisions even in the absence of business demand,
- Lead and continually evolve the technology transformation,
- Select and implement digital composable architectures and technologies,
- Leverage innovation and digitalization from the core of the business,
- Foster a culture of autonomy, accountability, and trust,
- Engage in the incremental and experimental development of everything,
- Implement digitally packaged business capabilities,
- Make systemic changes rather than planning every detail,
- Foster a culture of learning and knowledge to attract and develop talents,
- Consider interoperability in every decision and technology,
- Secure foundational, interoperable, and sustainable digital transformations,
- Establish product and value-driven organizations.

CIOs, CTOs, and CDOs must impact digital evolutionary transformations by promoting and implementing interoperable enterprise-wide foundational technologies, advocating and leading digital transformations, enabling collaboration, and protecting balanced investments into digital transformations from the core of the business. By doing so, they must ensure that organizations successfully navigate in systemic, incremental, and sustainable ways toward the ultimate goal of digital composable enterprises.

Business executives

Recommendation: leverage a balanced prioritizations, collaboration, and ownership culture and take responsibility to develop and implement competence and skill strategies.

- Realize and further scale promises and return on investments,
- Become tech-savvy leaders utilizing technologies in systemic ways,
- Develop and implement competence and skill strategies,
- Drive balanced ROI-inspired investments,
- Assume accountability for composability and interoperability, including tactical and strategic investments,
- Implement knowledge strategies to attract and develop new tech and data-inspired roles,
- Design packaged business capabilities,
- Assume distinct ownership for digital products, data, and information models,
- Avoid solving isolated business problems and assume more holistic thinking,
- Articulate and define their problems, NOT technologies or vendors to solve their problems,
- Embrace innovation by reusing and leveraging platform-enabled technologies.

Business executives must impact digital evolutionary transformations by exploring interoperable technologies founding the digital landscape, championing digital transformations, fostering collaboration, and securing balanced investments into digital transformations from the core of the business. By doing so, they must realize business cases and navigate the challenges and opportunities of sustainable digital business transformations toward the ultimate goals of digital composable enterprises. Their main responsibility is to bring tech, data, and business needs together. They must assume accountability for data, information, and new digital products as they have to scale their abilities to significantly improve the process from ideation to monetization while continually leveraging innovation and evolving the organization's culture.

Applied Technology Leadership
Ingo Paas, CIO & CDO, Green Cargo

Transformation of IT functions is essential to enable the transformation of the business

"To innovate and transform the business does require a fundamental transformation of IT, including its values, skills, principles, strategies, technologies, and overall approach to bring business innovation to life.

As Prof. Johan Magnusson confirmed, not disturbing the established order of CIOs and ignoring the necessity to radically but evolutionary shift and redevelop the purpose and role of IT will limit the success and impact of digital investments. Pursuing the goal of transforming the IT and tech functions is less about democratizing their physical belonging, such as moving IT into the business. It is not about that question, as this process will do the opposite of good. The role of IT (central – which I prefer, compared to decentral – a major risk of defragmentation) is to build platforms and democratize the utilization of tech and data. They must collaborate and help evolve the culture, governing for success, not for limitations. The IT function must provide the platforms, ensure scalability, and foster a climate of systemic and unrestricted innovation where constraints are minimized and value maximized.

At Green Cargo, we positioned this at the core of our IT transformation, empowering the business with governance and strategies rather than limiting their attempts moving forward, but with unavoidable exemptions. Disruptive future AI investments are aligned with our strategy and fully augmented into our digital composable architecture with innovative graph databases. When we meet with software companies or specialists in their technology field, we realize that our technology stack and its relentless interoperability, combined with the ability to navigate, execute, innovate, and scale, has led to easy decisions NOT to buy their packaged products or services anymore. We go stronger, faster, better, and deliver for lower costs by choosing and owning our technologies with ever-increasing levels of autonomy and accountability.

We will continue on this path moving forward where business and IT will master the process of seamless interoperability and composability by promoting ambidexterity everywhere."

Written by Ingo Paas, CIO & CDO, Green Cargo

Epilogue

This book is the first one addressing one of the most complex transformations all enterprises must undergo, while many have not even realized this fundamental need to transform. Recognizing and prioritizing composability can be a struggle for many enterprises, as it can be overwhelming to identify and understand the endless complexity of such undertakings.

While working on this project, I found the theory of digital composability quite challenging, even though we practiced this successfully and at a larger scale at Green Cargo. In comparison, little information or inspiration was available while I undertook the authoring process between January 2022 and March 2023.

However, while writing this book and translating practice into theory, I learned that the opposite is true. Accepting new thinking and determination during execution makes digital composability much less complicated than anticipated. Accomplishing enterprise composability from the core of the business is achievable and requires evolutionary strategies combined with continuity and discipline in execution.

Writing in plain English and developing this thought-provoking approach was my most stimulating and challenging experience ever. I had to apply severe self-criticism techniques to evolve into the new role and learn skills to become a professional writer, despite having no professional experience, editorial, or technical support. This journey was more difficult than I had anticipated, but it was worth every minute and became my life's most intensive learning period and intellectual challenge. I received brilliant feedback on individual chapters from the group of thought leaders, while Johan Magnusson gave me highly appreciated and valuable feedback on the entire project, which was instrumental in the book's development.

Finally, I found the courage to determine the status of "Mission Accomplished" on the evening of the 10th of April, 2023. I had to overcome the urge to continue reorganizing my thoughts, strategies, and observations for endless months to come and finally share and publish my work. As I wrote in the introduction, *"Ultimately, it is not about the outcome but the courage to do and achieve it anyhow"*.

Professor Johan Magnusson, PhD wrote in the introduction to this book: *"As such, the direction set out by the author of this book may be considered either trail-blazing or sacrilegious, in both interpretations deeply troubling to the established order. But this is a time for action, and there is ample support for the path proposed by Ingo Paas, both in emerging research and an increasing stream of practical examples from the industry."*

Hans van Grieken summed it up in Chapter Three, *"It appears that in his approach, Ingo has managed to solidly marry the more foundational and Talent Driven approach of Talent and Strategy Leaders to the far more agile, speedy and risk-tolerant"* approach of Fast Moving Experimenters."

Marc Dowd delivered another compelling message in Chapter Six, *"Digital transformation will fail to be a business differentiator if these lessons in this book are not understood and implemented with great leadership and skill."*

To my colleagues at Green Cargo: I want to express my deep appreciation for the exceptional individuals and leaders I worked alongside during my three and a half years at Green Cargo, particularly our IT and tech teams. Your outstanding leadership enabled us to transform from chaos into a true high-performance digital-first culture. I must also recognize the valuable support and partnership from my executive colleagues and our board of directors. I am especially grateful to our CEO, Ted Söderholm, for his faith and true leadership, championing our need for autonomy, accountability, and trust, which allowed us to achieve what seemed impossible at the outset of our transformation.

To my family: All my love and appreciation goes to my family for never giving up while jointly overcoming impossible difficulties during the global pandemic, thus supporting me in authoring this book.

To my readers: Thank you for reading this book which means a lot to me! As the author, I hope you found the time you spent valuable and that you could find inspiration, meaning, and purpose in your attempt to pursue digital composable transformations differently and more successfully.

Finally, this is the end of this book, but hopefully, a new beginning of YOUR digital composable journey pursuing the implementation of the next generation of "Digital Composable Enterprises". Thank you!

I wish you success!

Ingo Paas

– END –

Please scan this QR to get in touch to give feedback or request future updates.

RESOURCES AND REFERENCES

References

"The Rise of the Ambidextrous Organization - The Secret Revolution Happening Right Under Your Nose" by Zabiegalski, D. E., (2019, ISBN 9781646333400, Business Research Consulting)

"The Innovator's Dilemma: When New Technologies Cause Great Firms to Fail" by Clayton M. Christensen (1997, ISBN 9781633691780, Harvard Business Review Press)

"Hands-On Azure Digital Twins - A practical guide to building distributed IoT solutions", by Alexander Meijers (2022, ISBN 9781801073974, Packt Publishing)

"In the Age of AI - How AI and Emerging Technologies Are Disrupting Industries, Lives, and the Future of Work", by Sam Mieleke (2021, ISBN 9781637305263, New Degree Press)

"Sustainable Playbook for Technology Leaders – Design and implement sustainable IT practices and unlock sustainable business opportunities", by Niklas Sundberg (2022, ISBN978-1-80323-034-4, Packt Publishing)

"Building Evolutionary Architectures: Support Constant Change" by Neal Ford, Rebecca Parsons, and Patrick Kua. ISBN: 978-1491986363. Publisher: O'Reilly Media. Release date: 2017.

"Digital Transformation: Build Your Organization's Future for the Innovation Age" by Lindsay Herbert (2019, ISBN 9780749484702, Kogan Page)

"The Lean Enterprise: How to Make Agile and DevOps Work in Your Company" by Jez Humble, Joanne Molesky, and Barry O'Reilly (2020, ISBN: 978-1087861087, Addison-Wesley Professional)

"Platform Revolution: How Networked Markets Are Transforming the Economy and How to Make Them Work for You" by Geoffrey G. Parker, Marshall W. Van Alstyne, and Sangeet Paul Choudary (2016, ISBN 9780393354355, W. W. Norton & Company)

"Digital to the Core: Remastering Leadership for Your Industry, Your Enterprise, and Yourself" by Mark Raskino and Graham Waller (2015, ISBN 9781629560719, Gartner Press)

"The Startup Way: How Modern Companies Use Entrepreneurial Management to Transform Culture and Drive Long-Term Growth" by Eric Ries (2017, ISBN 9781101903209, Currency)

Resources

Hans van Grieken, e. a. (2017). *Dutch Digital DNA Demystified.* Deloitte.

Harry Markowitz. (1990). *The Modern Portfolio Theory.* 1990 Nobel Memorial Prize in Economic Sciences.

Colony, G. (2012). *The CIO's Dilemma: Balancing the Risks, Opportunities, and Investments of IT.* Forrester Research.

The Institute of Risk Management. (2012). *Risk Culture.* The Institute of Risk Management.

Gartner. (2021). *Combine, Cluster, Complement: 3 Fundamentals of Combinatorial Digital Innovation.* Hämtat från Gartner.com: https://www.gartner.com/smarterwithgartner/combine-cluster-complement-3-fundamentals-of-combinatorial-digital-innovation

Gartner. (2021). *Gartner Survey of Over 2,000 CIOs Reveals the Need for Enterprises to Embrace Business Composability in 2022.* Gartner.

Gartner. (u.d.). *Execute Your Cloud Strategy With a Cloud Center of Excellence.* Gartner.com: https://www.gartner.com/smarterwithgartner/execute-your-cloud-strategy-with-a-cloud-center-of-excellence

MIT Technology Review Insights & Databricks. (2021). *Building a high performance data and AI organization.*

Viima.com. (September 2018). Hämtat från https://www.viima.com/blog/innovation-management-models

Institute of Risk Management. (u.d.). *Risk culture Framework.* Institute of Risk Management.

Markets and Markets. (2021). *Global Cloud Market by 2023.* MarketsandMarkets.

Matthew C. Le Merle. (2017). *Corporate Innovation in the Fifth Era: Lessons from Alphabet/Google, Amazon, Apple, Facebook, and Microsoft.* Cartwright Publishing.

Generative AI: Hype, or truly transformative? (2023)*, Goldman Sachs, Global Marco Research*

Table of Figures

Table of content

Made in United States
Orlando, FL
21 July 2023

35351732R00295